D0110041

Van Von Hunter Vol. 2
Created by Ron Kaulfersch and Mike Schwark

Production Artist - Jason Milligan
Cover Artists - Mike Schwark
Cover Design - Raymond Makowski

Editor - Lillian Diaz-Przybyl
Digital Imaging Manager - Chris Buford
Production Managers - Jennifer Miller and Mutsumi Miyazaki
Managing Editor - Jill Freshney
Editorial Director - Jeremy Ross
VP of Production - Ron Klamert
Publisher and E.I.C. - Mike Kiley
President and C.O.O. - John Parker
C.E.O. - Stuart Levy

A  Manga

TOKYOPOP Inc.
5900 Wilshire Blvd. Suite 2000
Los Angeles, CA 90036

E-mail: info@TOKYOPOP.com
Come visit us online at www.TOKYOPOP.com

ISBN: 1-59532-693-6

First TOKYOPOP printing: September 2005
10 9 8 7 6 5 4 3 2 1
Printed in the USA

VAN VON HUNTER

VOL. 2

BY
RON KAULFERSCH
AND
MIKE SCHWARK

HAMBURG // LONDON // LOS ANGELES // TOKYO

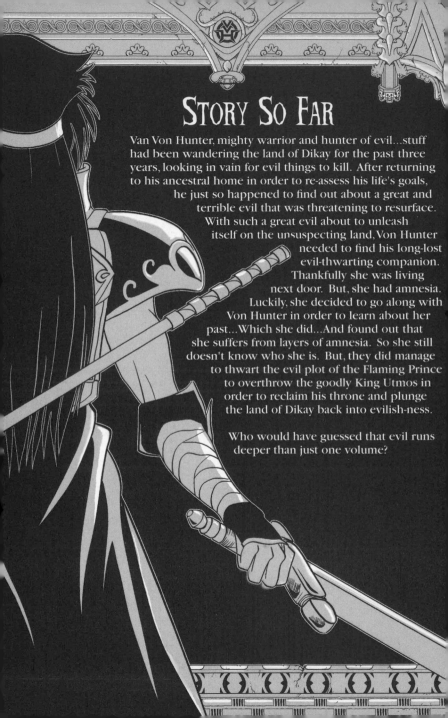

STORY SO FAR

Van Von Hunter, mighty warrior and hunter of evil...stuff
had been wandering the land of Dikay for the past three
years, looking in vain for evil things to kill. After returning
to his ancestral home in order to re-assess his life's goals,
he just so happened to find out about a great and
terrible evil that was threatening to resurface.
With such a great evil about to unleash
itself on the unsuspecting land, Von Hunter
needed to find his long-lost
evil-thwarting companion.
Thankfully she was living
next door. But, she had amnesia.
Luckily, she decided to go along with
Von Hunter in order to learn about her
past...Which she did...And found out that
she suffers from layers of amnesia. So she still
doesn't know who she is. But, they did manage
to thwart the evil plot of the Flaming Prince
to overthrow the goodly King Utmos in
order to reclaim his throne and plunge
the land of Dikay back into evilish-ness.

Who would have guessed that evil runs
deeper than just one volume?

1

WHEN ZOMBIE HORDES COME MARCHING IN, RRAH, HURRAH!

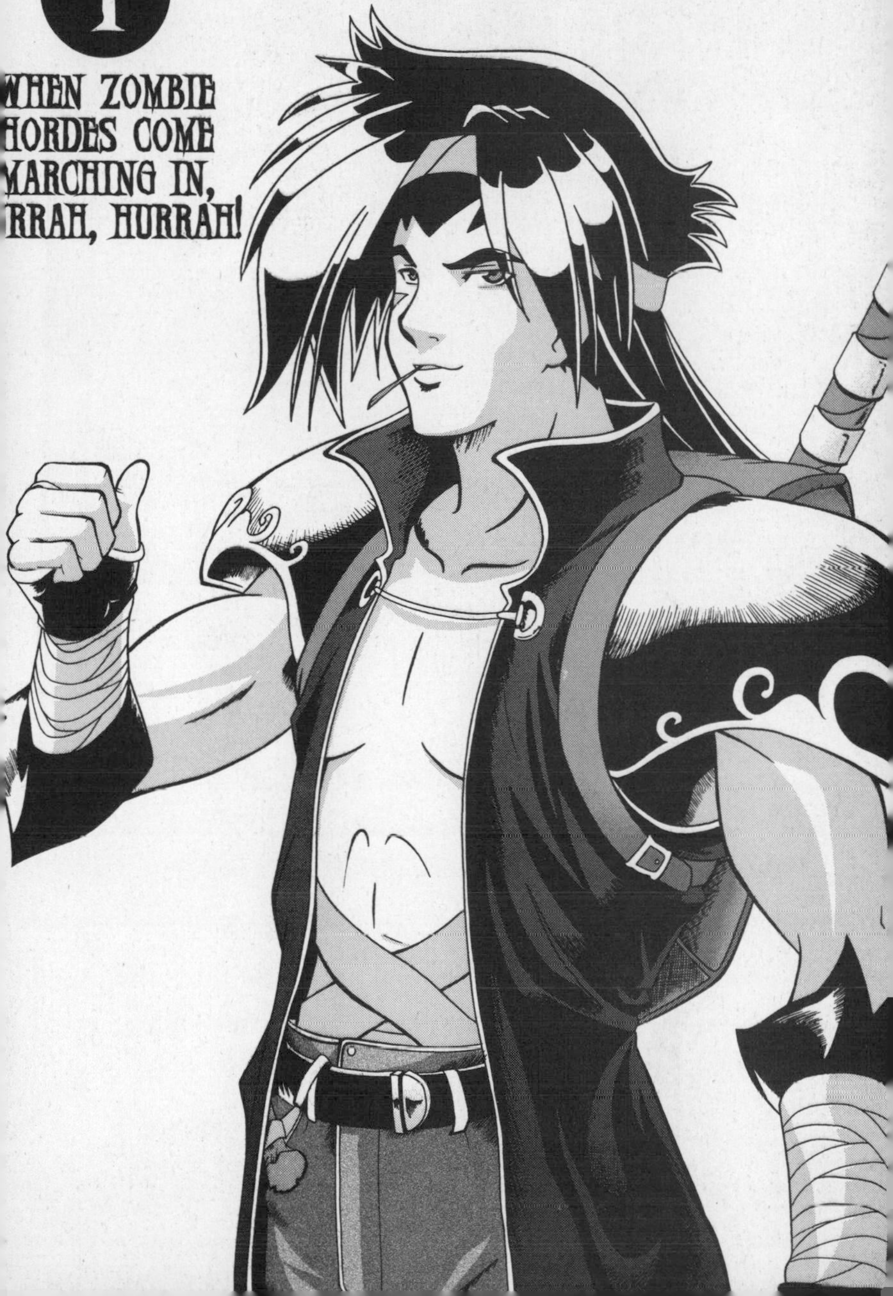

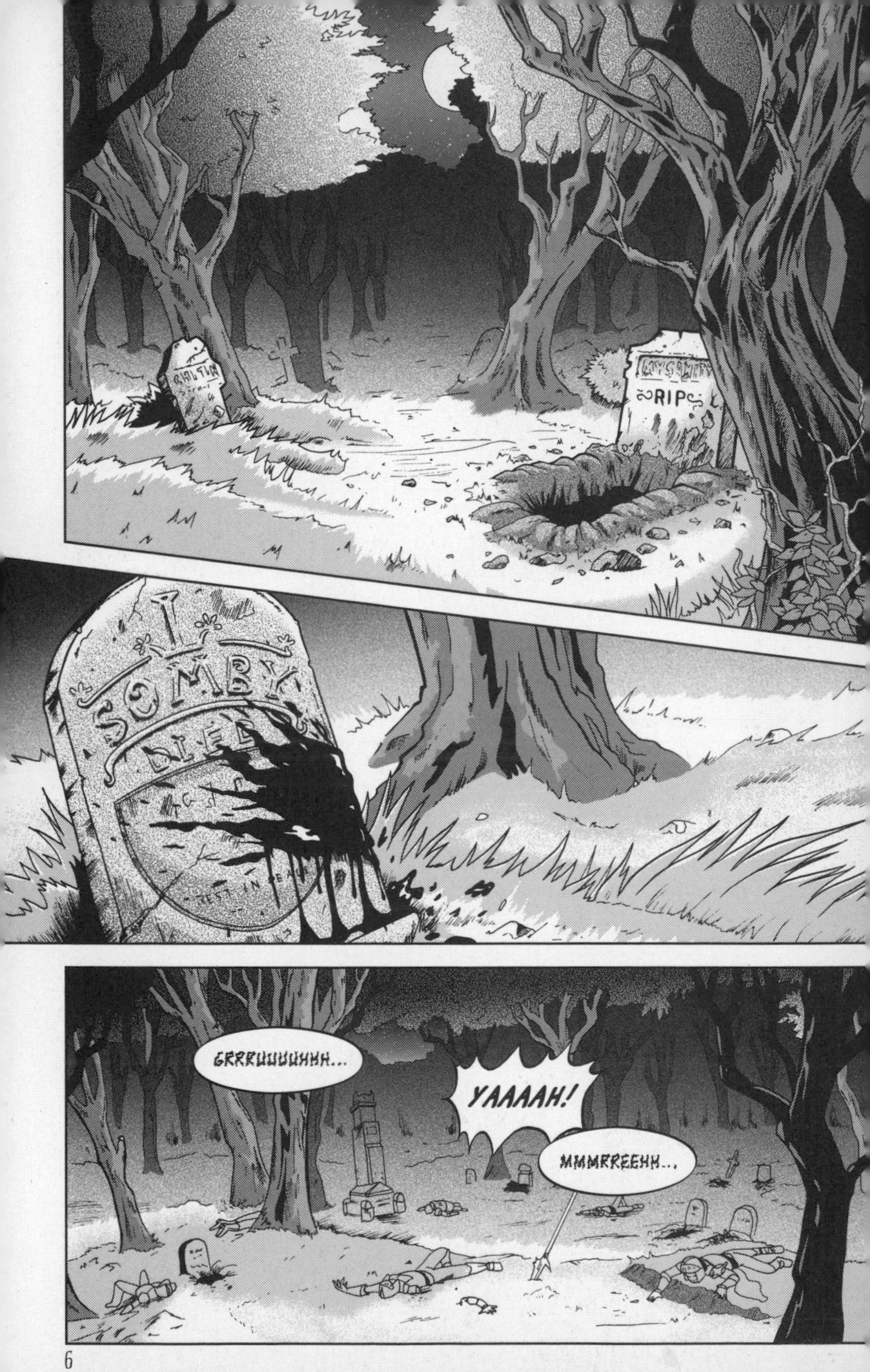
RIP
SOMBY
GRRRUUUUHHH...
YAAAAH!
MMMRREEHH...

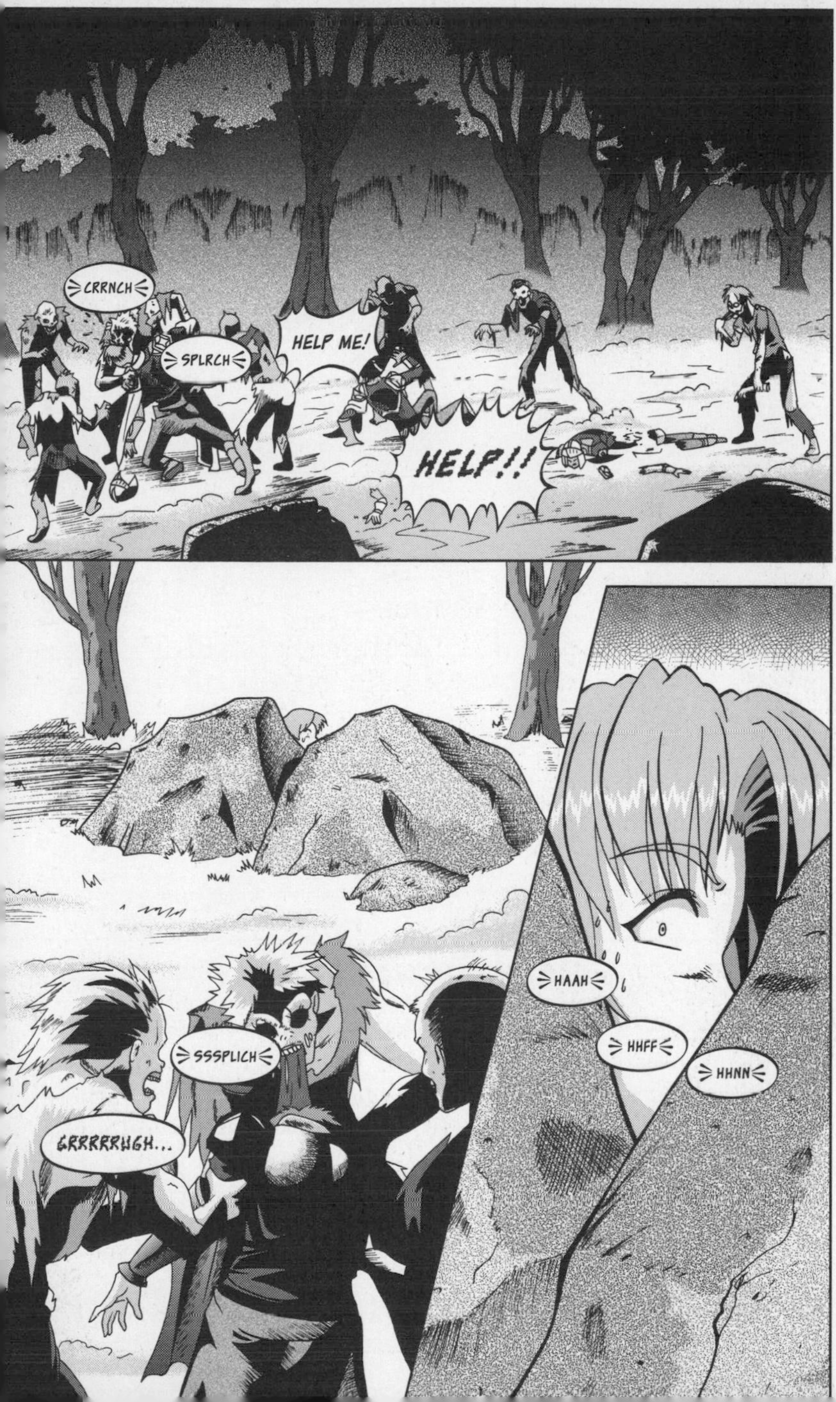

CRRNCH
SPLRCH
HELP ME!
HELP!!
SSSPLICH
GRRRRRUGH...
HAAH
HHFF
HHNN

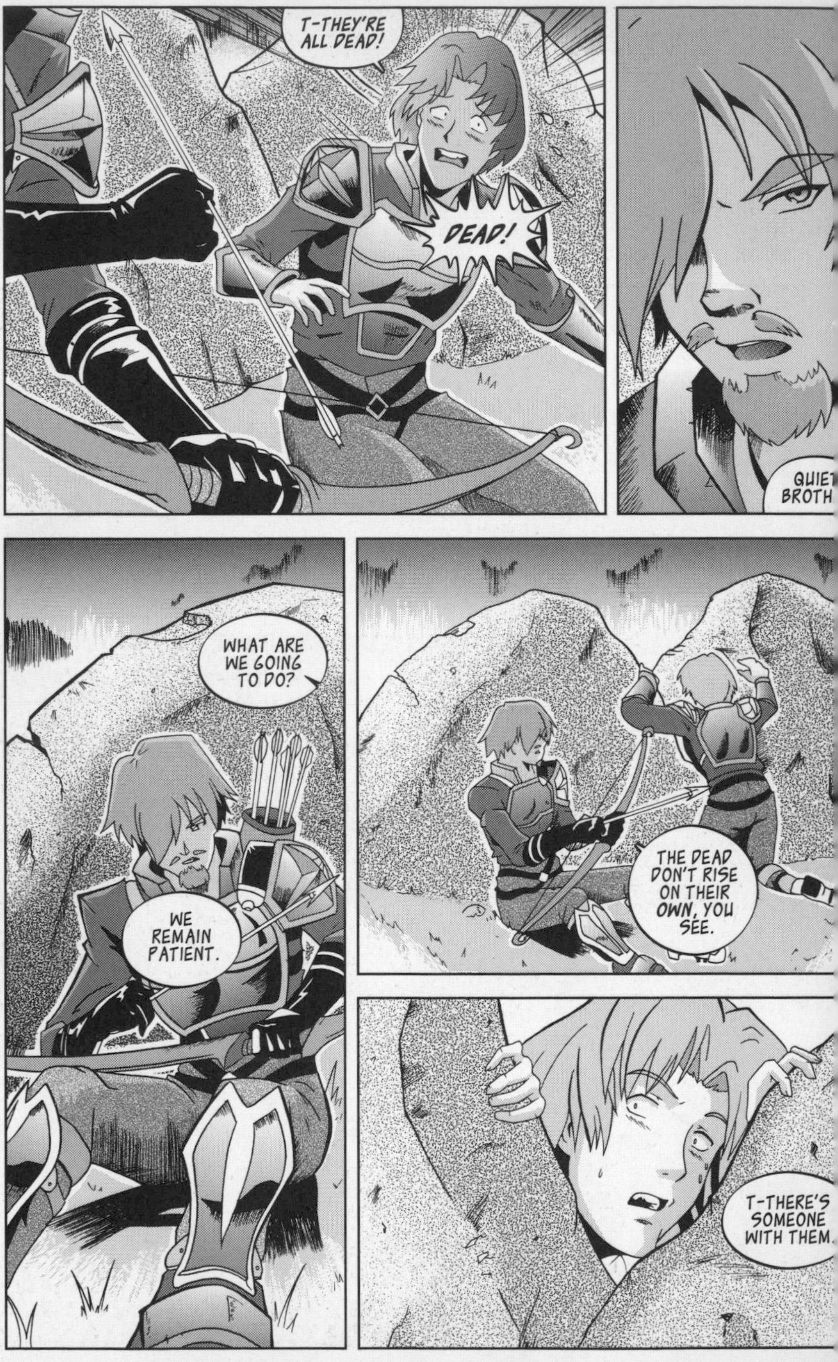
T-THEY'RE ALL DEAD!
DEAD!
QUIET BROTH
WHAT ARE WE GOING TO DO?
WE REMAIN PATIENT.
THE DEAD DON'T RISE ON THEIR OWN, YOU SEE.
T-THERE'S SOMEONE WITH THEM.

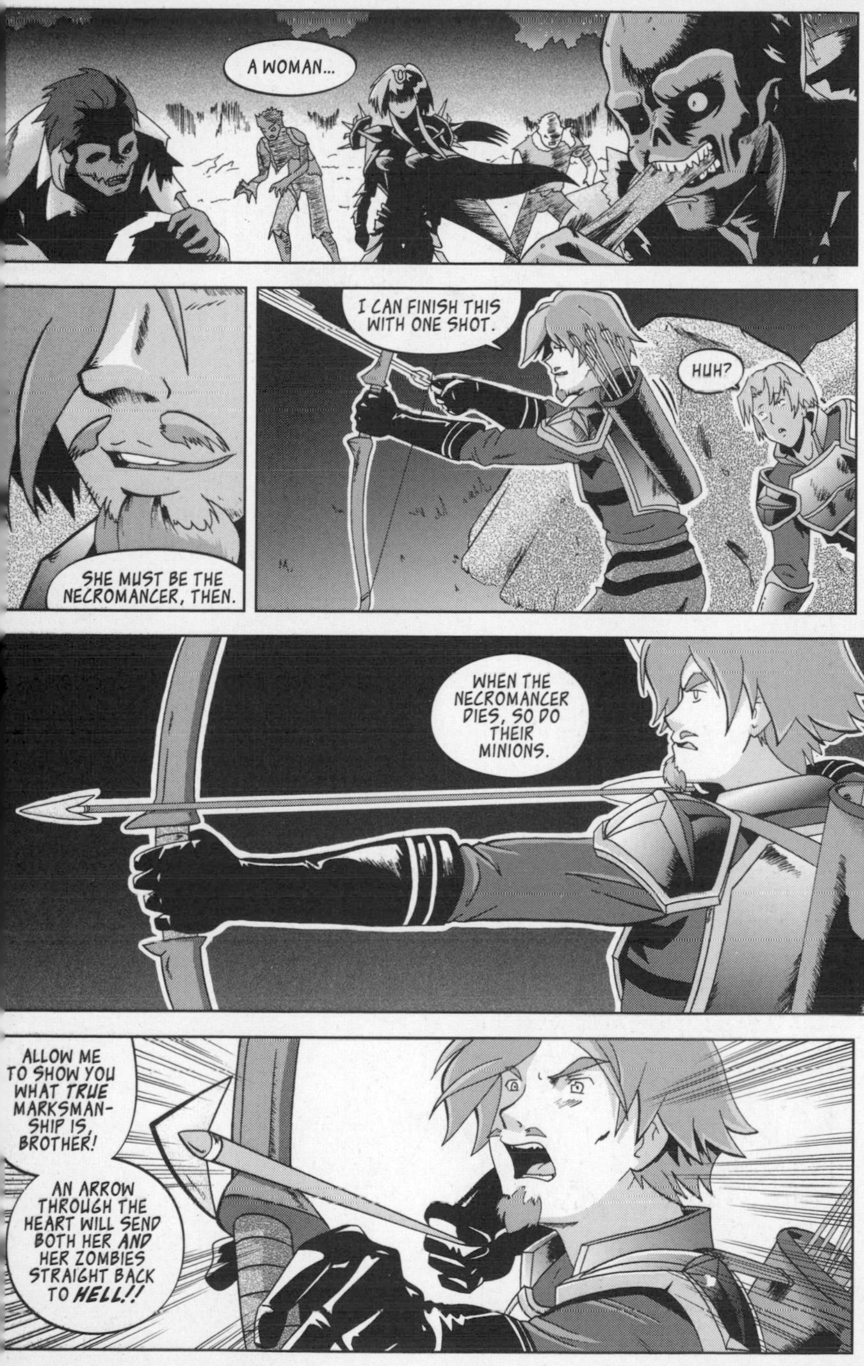
A WOMAN...
SHE MUST BE THE NECROMANCER, THEN.
I CAN FINISH THIS WITH ONE SHOT.
HUH?
WHEN THE NECROMANCER DIES, SO DO THEIR MINIONS.
ALLOW ME TO SHOW YOU WHAT *TRUE* MARKSMAN-SHIP IS, BROTHER!
AN ARROW THROUGH THE HEART WILL SEND BOTH HER *AND* HER ZOMBIES STRAIGHT BACK TO ***HELL!!***

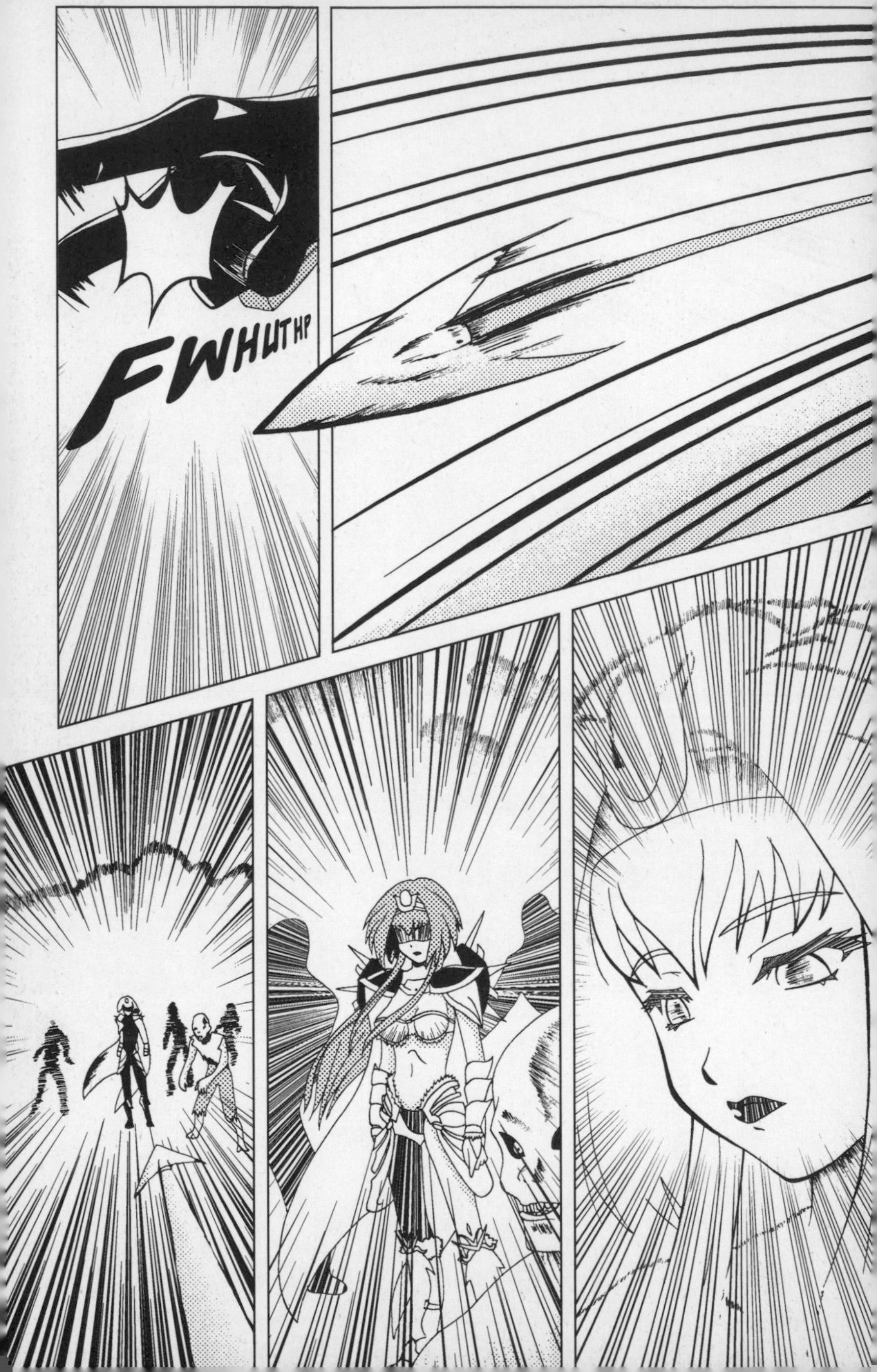
FWHUTHP

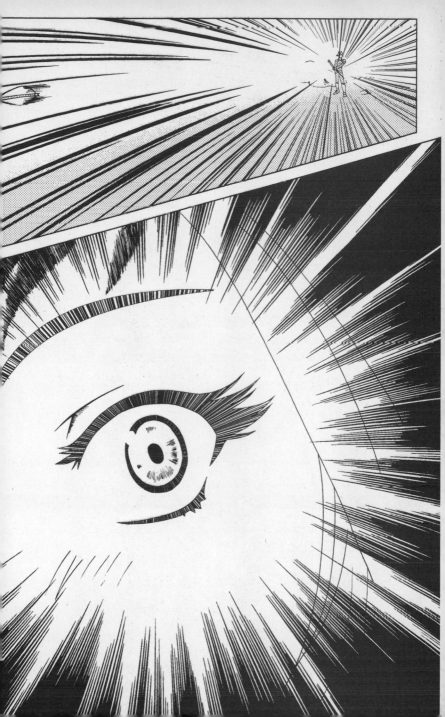

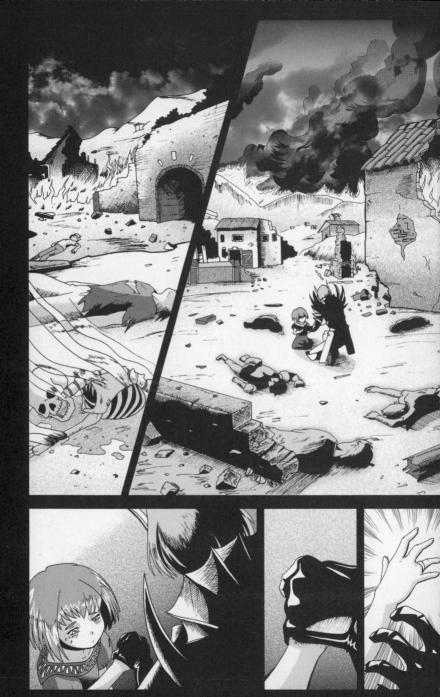

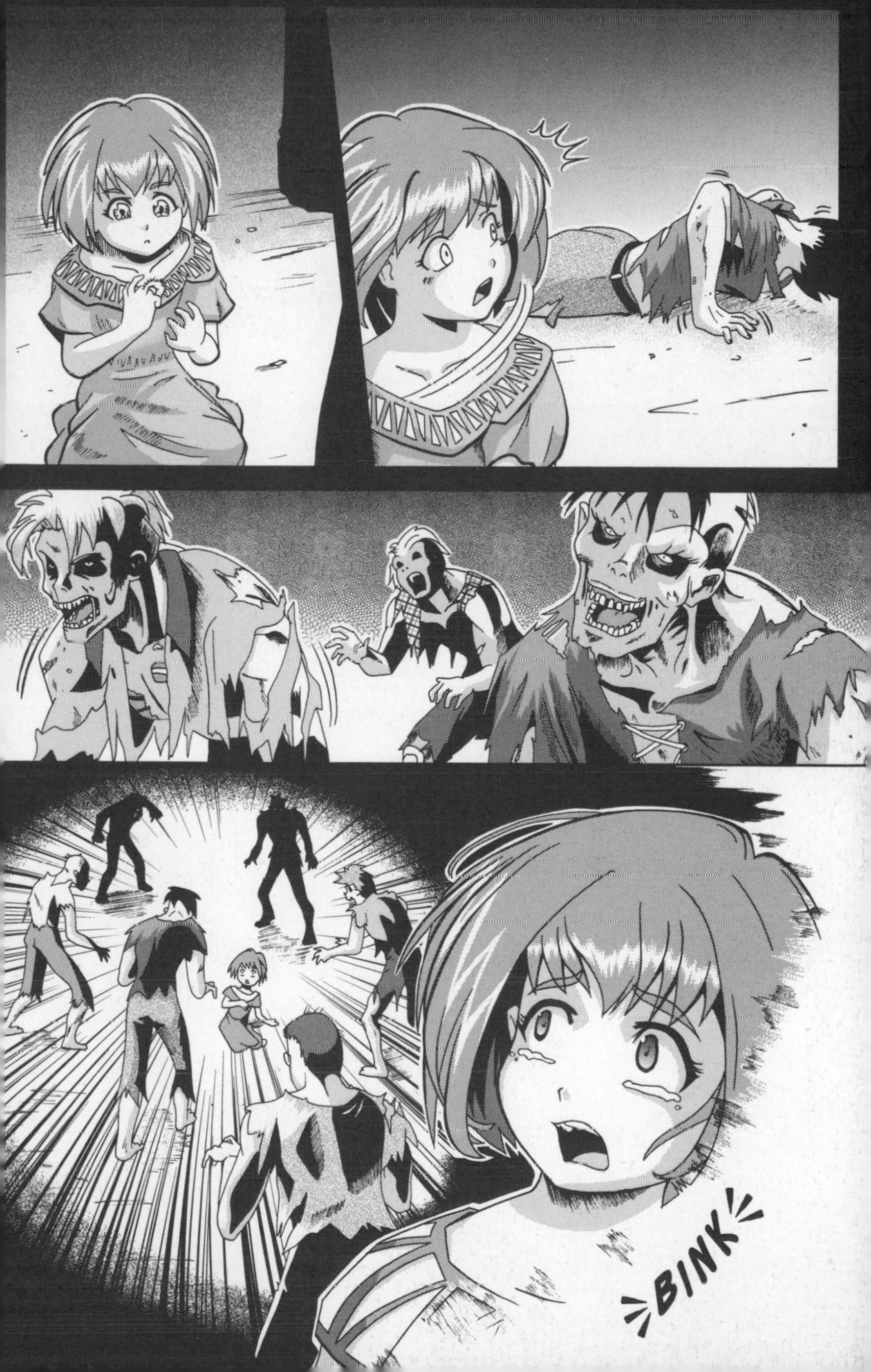
BINK

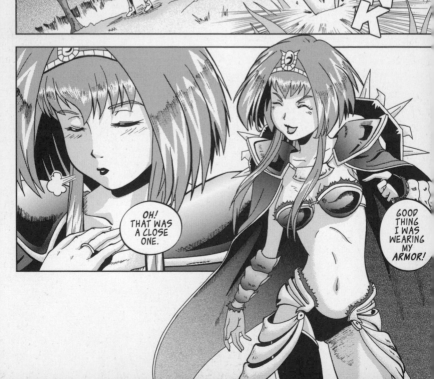

OH! THAT WAS A CLOSE ONE.

GOOD THING I WAS WEARING MY ARMOR!

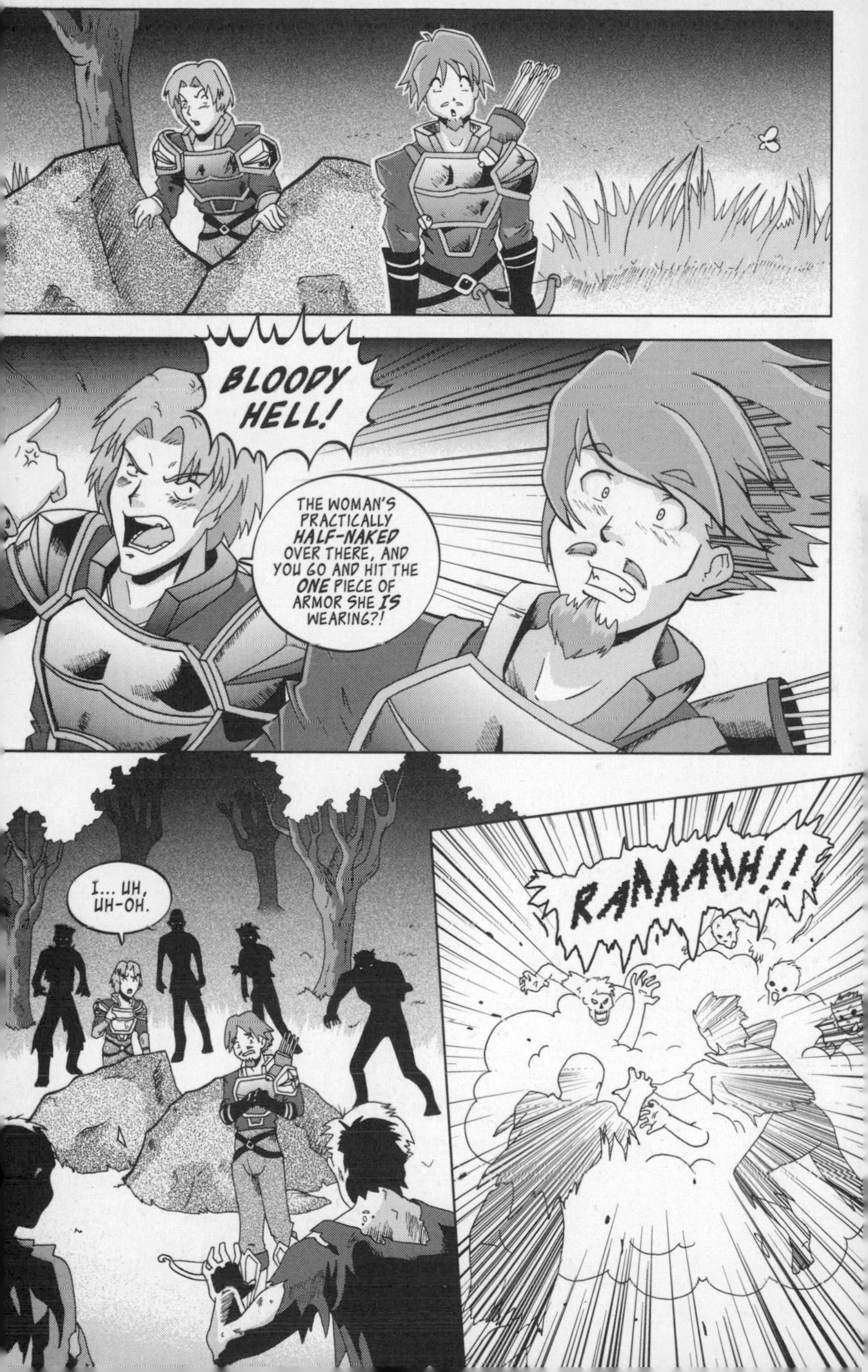
BLOODY HELL!
THE WOMAN'S PRACTICALLY HALF-NAKED OVER THERE, AND YOU GO AND HIT THE ONE PIECE OF ARMOR SHE IS WEARING?!
I... UH, UH-OH.
RAAAAHH!!

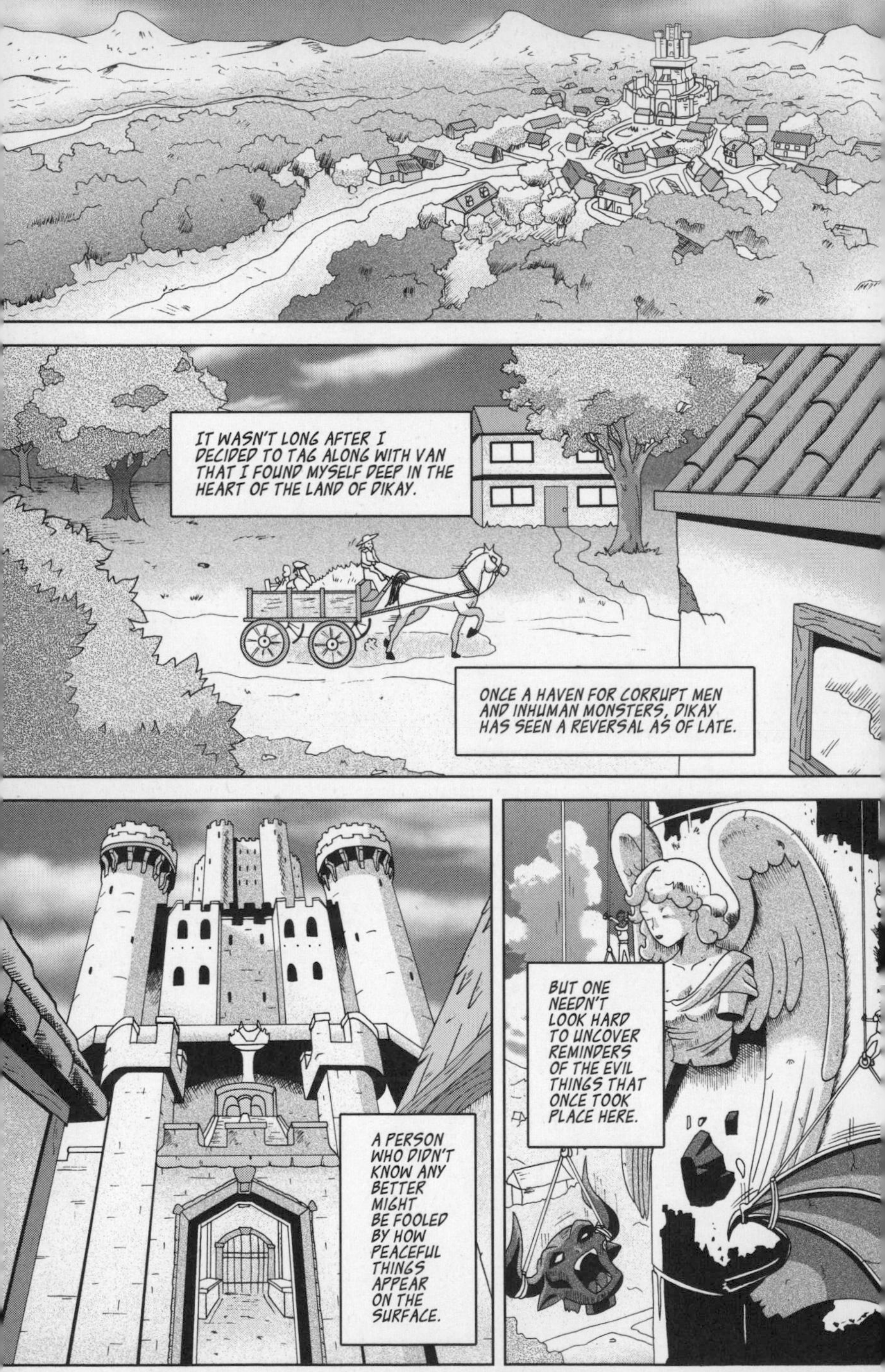
IT WASN'T LONG AFTER I DECIDED TO TAG ALONG WITH VAN THAT I FOUND MYSELF DEEP IN THE HEART OF THE LAND OF DIKAY.
ONCE A HAVEN FOR CORRUPT MEN AND INHUMAN MONSTERS, DIKAY HAS SEEN A REVERSAL AS OF LATE.
A PERSON WHO DIDN'T KNOW ANY BETTER MIGHT BE FOOLED BY HOW PEACEFUL THINGS APPEAR ON THE SURFACE.
BUT ONE NEEDN'T LOOK HARD TO UNCOVER REMINDERS OF THE EVIL THINGS THAT ONCE TOOK PLACE HERE.

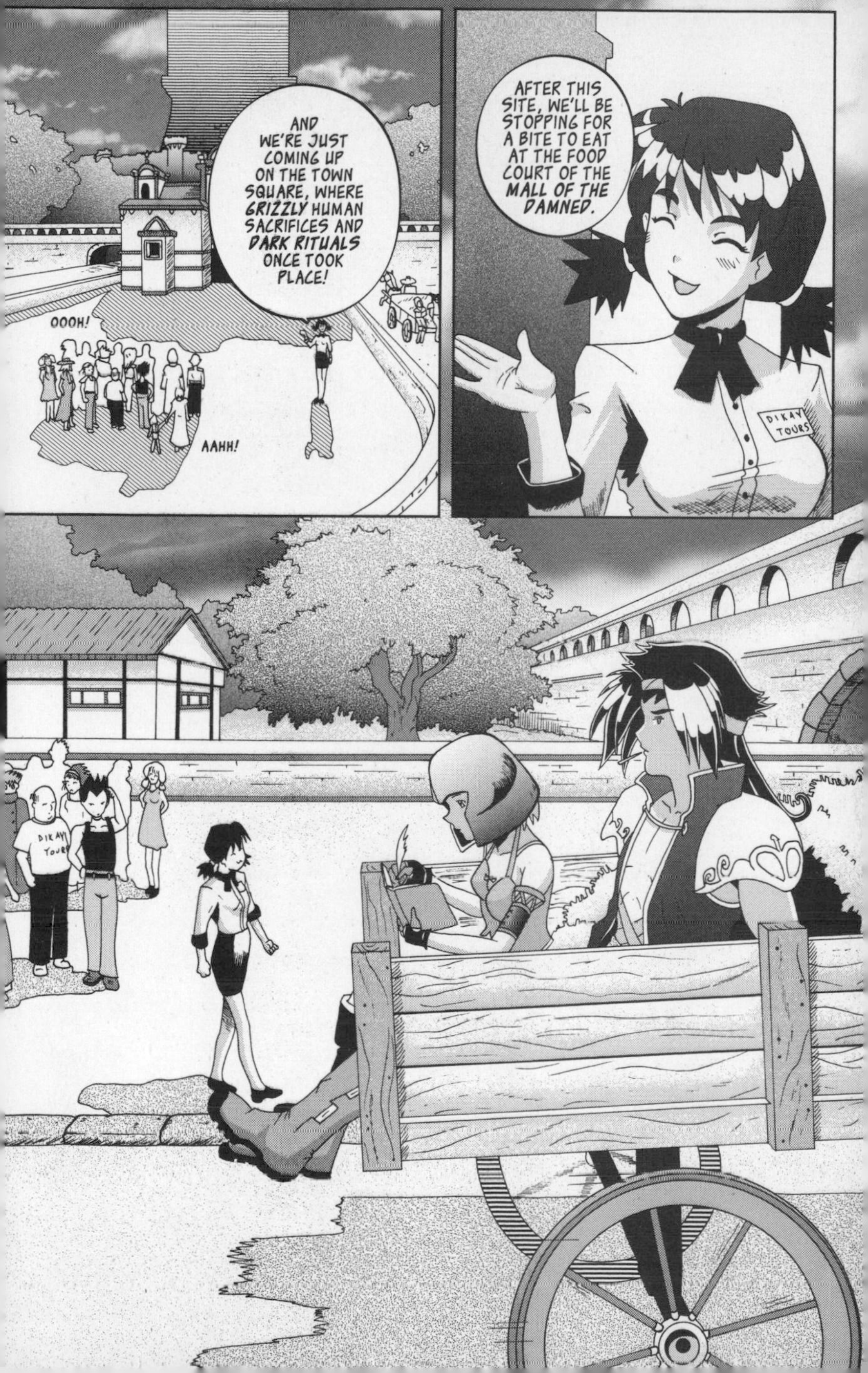
AND WE'RE JUST COMING UP ON THE TOWN SQUARE, WHERE GRIZZLY HUMAN SACRIFICES AND DARK RITUALS ONCE TOOK PLACE!
OOOH!
AAHH!
AFTER THIS SITE, WE'LL BE STOPPING FOR A BITE TO EAT AT THE FOOD COURT OF THE MALL OF THE DAMNED.
DIKAY TOURS

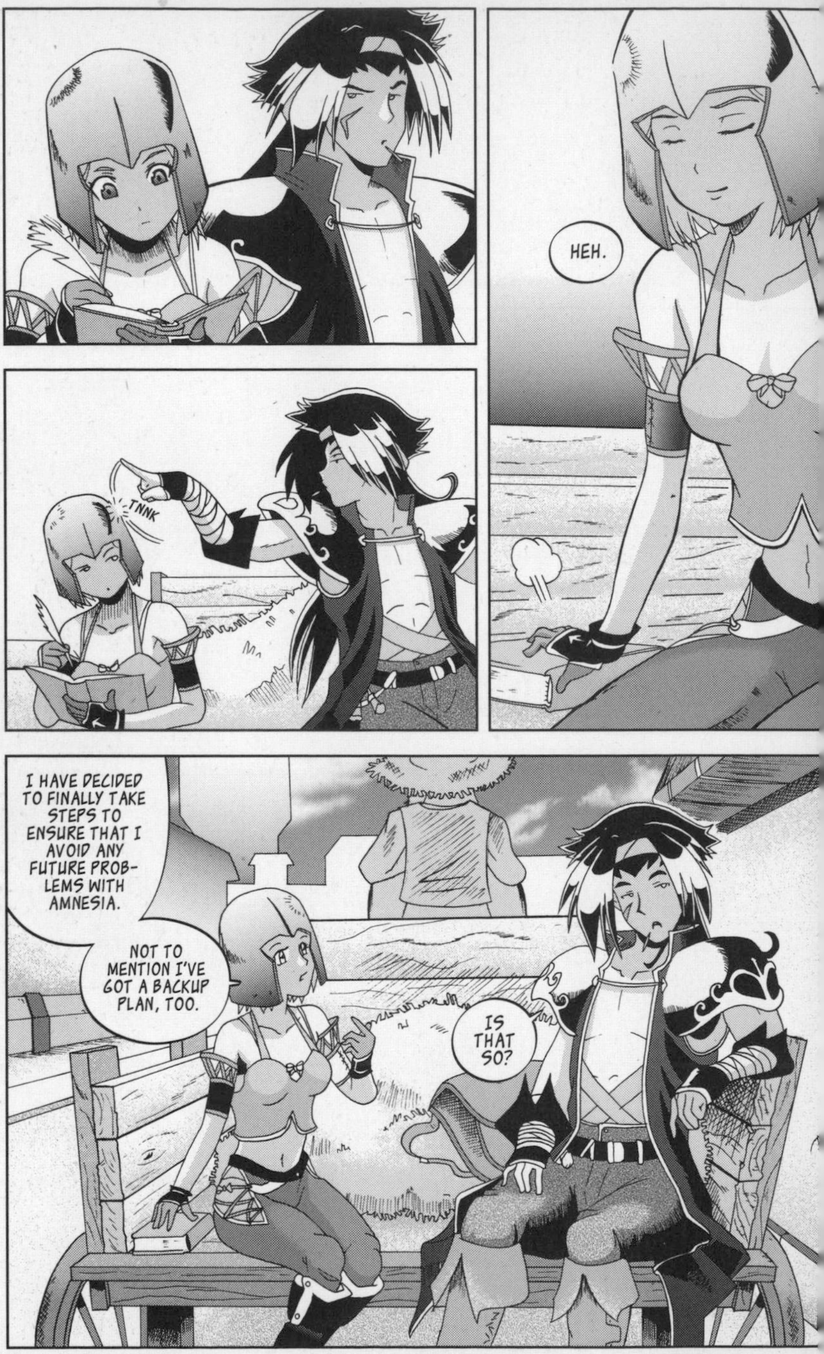
HEH.
TNNK
I HAVE DECIDED TO FINALLY TAKE STEPS TO ENSURE THAT I AVOID ANY FUTURE PROB-LEMS WITH AMNESIA.
NOT TO MENTION I'VE GOT A BACKUP PLAN, TOO.
IS THAT SO?

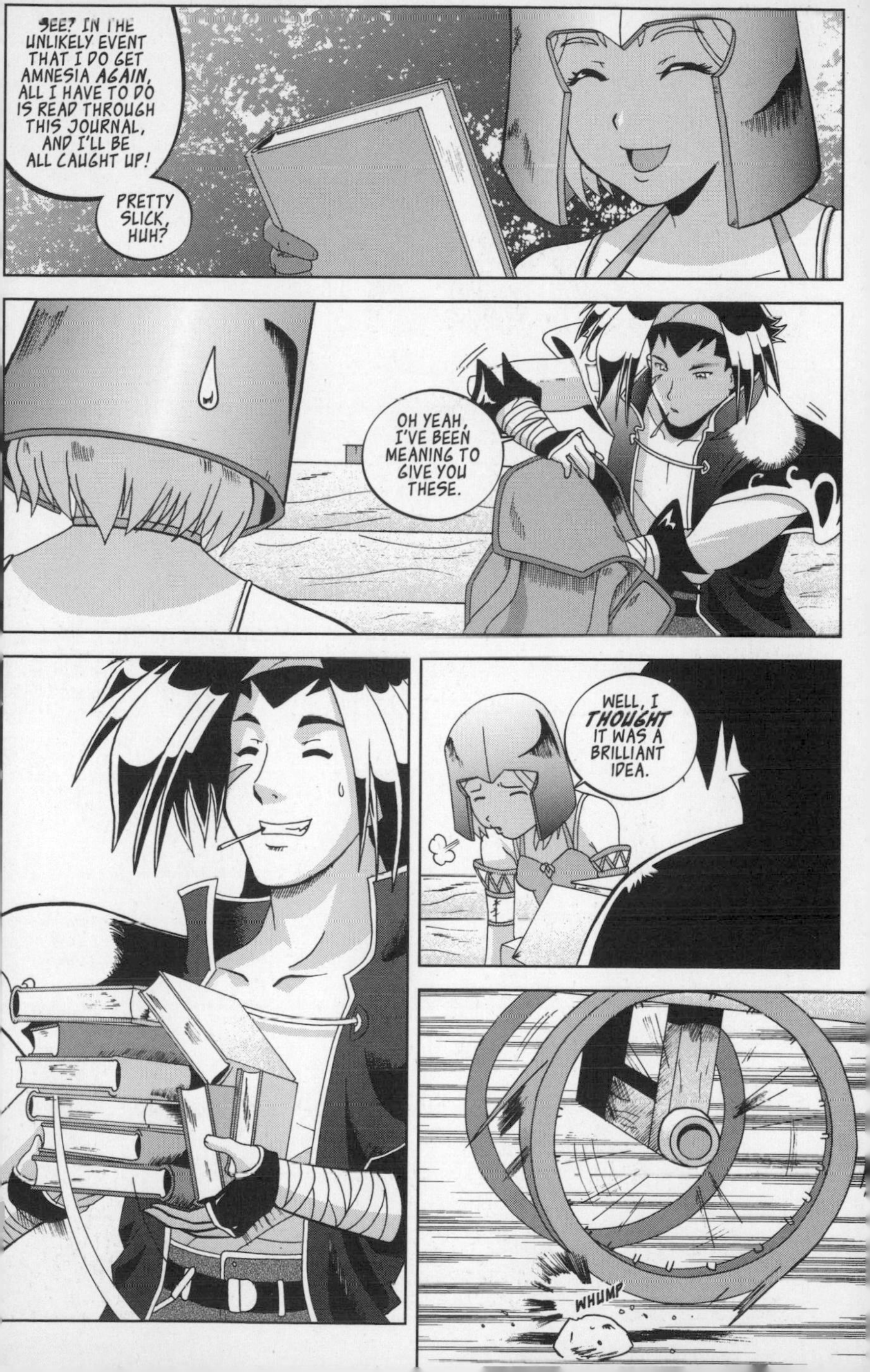
SEE? IN THE UNLIKELY EVENT THAT I DO GET AMNESIA AGAIN, ALL I HAVE TO DO IS READ THROUGH THIS JOURNAL, AND I'LL BE ALL CAUGHT UP!
PRETTY SLICK, HUH?
OH YEAH, I'VE BEEN MEANING TO GIVE YOU THESE.
WELL, I THOUGHT IT WAS A BRILLIANT IDEA.
WHUMP

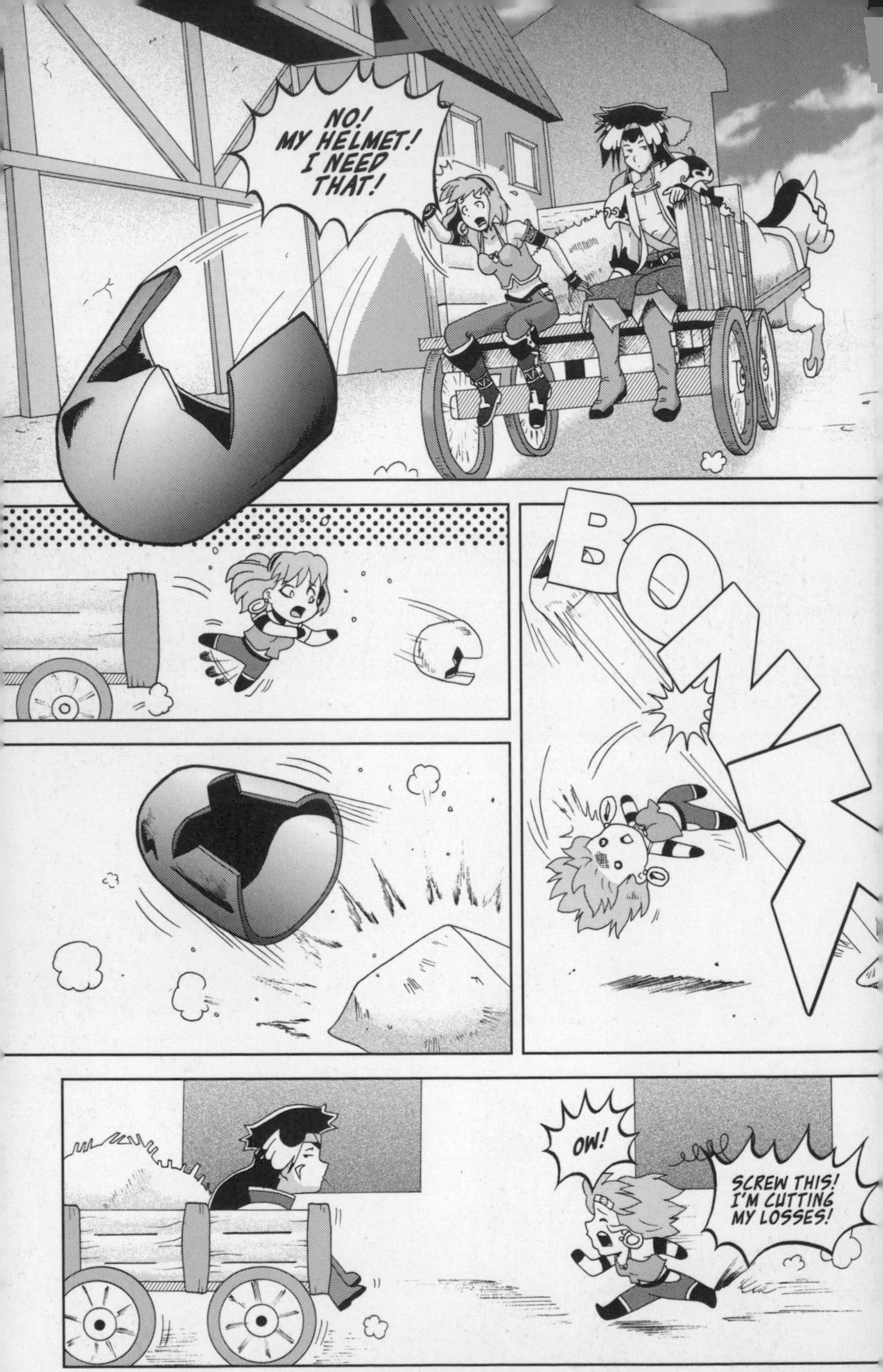
NO! MY HELMET! I NEED THAT!
BONK
OW!
SCREW THIS! I'M CUTTING MY LOSSES!

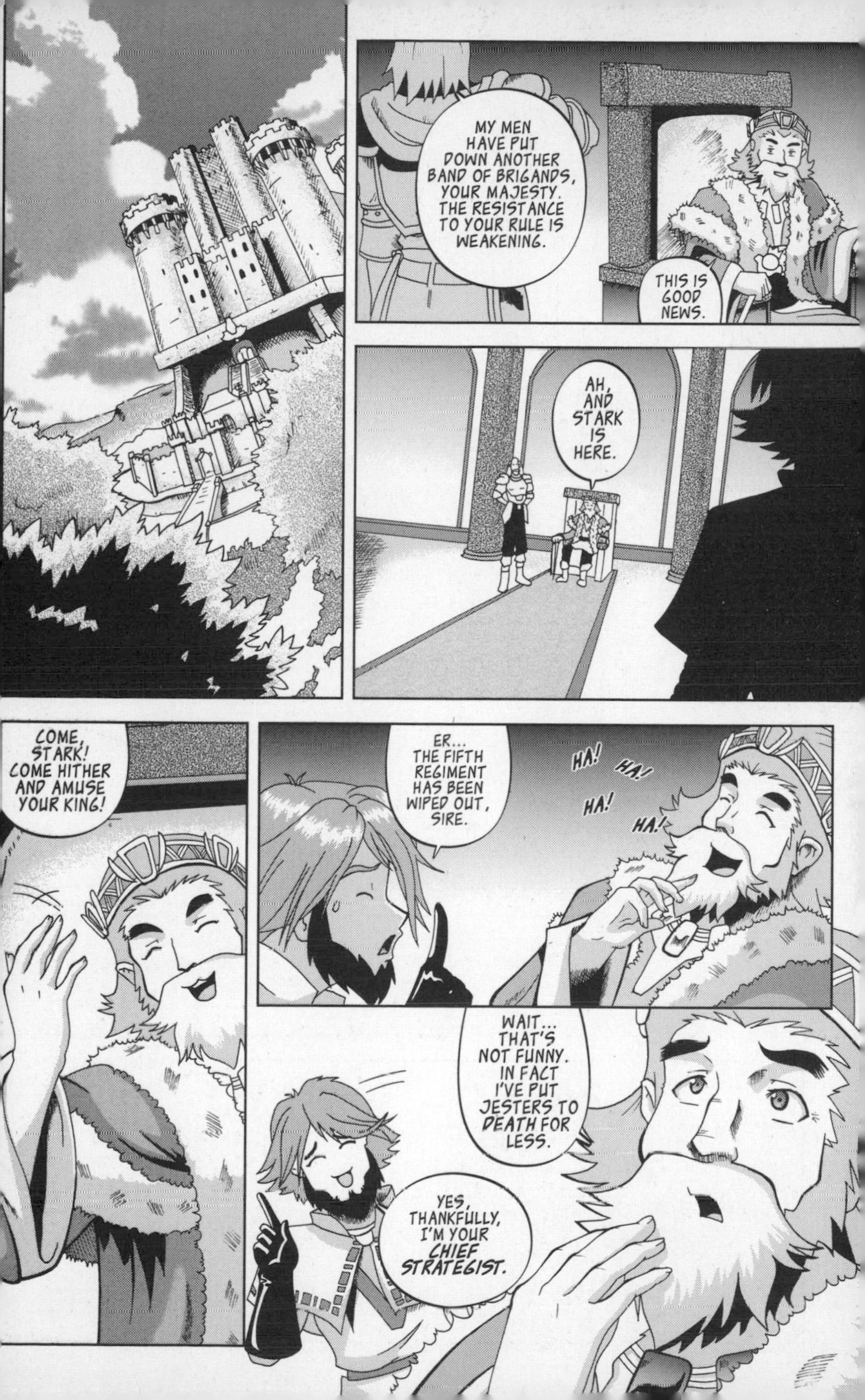
MY MEN HAVE PUT DOWN ANOTHER BAND OF BRIGANDS, YOUR MAJESTY. THE RESISTANCE TO YOUR RULE IS WEAKENING.
THIS IS GOOD NEWS.
AH, AND STARK IS HERE.
COME, STARK! COME HITHER AND AMUSE YOUR KING!
ER... THE FIFTH REGIMENT HAS BEEN WIPED OUT, SIRE.
HA! HA! HA! HA!
WAIT... THAT'S NOT FUNNY. IN FACT I'VE PUT JESTERS TO DEATH FOR LESS.
YES, THANKFULLY, I'M YOUR CHIEF STRATEGIST.

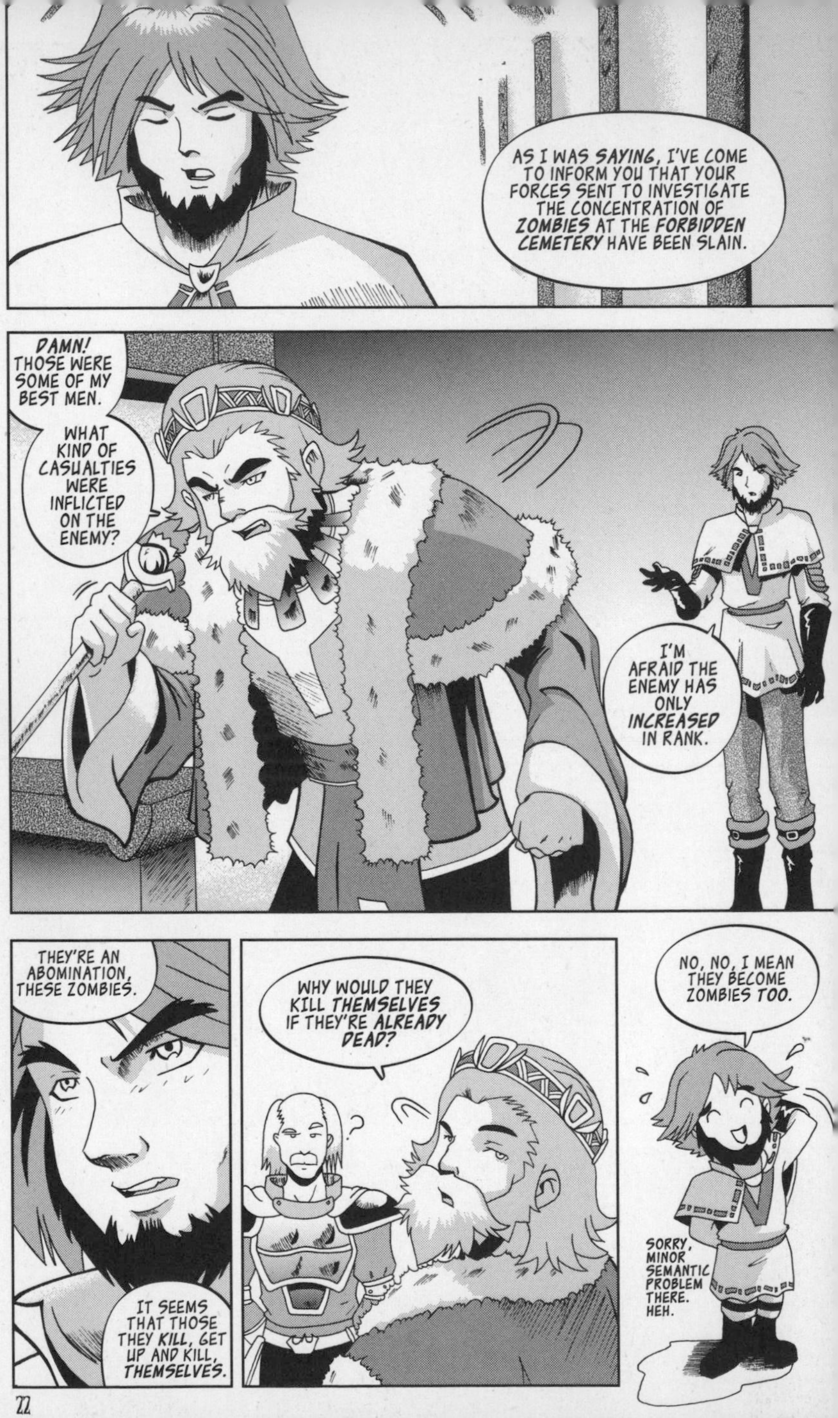
AS I WAS SAYING, I'VE COME TO INFORM YOU THAT YOUR FORCES SENT TO INVESTIGATE THE CONCENTRATION OF ZOMBIES AT THE FORBIDDEN CEMETERY HAVE BEEN SLAIN.
DAMN! THOSE WERE SOME OF MY BEST MEN.
WHAT KIND OF CASUALTIES WERE INFLICTED ON THE ENEMY?
I'M AFRAID THE ENEMY HAS ONLY INCREASED IN RANK.
THEY'RE AN ABOMINATION, THESE ZOMBIES.
IT SEEMS THAT THOSE THEY KILL, GET UP AND KILL, THEMSELVES.
WHY WOULD THEY KILL THEMSELVES IF THEY'RE ALREADY DEAD?
NO, NO, I MEAN THEY BECOME ZOMBIES TOO.
SORRY, MINOR SEMANTIC PROBLEM THERE. HEH.

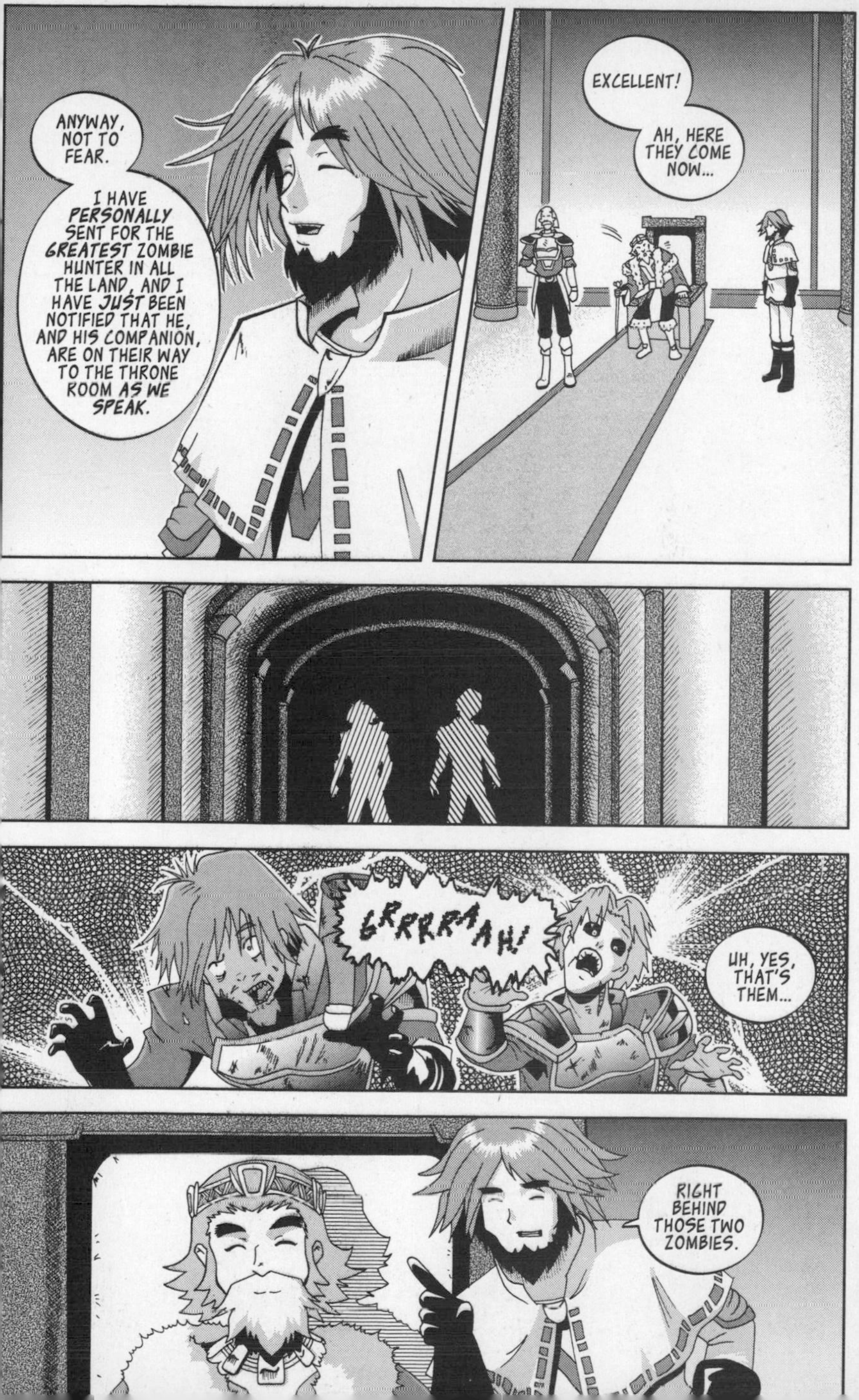
ANYWAY, NOT TO FEAR.
I HAVE PERSONALLY SENT FOR THE GREATEST ZOMBIE HUNTER IN ALL THE LAND, AND I HAVE JUST BEEN NOTIFIED THAT HE, AND HIS COMPANION, ARE ON THEIR WAY TO THE THRONE ROOM AS WE SPEAK.
EXCELLENT!
AH, HERE THEY COME NOW...
GRRRRAAH!
UH, YES, THAT'S THEM...
RIGHT BEHIND THOSE TWO ZOMBIES.

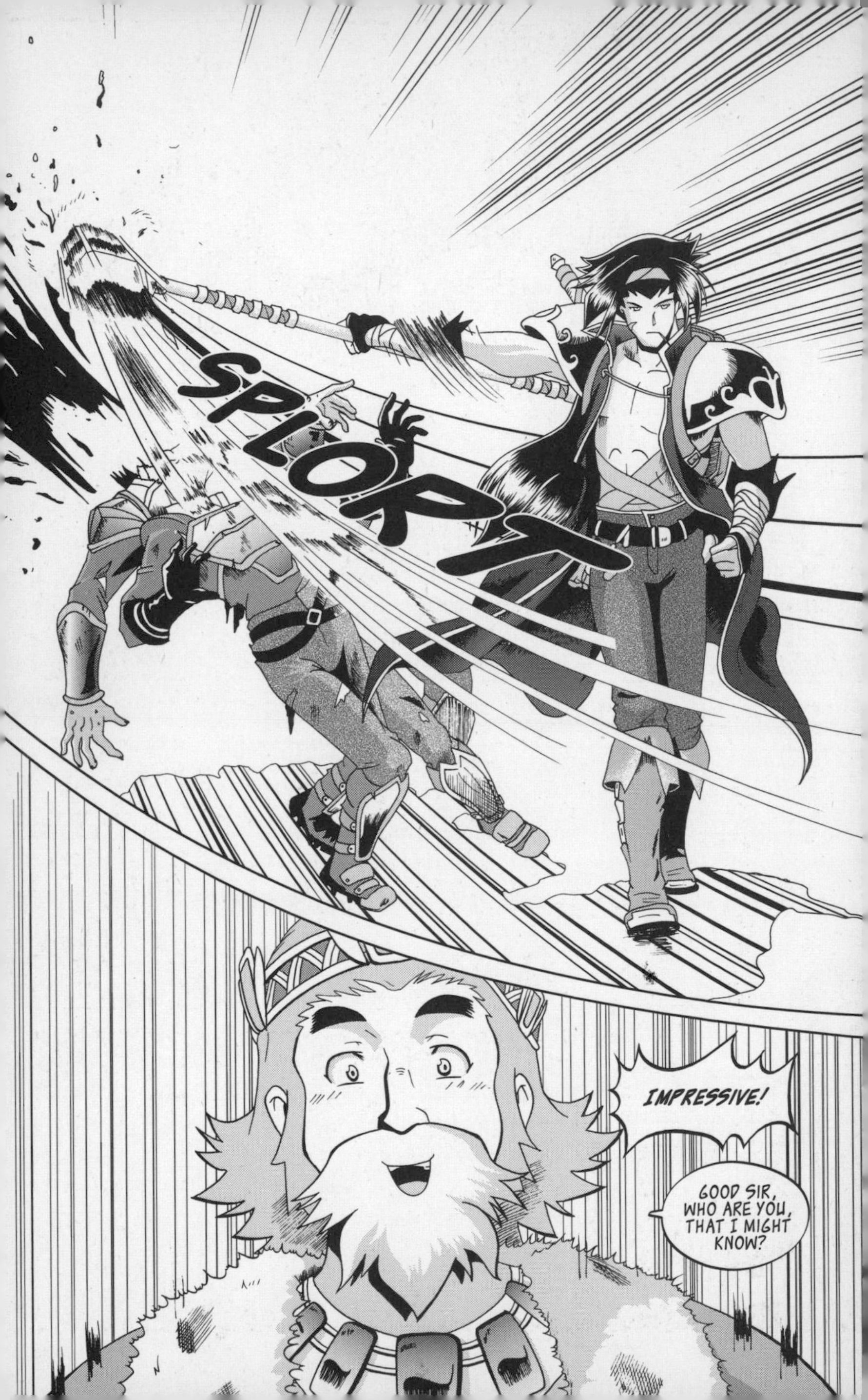
SPLORT
IMPRESSIVE!
GOOD SIR, WHO ARE YOU, THAT I MIGHT KNOW?

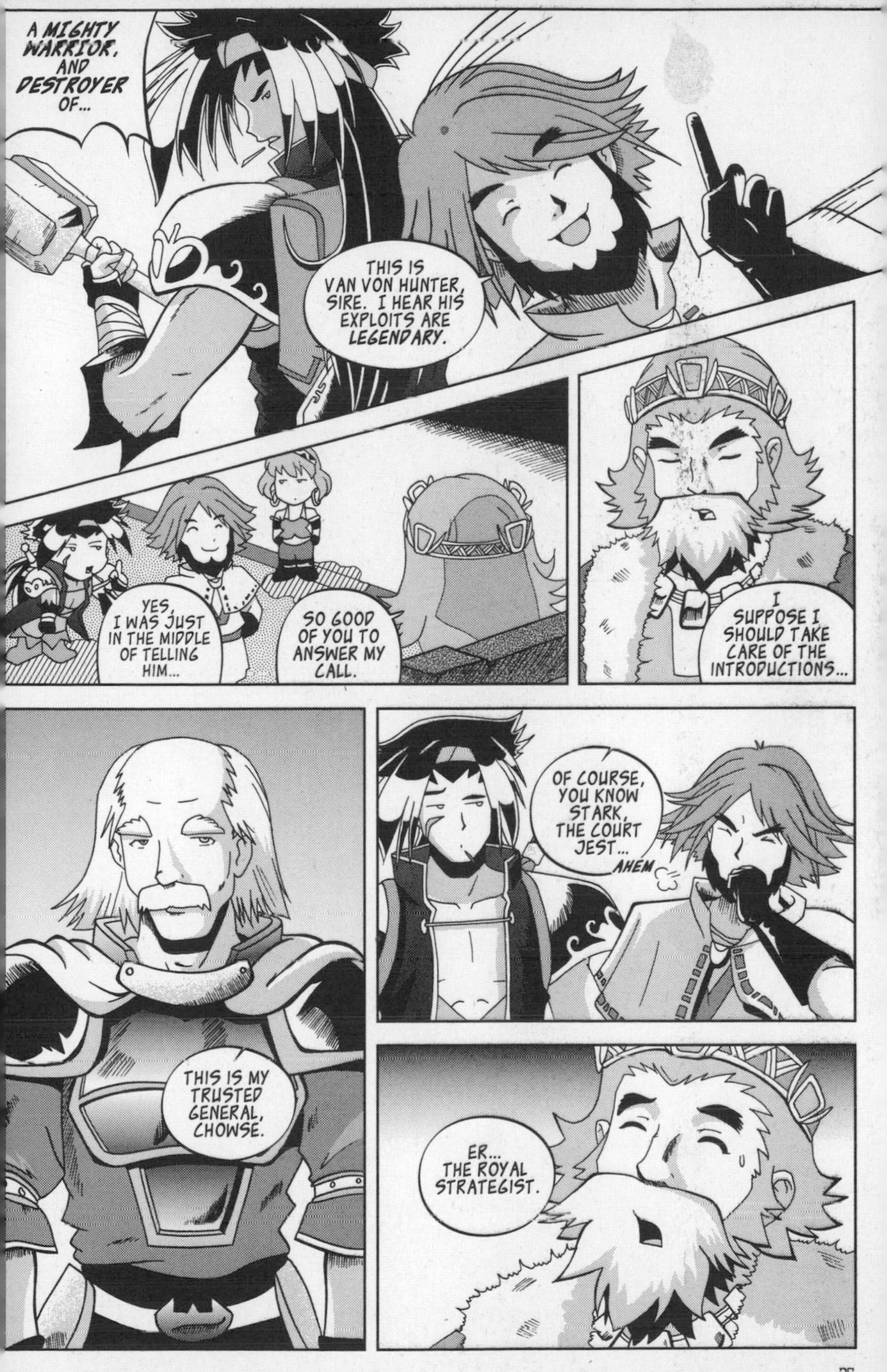
A MIGHTY WARRIOR, AND DESTROYER OF...
THIS IS VAN VON HUNTER, SIRE. I HEAR HIS EXPLOITS ARE LEGENDARY.
YES, I WAS JUST IN THE MIDDLE OF TELLING HIM...
SO GOOD OF YOU TO ANSWER MY CALL.
I SUPPOSE I SHOULD TAKE CARE OF THE INTRODUCTIONS...
THIS IS MY TRUSTED GENERAL, CHOWSE.
OF COURSE, YOU KNOW STARK, THE COURT JEST...
AHEM
ER... THE ROYAL STRATEGIST.

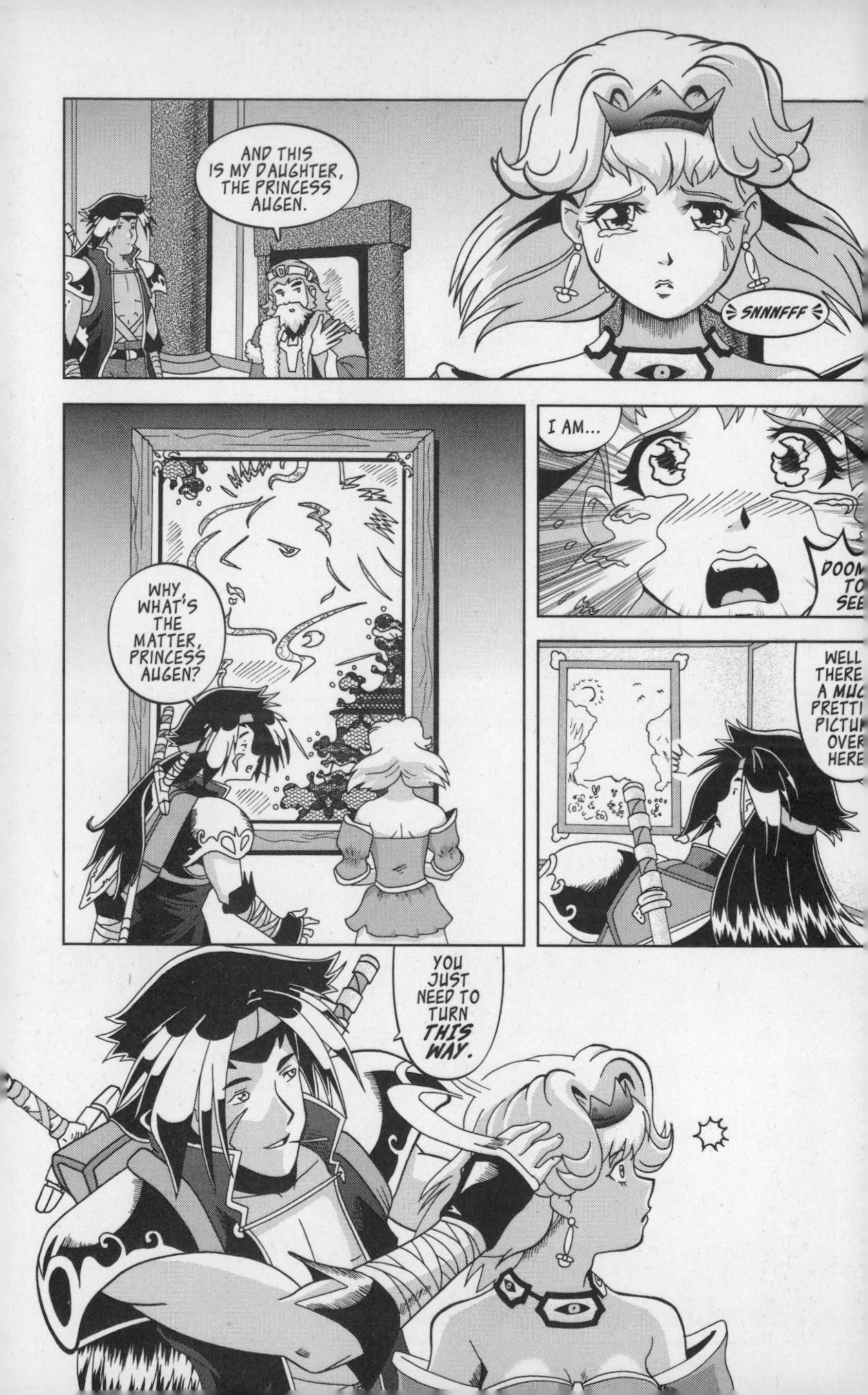
AND THIS IS MY DAUGHTER, THE PRINCESS AUGEN.
SNNNFFF
WHY, WHAT'S THE MATTER, PRINCESS AUGEN?
I AM...
DOOM TO SEE
WELL THERE A MUC PRETTI PICTUI OVER HERE
YOU JUST NEED TO TURN **THIS WAY.**

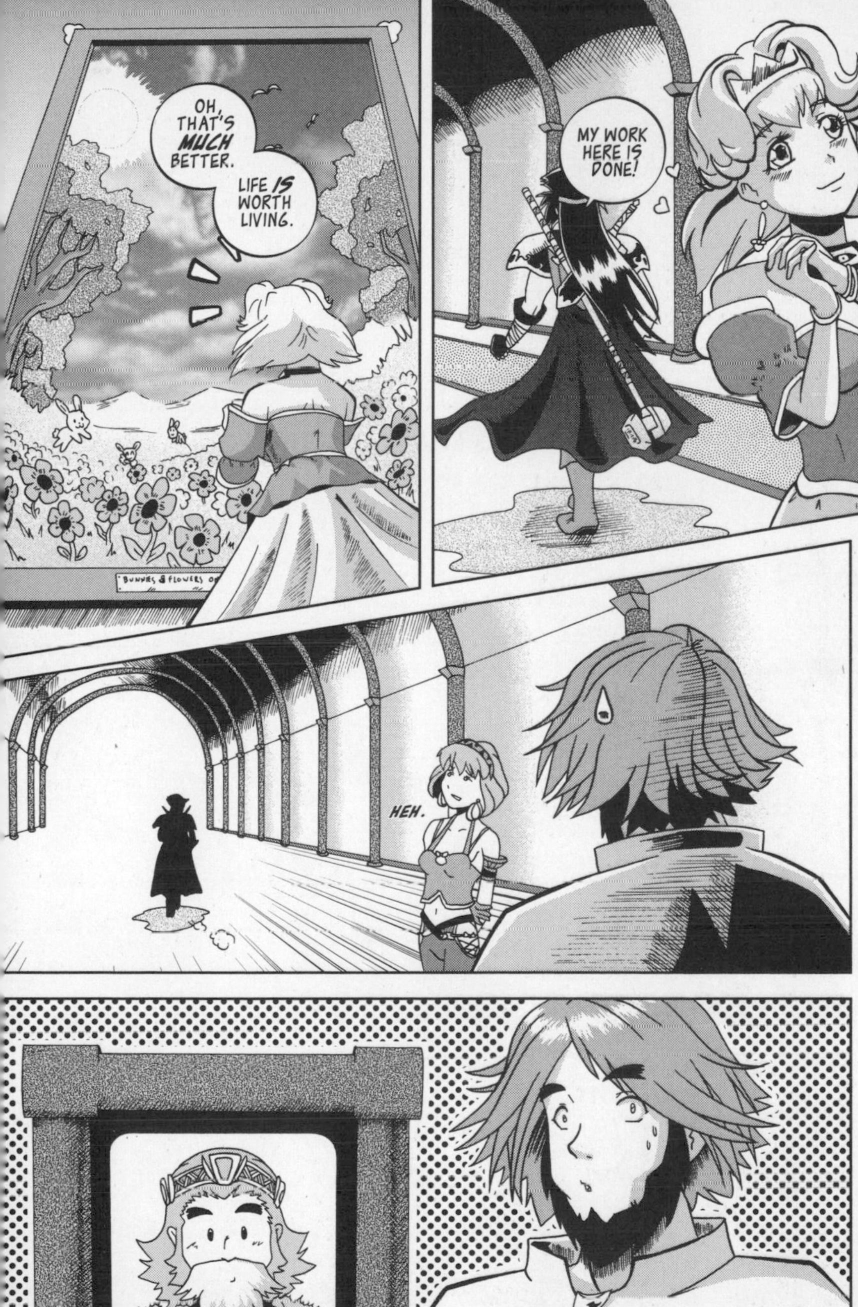
OH, THAT'S *MUCH* BETTER.
LIFE *IS* WORTH LIVING.
MY WORK HERE IS DONE!
HEH.

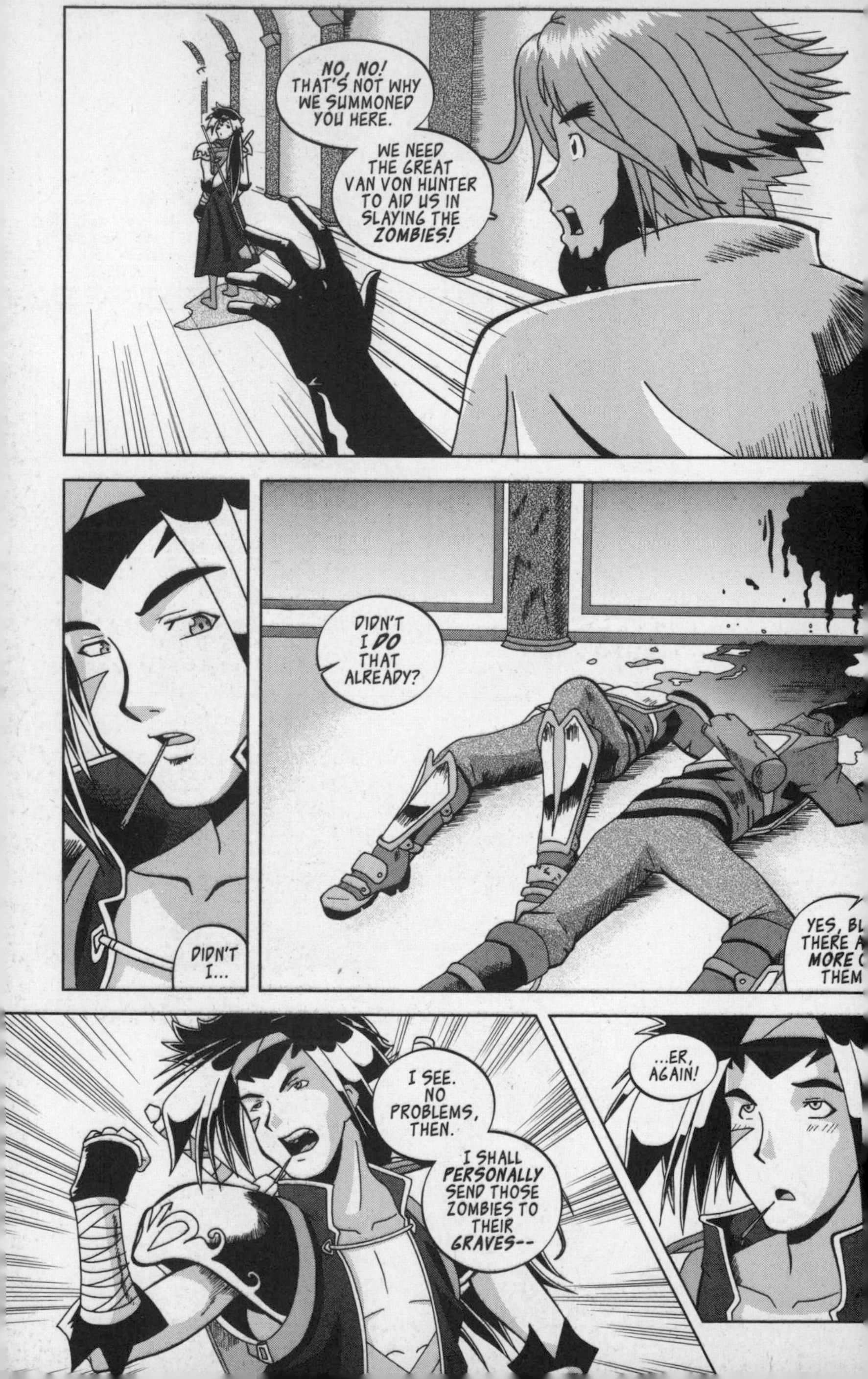
NO, NO! THAT'S NOT WHY WE SUMMONED YOU HERE.
WE NEED THE GREAT VAN VON HUNTER TO AID US IN SLAYING THE ZOMBIES!
DIDN'T I...
DIDN'T I DO THAT ALREADY?
YES, BU THERE A MORE O THEM
I SEE. NO PROBLEMS, THEN.
I SHALL PERSONALLY SEND THOSE ZOMBIES TO THEIR GRAVES--
...ER, AGAIN!

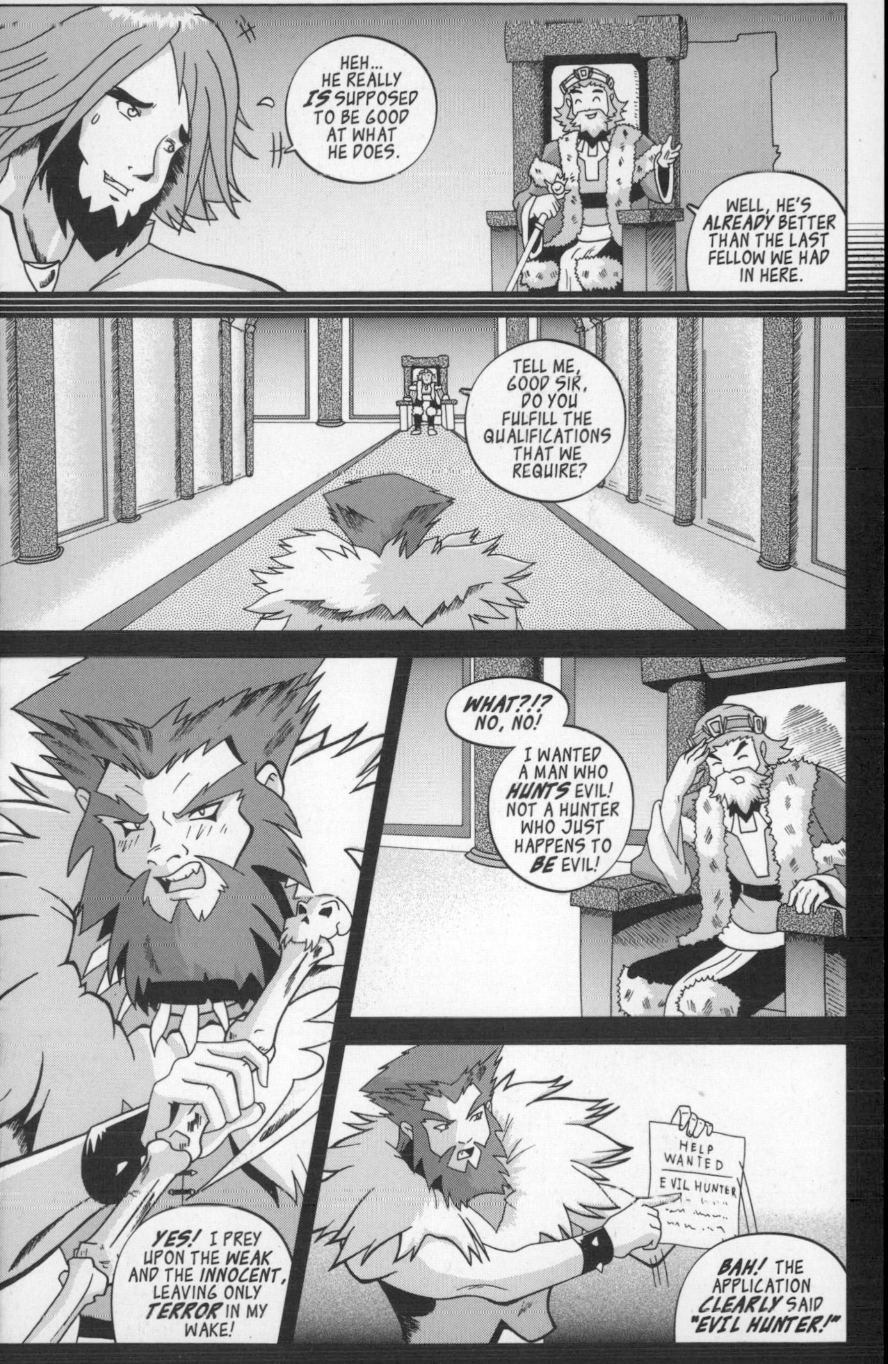
HEH... HE REALLY IS SUPPOSED TO BE GOOD AT WHAT HE DOES.
WELL, HE'S ALREADY BETTER THAN THE LAST FELLOW WE HAD IN HERE.
TELL ME, GOOD SIR, DO YOU FULFILL THE QUALIFICATIONS THAT WE REQUIRE?
YES! I PREY UPON THE WEAK AND THE INNOCENT, LEAVING ONLY TERROR IN MY WAKE!
WHAT?!? NO, NO!
I WANTED A MAN WHO HUNTS EVIL! NOT A HUNTER WHO JUST HAPPENS TO BE EVIL!
HELP WANTED
EVIL HUNTER
BAH! THE APPLICATION CLEARLY SAID "EVIL HUNTER!"

2

FOR THE SAKE OF APPEARANCES, WE MIGHT AS WELL HAVE A QUEST.

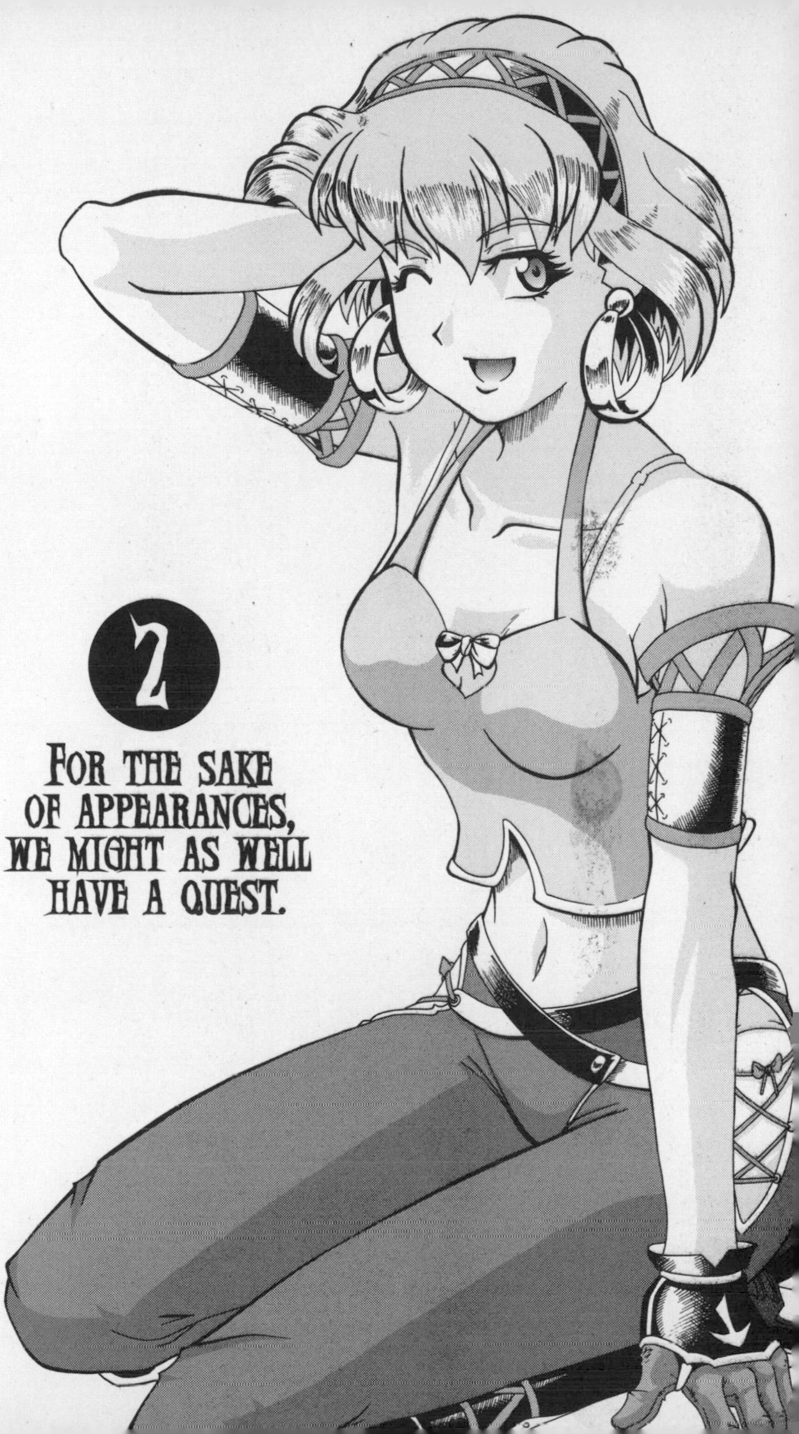

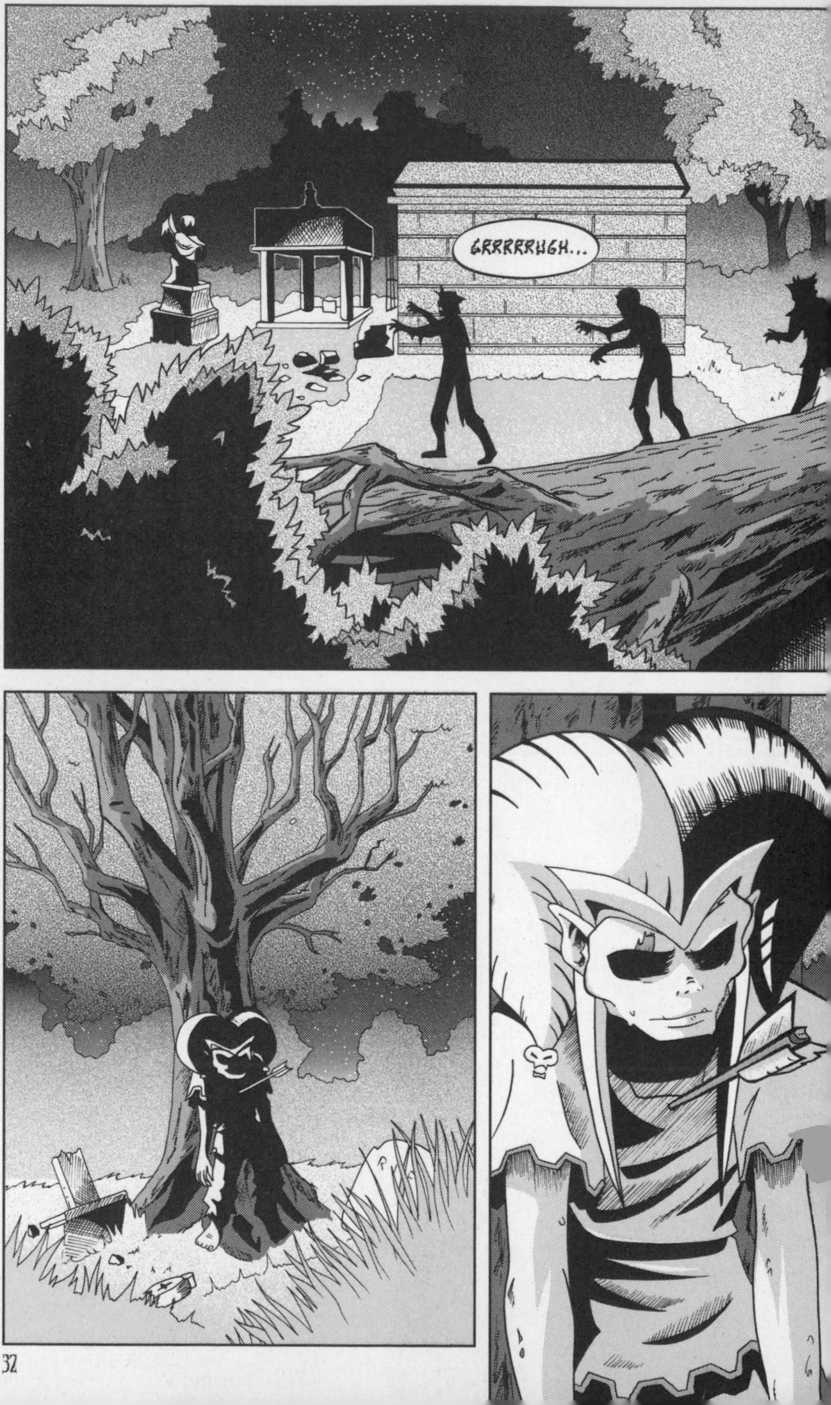
GRRRRRUGH...

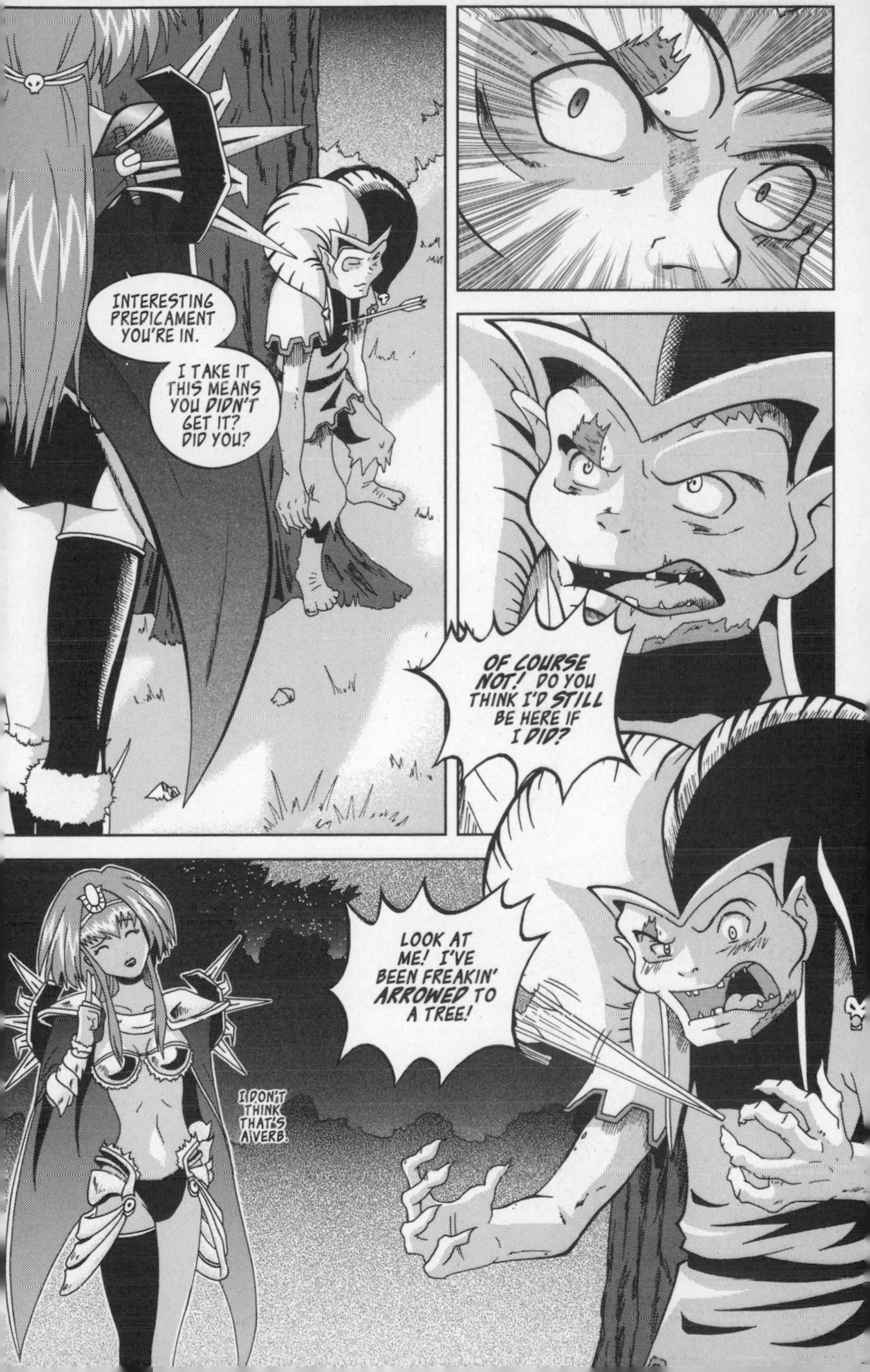
INTERESTING PREDICAMENT YOU'RE IN.
I TAKE IT THIS MEANS YOU *DIDN'T* GET IT? DID YOU?
OF COURSE NOT! DO YOU THINK I'D *STILL* BE HERE IF I *DID?*
LOOK AT ME! I'VE BEEN FREAKIN' *ARROWED* TO A TREE!
I DON'T THINK THAT'S A VERB.

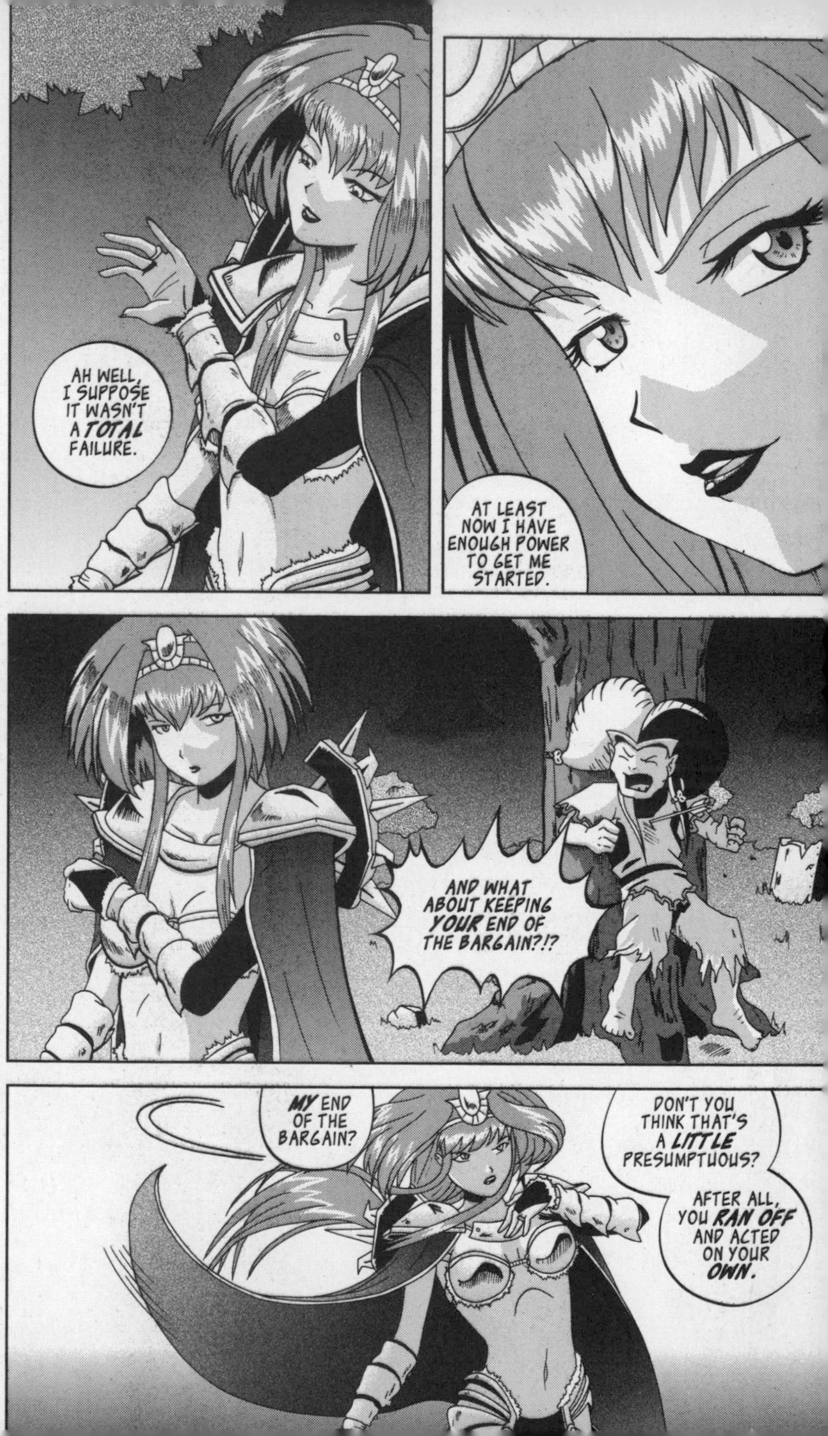
AH WELL, I SUPPOSE IT WASN'T A TOTAL FAILURE.
AT LEAST NOW I HAVE ENOUGH POWER TO GET ME STARTED.
AND WHAT ABOUT KEEPING YOUR END OF THE BARGAIN?!?
MY END OF THE BARGAIN?
DON'T YOU THINK THAT'S A LITTLE PRESUMPTUOUS?
AFTER ALL, YOU RAN OFF AND ACTED ON YOUR OWN.

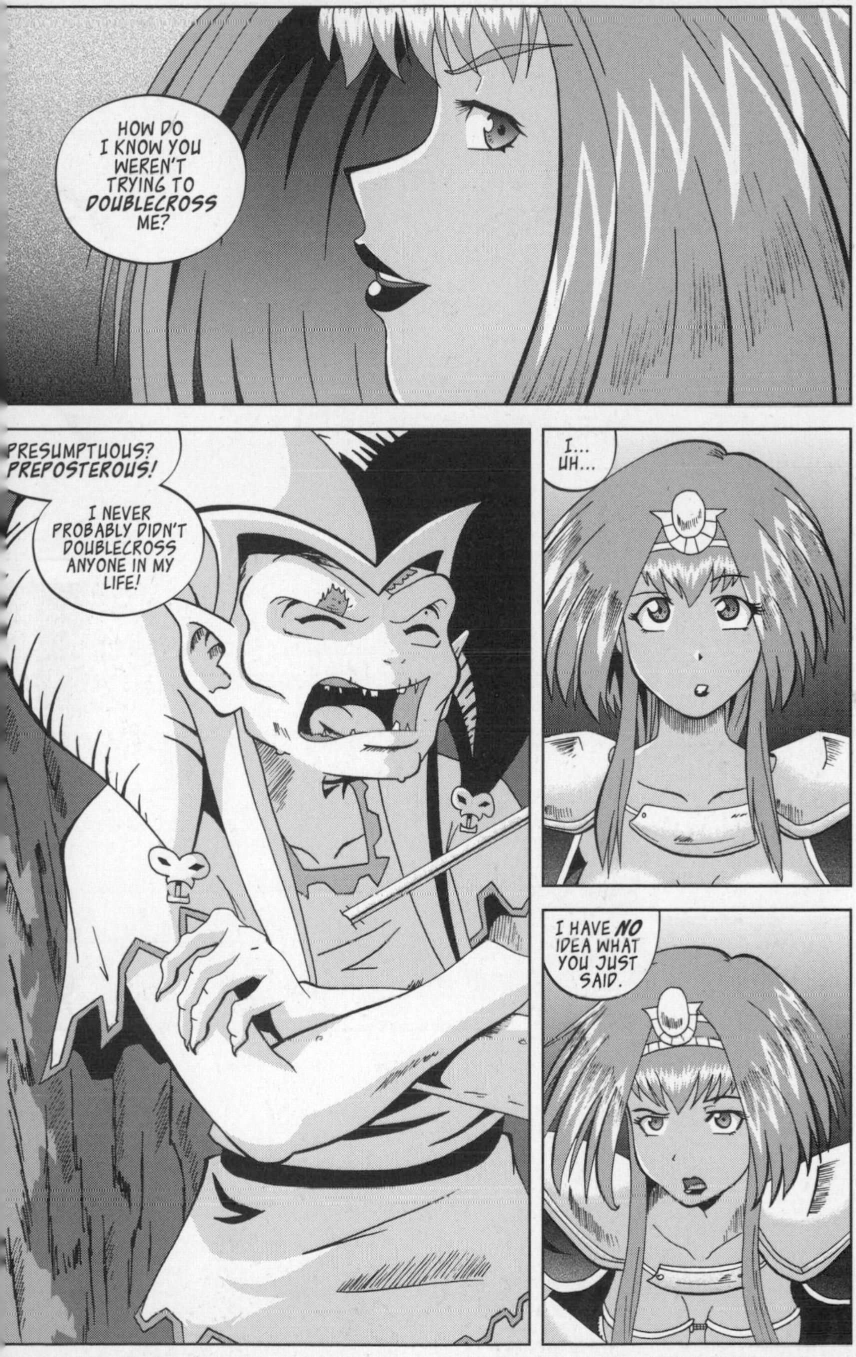
HOW DO I KNOW YOU WEREN'T TRYING TO DOUBLECROSS ME?
PRESUMPTUOUS? PREPOSTEROUS!
I NEVER PROBABLY DIDN'T DOUBLECROSS ANYONE IN MY LIFE!
I... UH...
I HAVE NO IDEA WHAT YOU JUST SAID.

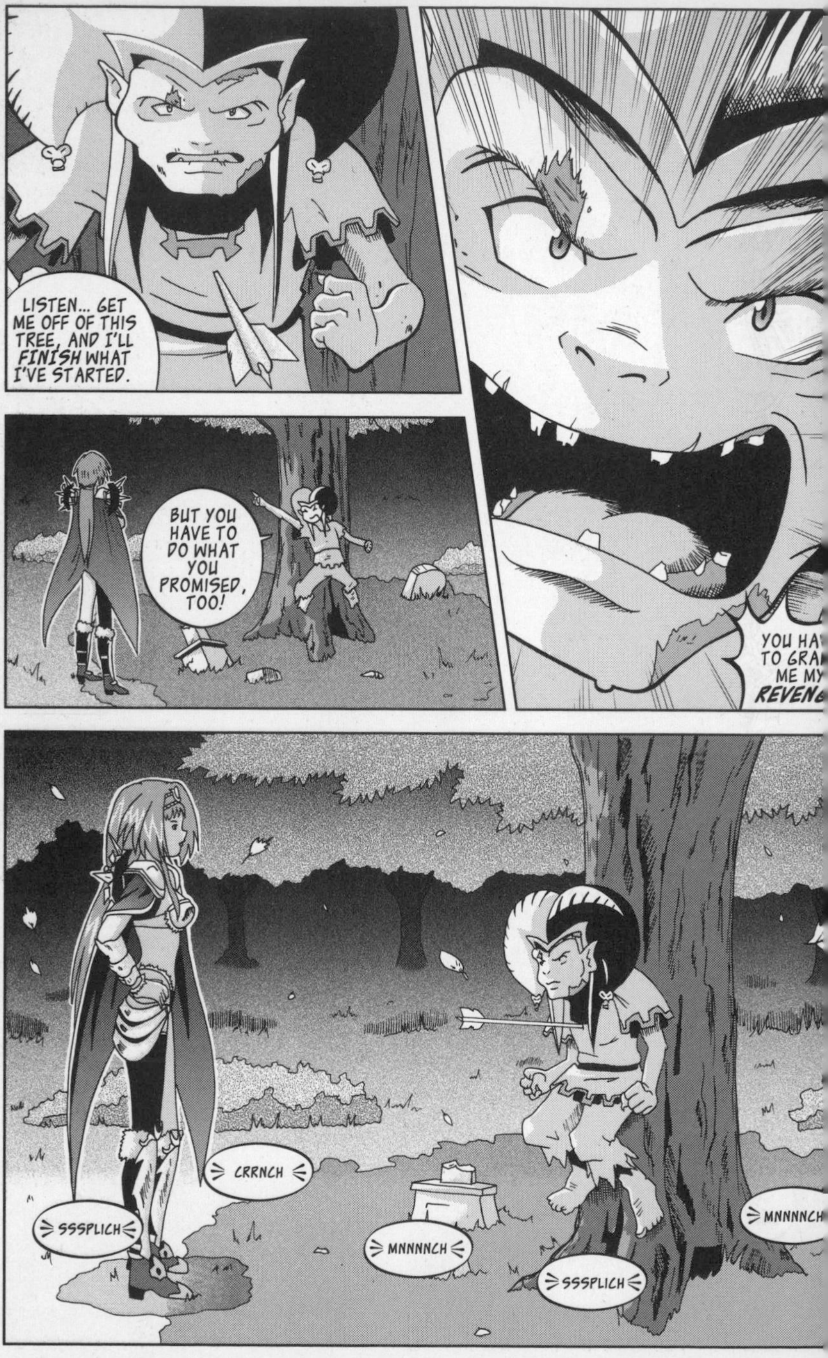

LISTEN... GET ME OFF OF THIS TREE, AND I'LL *FINISH* WHAT I'VE STARTED.
YOU HA TO GRA ME MY *REVEN*
BUT YOU HAVE TO DO WHAT YOU PROMISED, TOO!
CRRNCH
SSSPLICH
MNNNNCH
SSSPLICH
MNNNNCH

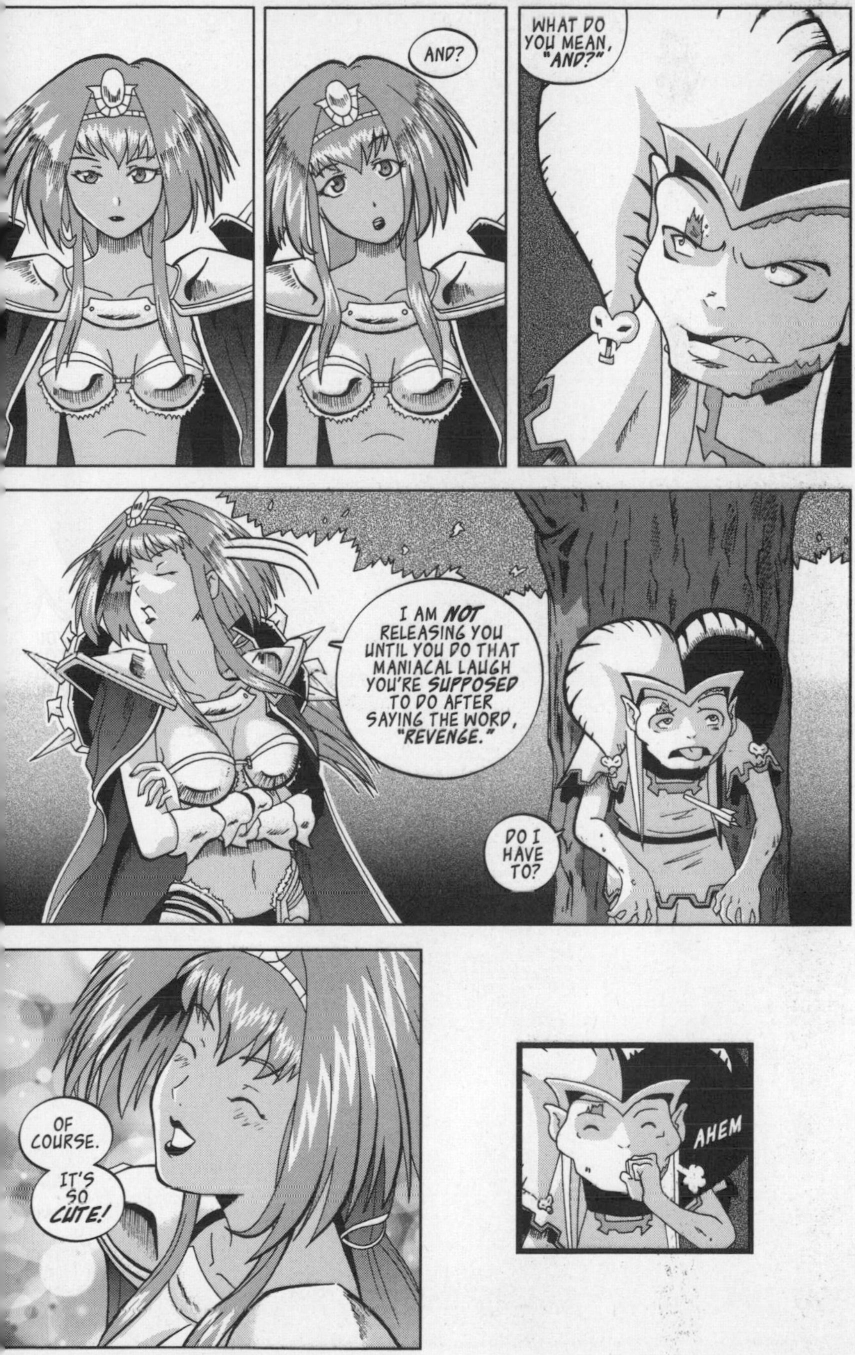
AND?
WHAT DO YOU MEAN, "AND?"
I AM NOT RELEASING YOU UNTIL YOU DO THAT MANIACAL LAUGH YOU'RE SUPPOSED TO DO AFTER SAYING THE WORD, "REVENGE."
DO I HAVE TO?
OF COURSE.
IT'S SO CUTE!
AHEM

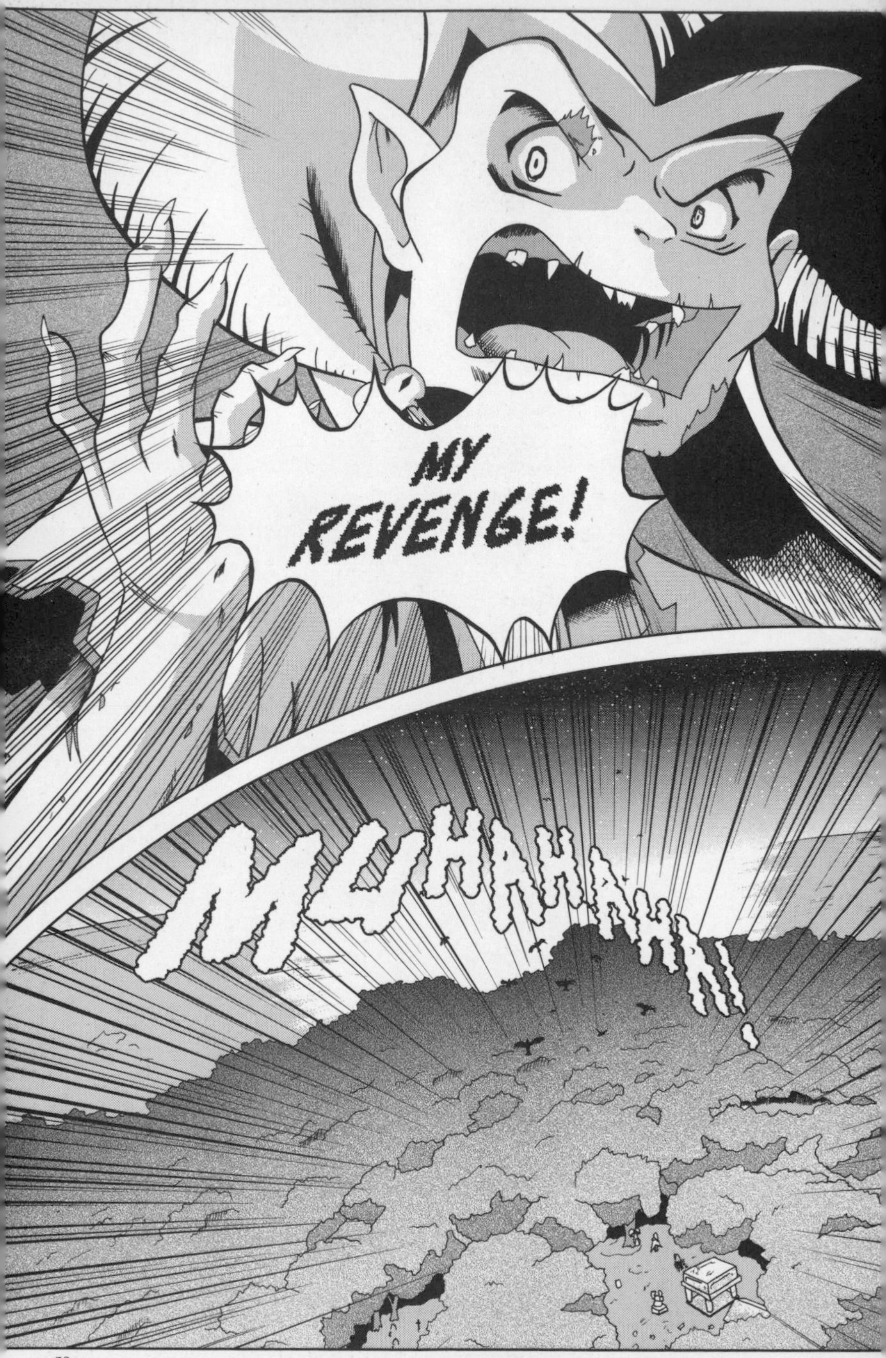
MY REVENGE!
MUHAHAHAHA!

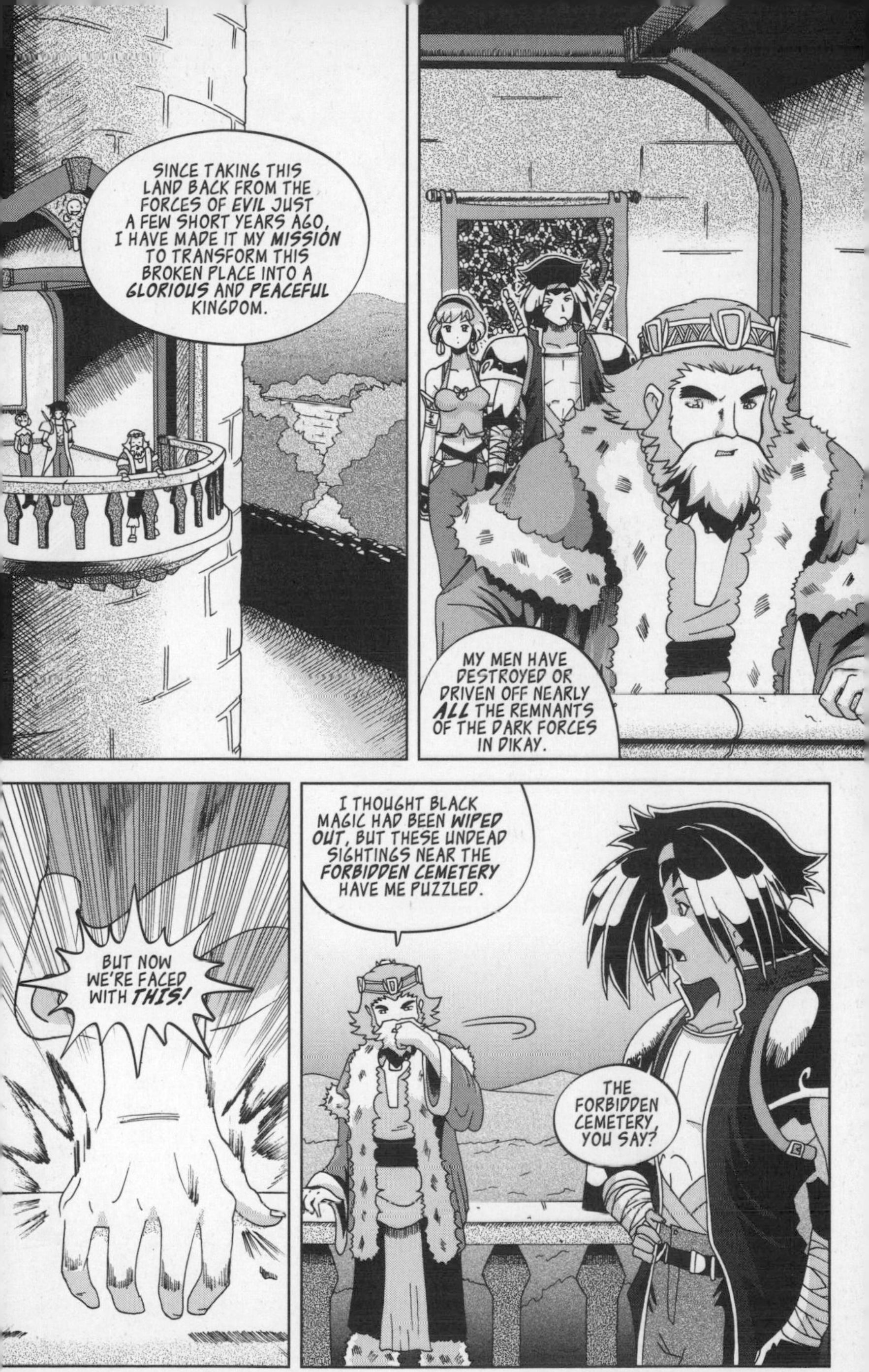
SINCE TAKING THIS LAND BACK FROM THE FORCES OF EVIL JUST A FEW SHORT YEARS AGO, I HAVE MADE IT MY MISSION TO TRANSFORM THIS BROKEN PLACE INTO A GLORIOUS AND PEACEFUL KINGDOM.
MY MEN HAVE DESTROYED OR DRIVEN OFF NEARLY ALL THE REMNANTS OF THE DARK FORCES IN DIKAY.
BUT NOW WE'RE FACED WITH THIS!
I THOUGHT BLACK MAGIC HAD BEEN WIPED OUT, BUT THESE UNDEAD SIGHTINGS NEAR THE FORBIDDEN CEMETERY HAVE ME PUZZLED.
THE FORBIDDEN CEMETERY, YOU SAY?

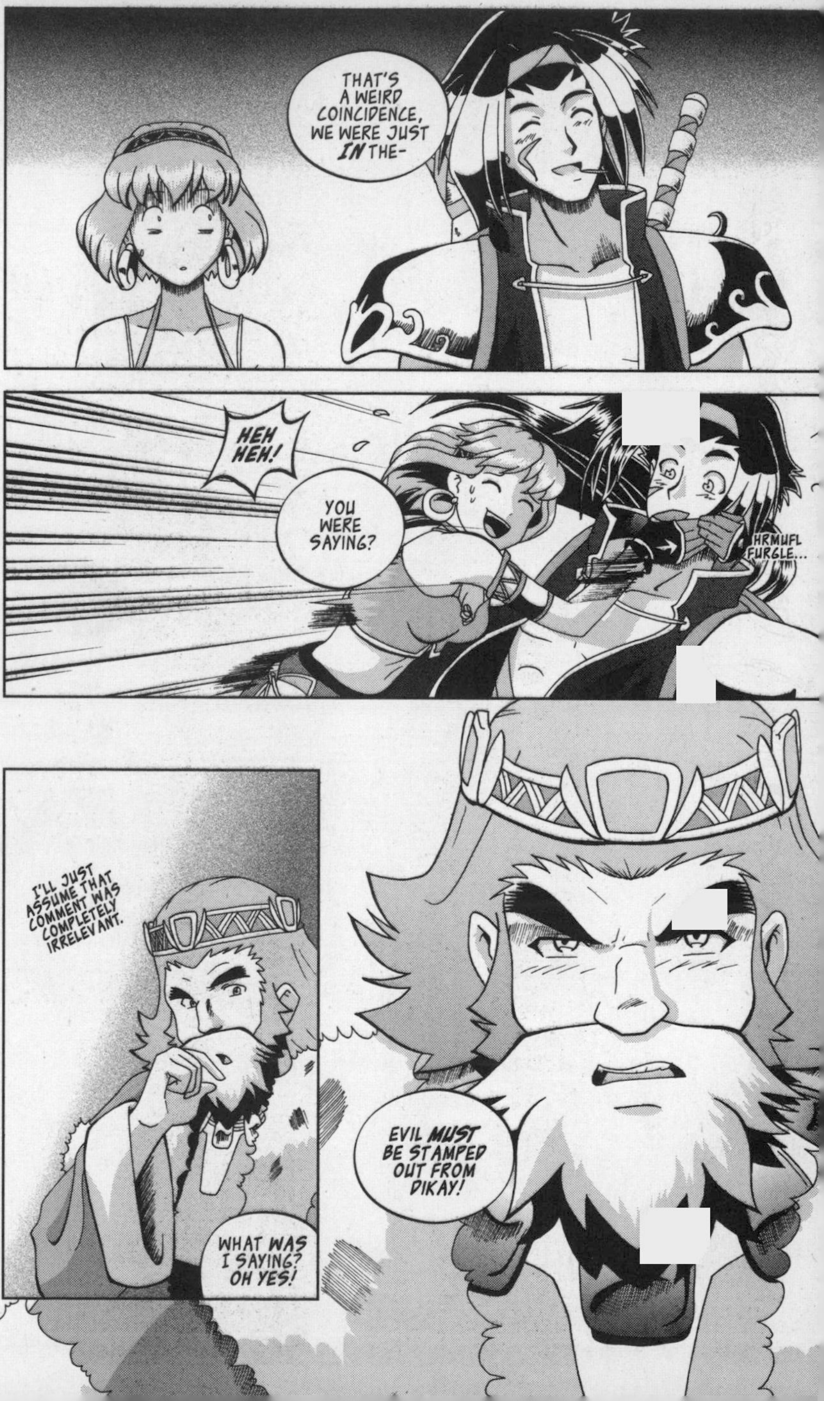
THAT'S A WEIRD COINCIDENCE, WE WERE JUST IN THE-
HEH HEH!
YOU WERE SAYING?
HRMUFL FURGLE...
I'LL JUST ASSUME THAT COMMENT WAS COMPLETELY IRRELEVANT.
WHAT WAS I SAYING? OH YES!
EVIL MUST BE STAMPED OUT FROM DIKAY!

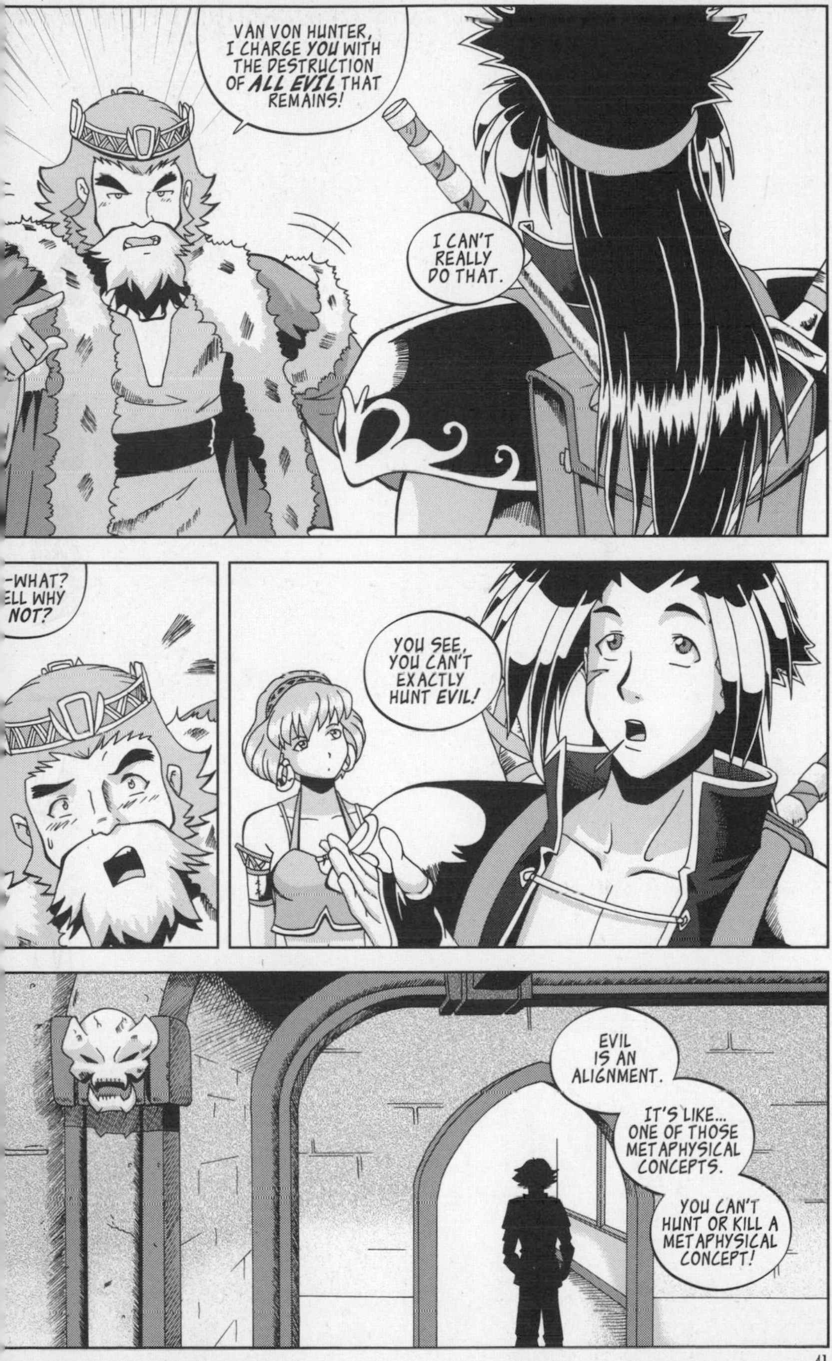
VAN VON HUNTER, I CHARGE YOU WITH THE DESTRUCTION OF ALL EVIL THAT REMAINS!
I CAN'T REALLY DO THAT.
-WHAT? ELL WHY NOT?
YOU SEE, YOU CAN'T EXACTLY HUNT EVIL!
EVIL IS AN ALIGNMENT.
IT'S LIKE... ONE OF THOSE METAPHYSICAL CONCEPTS.
YOU CAN'T HUNT OR KILL A METAPHYSICAL CONCEPT!

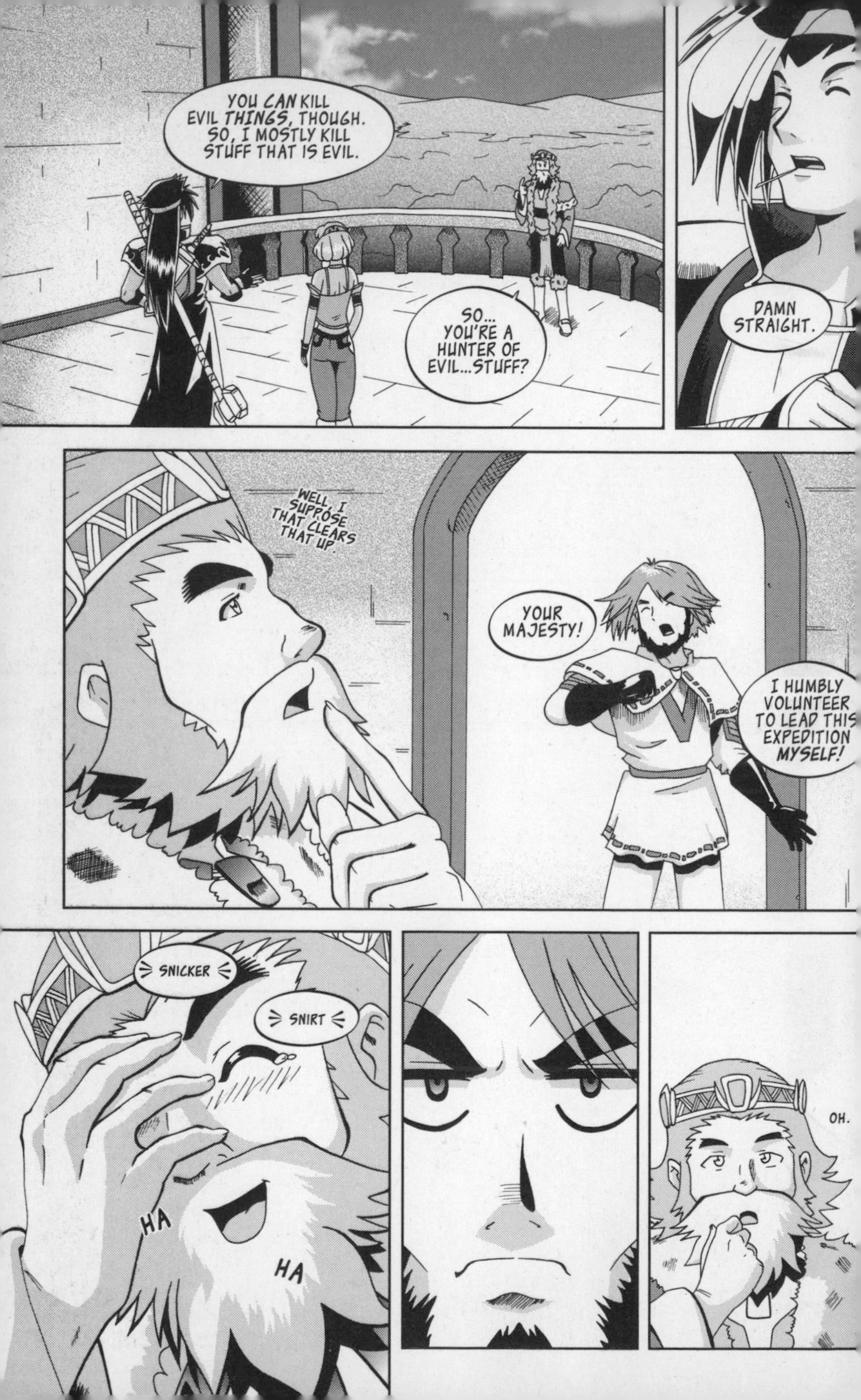
YOU CAN KILL EVIL THINGS, THOUGH. SO, I MOSTLY KILL STUFF THAT IS EVIL.
SO... YOU'RE A HUNTER OF EVIL...STUFF?
DAMN STRAIGHT.
WELL, I SUPPOSE THAT CLEARS THAT UP.
YOUR MAJESTY!
I HUMBLY VOLUNTEER TO LEAD THIS EXPEDITION MYSELF!
SNICKER
SNIRT
HA
HA
OH.

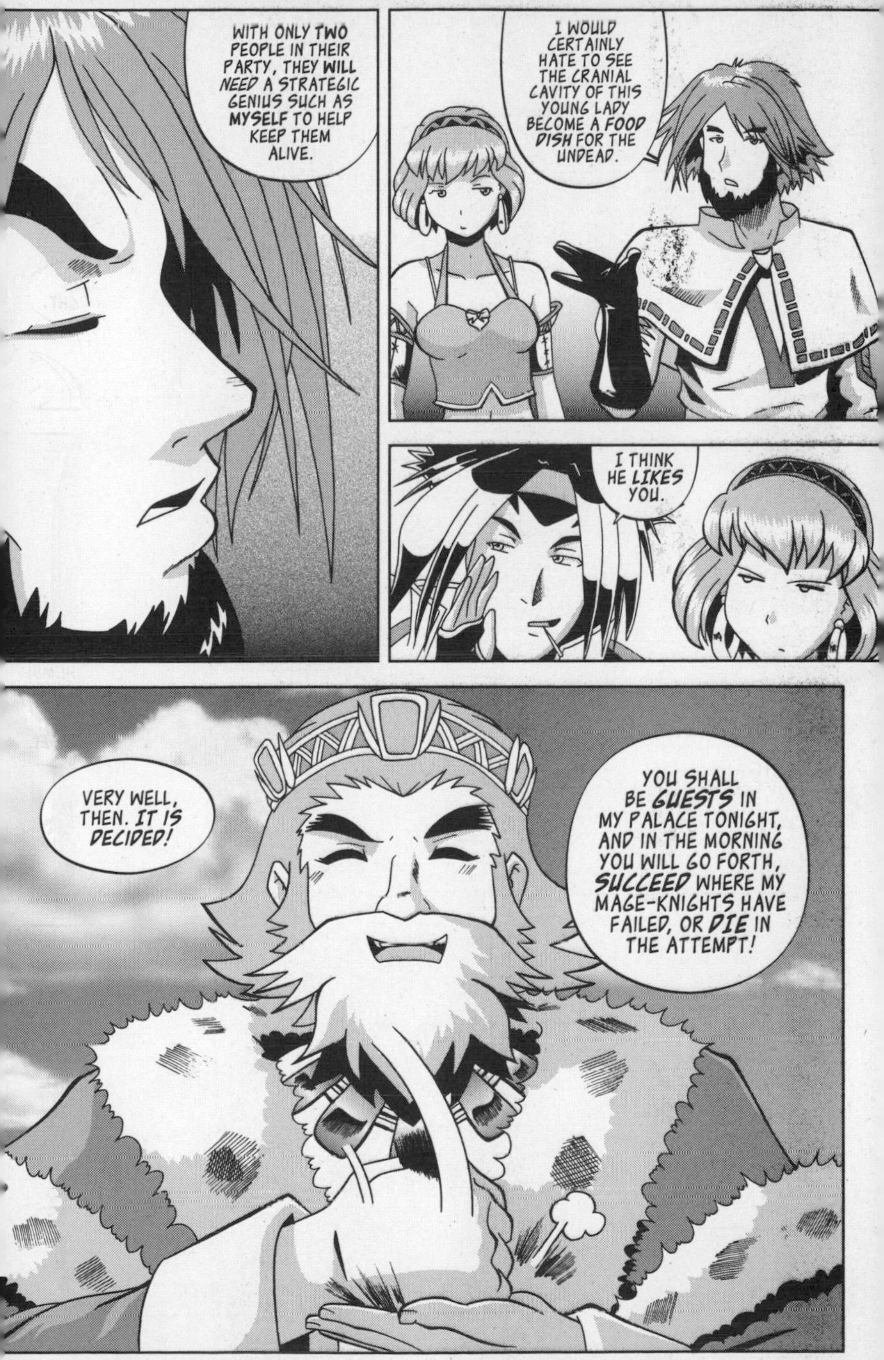
WITH ONLY TWO PEOPLE IN THEIR PARTY, THEY WILL NEED A STRATEGIC GENIUS SUCH AS MYSELF TO HELP KEEP THEM ALIVE.
I WOULD CERTAINLY HATE TO SEE THE CRANIAL CAVITY OF THIS YOUNG LADY BECOME A FOOD DISH FOR THE UNDEAD.
I THINK HE LIKES YOU.
VERY WELL, THEN. IT IS DECIDED!
YOU SHALL BE GUESTS IN MY PALACE TONIGHT, AND IN THE MORNING YOU WILL GO FORTH, SUCCEED WHERE MY MAGE-KNIGHTS HAVE FAILED, OR DIE IN THE ATTEMPT!

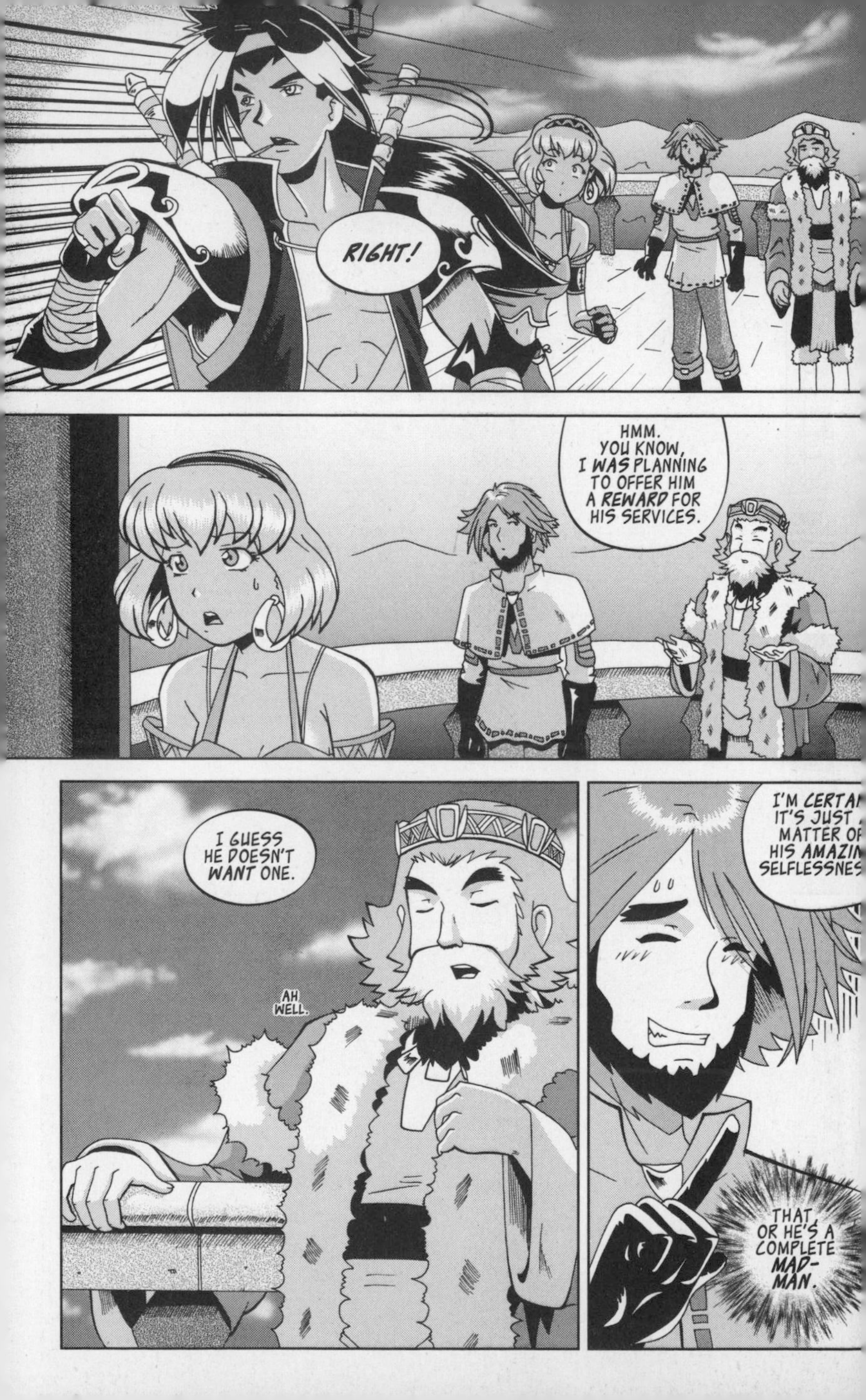
RIGHT!
HMM. YOU KNOW, I WAS PLANNING TO OFFER HIM A REWARD FOR HIS SERVICES.
I GUESS HE DOESN'T WANT ONE.
AH WELL.
I'M CERTA IT'S JUST MATTER OF HIS AMAZI SELFLESSNES
THAT OR HE'S A COMPLETE MAD-MAN.

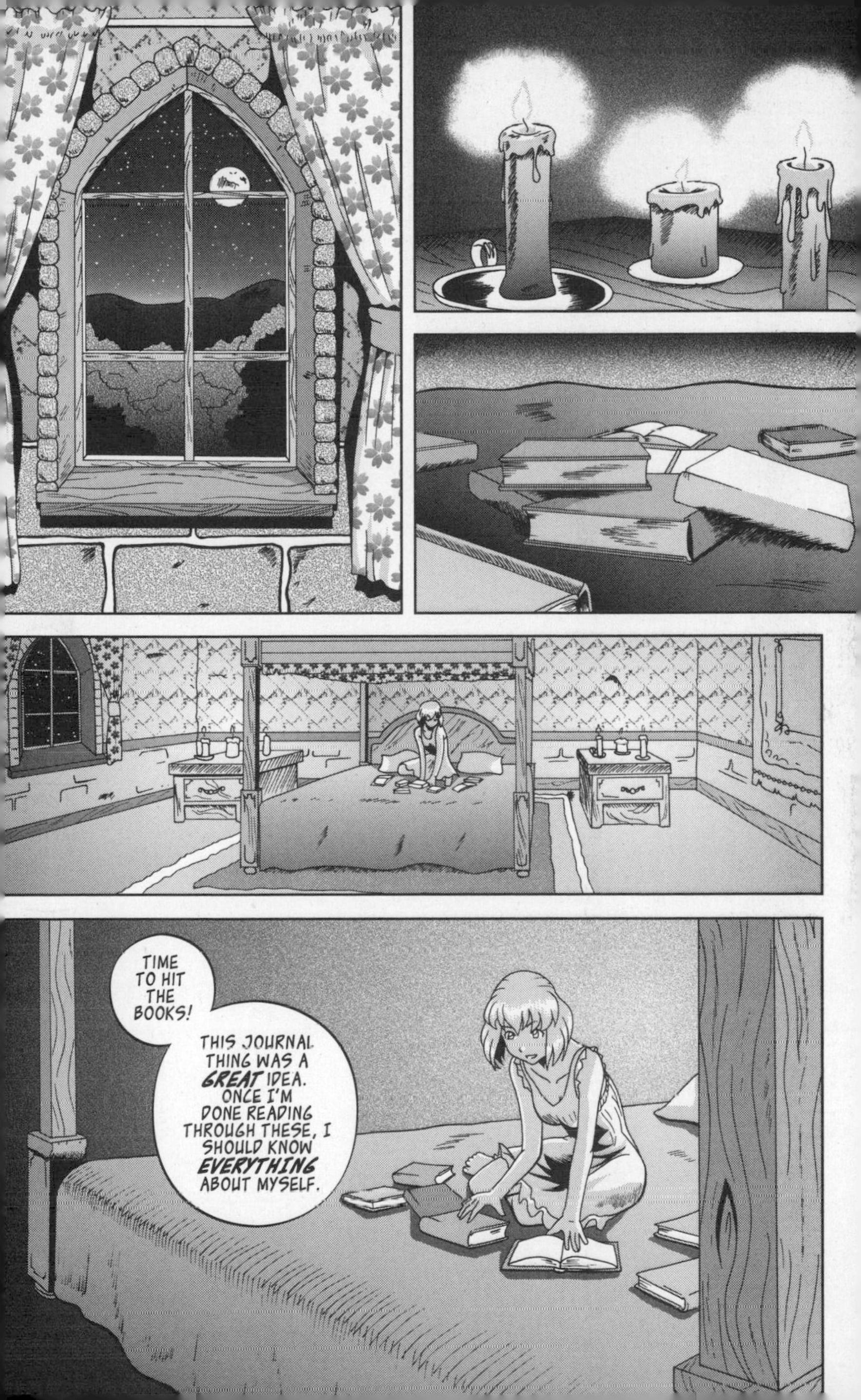
TIME TO HIT THE BOOKS!
THIS JOURNAL THING WAS A GREAT IDEA. ONCE I'M DONE READING THROUGH THESE, I SHOULD KNOW EVERYTHING ABOUT MYSELF.

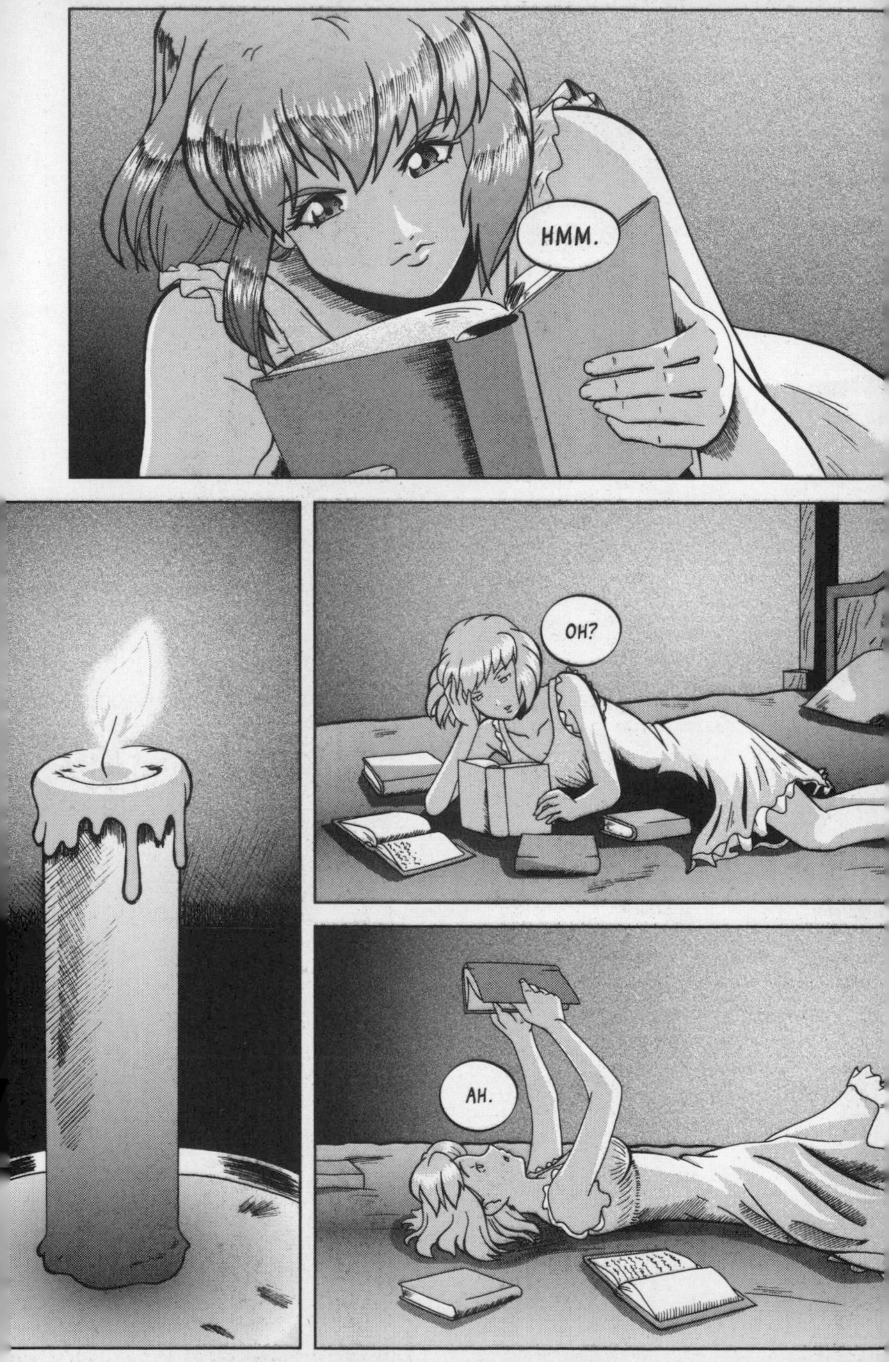
HMM.
OH?
AH.

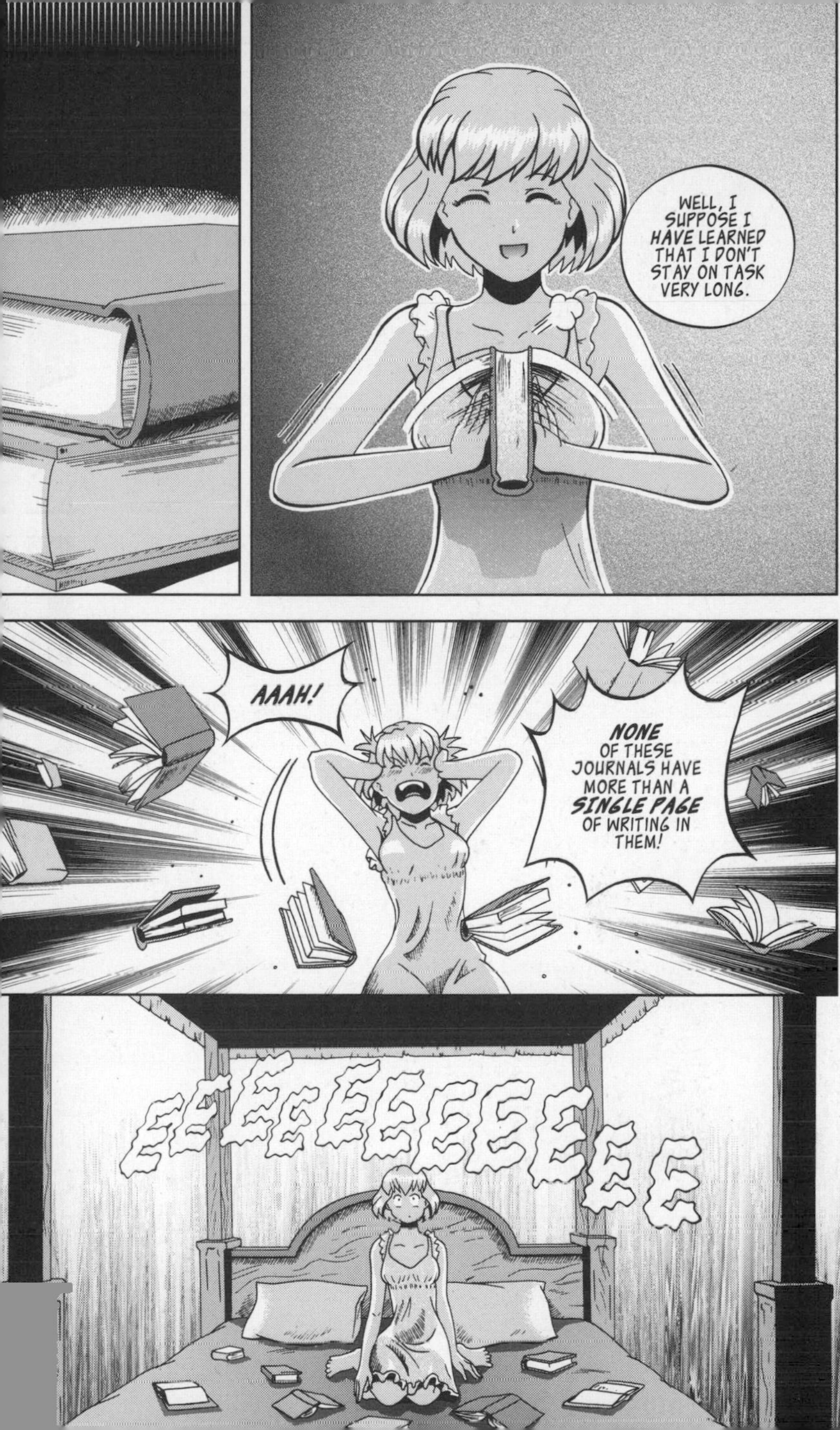
WELL, I SUPPOSE I *HAVE* LEARNED THAT I DON'T STAY ON TASK VERY LONG.
AAAH!
NONE OF THESE JOURNALS HAVE MORE THAN A *SINGLE PAGE* OF WRITING IN THEM!
EEEEEEEEEEEEEE

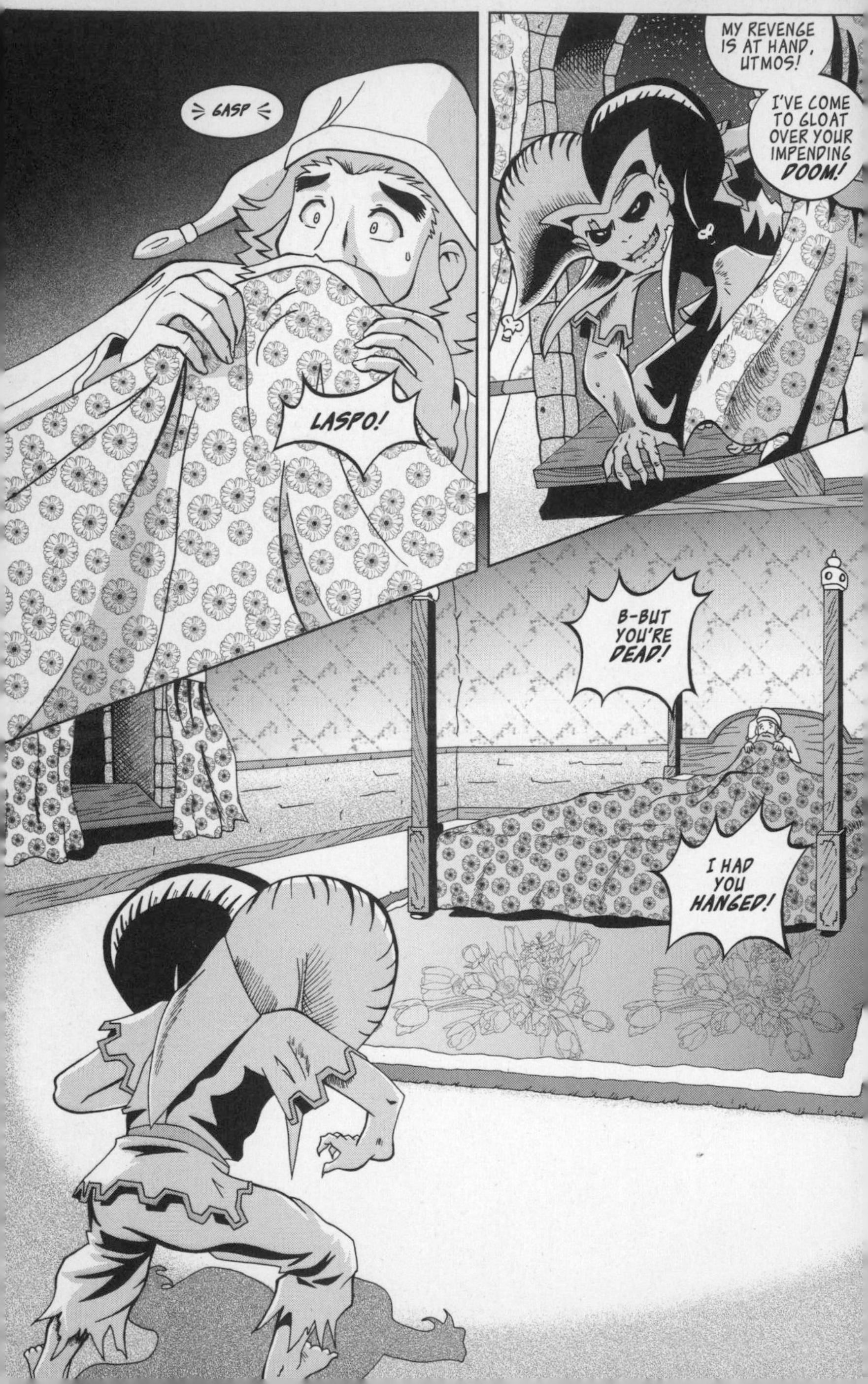
GASP
LASPO!
MY REVENGE IS AT HAND, UTMOS!
I'VE COME TO GLOAT OVER YOUR IMPENDING DOOM!
B-BUT YOU'RE DEAD!
I HAD YOU HANGED!

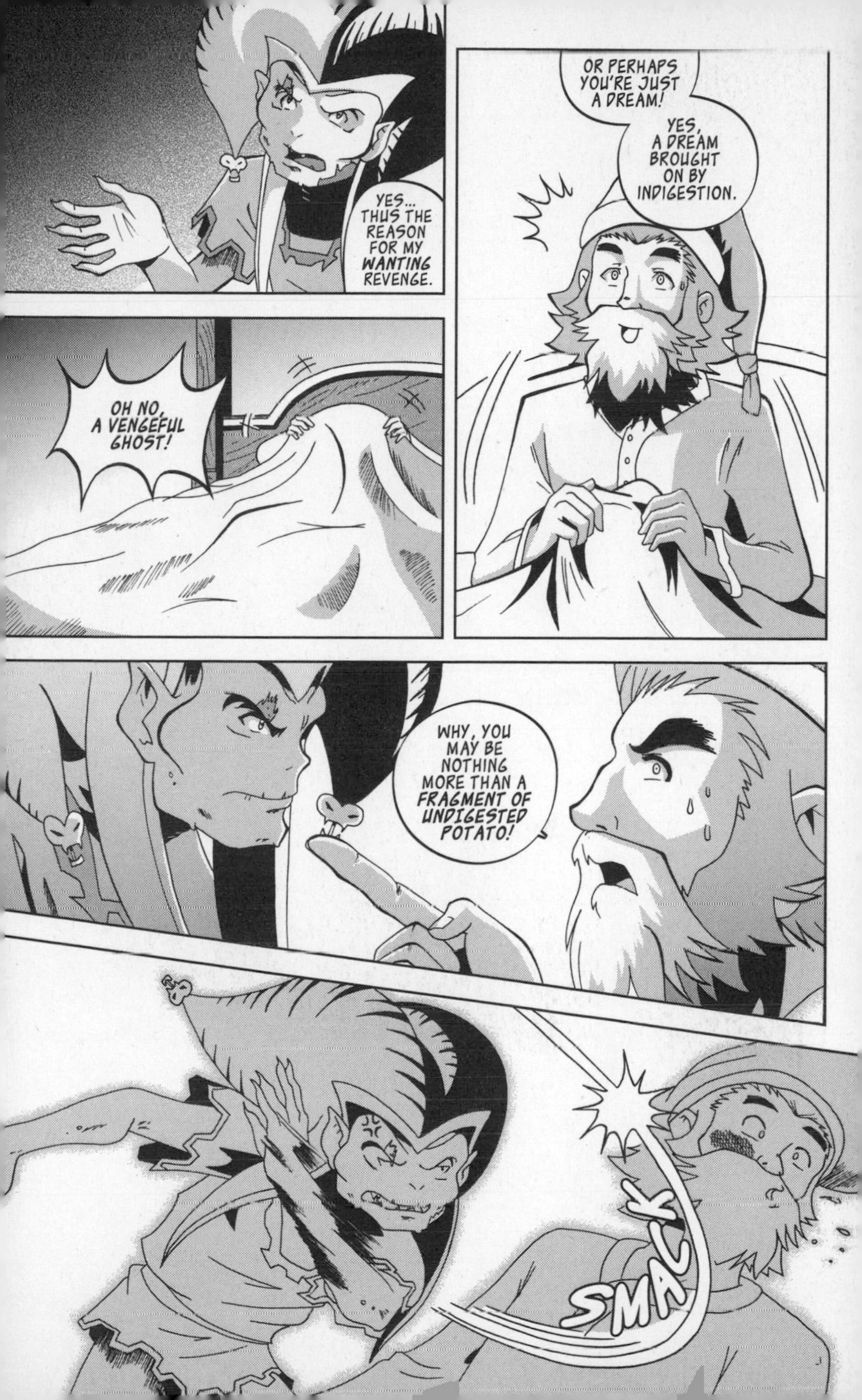
YES... THUS THE REASON FOR MY WANTING REVENGE.
OR PERHAPS YOU'RE JUST A DREAM!
YES, A DREAM BROUGHT ON BY INDIGESTION.
OH NO, A VENGEFUL GHOST!
WHY, YOU MAY BE NOTHING MORE THAN A FRAGMENT OF UNDIGESTED POTATO!
SMACK

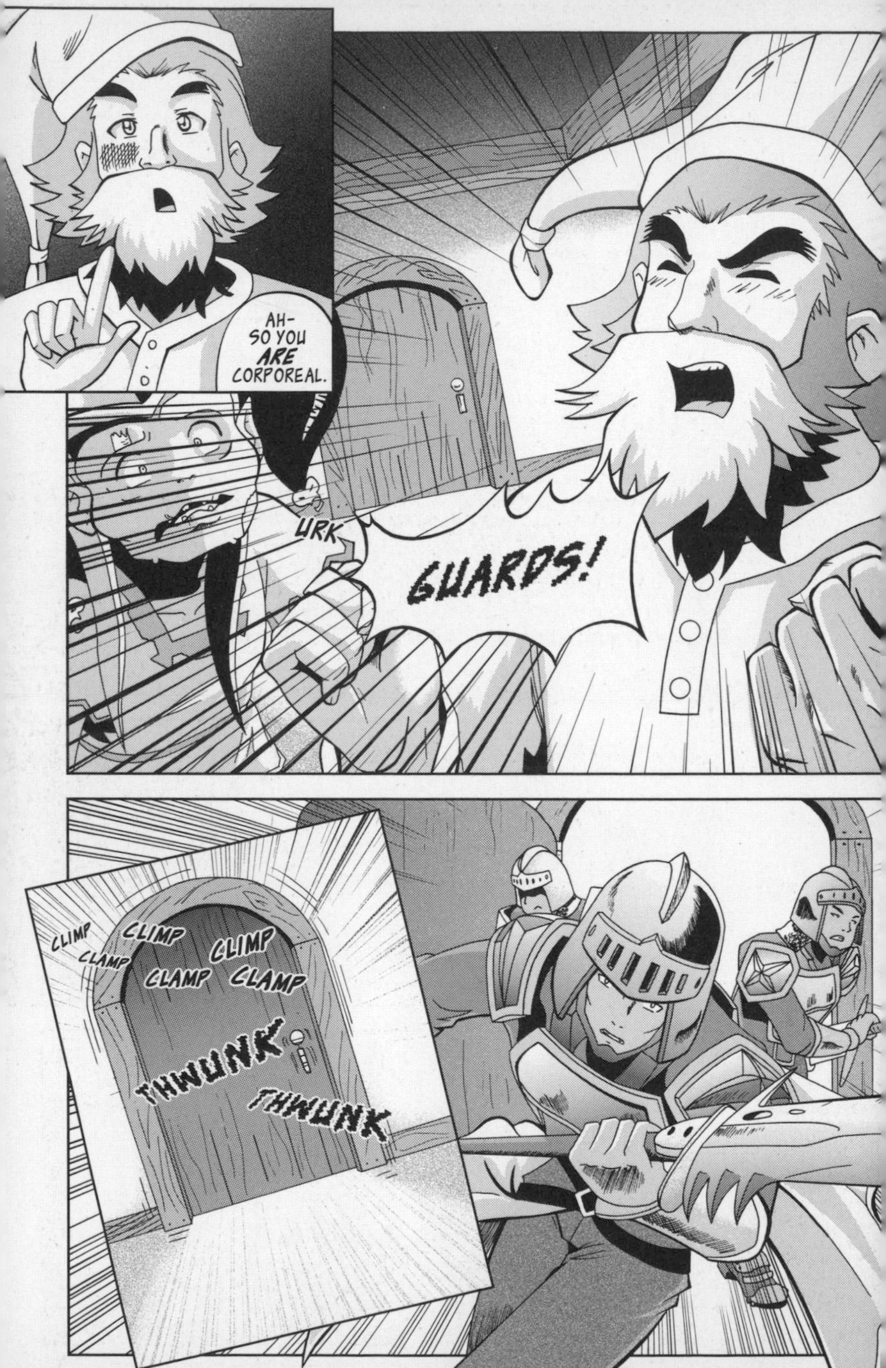

AH- SO YOU ARE CORPOREAL.
URK
GUARDS!
CLIMP CLAMP CLIMP CLAMP CLIMP CLAMP
THWUNK
THWUNK

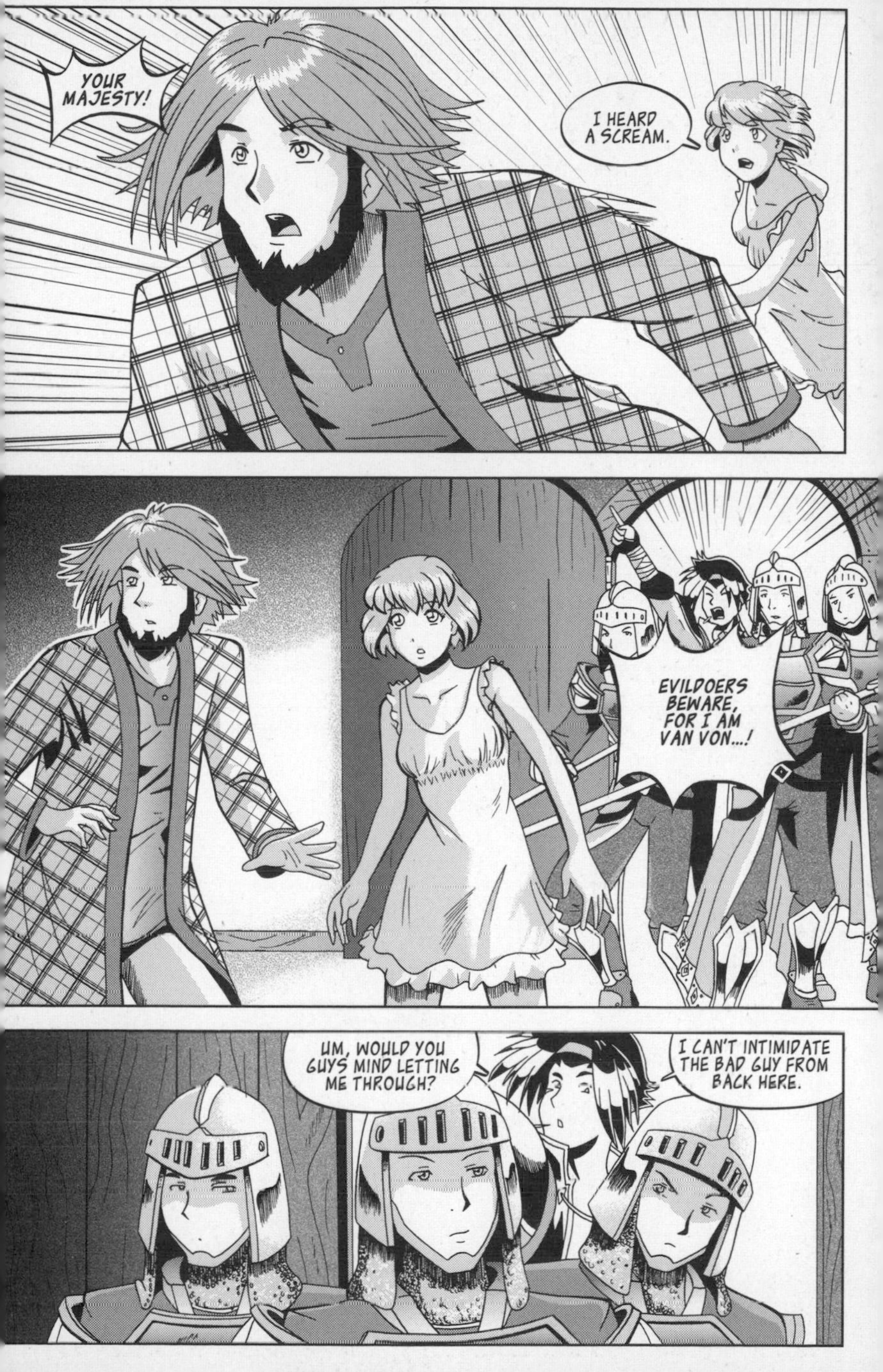
YOUR MAJESTY!
I HEARD A SCREAM.
EVILDOERS BEWARE, FOR I AM VAN VON...!
UM, WOULD YOU GUYS MIND LETTING ME THROUGH?
I CAN'T INTIMIDATE THE BAD GUY FROM BACK HERE.

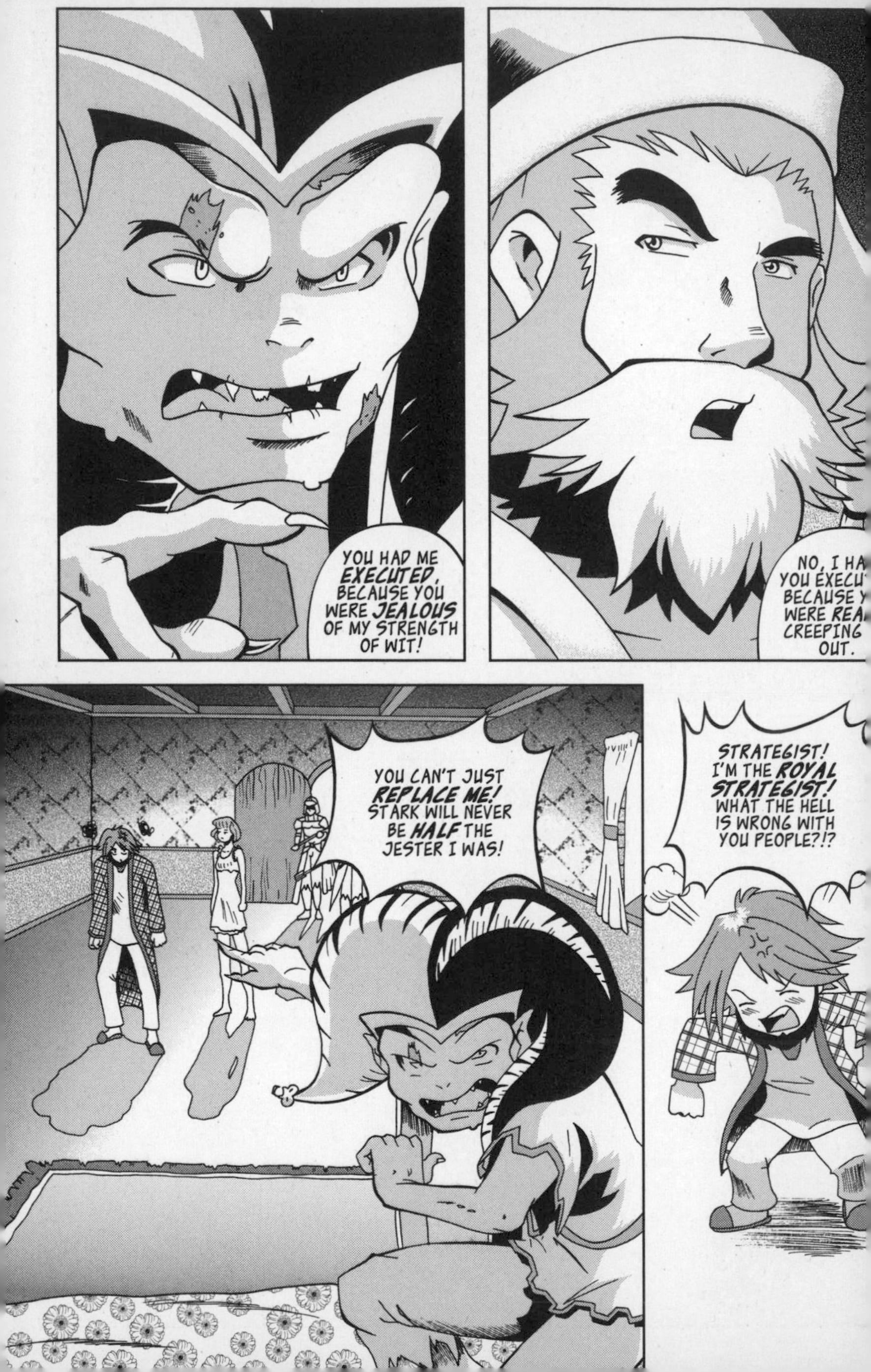
YOU HAD ME EXECUTED, BECAUSE YOU WERE JEALOUS OF MY STRENGTH OF WIT!
NO, I HA YOU EXECUT BECAUSE Y WERE REA CREEPING OUT.
YOU CAN'T JUST REPLACE ME! STARK WILL NEVER BE HALF THE JESTER I WAS!
STRATEGIST! I'M THE ROYAL STRATEGIST! WHAT THE HELL IS WRONG WITH YOU PEOPLE?!?

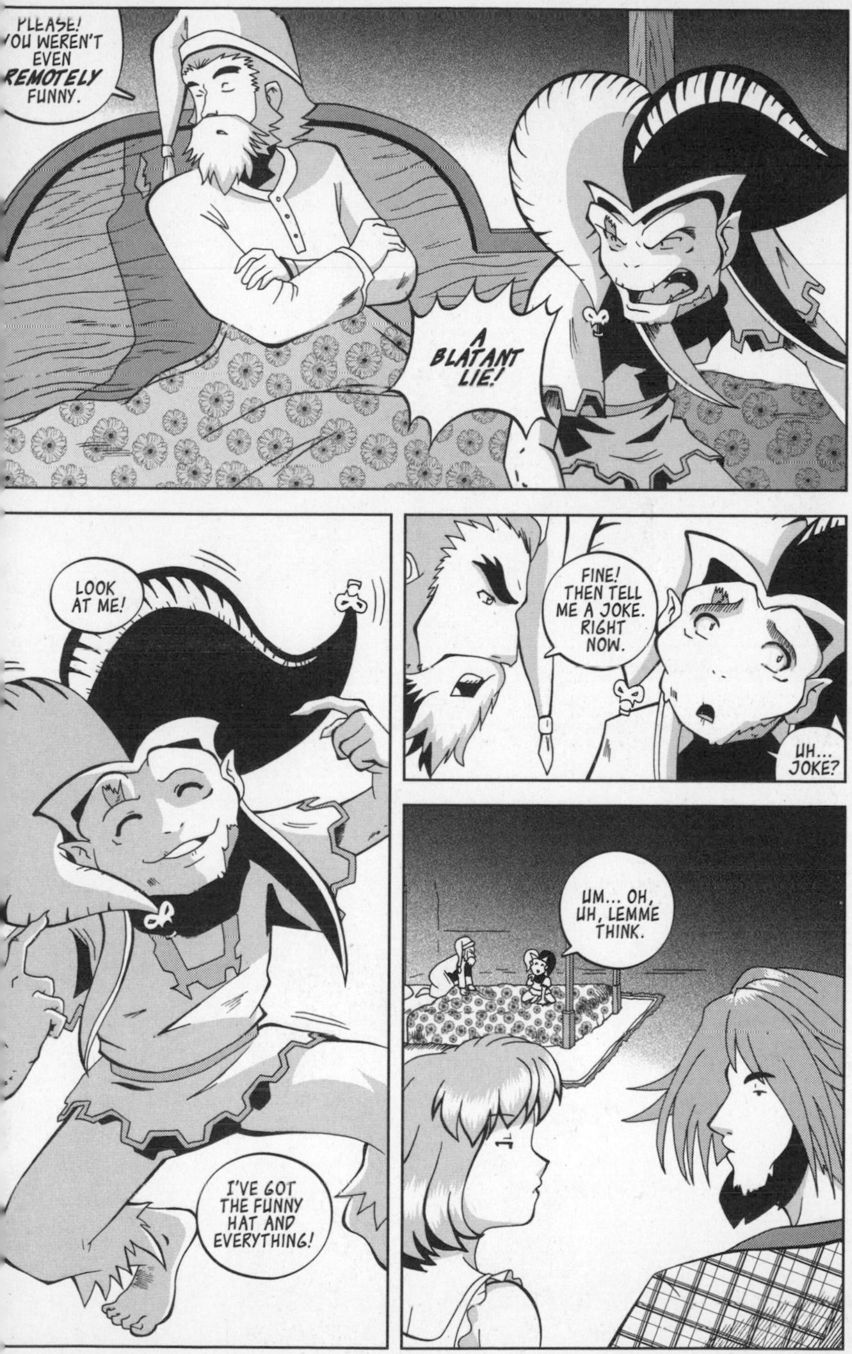
PLEASE! YOU WEREN'T EVEN REMOTELY FUNNY.
A BLATANT LIE!
LOOK AT ME!
I'VE GOT THE FUNNY HAT AND EVERYTHING!
FINE! THEN TELL ME A JOKE. RIGHT NOW.
UH... JOKE?
UM... OH, UH, LEMME THINK.

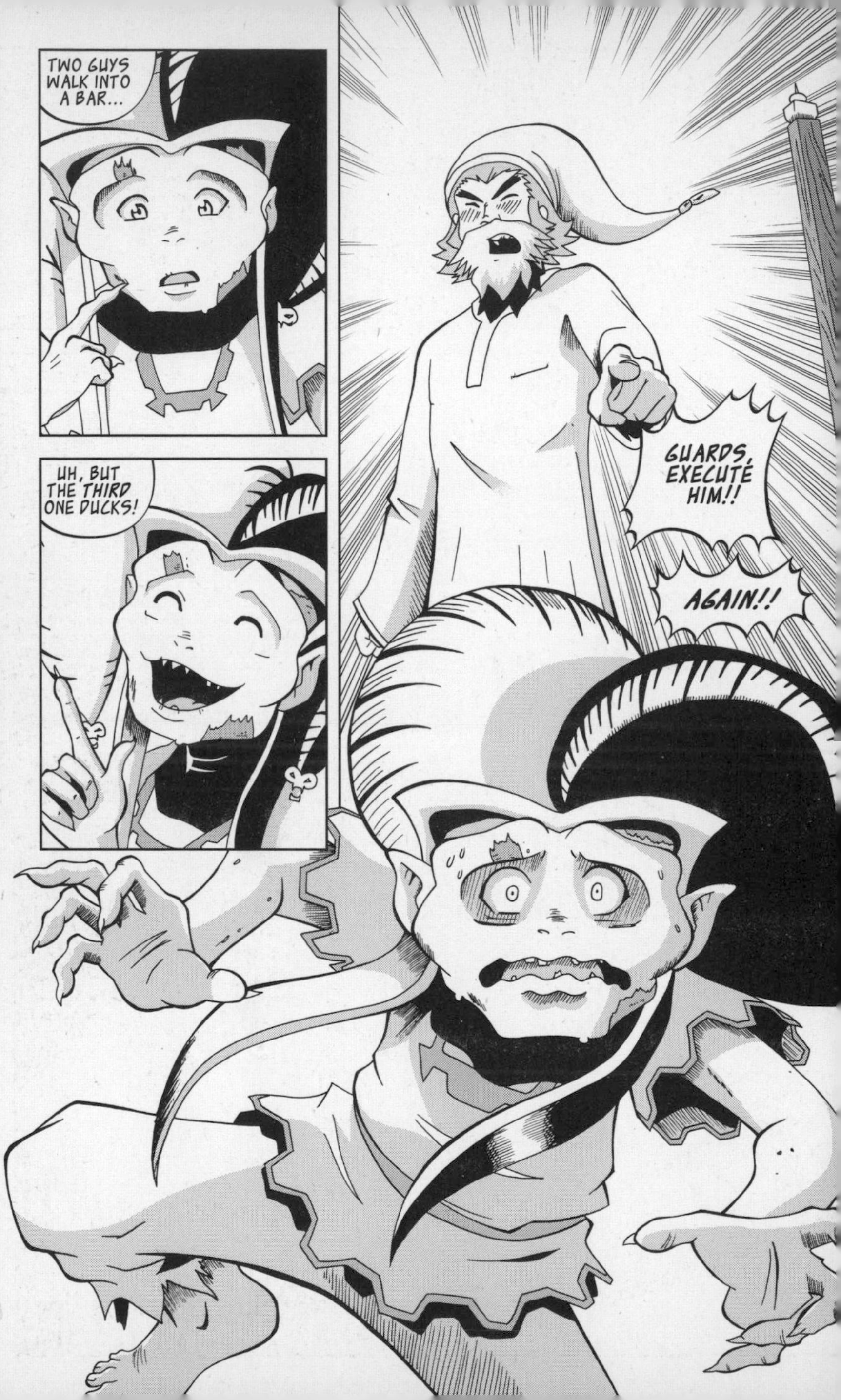
TWO GUYS WALK INTO A BAR...
UH, BUT THE *THIRD* ONE DUCKS!
GUARDS, EXECUTE HIM!!
AGAIN!!

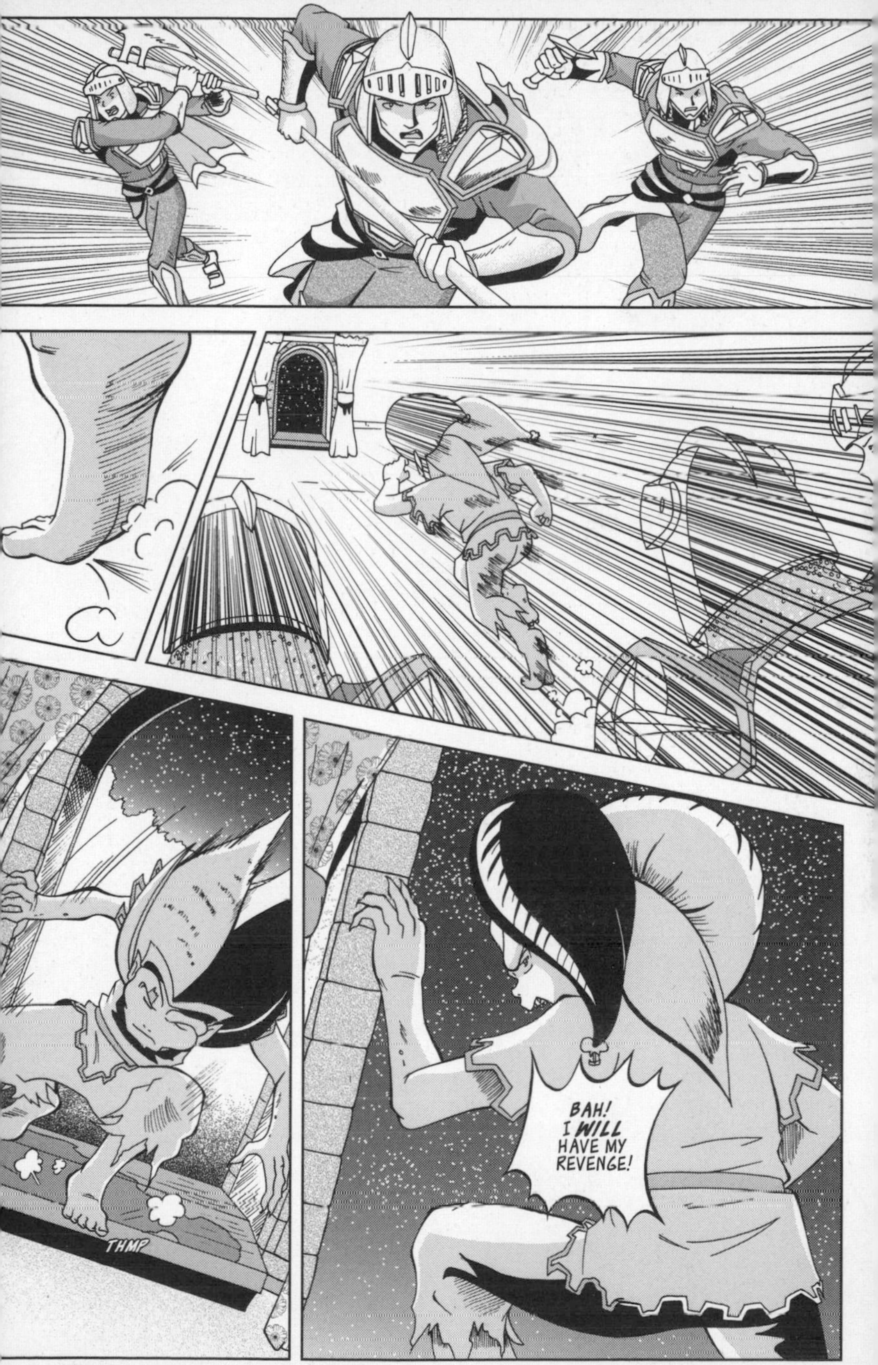
THMP
BAH! I WILL HAVE MY REVENGE!

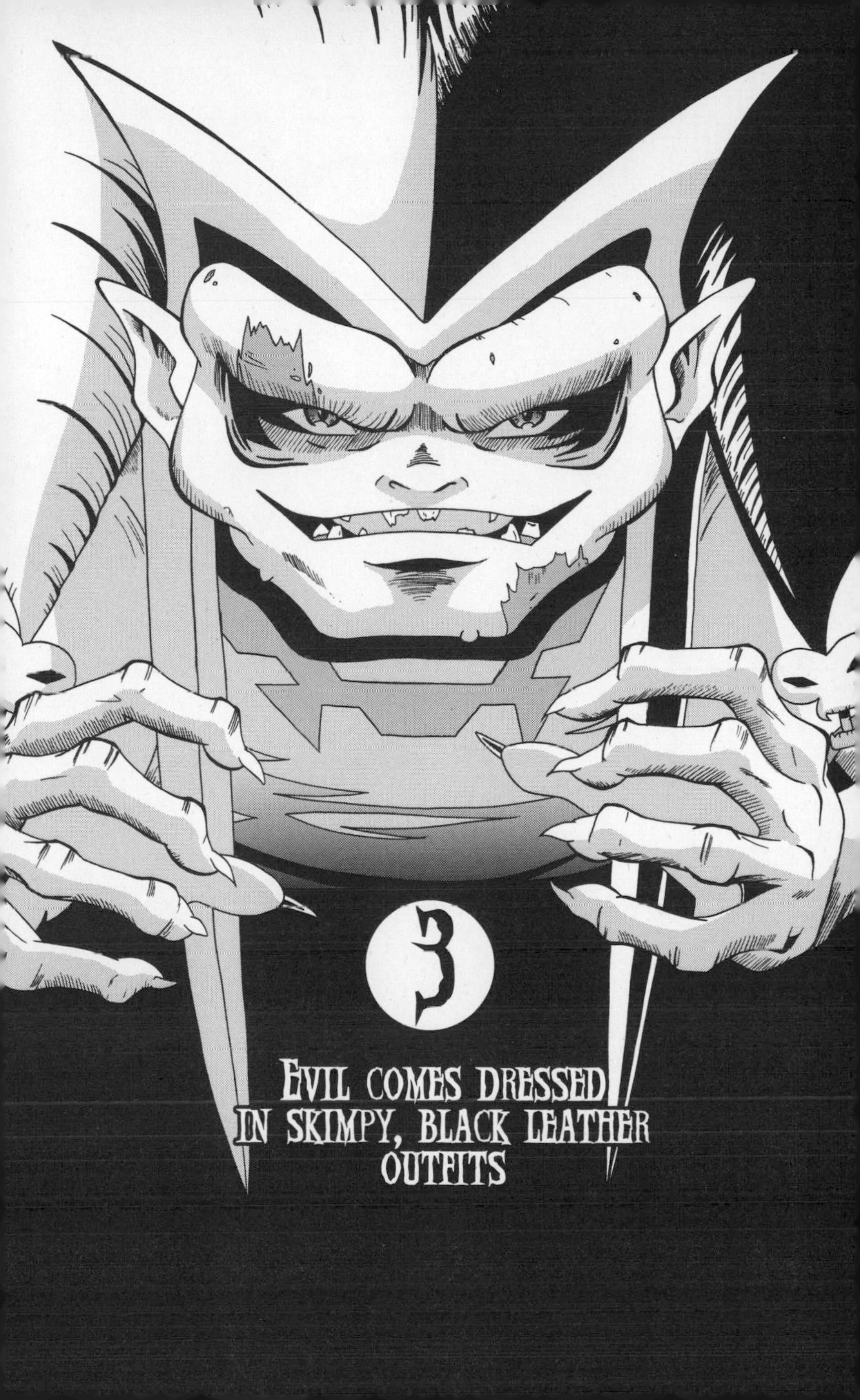
3
EVIL COMES DRESSED
IN SKIMPY, BLACK LEATHER
OUTFITS

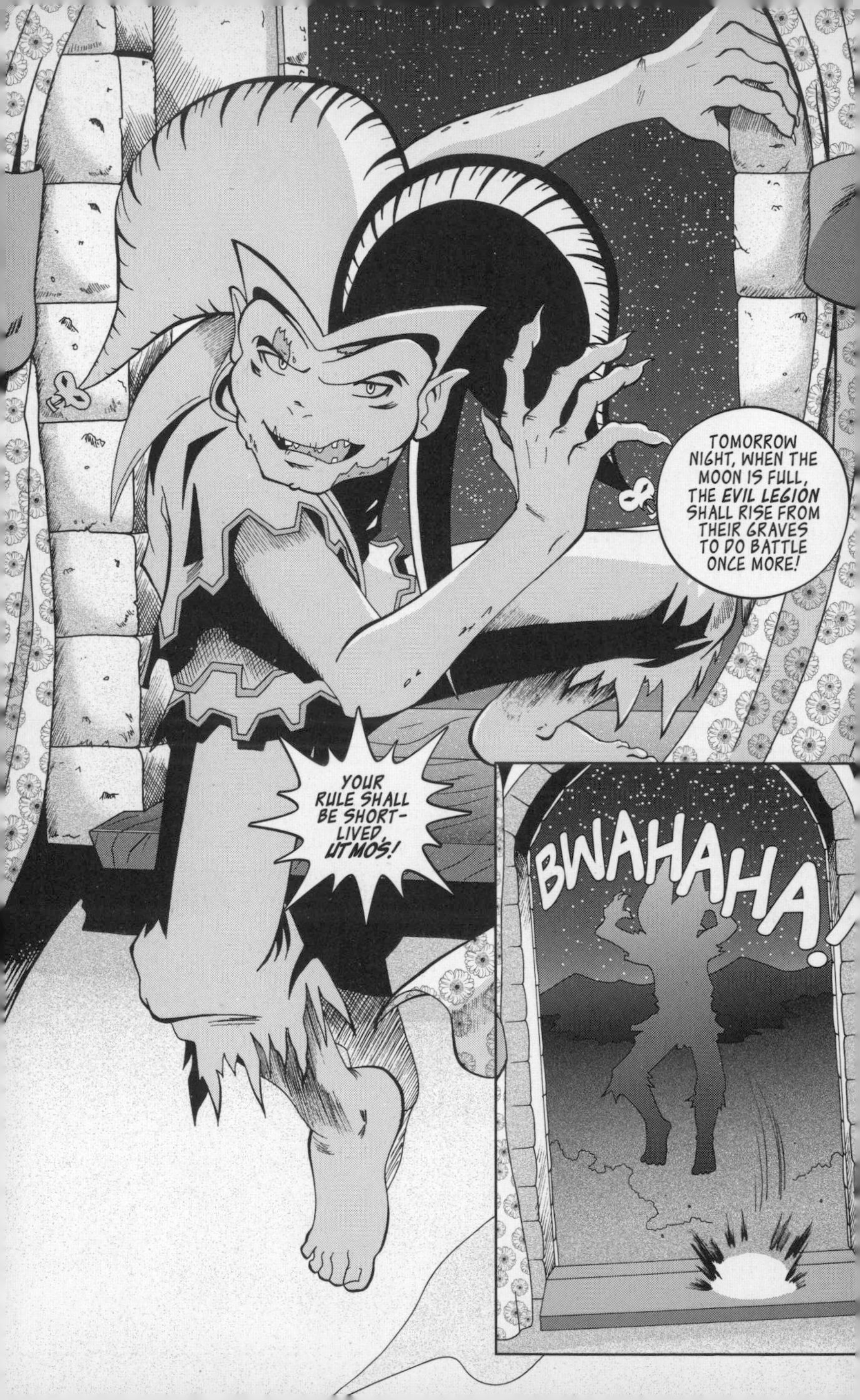
TOMORROW NIGHT, WHEN THE MOON IS FULL, THE *EVIL LEGION* SHALL RISE FROM THEIR GRAVES TO DO BATTLE ONCE MORE!
YOUR RULE SHALL BE SHORT-LIVED, *UTMOS*!
BWAHAHA!

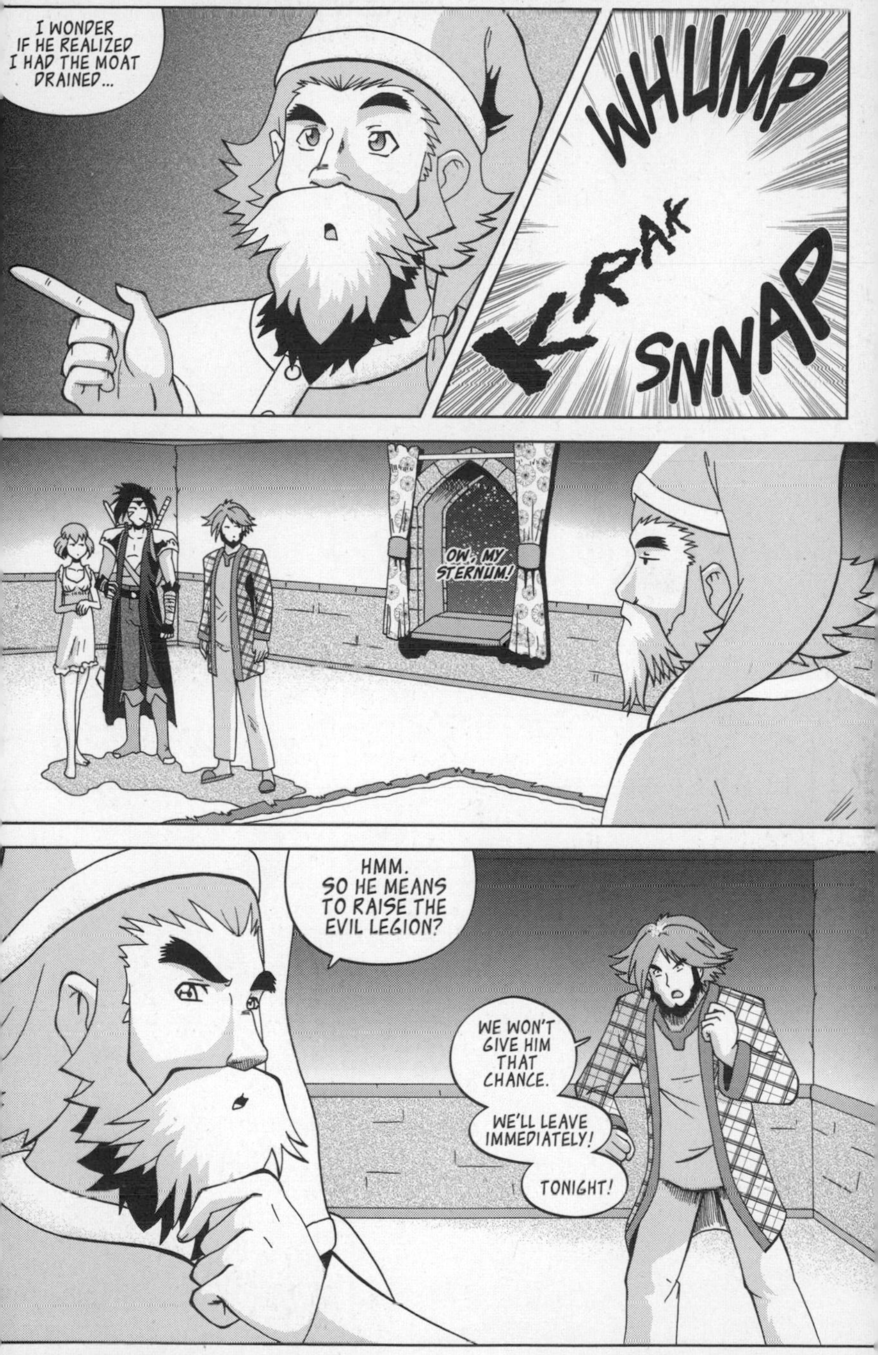
I WONDER IF HE REALIZED I HAD THE MOAT DRAINED...
WHUMP
KRAK
SNNAP
OW, MY STERNUM!
HMM. SO HE MEANS TO RAISE THE EVIL LEGION?
WE WON'T GIVE HIM THAT CHANCE.
WE'LL LEAVE IMMEDIATELY!
TONIGHT!

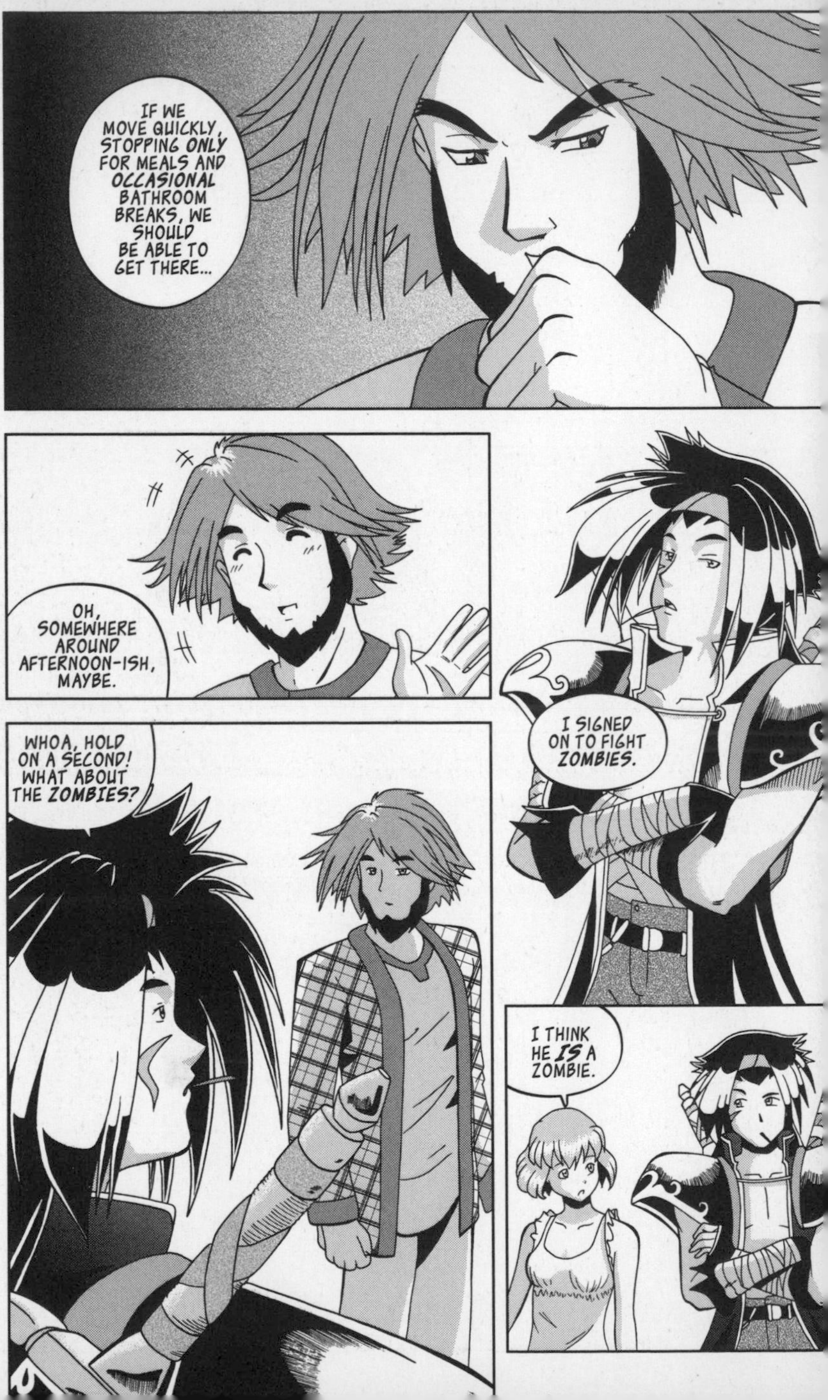
IF WE MOVE QUICKLY, STOPPING ONLY FOR MEALS AND OCCASIONAL BATHROOM BREAKS, WE SHOULD BE ABLE TO GET THERE...
OH, SOMEWHERE AROUND AFTERNOON-ISH, MAYBE.
I SIGNED ON TO FIGHT ZOMBIES.
WHOA, HOLD ON A SECOND! WHAT ABOUT THE ZOMBIES?
I THINK HE IS A ZOMBIE.

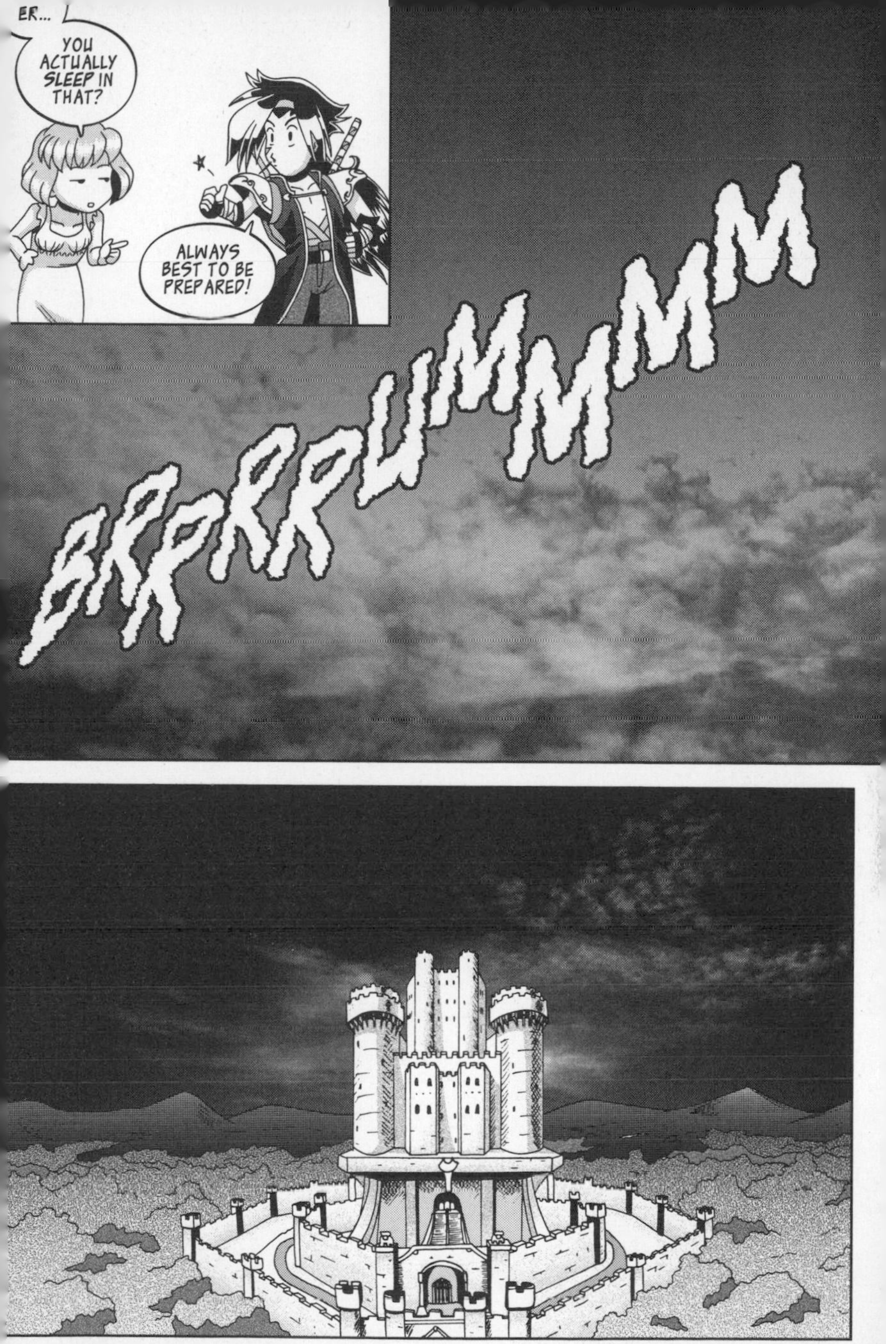
ER...
YOU ACTUALLY SLEEP IN THAT?
ALWAYS BEST TO BE PREPARED!
BRRRRUMMMMM

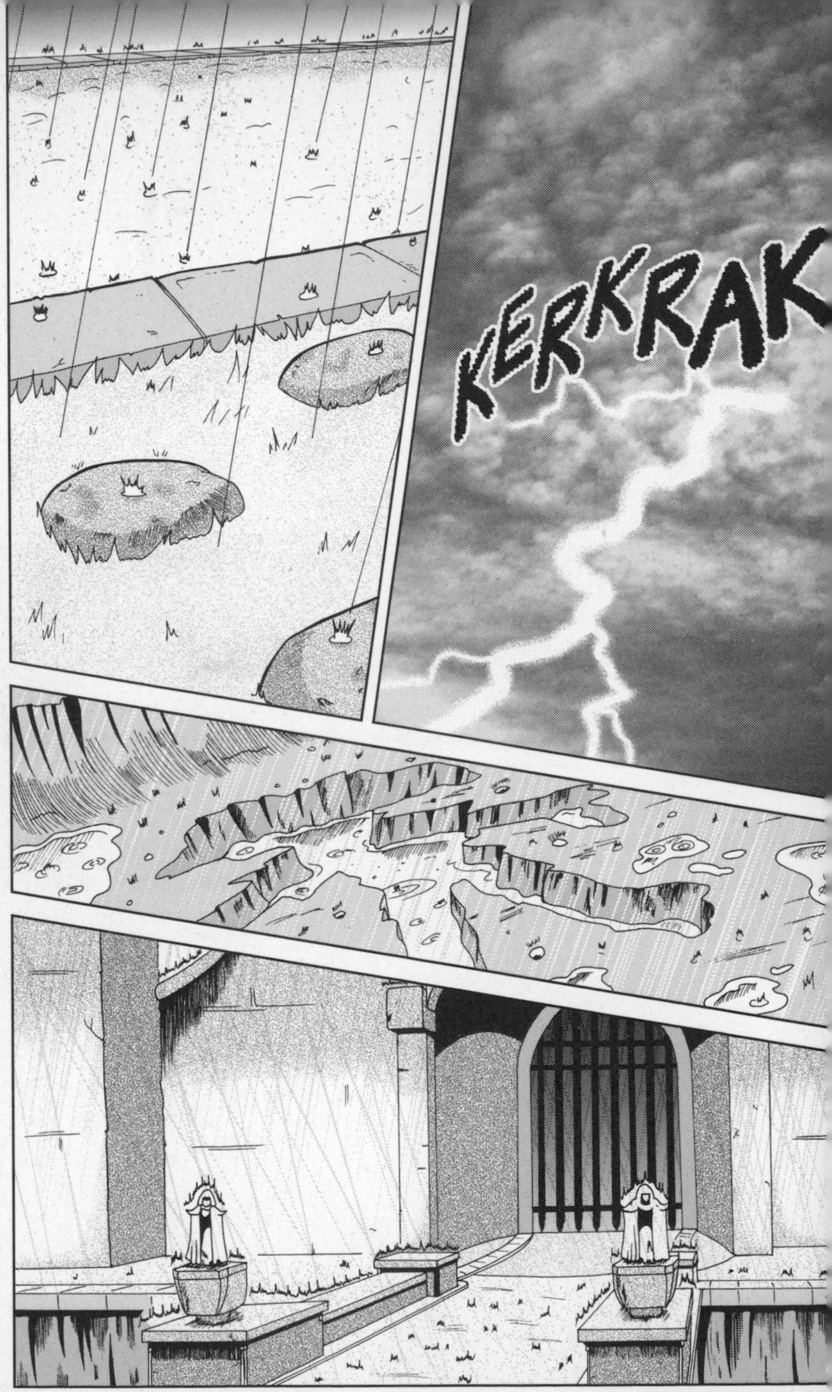
KERKRAK

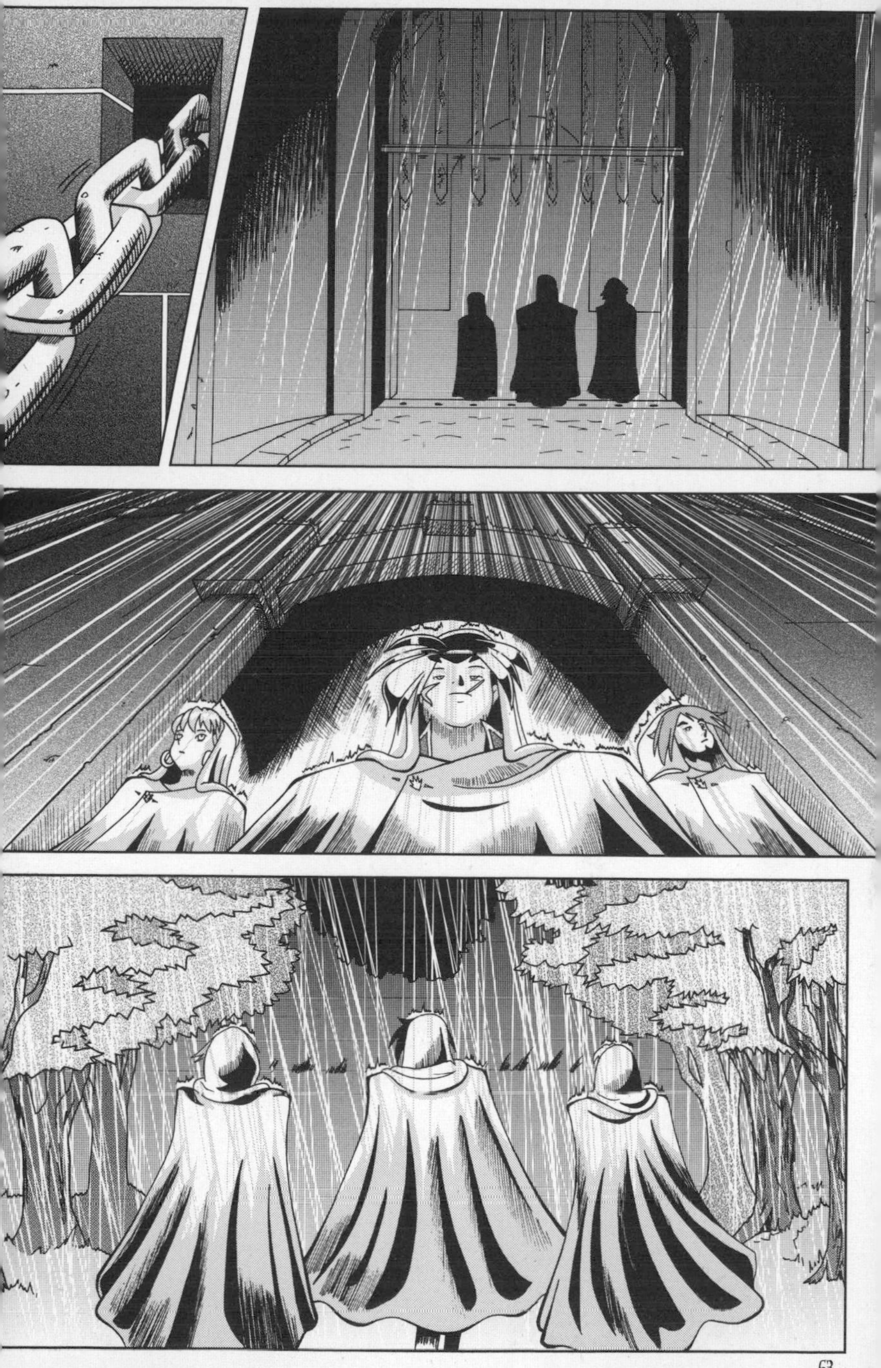

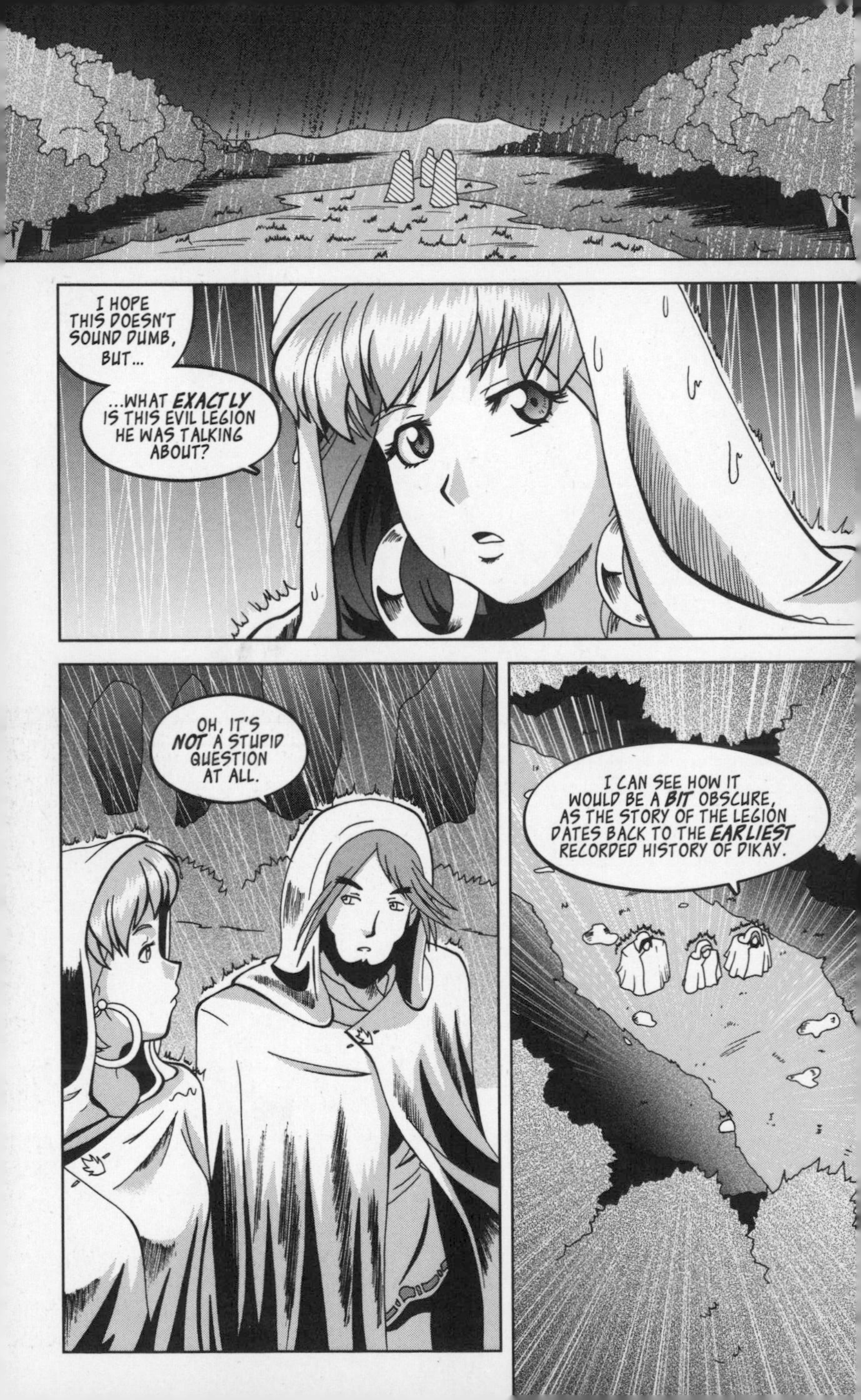
I HOPE THIS DOESN'T SOUND DUMB, BUT...
...WHAT **EXACTLY** IS THIS EVIL LEGION HE WAS TALKING ABOUT?
OH, IT'S **NOT** A STUPID QUESTION AT ALL.
I CAN SEE HOW IT WOULD BE A **BIT** OBSCURE, AS THE STORY OF THE LEGION DATES BACK TO THE **EARLIEST** RECORDED HISTORY OF DIKAY.

IT'S REALLY PART OF THE TALE OF THE *CORRUPT* SHAMAN, KUULATS.

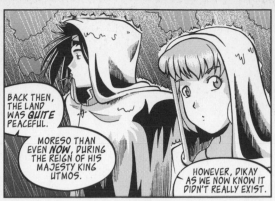

BACK THEN, THE LAND WAS *QUITE* PEACEFUL.

MORESO THAN EVEN *NOW*, DURING THE REIGN OF HIS MAJESTY KING UTMOS.

HOWEVER, DIKAY AS WE NOW KNOW IT DIDN'T REALLY EXIST.

IN ITS PLACE WAS AN ASSORTMENT OF INSIGNIFICANT PROVINCES, WHICH, ON THEIR OWN, HELD *VERY LITTLE* POLITICAL WEIGHT.

THE CORRUPT SHAMAN, KUULATS, HAD A DARK VISION FOR THE LAND.

IT WAS HIS DESIRE TO SEE THE FRACTURED PROVINCES UNITED TOGETHER UNDER A SINGLE BANNER...

HIS BANNER!

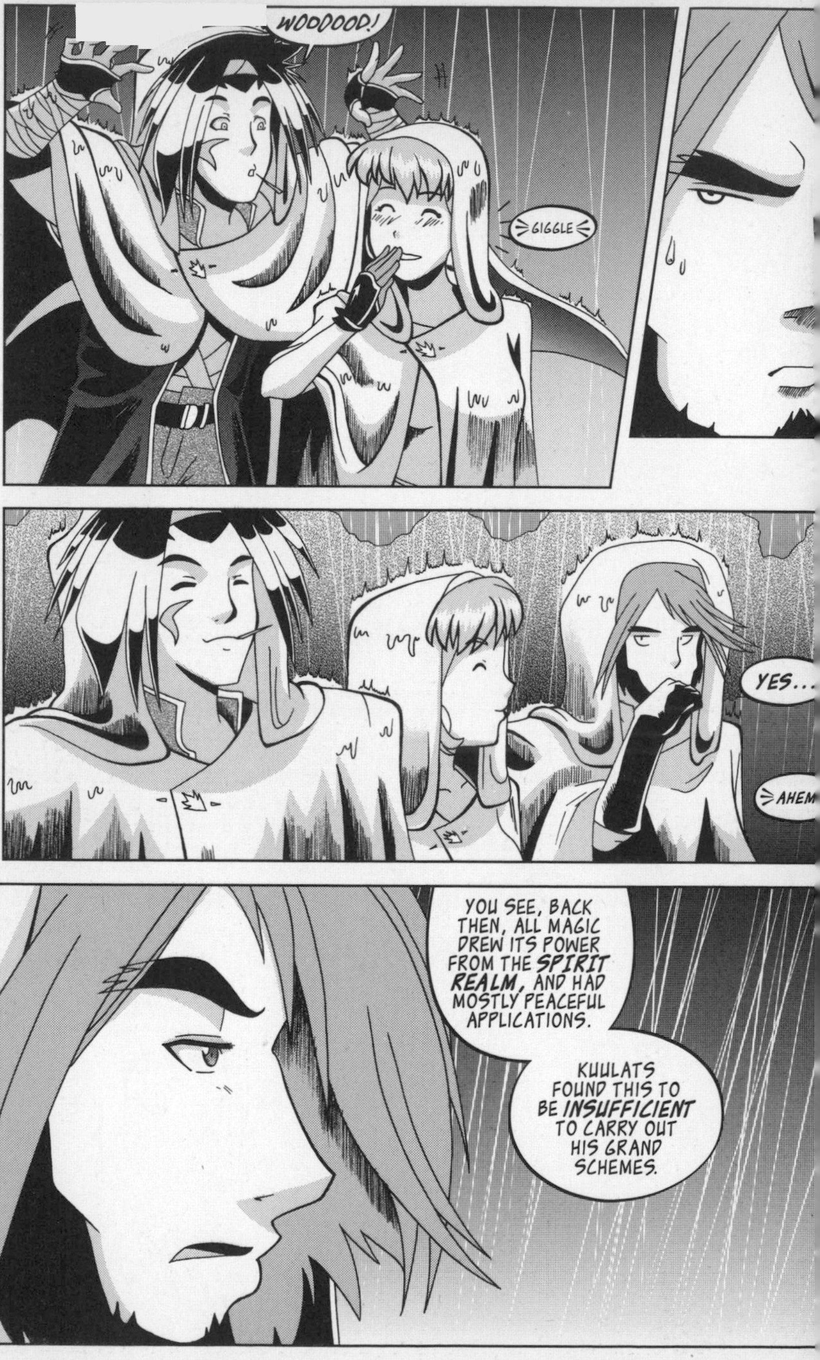
WOOOOOD!
GIGGLE
YES...
AHEM
YOU SEE, BACK THEN, ALL MAGIC DREW ITS POWER FROM THE SPIRIT REALM, AND HAD MOSTLY PEACEFUL APPLICATIONS.
KUULATS FOUND THIS TO BE INSUFFICIENT TO CARRY OUT HIS GRAND SCHEMES.

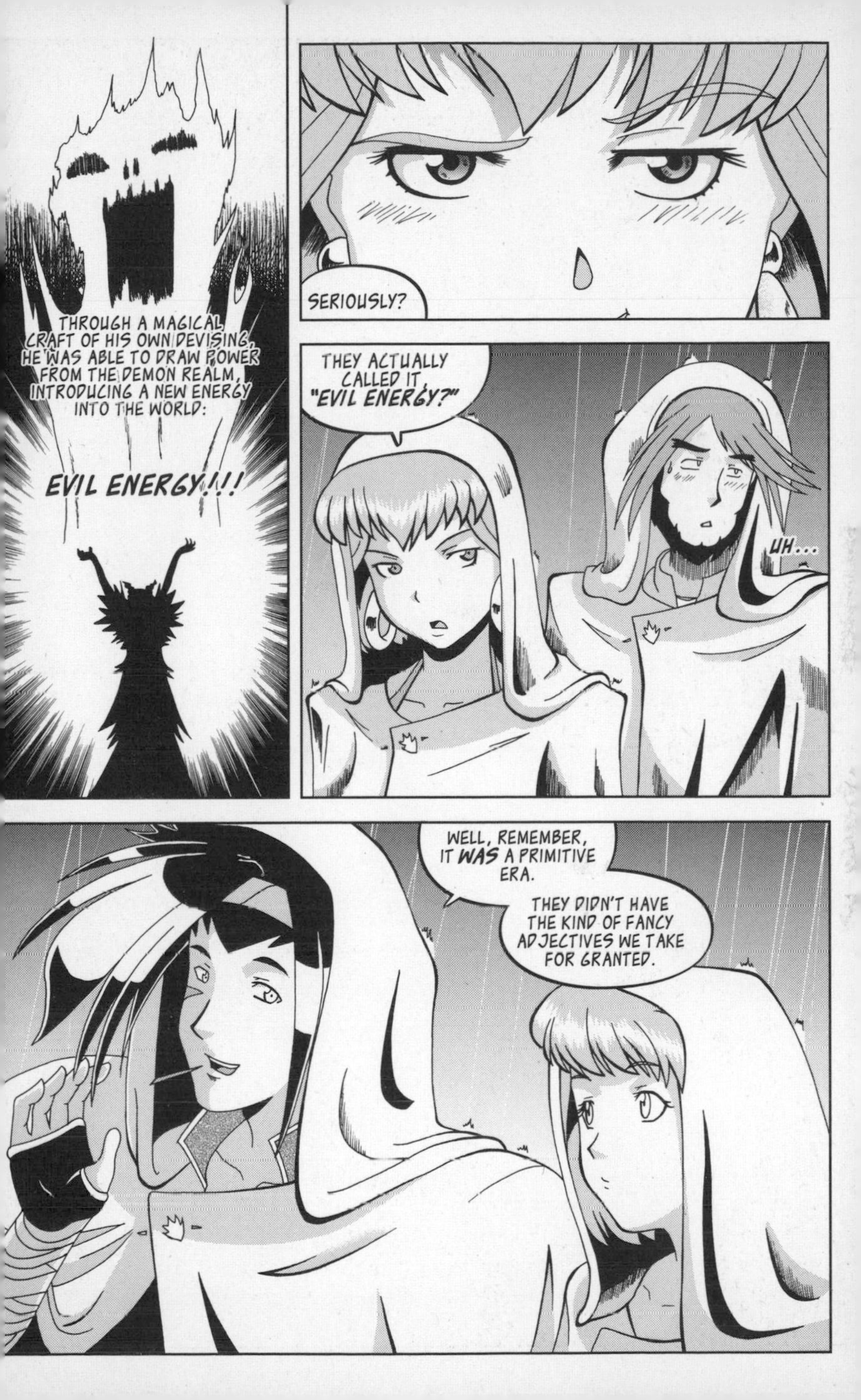
THROUGH A MAGICAL CRAFT OF HIS OWN DEVISING, HE WAS ABLE TO DRAW POWER FROM THE DEMON REALM, INTRODUCING A NEW ENERGY INTO THE WORLD:
EVIL ENERGY!!!
SERIOUSLY?
THEY ACTUALLY CALLED IT "EVIL ENERGY?"
UH...
WELL, REMEMBER, IT WAS A PRIMITIVE ERA.
THEY DIDN'T HAVE THE KIND OF FANCY ADJECTIVES WE TAKE FOR GRANTED.

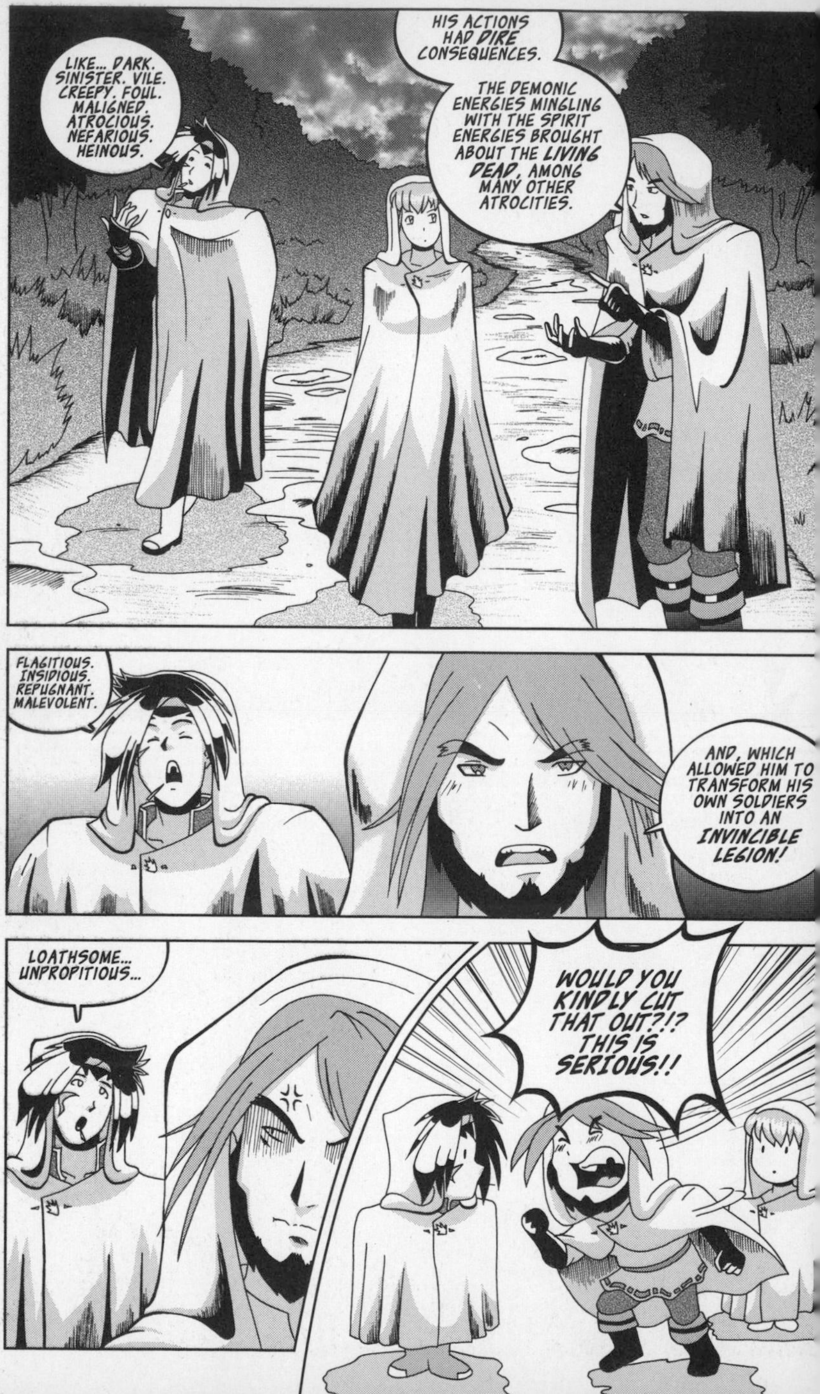
LIKE... DARK. SINISTER. VILE. CREEPY. FOUL. MALIGNED. ATROCIOUS. NEFARIOUS. HEINOUS.
HIS ACTIONS HAD DIRE CONSEQUENCES.
THE DEMONIC ENERGIES MINGLING WITH THE SPIRIT ENERGIES BROUGHT ABOUT THE LIVING DEAD, AMONG MANY OTHER ATROCITIES.
FLAGITIOUS. INSIDIOUS. REPUGNANT. MALEVOLENT.
AND, WHICH ALLOWED HIM TO TRANSFORM HIS OWN SOLDIERS INTO AN INVINCIBLE LEGION!
LOATHSOME... UNPROPITIOUS...
WOULD YOU KINDLY CUT THAT OUT?!? THIS IS SERIOUS!!

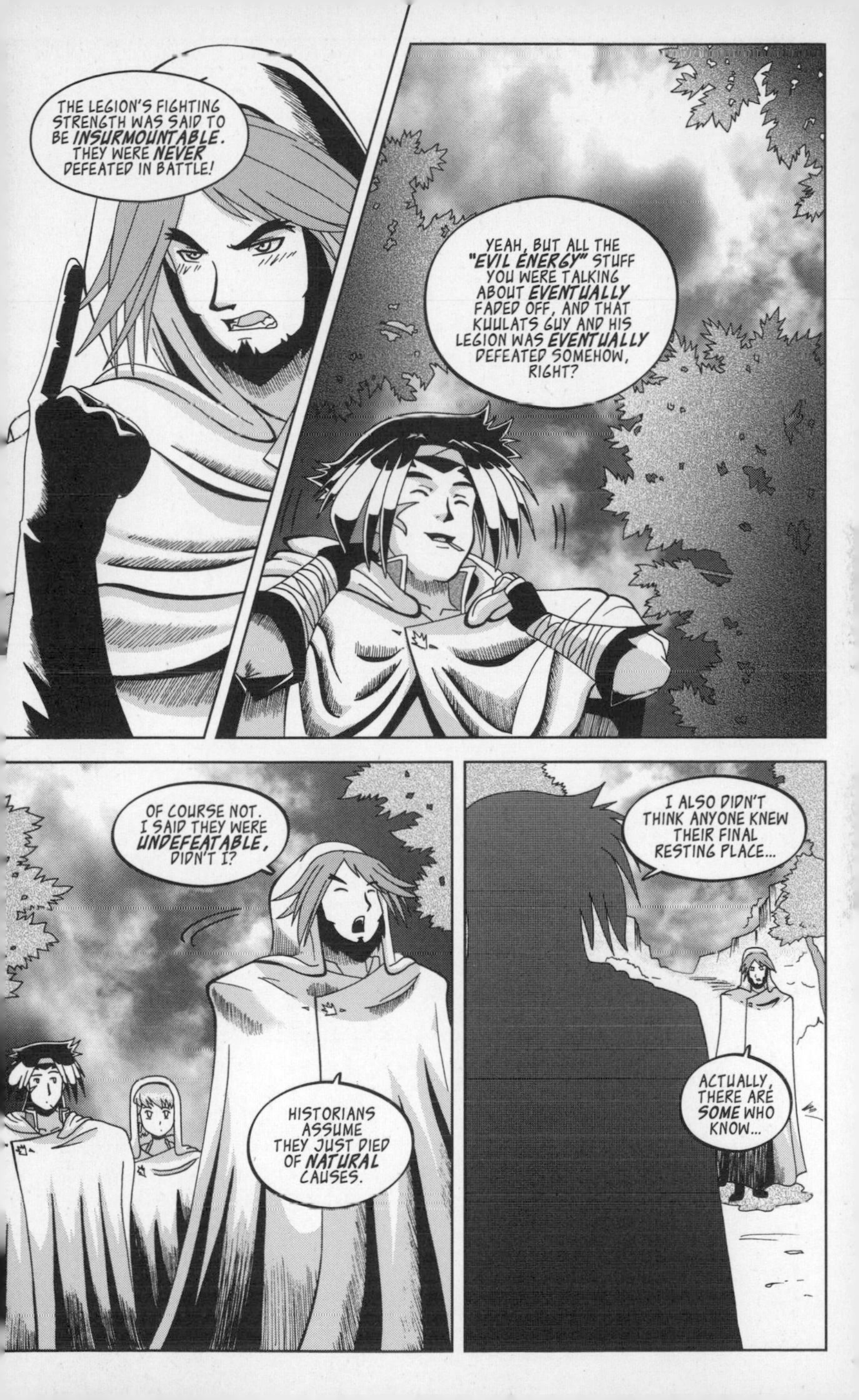
THE LEGION'S FIGHTING STRENGTH WAS SAID TO BE INSURMOUNTABLE. THEY WERE NEVER DEFEATED IN BATTLE!
YEAH, BUT ALL THE "EVIL ENERGY" STUFF YOU WERE TALKING ABOUT EVENTUALLY FADED OFF, AND THAT KUULATS GUY AND HIS LEGION WAS EVENTUALLY DEFEATED SOMEHOW, RIGHT?
OF COURSE NOT. I SAID THEY WERE UNDEFEATABLE, DIDN'T I?
HISTORIANS ASSUME THEY JUST DIED OF NATURAL CAUSES.
I ALSO DIDN'T THINK ANYONE KNEW THEIR FINAL RESTING PLACE...
ACTUALLY, THERE ARE SOME WHO KNOW...

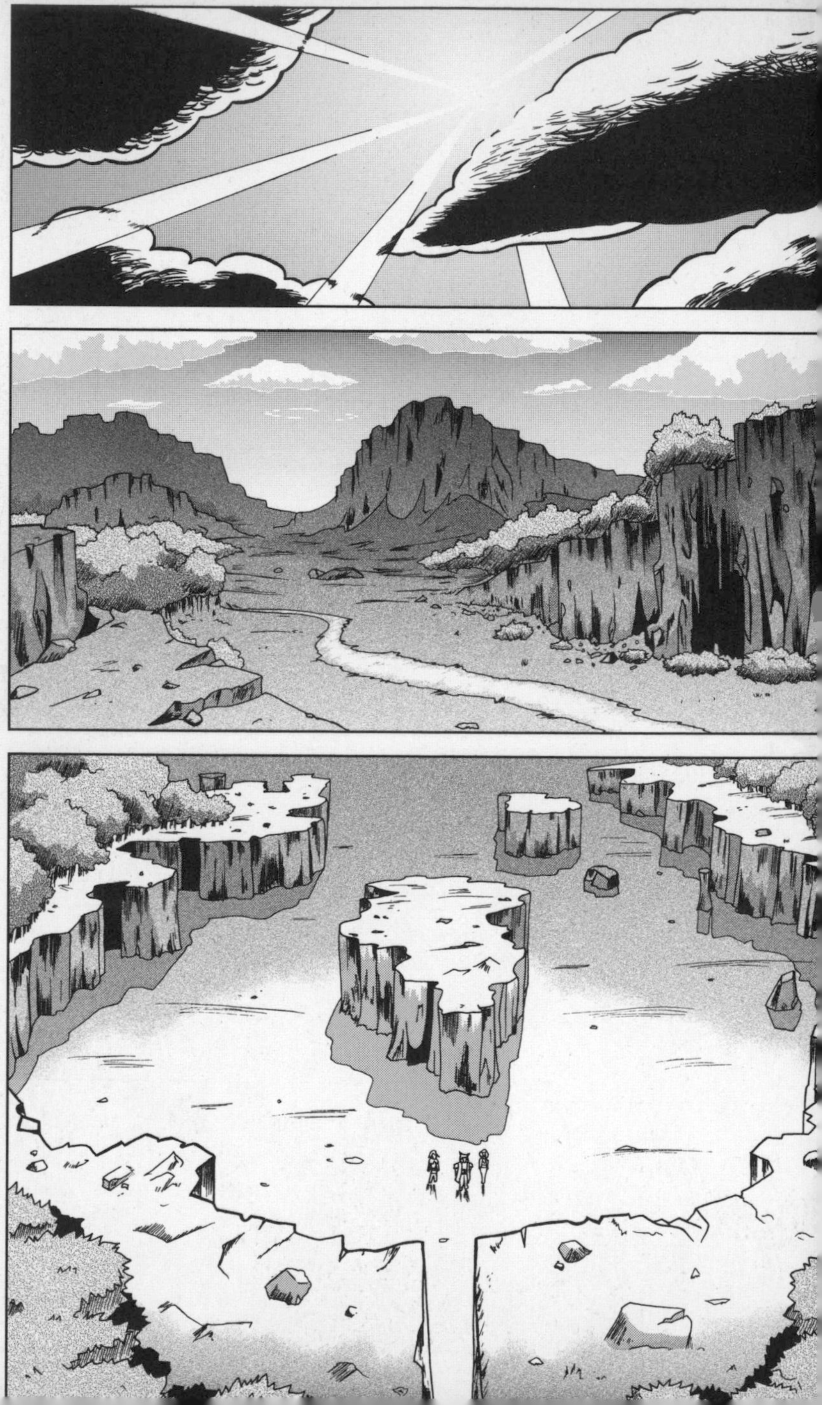

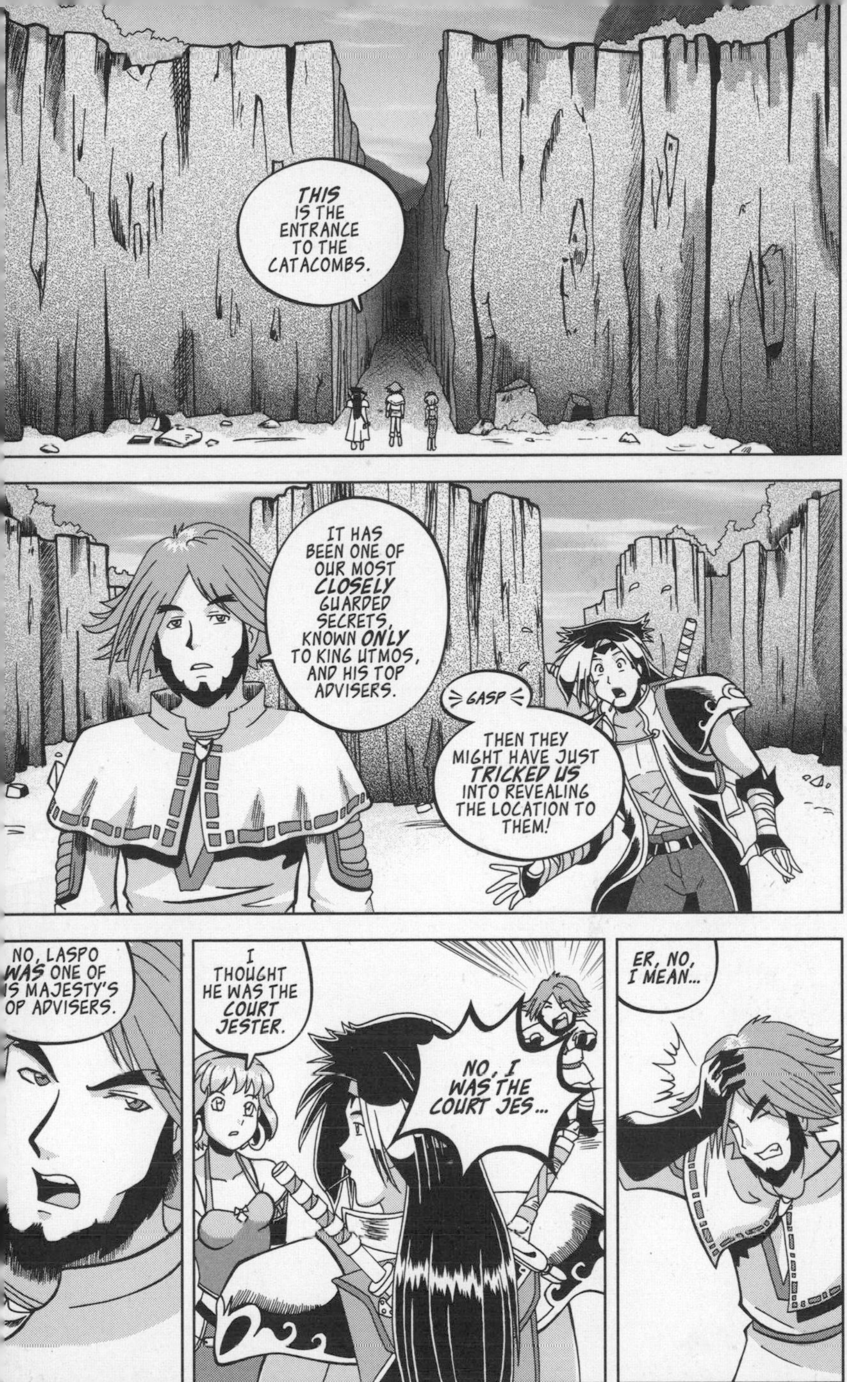
THIS IS THE ENTRANCE TO THE CATACOMBS.
IT HAS BEEN ONE OF OUR MOST CLOSELY GUARDED SECRETS, KNOWN ONLY TO KING UTMOS, AND HIS TOP ADVISERS.
GASP
THEN THEY MIGHT HAVE JUST TRICKED US INTO REVEALING THE LOCATION TO THEM!
NO, LASPO WAS ONE OF IS MAJESTY'S OP ADVISERS.
I THOUGHT HE WAS THE COURT JESTER.
NO, I WAS THE COURT JES...
ER, NO, I MEAN...

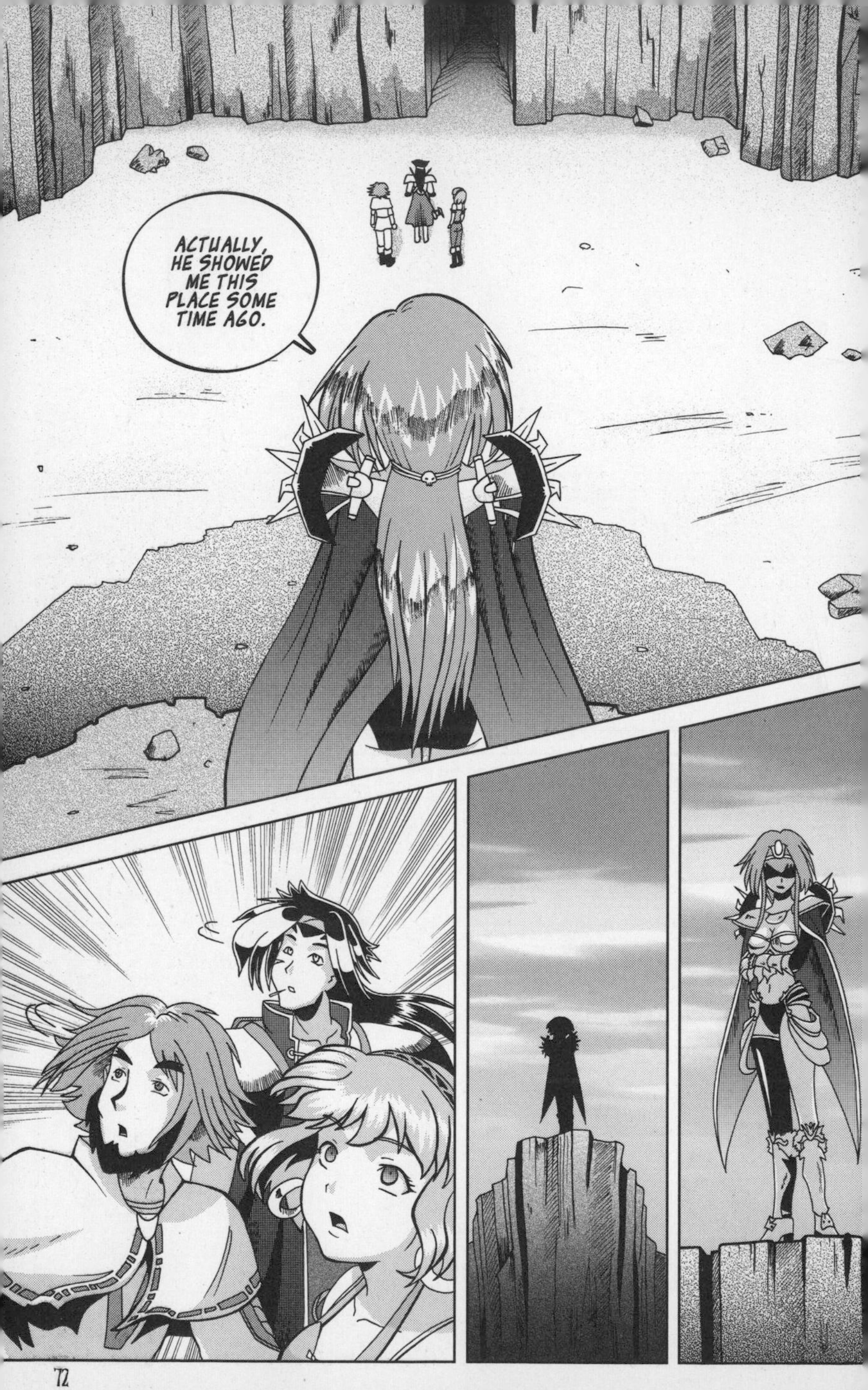
ACTUALLY, HE SHOWED ME THIS PLACE SOME TIME AGO.

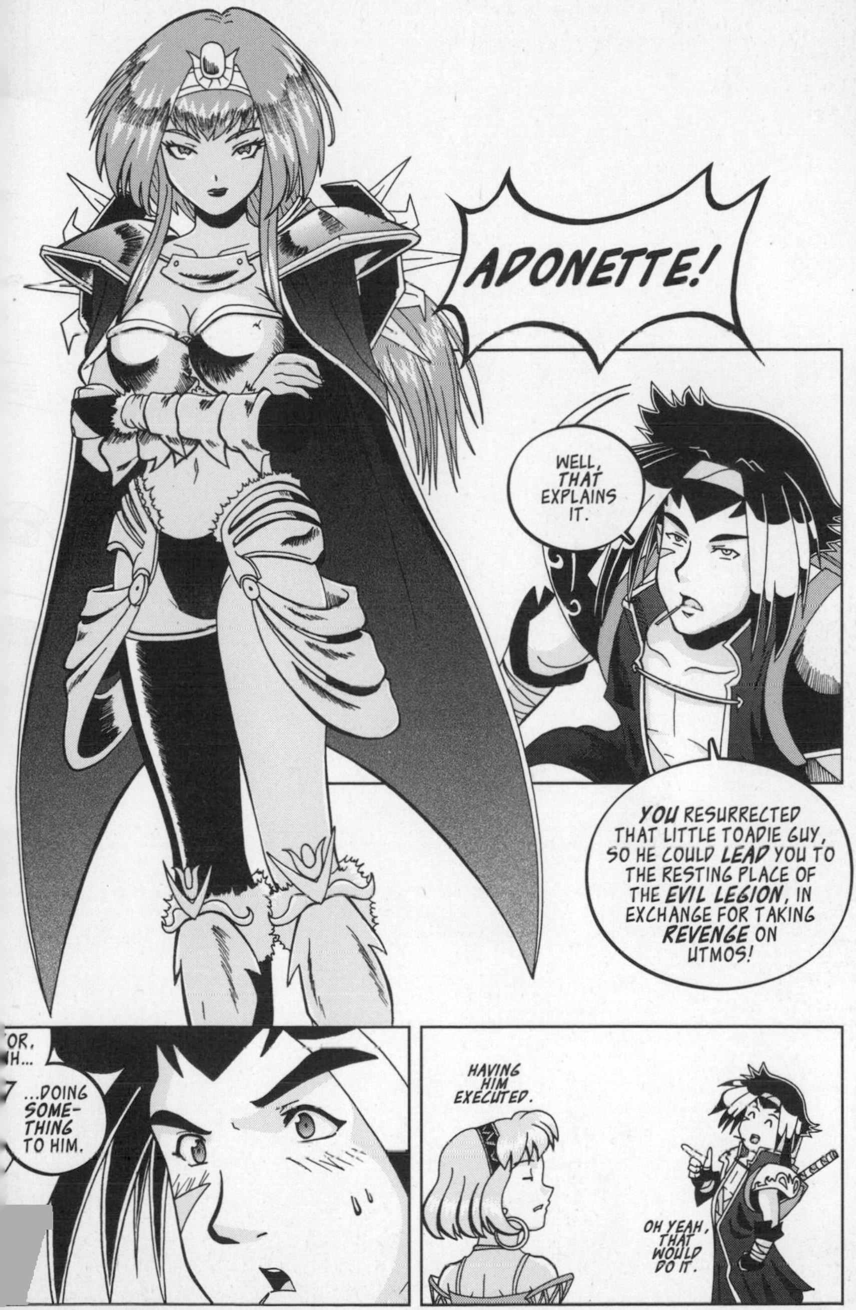
ADONETTE!
WELL, THAT EXPLAINS IT.
YOU RESURRECTED THAT LITTLE TOADIE GUY, SO HE COULD LEAD YOU TO THE RESTING PLACE OF THE EVIL LEGION, IN EXCHANGE FOR TAKING REVENGE ON UTMOS!
OR, H...
...DOING SOME-THING TO HIM.
HAVING HIM EXECUTED.
OH YEAH, THAT WOULD DO IT.

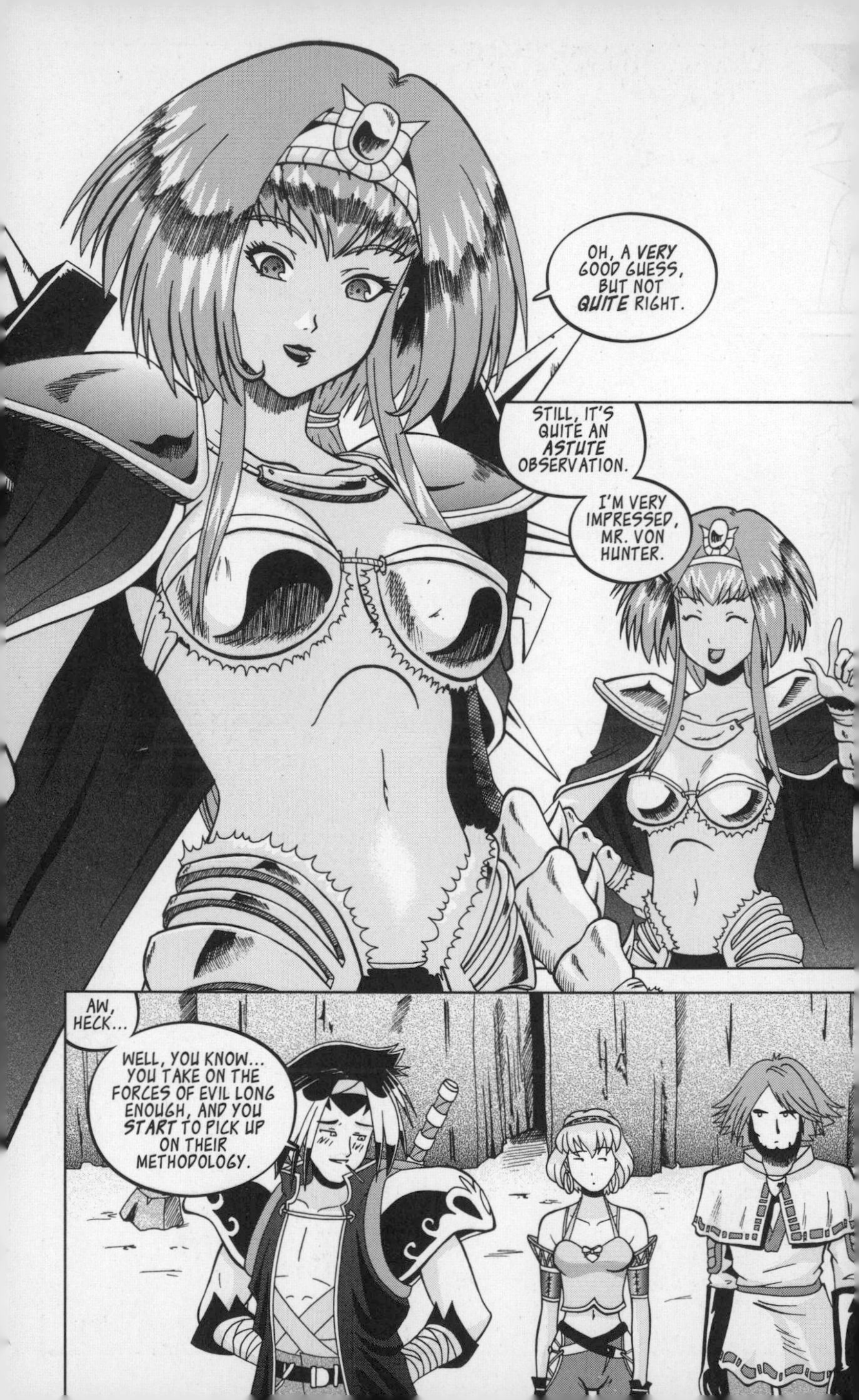
OH, A VERY GOOD GUESS, BUT NOT QUITE RIGHT.
STILL, IT'S QUITE AN ASTUTE OBSERVATION.
I'M VERY IMPRESSED, MR. VON HUNTER.
AW, HECK...
WELL, YOU KNOW... YOU TAKE ON THE FORCES OF EVIL LONG ENOUGH, AND YOU START TO PICK UP ON THEIR METHODOLOGY.

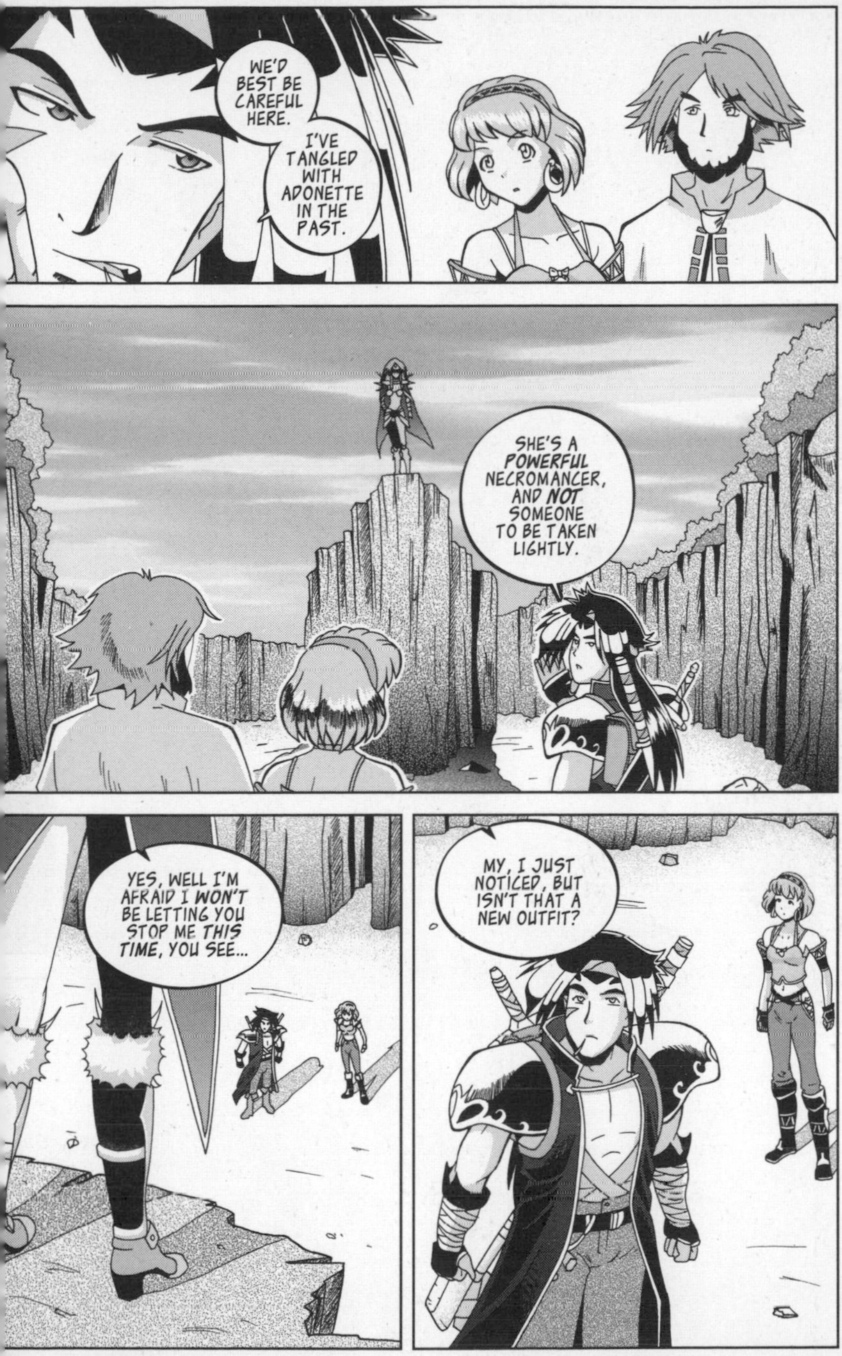
WE'D BEST BE CAREFUL HERE.
I'VE TANGLED WITH ADONETTE IN THE PAST.
SHE'S A **POWERFUL** NECROMANCER, AND **NOT** SOMEONE TO BE TAKEN LIGHTLY.
YES, WELL I'M AFRAID I **WON'T** BE LETTING YOU STOP ME **THIS TIME**, YOU SEE...
MY, I JUST NOTICED, BUT ISN'T THAT A NEW OUTFIT?

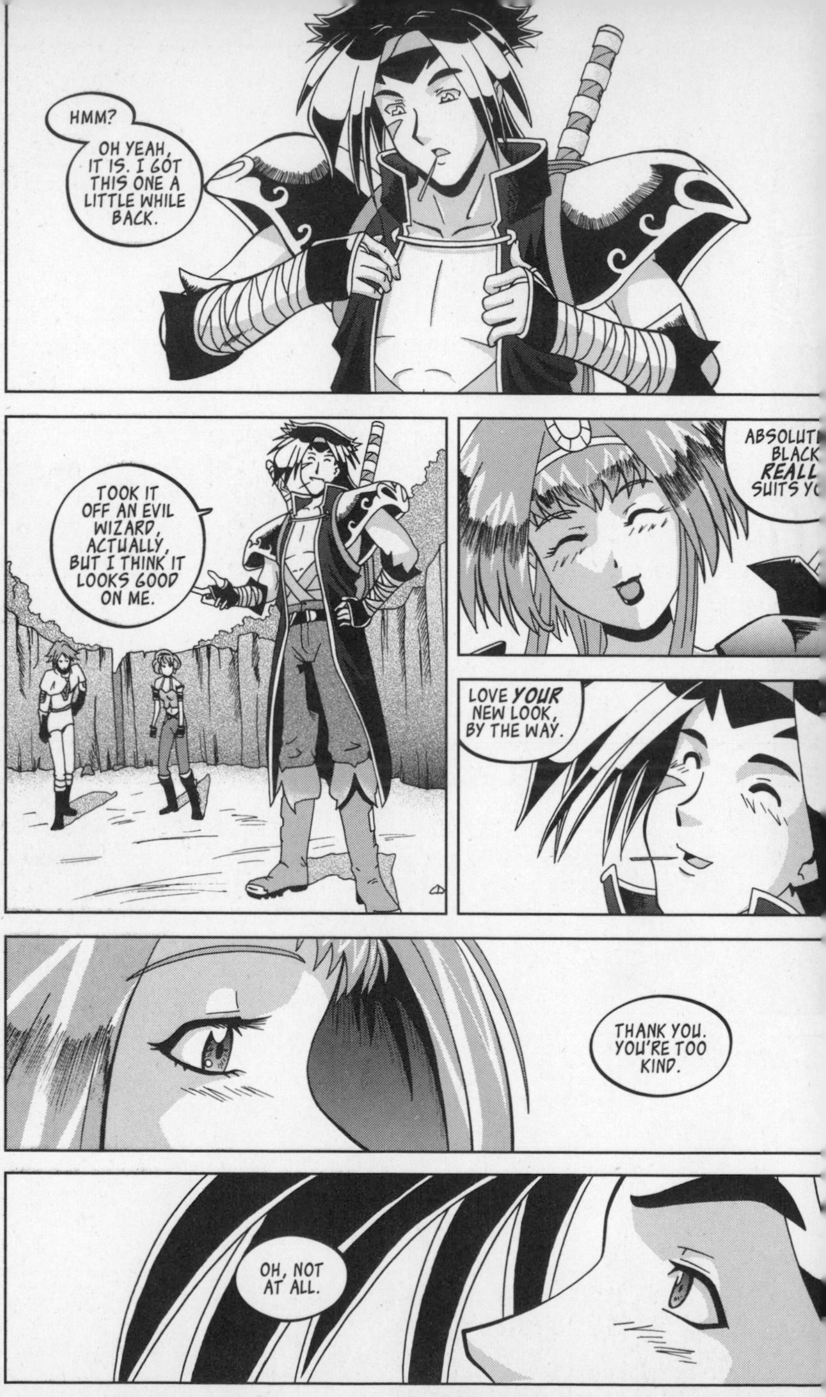
HMM?
OH YEAH, IT IS. I GOT THIS ONE A LITTLE WHILE BACK.
TOOK IT OFF AN EVIL WIZARD, ACTUALLY, BUT I THINK IT LOOKS GOOD ON ME.
ABSOLUT BLACK REALL SUITS YO
LOVE YOUR NEW LOOK, BY THE WAY.
THANK YOU. YOU'RE TOO KIND.
OH, NOT AT ALL.

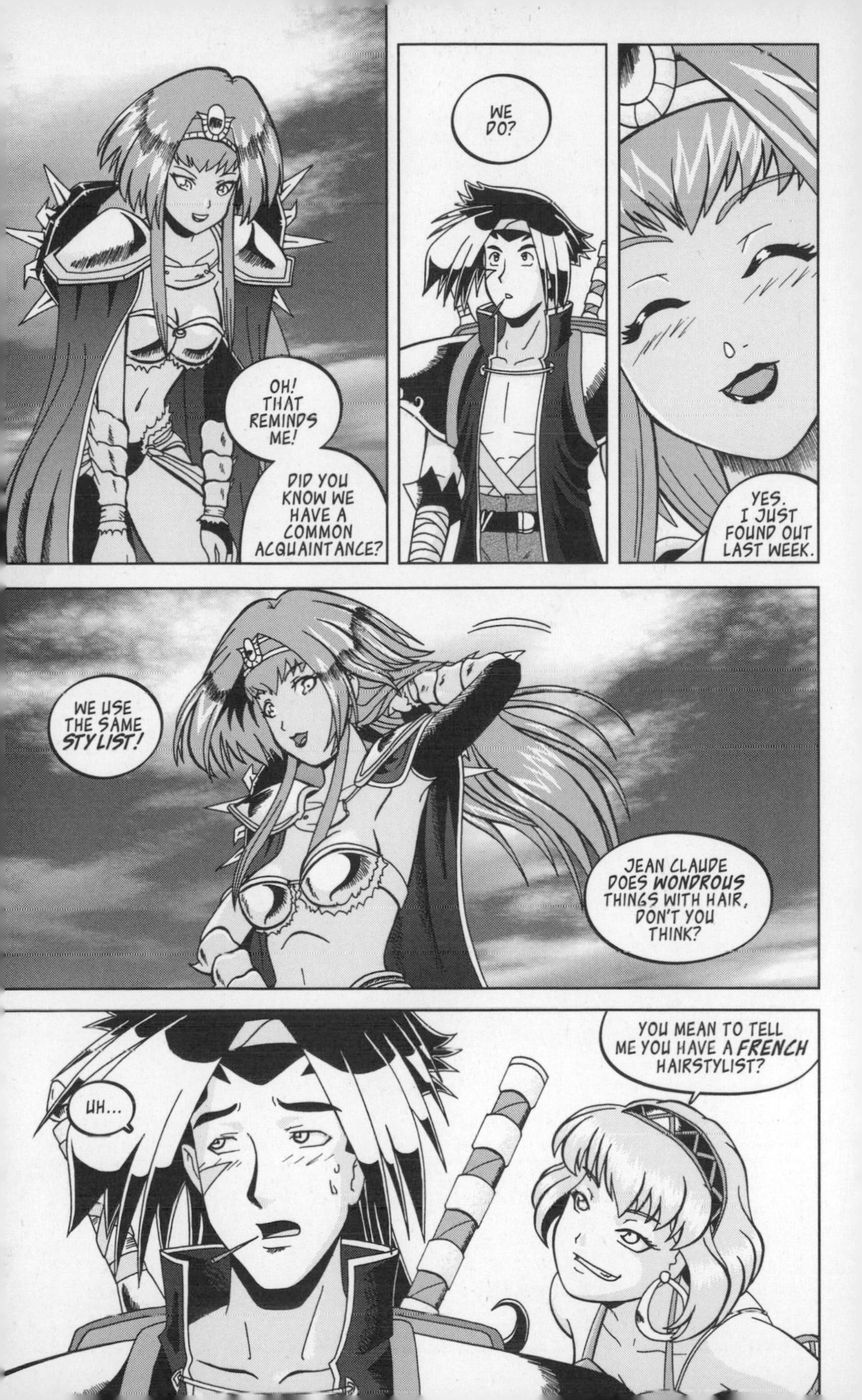
OH! THAT REMINDS ME!
DID YOU KNOW WE HAVE A COMMON ACQUAINTANCE?
WE DO?
YES. I JUST FOUND OUT LAST WEEK.
WE USE THE SAME STYLIST!
JEAN CLAUDE DOES WONDROUS THINGS WITH HAIR, DON'T YOU THINK?
UH...
YOU MEAN TO TELL ME YOU HAVE A FRENCH HAIRSTYLIST?

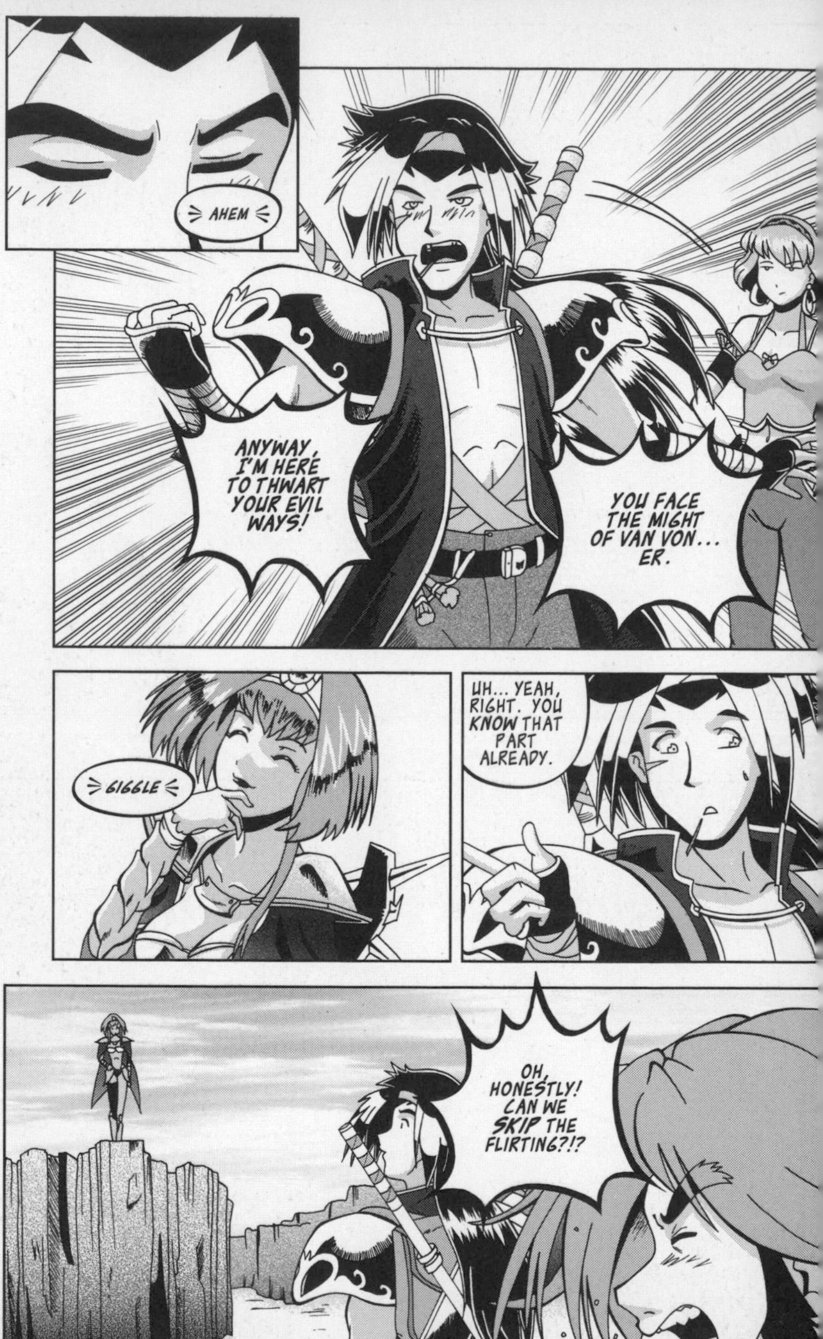
AHEM
ANYWAY, I'M HERE TO THWART YOUR EVIL WAYS!
YOU FACE THE MIGHT OF VAN VON... ER.
GIGGLE
UH... YEAH, RIGHT. YOU KNOW THAT PART ALREADY.
OH, HONESTLY! CAN WE SKIP THE FLIRTING?!?

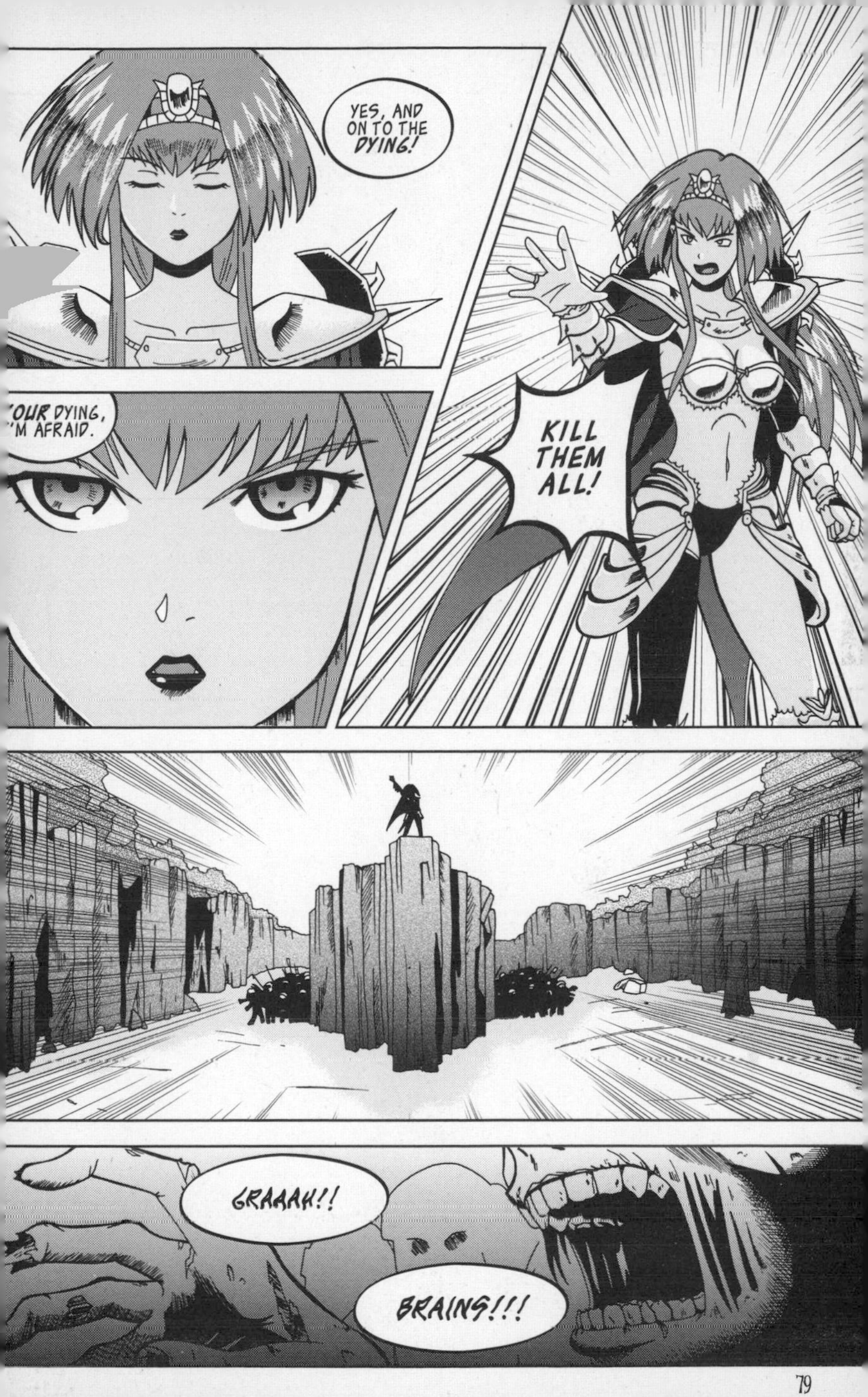

YES, AND ON TO THE DYING!
YOUR DYING, I'M AFRAID.
KILL THEM ALL!
GRAAAH!!
BRAINS!!!

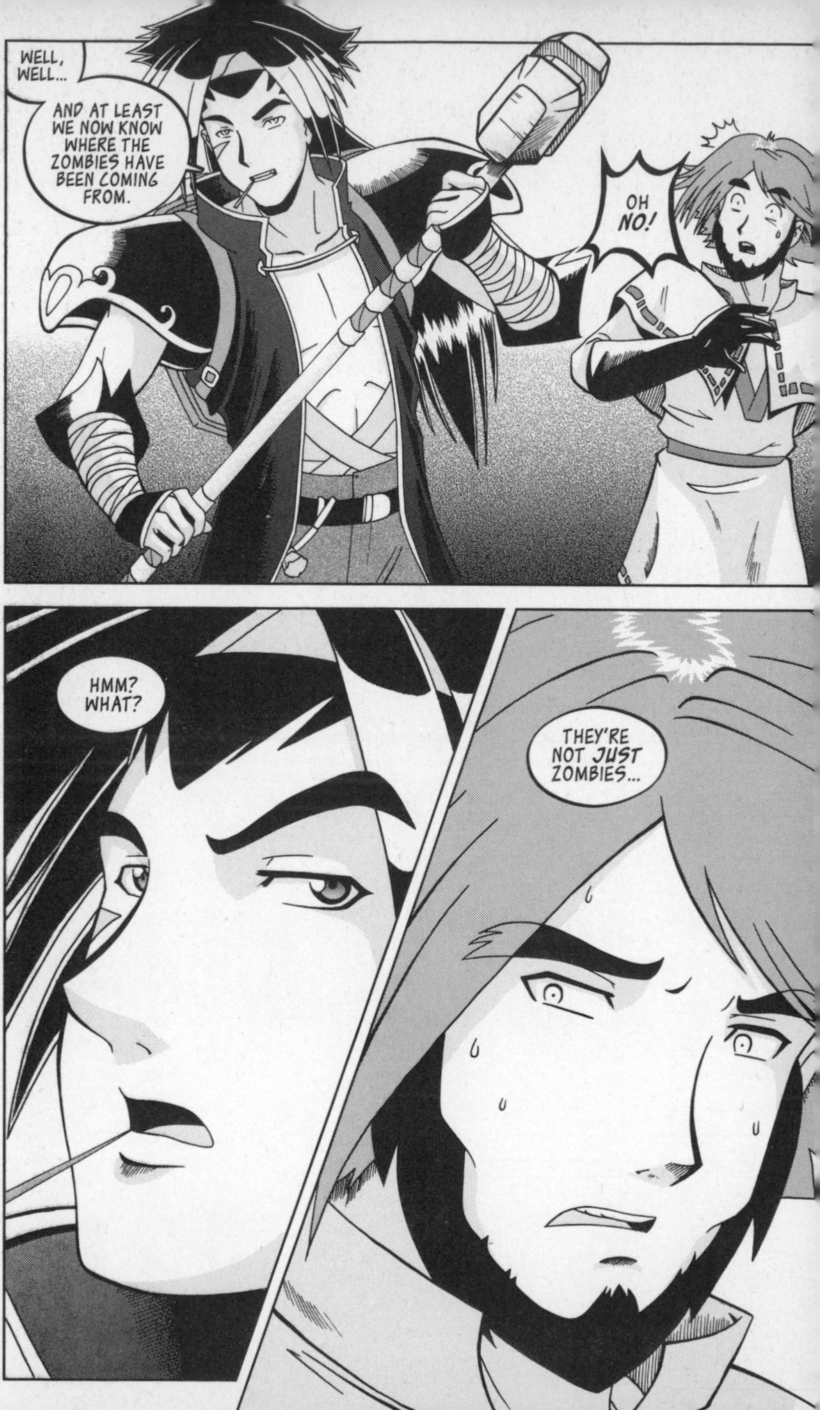
WELL, WELL...
AND AT LEAST WE NOW KNOW WHERE THE ZOMBIES HAVE BEEN COMING FROM.
OH NO!
HMM? WHAT?
THEY'RE NOT JUST ZOMBIES...

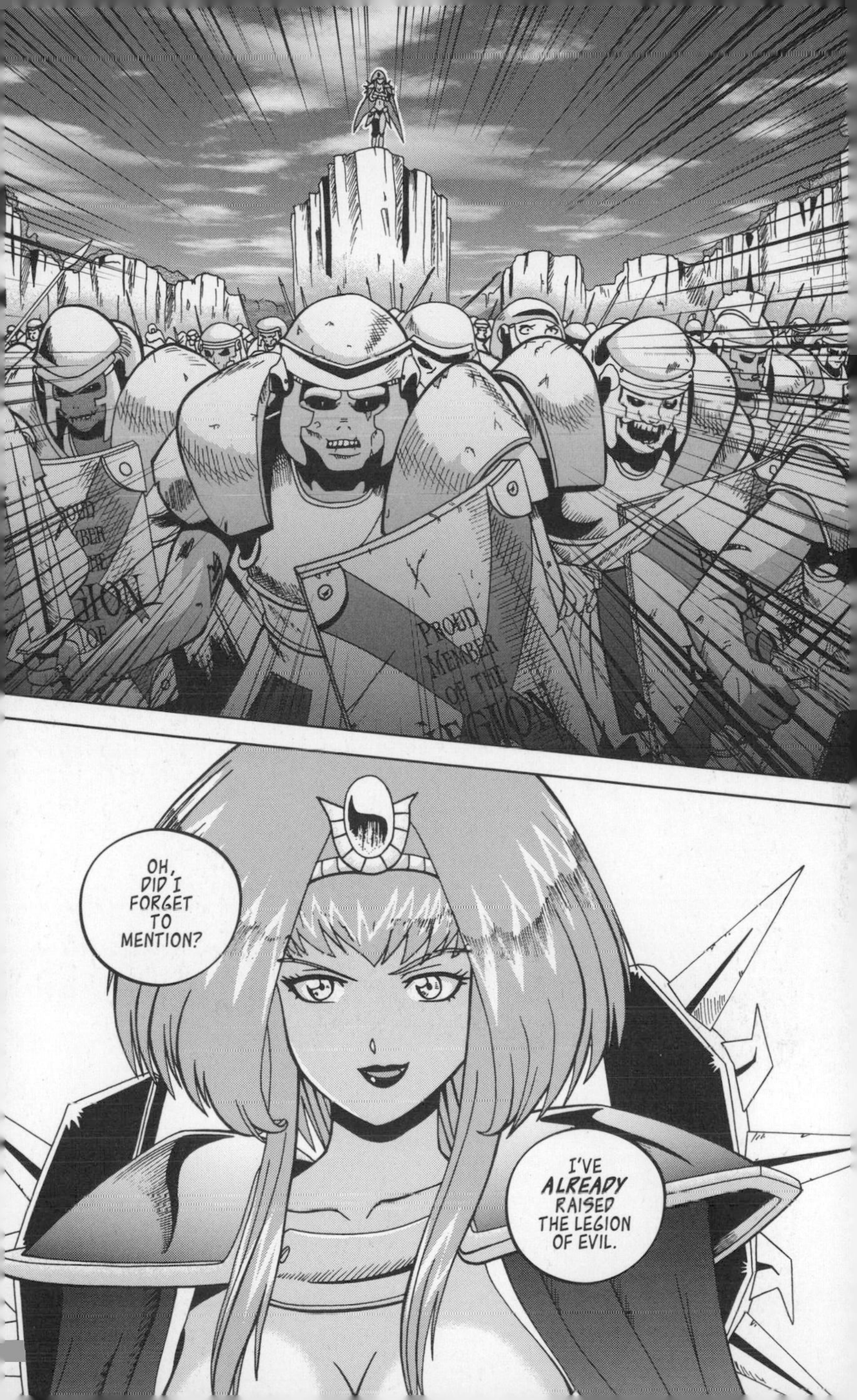
PROUD MEMBER OF THE LEGION
OH, DID I FORGET TO MENTION?
I'VE ALREADY RAISED THE LEGION OF EVIL.

4

HEY, I RECOGNIZE THAT STONE!

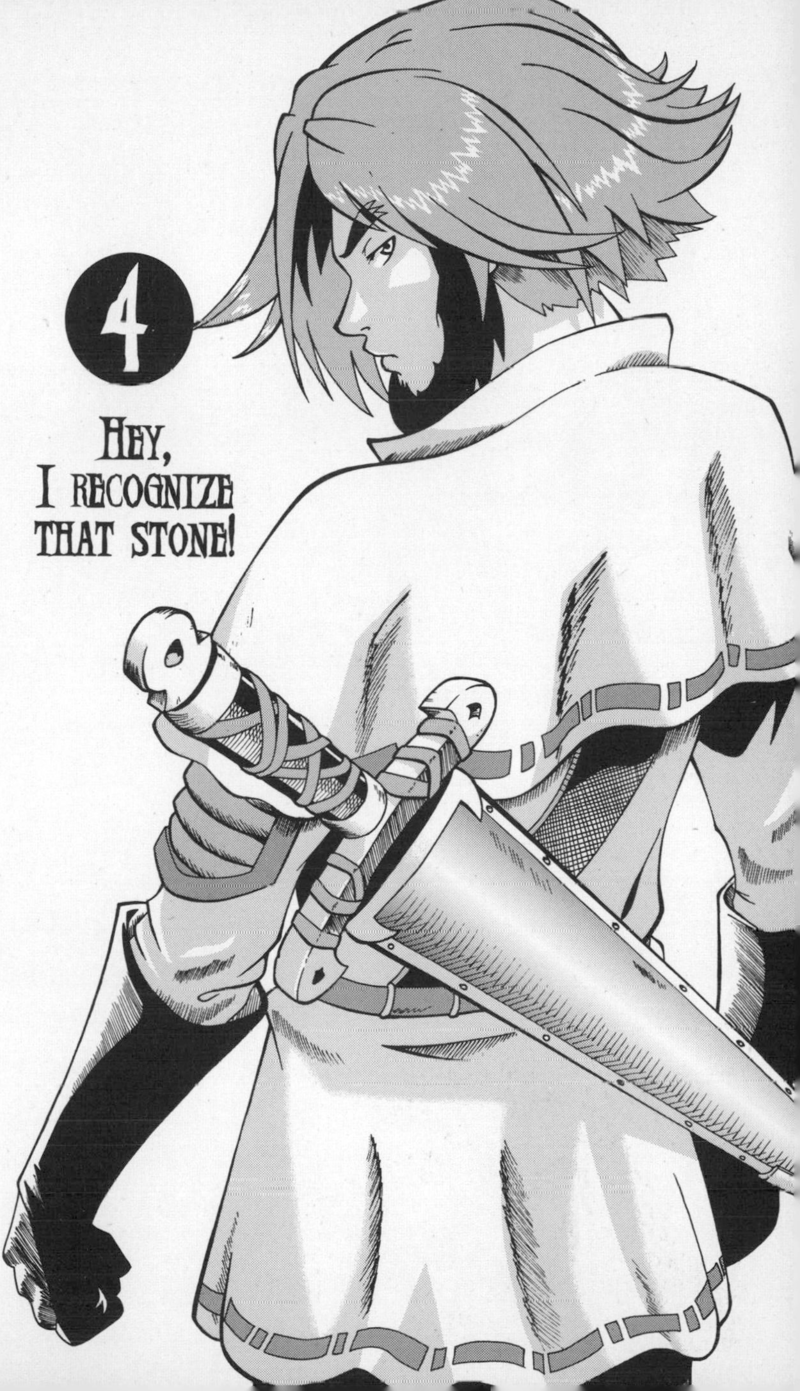

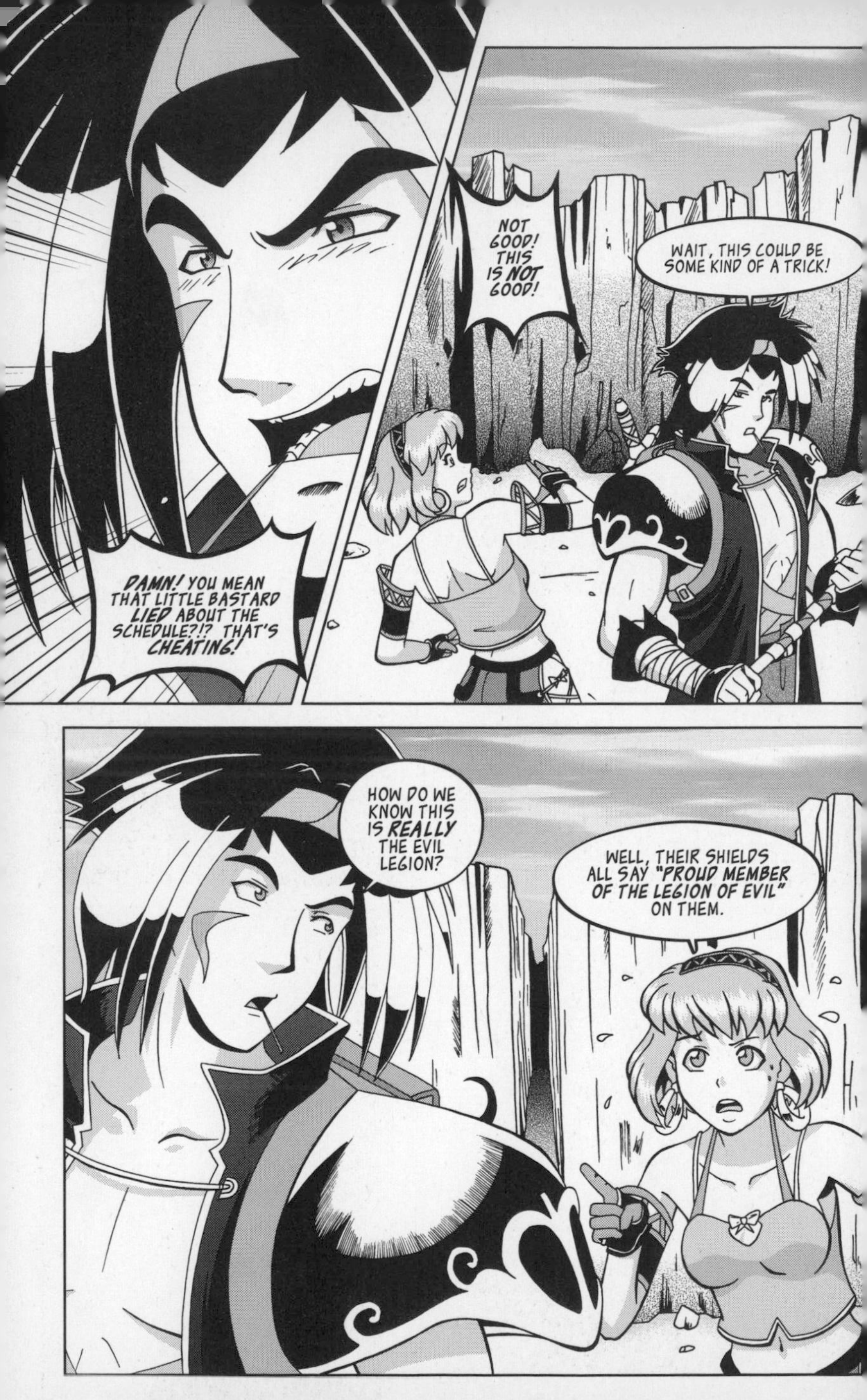
DAMN! YOU MEAN THAT LITTLE BASTARD LIED ABOUT THE SCHEDULE?!? THAT'S CHEATING!
NOT GOOD! THIS IS NOT GOOD!
WAIT, THIS COULD BE SOME KIND OF A TRICK!
HOW DO WE KNOW THIS IS REALLY THE EVIL LEGION?
WELL, THEIR SHIELDS ALL SAY "PROUD MEMBER OF THE LEGION OF EVIL" ON THEM.

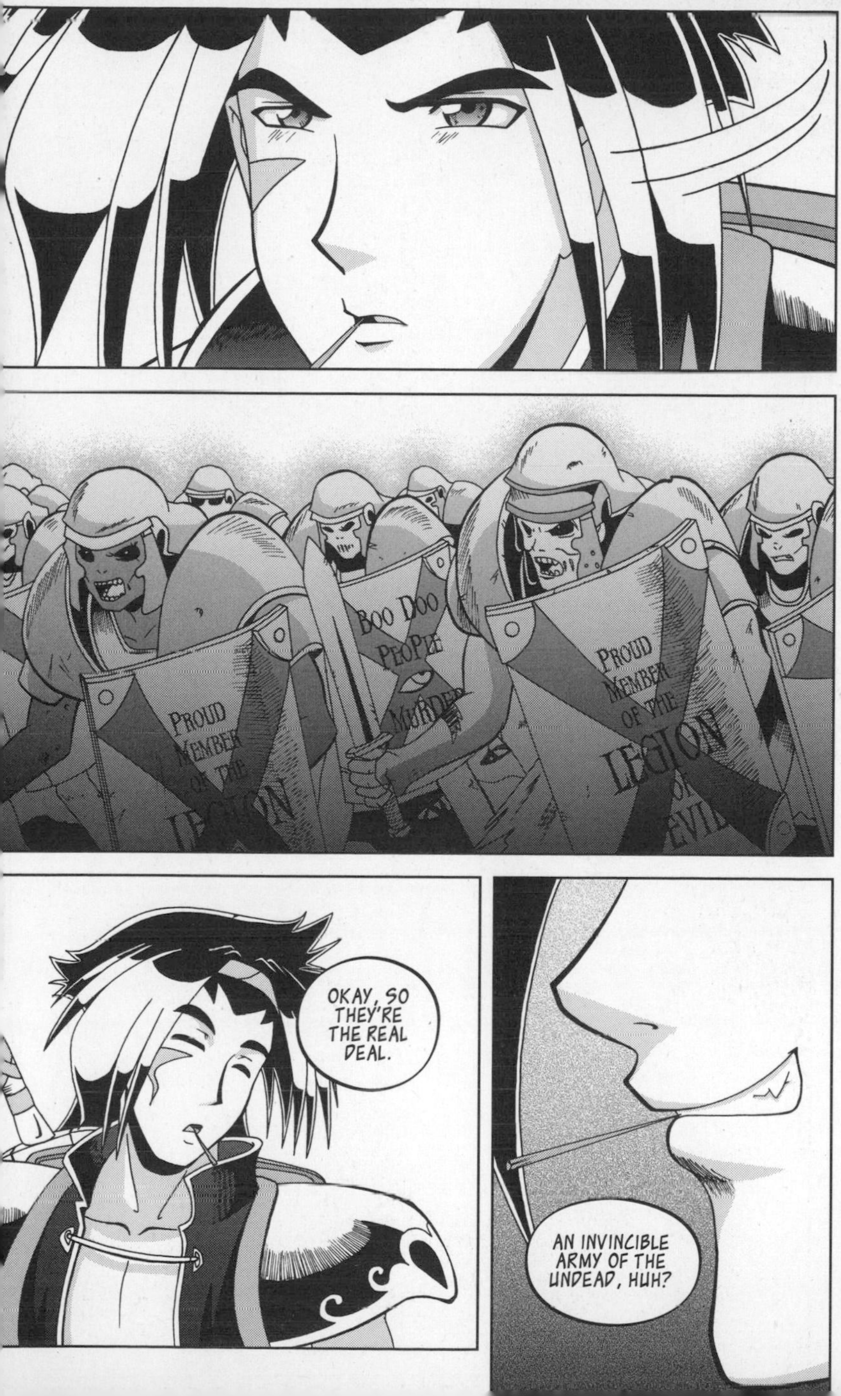
PROUD MEMBER OF THE
BOO DOO PEOPLE MURDER
PROUD MEMBER OF THE LEGION
OKAY, SO THEY'RE THE REAL DEAL.
AN INVINCIBLE ARMY OF THE UNDEAD, HUH?

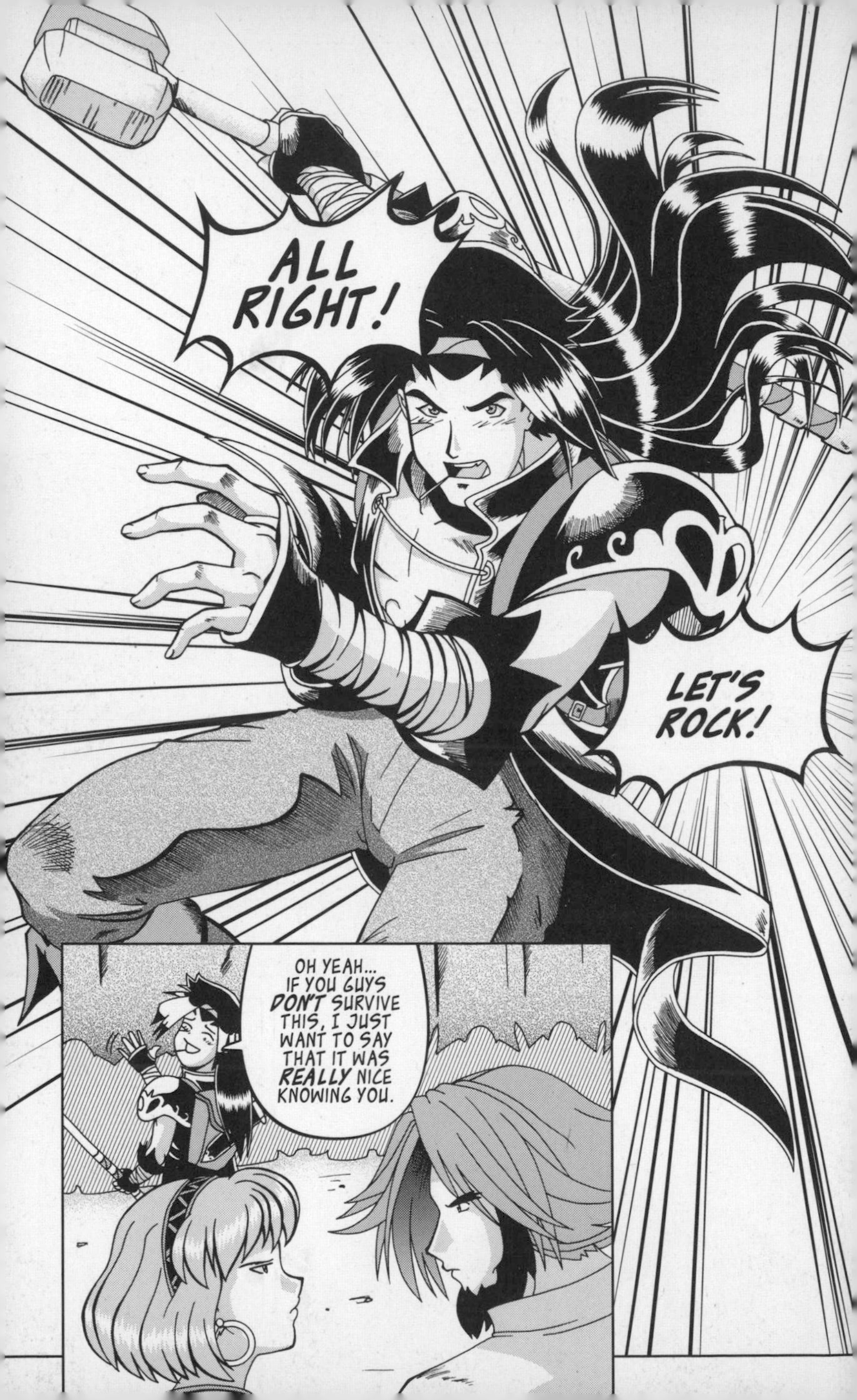
ALL RIGHT!
LET'S ROCK!
OH YEAH... IF YOU GUYS DON'T SURVIVE THIS, I JUST WANT TO SAY THAT IT WAS REALLY NICE KNOWING YOU.

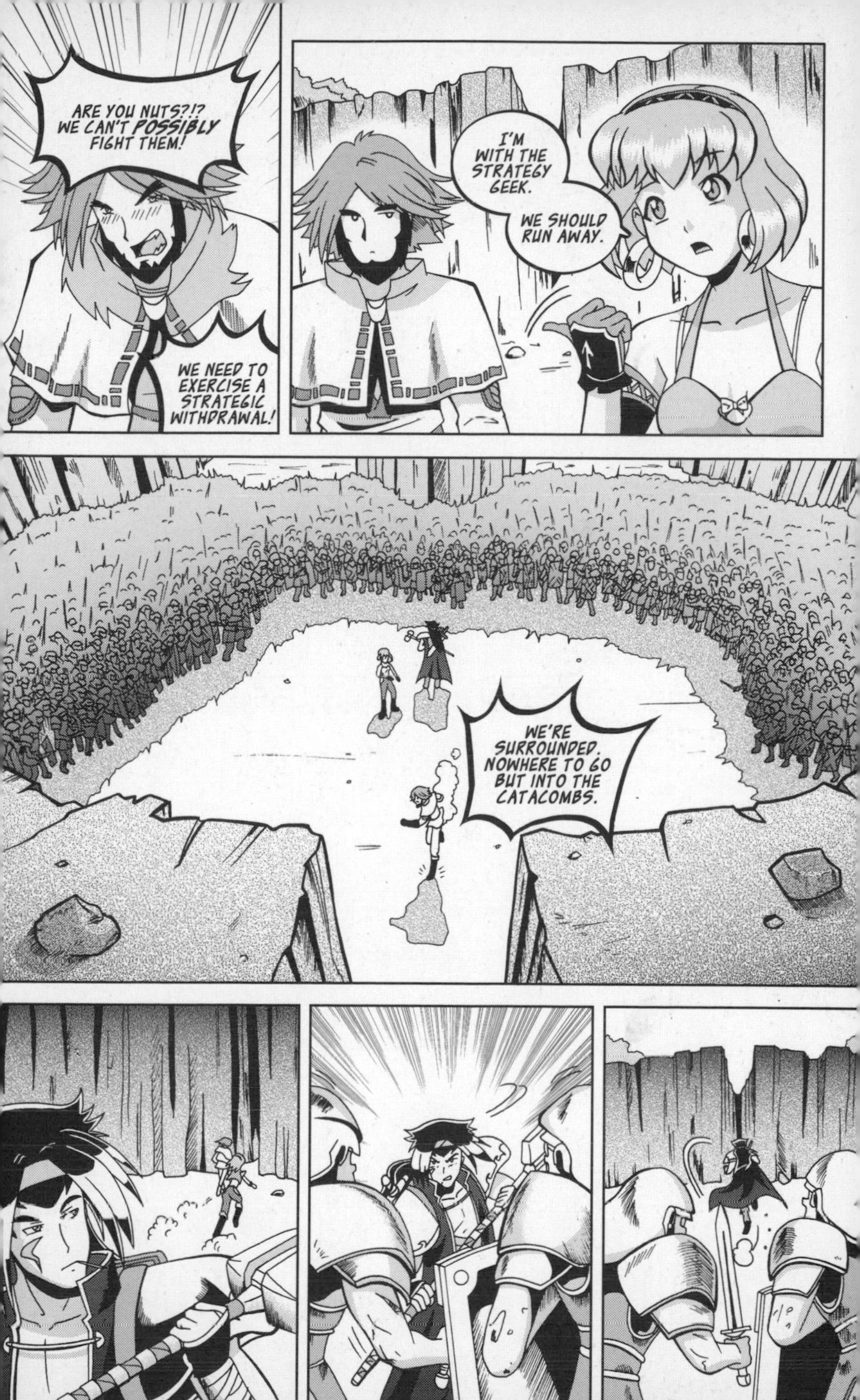
ARE YOU NUTS?!? WE CAN'T POSSIBLY FIGHT THEM!
WE NEED TO EXERCISE A STRATEGIC WITHDRAWAL!
I'M WITH THE STRATEGY GEEK.
WE SHOULD RUN AWAY.
WE'RE SURROUNDED. NOWHERE TO GO BUT INTO THE CATACOMBS.

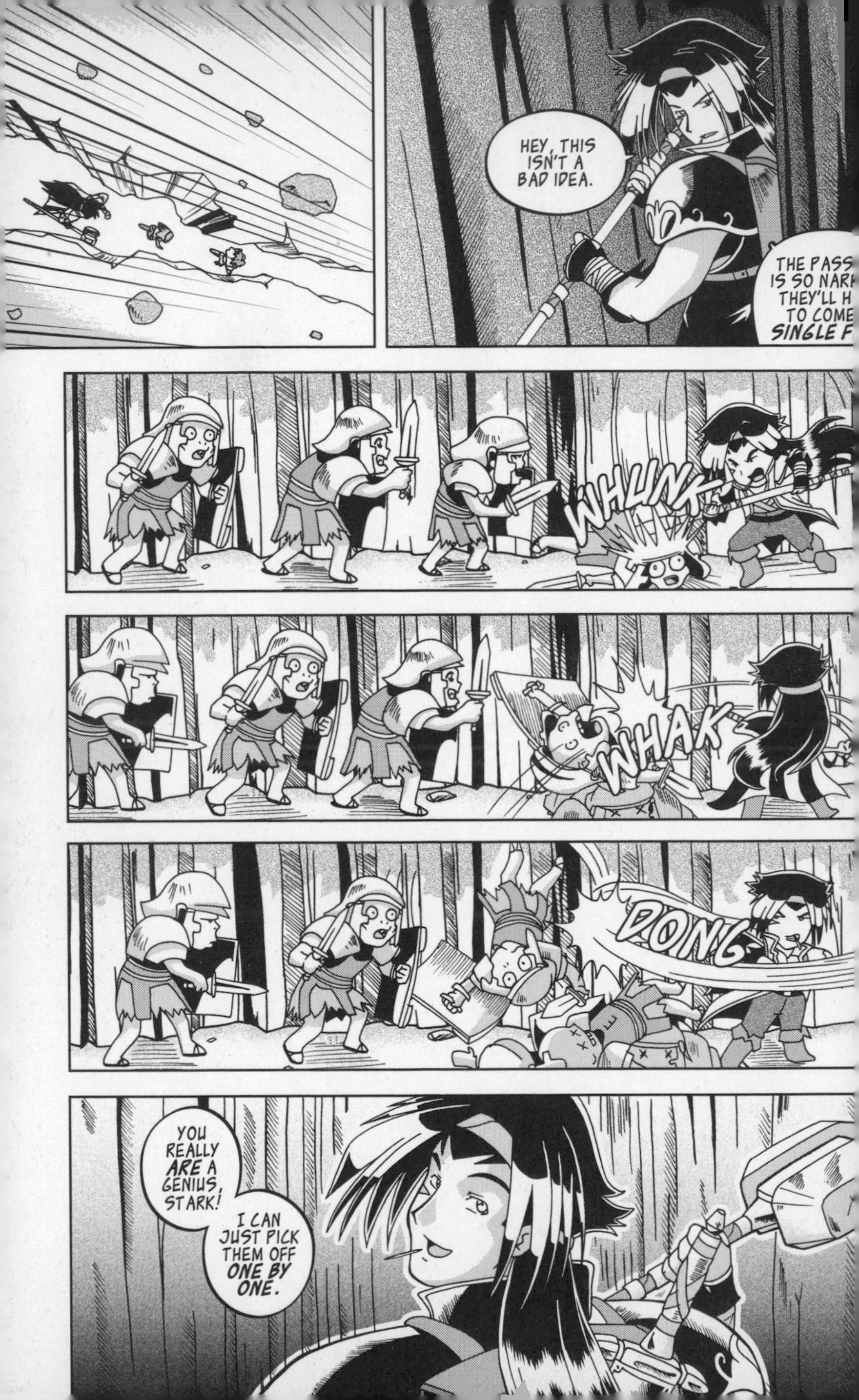
HEY, THIS ISN'T A BAD IDEA.
THE PASS IS SO NAR THEY'LL H TO COME SINGLE F
WHUNK
WHAK
DONG
YOU REALLY ARE A GENIUS, STARK!
I CAN JUST PICK THEM OFF ONE BY ONE.

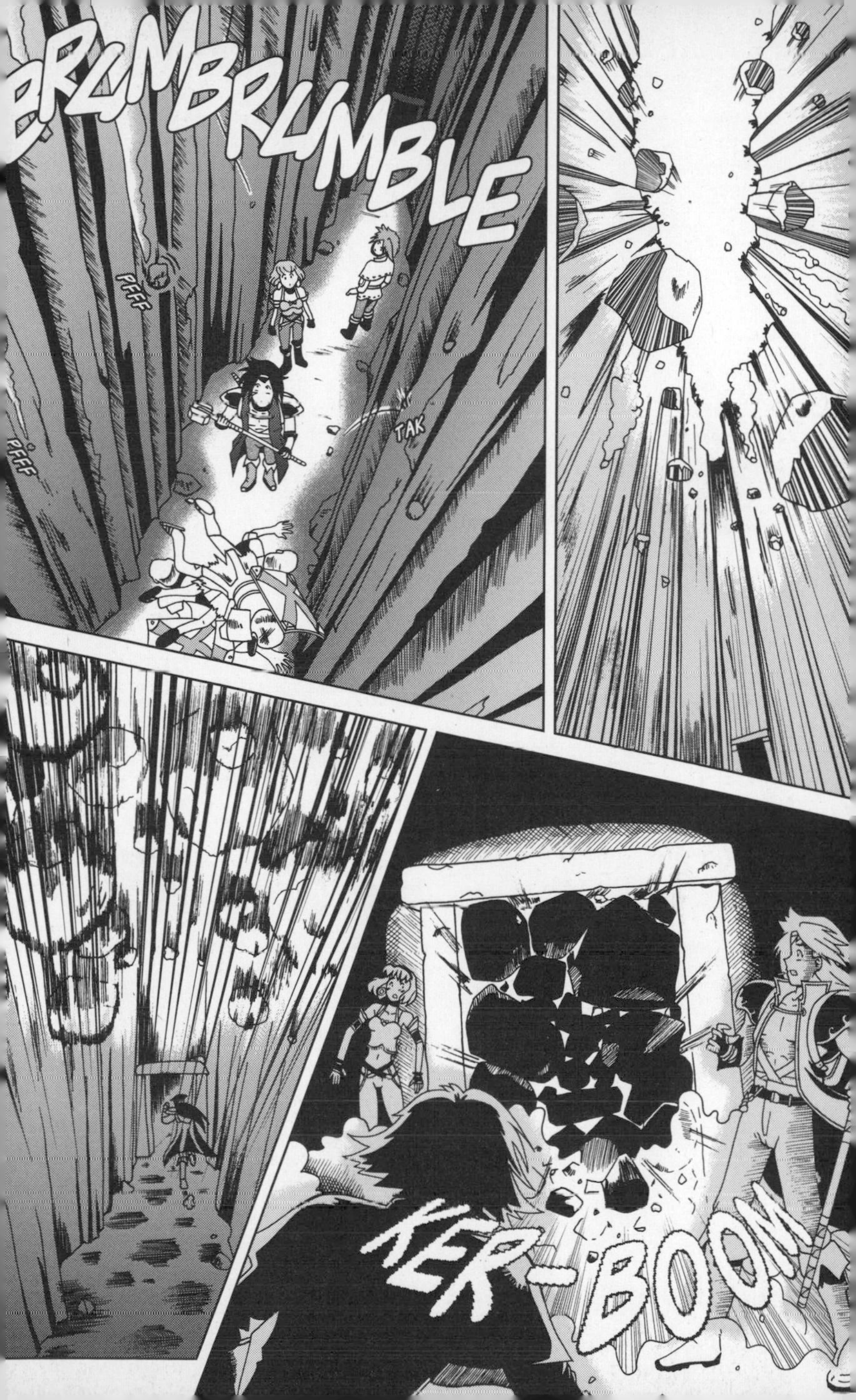
BRUMBRUMBLE
PFFF
TAK
PFFF
KER-BOOM

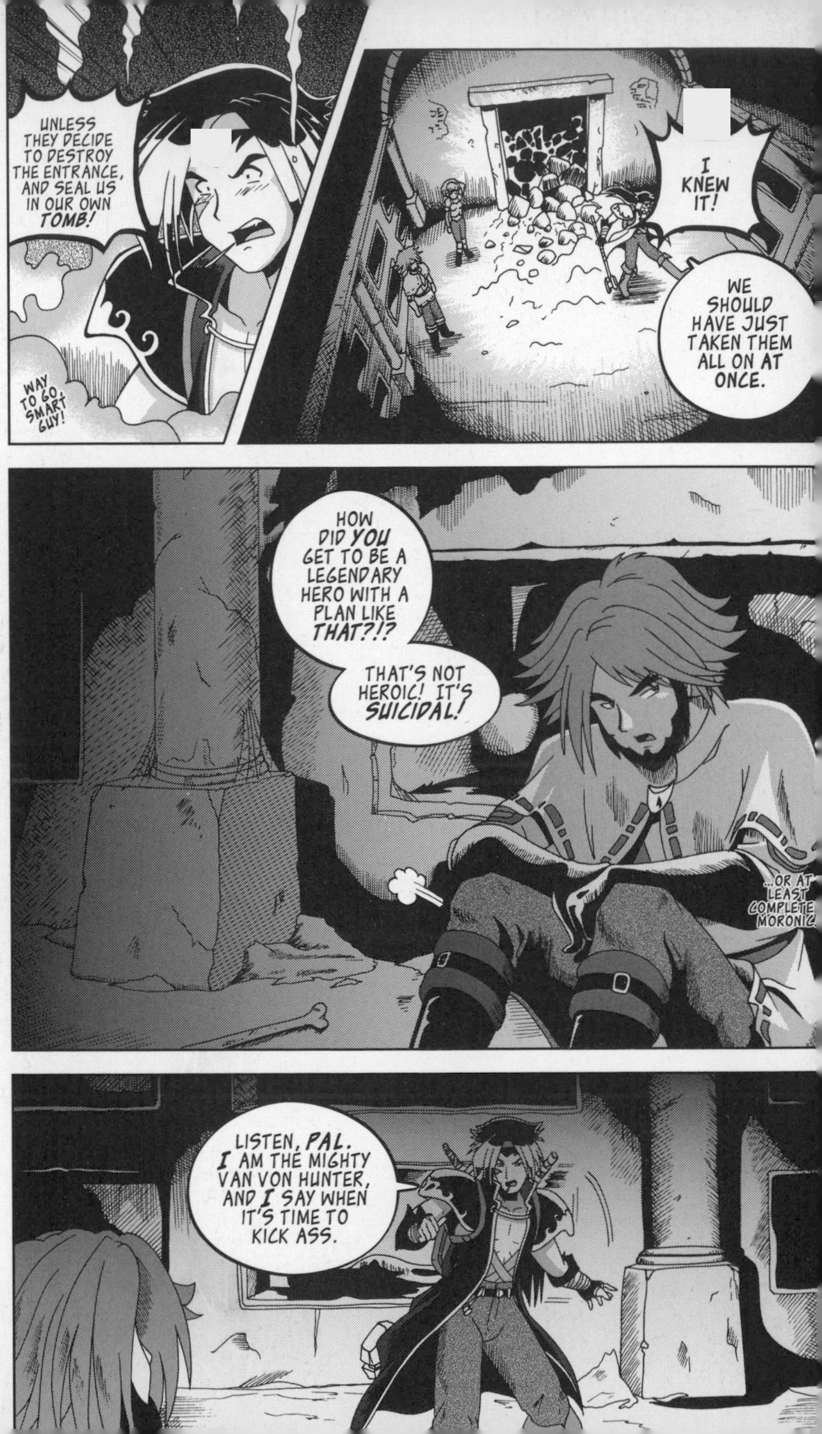

UNLESS THEY DECIDE TO DESTROY THE ENTRANCE, AND SEAL US IN OUR OWN TOMB!
WAY TO GO, SMART GUY!
I KNEW IT!
WE SHOULD HAVE JUST TAKEN THEM ALL ON AT ONCE.
HOW DID YOU GET TO BE A LEGENDARY HERO WITH A PLAN LIKE THAT?!?
THAT'S NOT HEROIC! IT'S SUICIDAL!
...OR AT LEAST COMPLETELY MORONIC.
LISTEN, PAL. I AM THE MIGHTY VAN VON HUNTER, AND I SAY WHEN IT'S TIME TO KICK ASS.

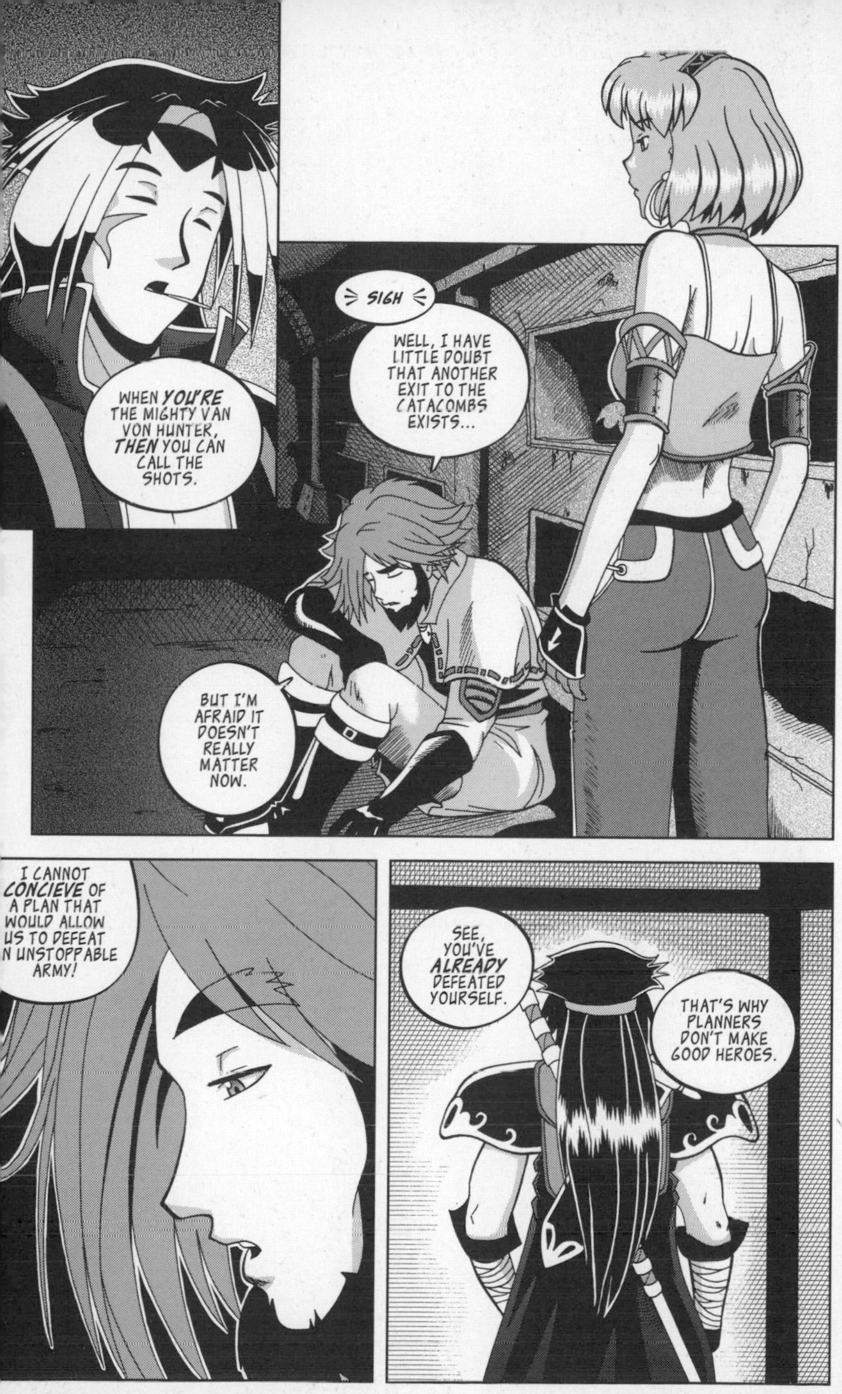
WHEN YOU'RE THE MIGHTY VAN VON HUNTER, THEN YOU CAN CALL THE SHOTS.
SIGH
WELL, I HAVE LITTLE DOUBT THAT ANOTHER EXIT TO THE CATACOMBS EXISTS...
BUT I'M AFRAID IT DOESN'T REALLY MATTER NOW.
I CANNOT CONCIEVE OF A PLAN THAT WOULD ALLOW US TO DEFEAT N UNSTOPPABLE ARMY!
SEE, YOU'VE ALREADY DEFEATED YOURSELF.
THAT'S WHY PLANNERS DON'T MAKE GOOD HEROES.

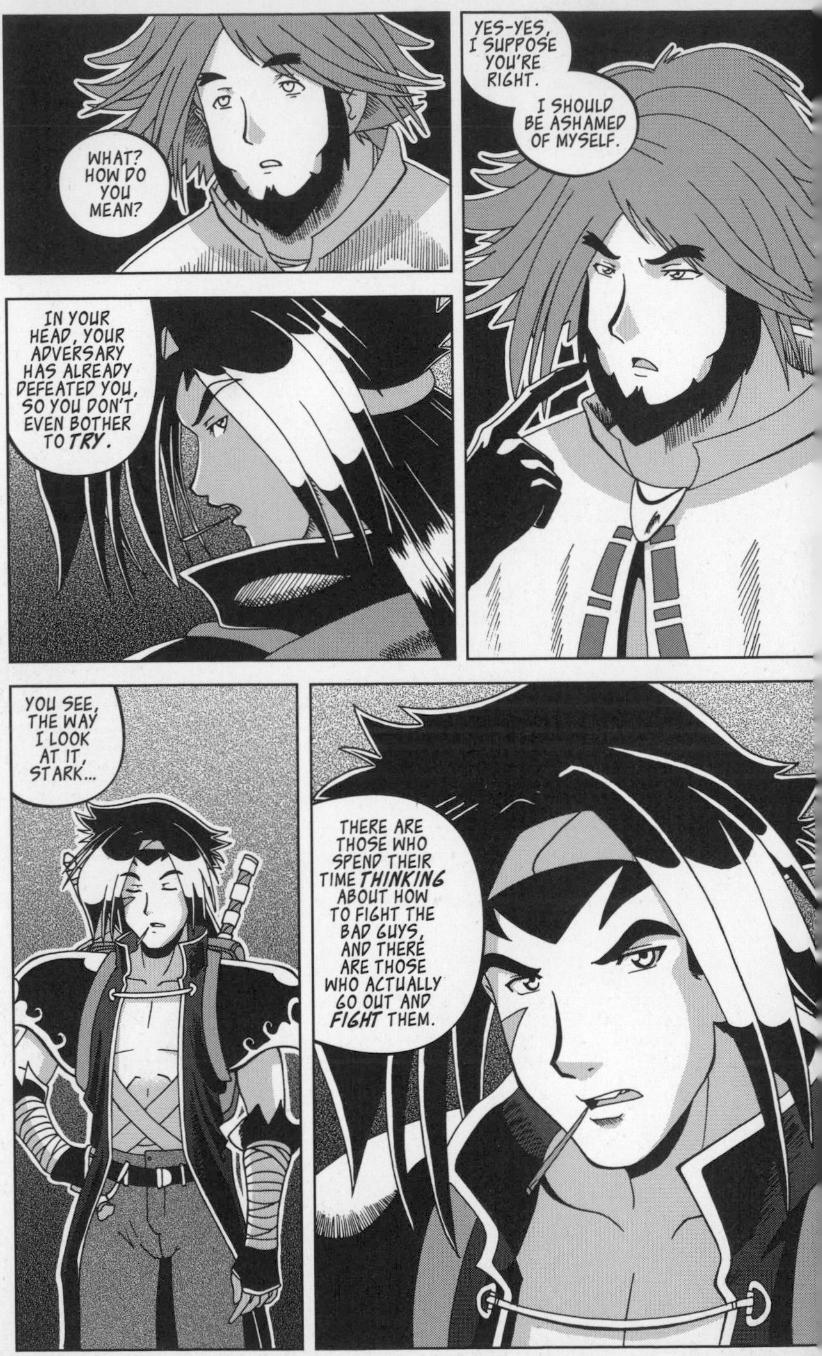
WHAT? HOW DO YOU MEAN?
YES-YES, I SUPPOSE YOU'RE RIGHT.
I SHOULD BE ASHAMED OF MYSELF.
IN YOUR HEAD, YOUR ADVERSARY HAS ALREADY DEFEATED YOU, SO YOU DON'T EVEN BOTHER TO *TRY*.
YOU SEE, THE WAY I LOOK AT IT, STARK...
THERE ARE THOSE WHO SPEND THEIR TIME *THINKING* ABOUT HOW TO FIGHT THE BAD GUYS, AND THERE ARE THOSE WHO ACTUALLY GO OUT AND *FIGHT* THEM.

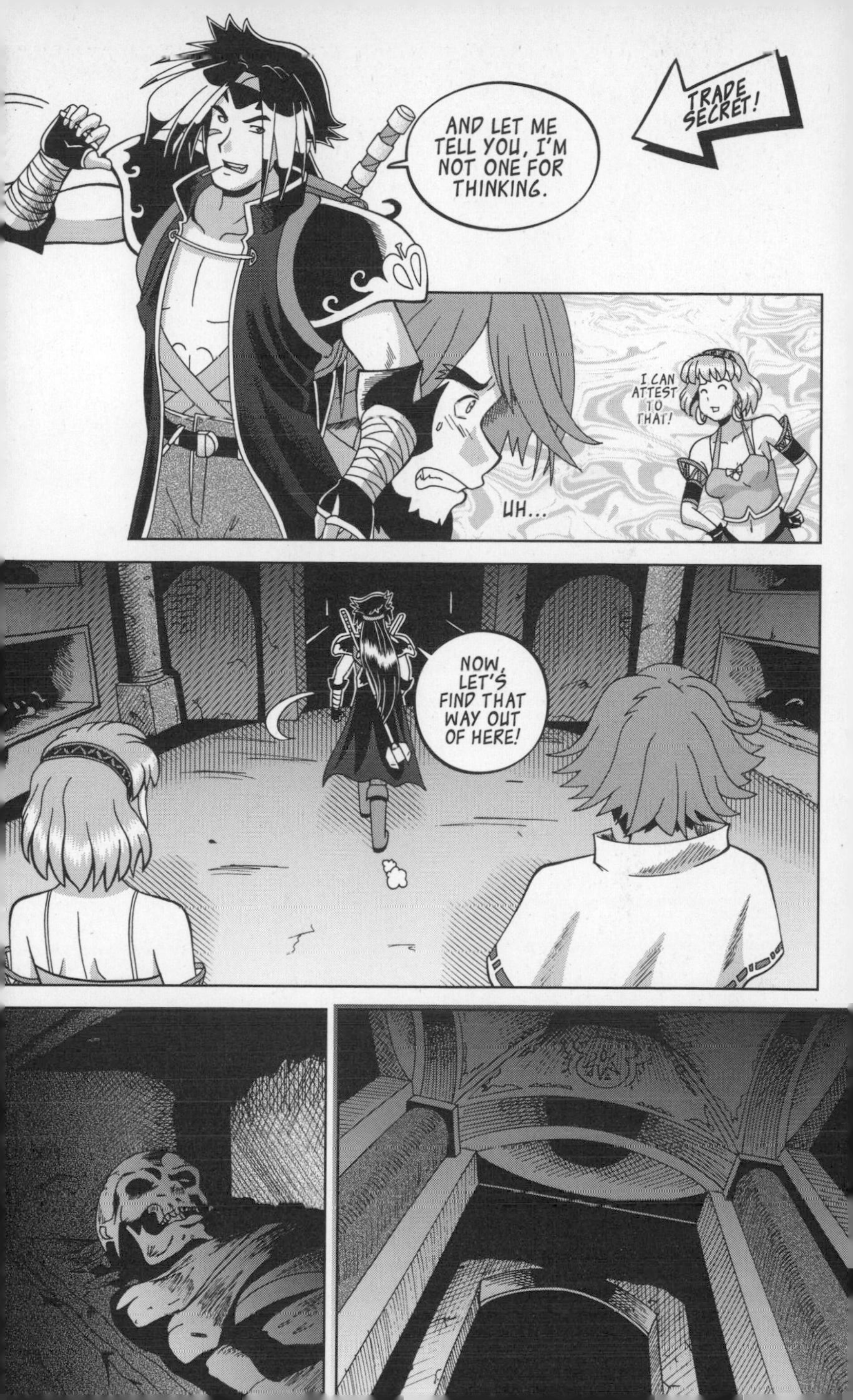
AND LET ME TELL YOU, I'M NOT ONE FOR THINKING.
TRADE SECRET!
UH...
I CAN ATTEST TO THAT!
NOW, LET'S FIND THAT WAY OUT OF HERE!

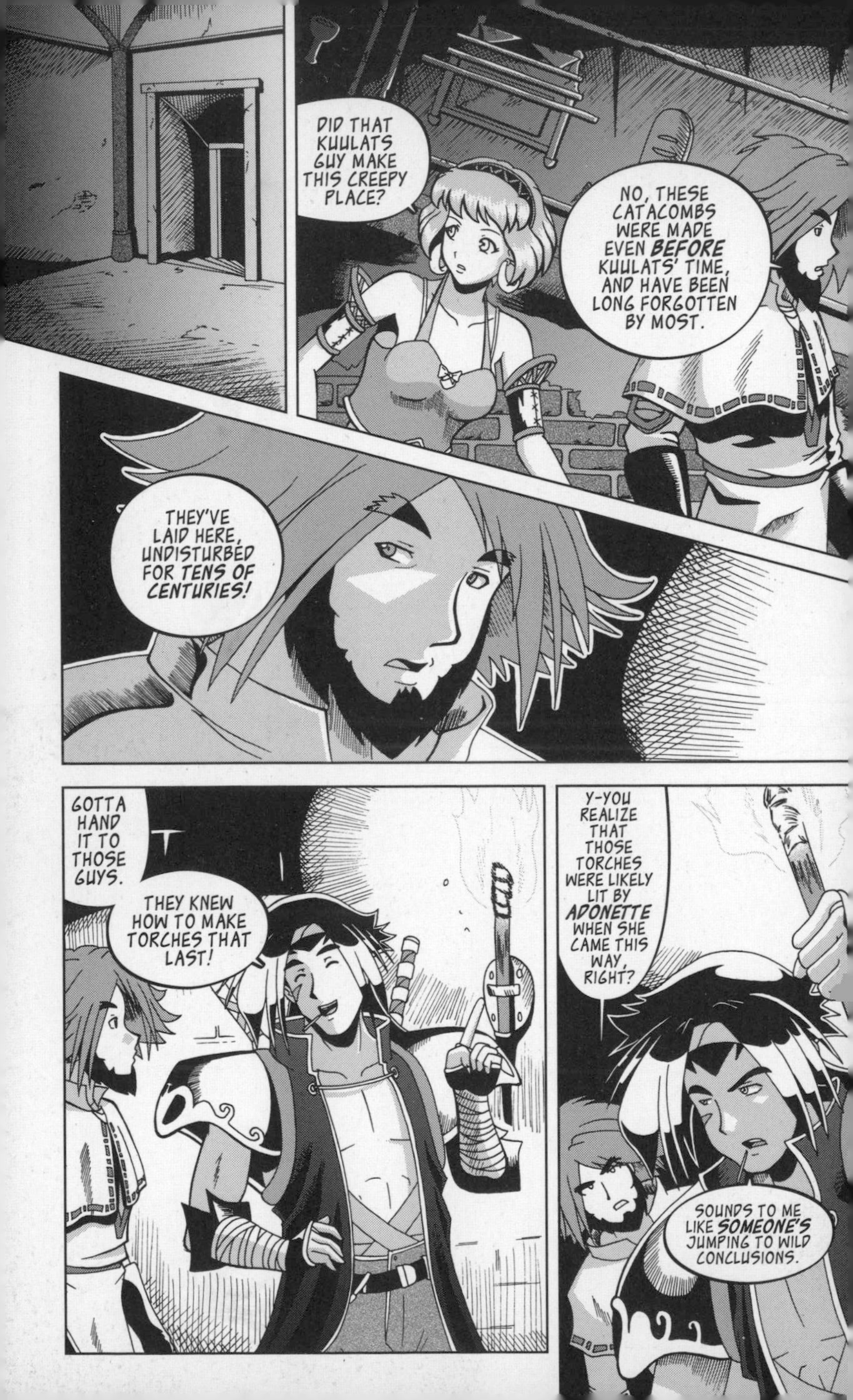
DID THAT KUULATS GUY MAKE THIS CREEPY PLACE?
NO, THESE CATACOMBS WERE MADE EVEN BEFORE KUULATS' TIME, AND HAVE BEEN LONG FORGOTTEN BY MOST.
THEY'VE LAID HERE, UNDISTURBED FOR TENS OF CENTURIES!
GOTTA HAND IT TO THOSE GUYS.
THEY KNEW HOW TO MAKE TORCHES THAT LAST!
Y-YOU REALIZE THAT THOSE TORCHES WERE LIKELY LIT BY ADONETTE WHEN SHE CAME THIS WAY, RIGHT?
SOUNDS TO ME LIKE SOMEONE'S JUMPING TO WILD CONCLUSIONS.

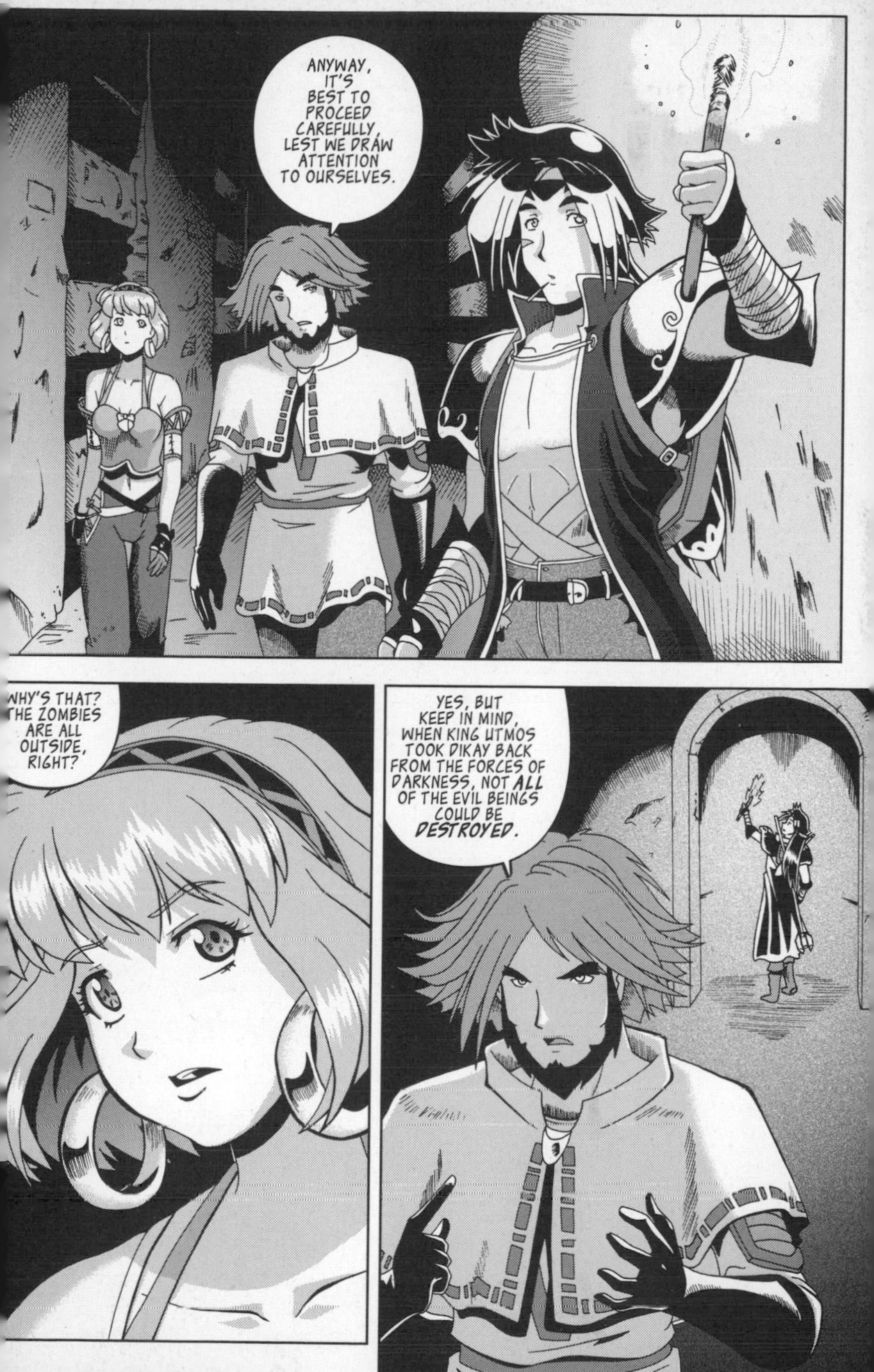
ANYWAY, IT'S BEST TO PROCEED CAREFULLY, LEST WE DRAW ATTENTION TO OURSELVES.
WHY'S THAT? THE ZOMBIES ARE ALL OUTSIDE, RIGHT?
YES, BUT KEEP IN MIND, WHEN KING UTMOS TOOK DIKAY BACK FROM THE FORCES OF DARKNESS, NOT ALL OF THE EVIL BEINGS COULD BE DESTROYED.

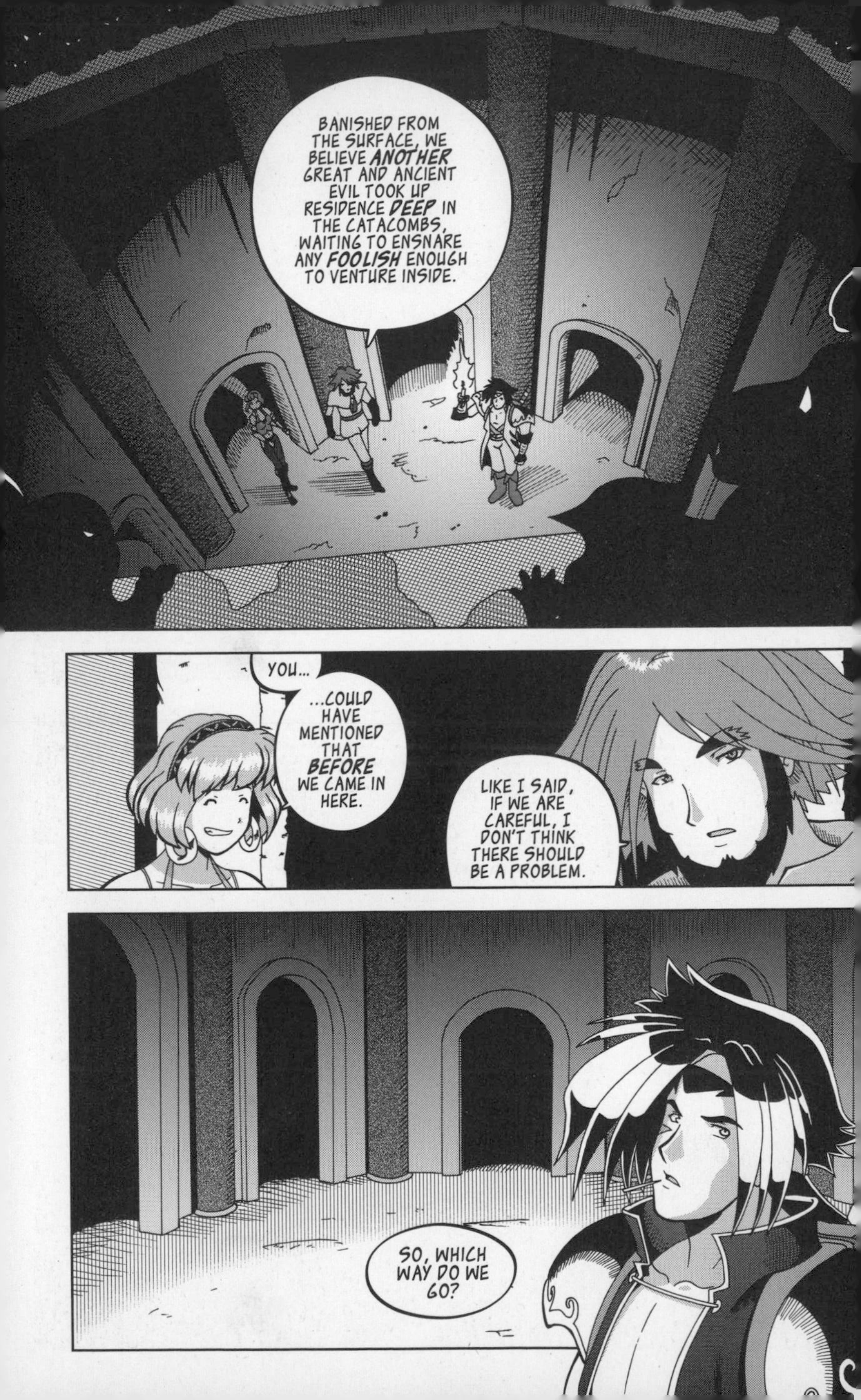
BANISHED FROM THE SURFACE, WE BELIEVE ANOTHER GREAT AND ANCIENT EVIL TOOK UP RESIDENCE DEEP IN THE CATACOMBS, WAITING TO ENSNARE ANY FOOLISH ENOUGH TO VENTURE INSIDE.
YOU...
...COULD HAVE MENTIONED THAT BEFORE WE CAME IN HERE.
LIKE I SAID, IF WE ARE CAREFUL, I DON'T THINK THERE SHOULD BE A PROBLEM.
SO, WHICH WAY DO WE GO?

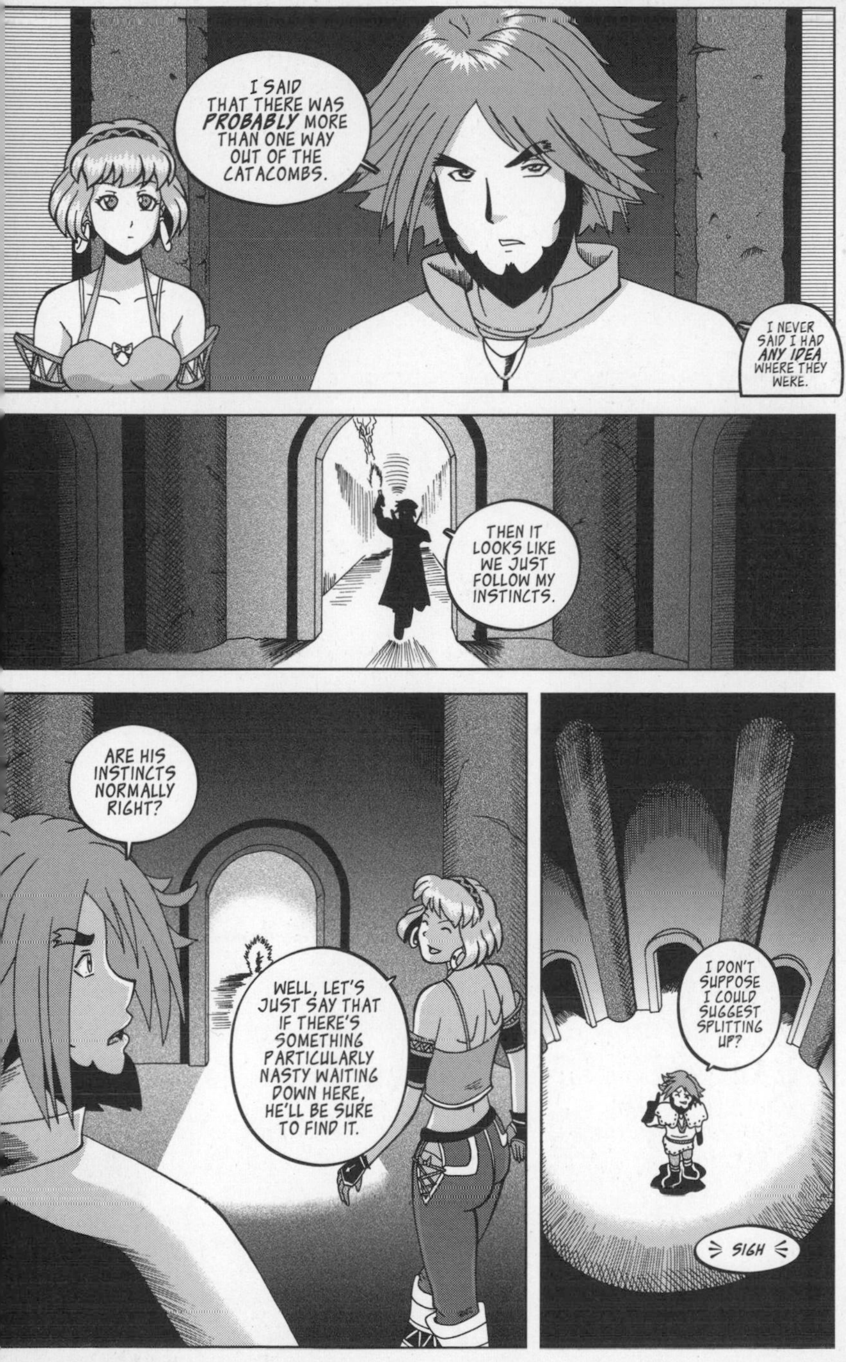
I SAID THAT THERE WAS PROBABLY MORE THAN ONE WAY OUT OF THE CATACOMBS.
I NEVER SAID I HAD ANY IDEA WHERE THEY WERE.
THEN IT LOOKS LIKE WE JUST FOLLOW MY INSTINCTS.
ARE HIS INSTINCTS NORMALLY RIGHT?
WELL, LET'S JUST SAY THAT IF THERE'S SOMETHING PARTICULARLY NASTY WAITING DOWN HERE, HE'LL BE SURE TO FIND IT.
I DON'T SUPPOSE I COULD SUGGEST SPLITTING UP?
SIGH

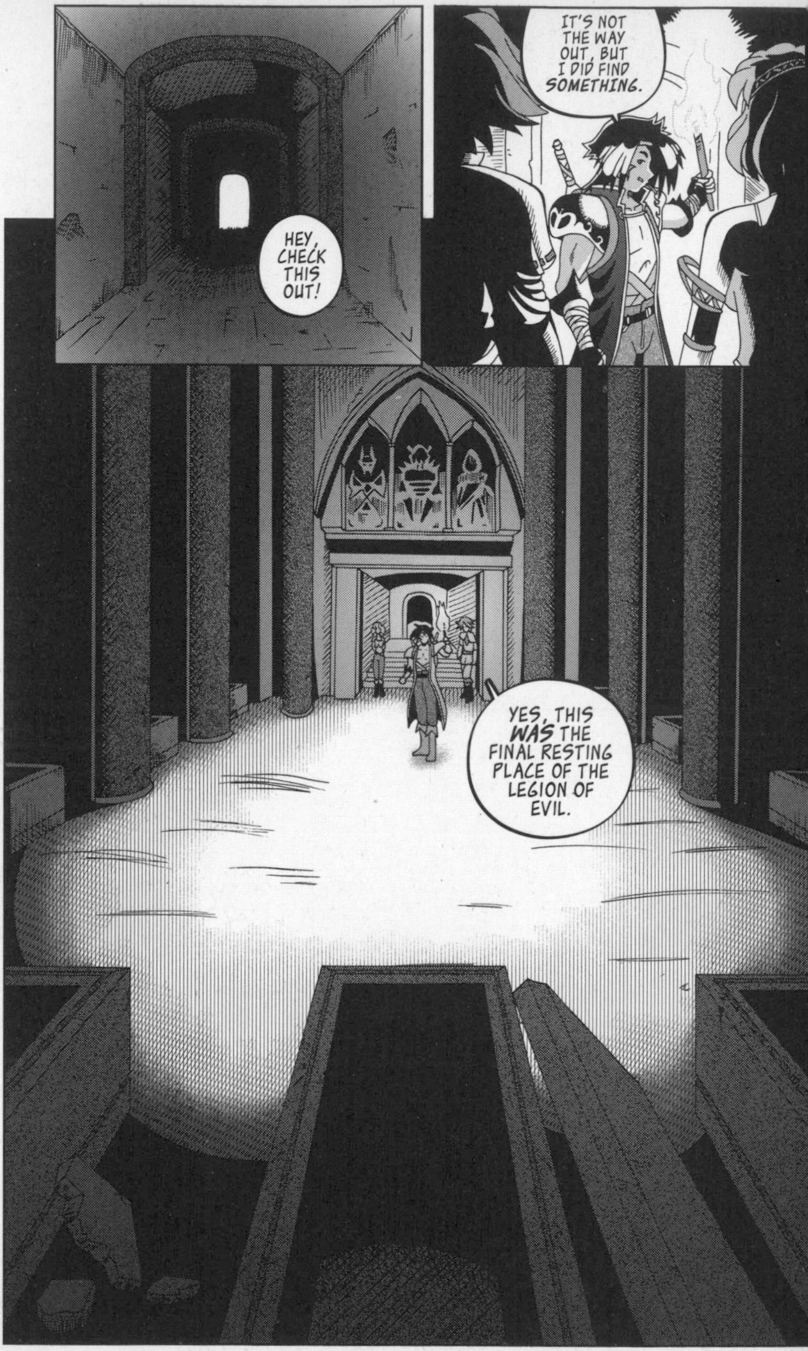
HEY, CHECK THIS OUT!
IT'S NOT THE WAY OUT, BUT I DID FIND SOMETHING.
YES, THIS WAS THE FINAL RESTING PLACE OF THE LEGION OF EVIL.

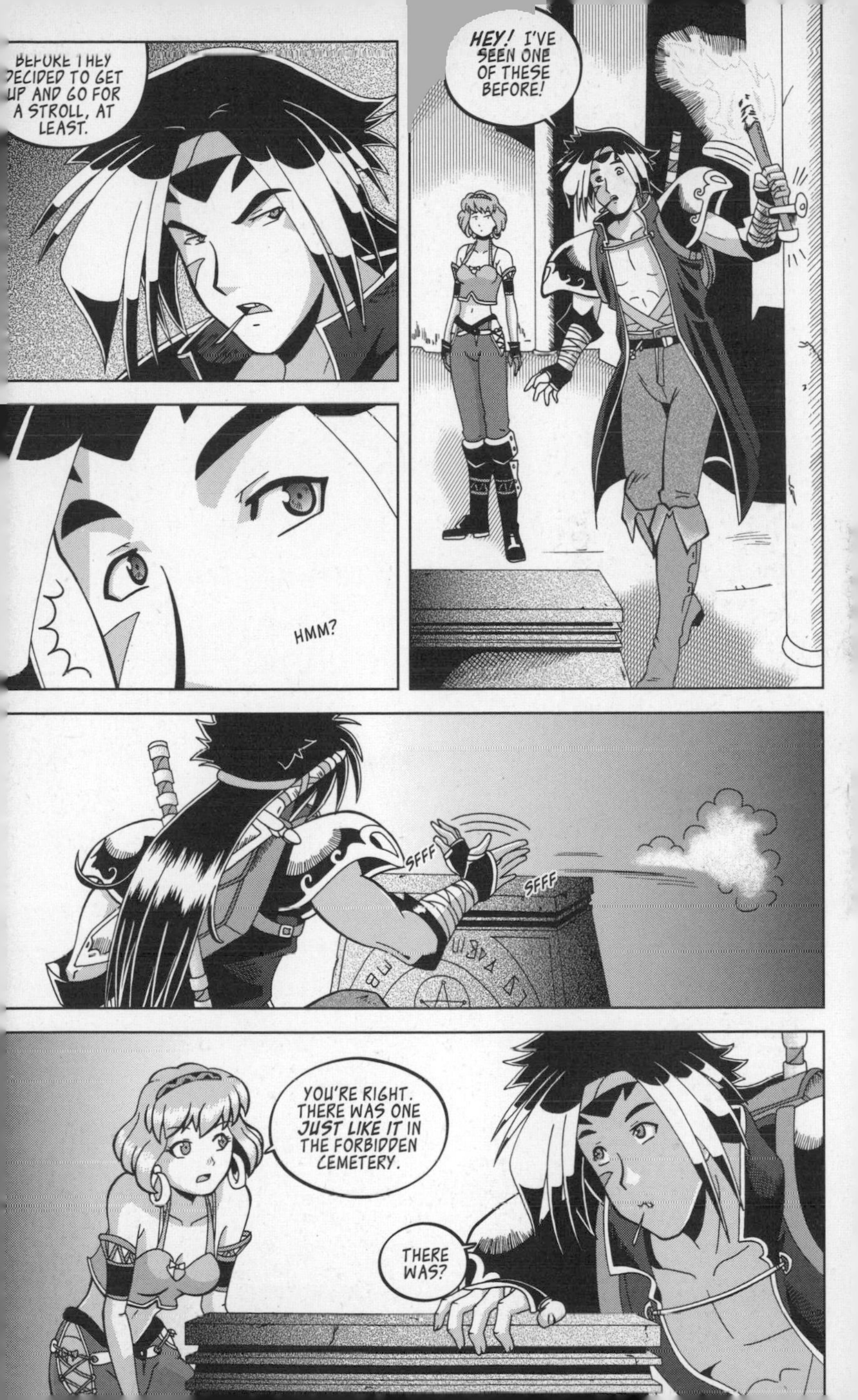
BEFORE THEY DECIDED TO GET UP AND GO FOR A STROLL, AT LEAST.
HMM?
HEY! I'VE SEEN ONE OF THESE BEFORE!
SFFF
SFFF
YOU'RE RIGHT. THERE WAS ONE JUST LIKE IT IN THE FORBIDDEN CEMETERY.
THERE WAS?

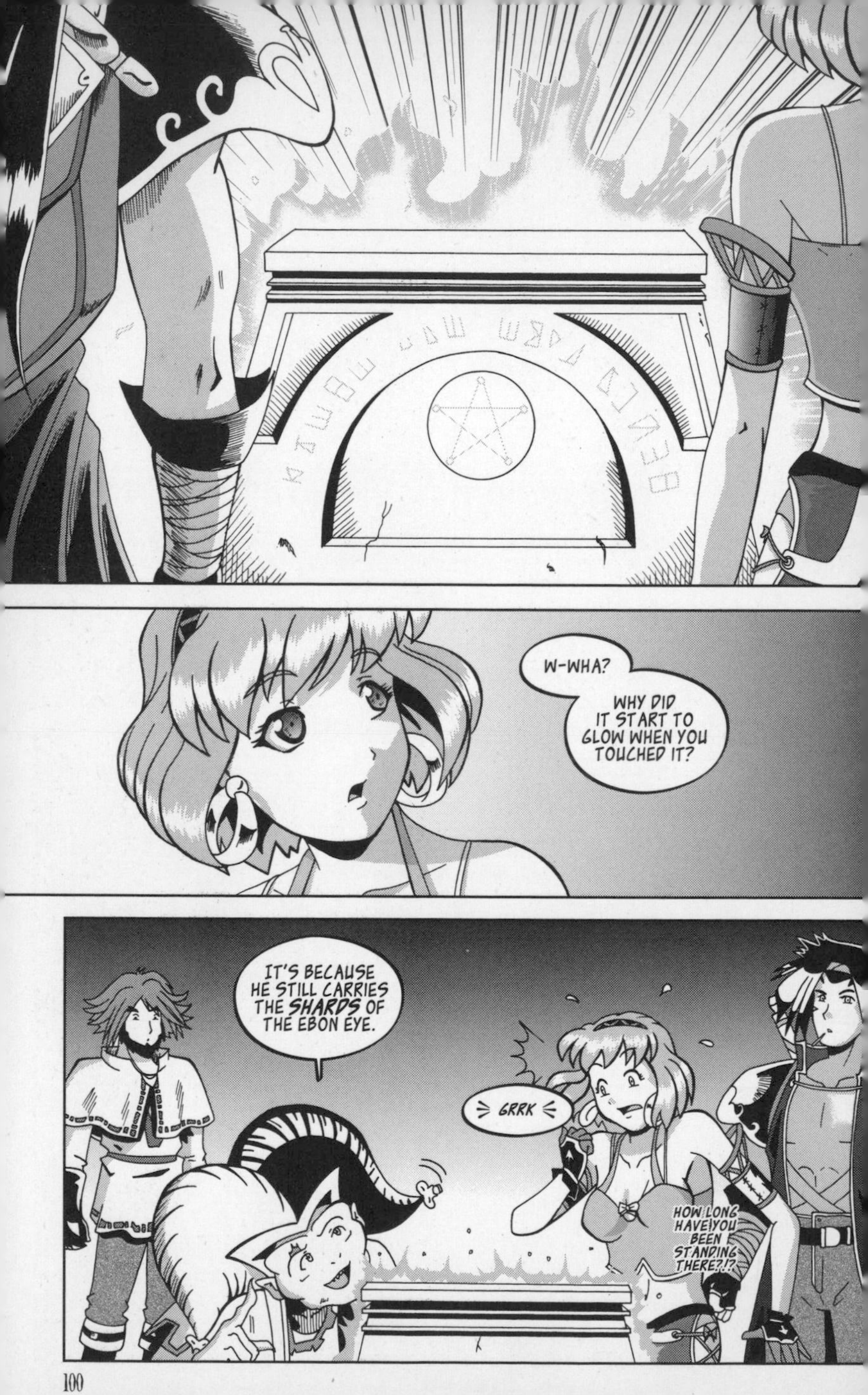
W-WHA?
WHY DID IT START TO GLOW WHEN YOU TOUCHED IT?
IT'S BECAUSE HE STILL CARRIES THE SHARDS OF THE EBON EYE.
GRRK
HOW LONG HAVE YOU BEEN STANDING THERE?!?

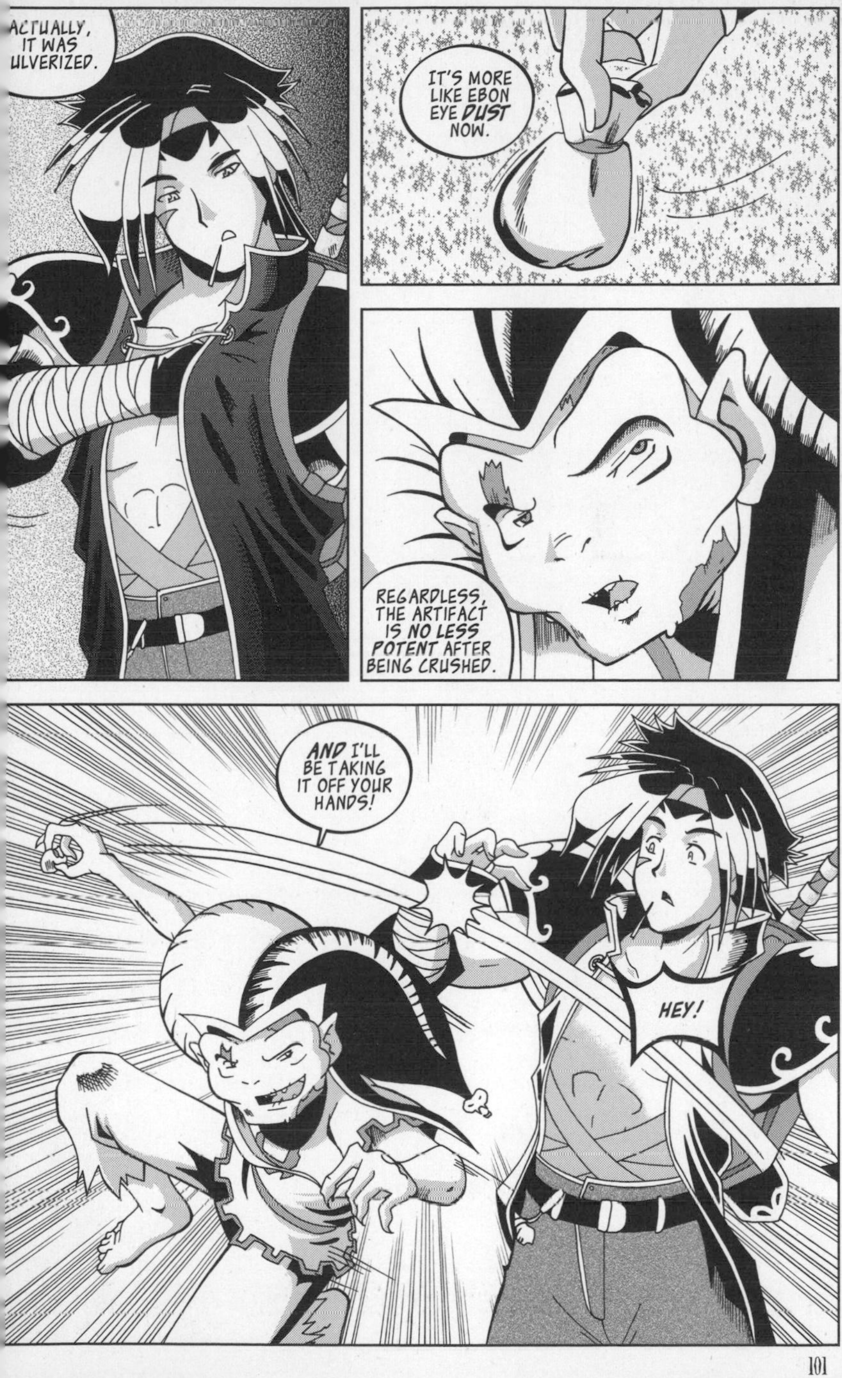
ACTUALLY, IT WAS ULVERIZED.
IT'S MORE LIKE EBON EYE DUST NOW.
REGARDLESS, THE ARTIFACT IS NO LESS POTENT AFTER BEING CRUSHED.
AND I'LL BE TAKING IT OFF YOUR HANDS!
HEY!

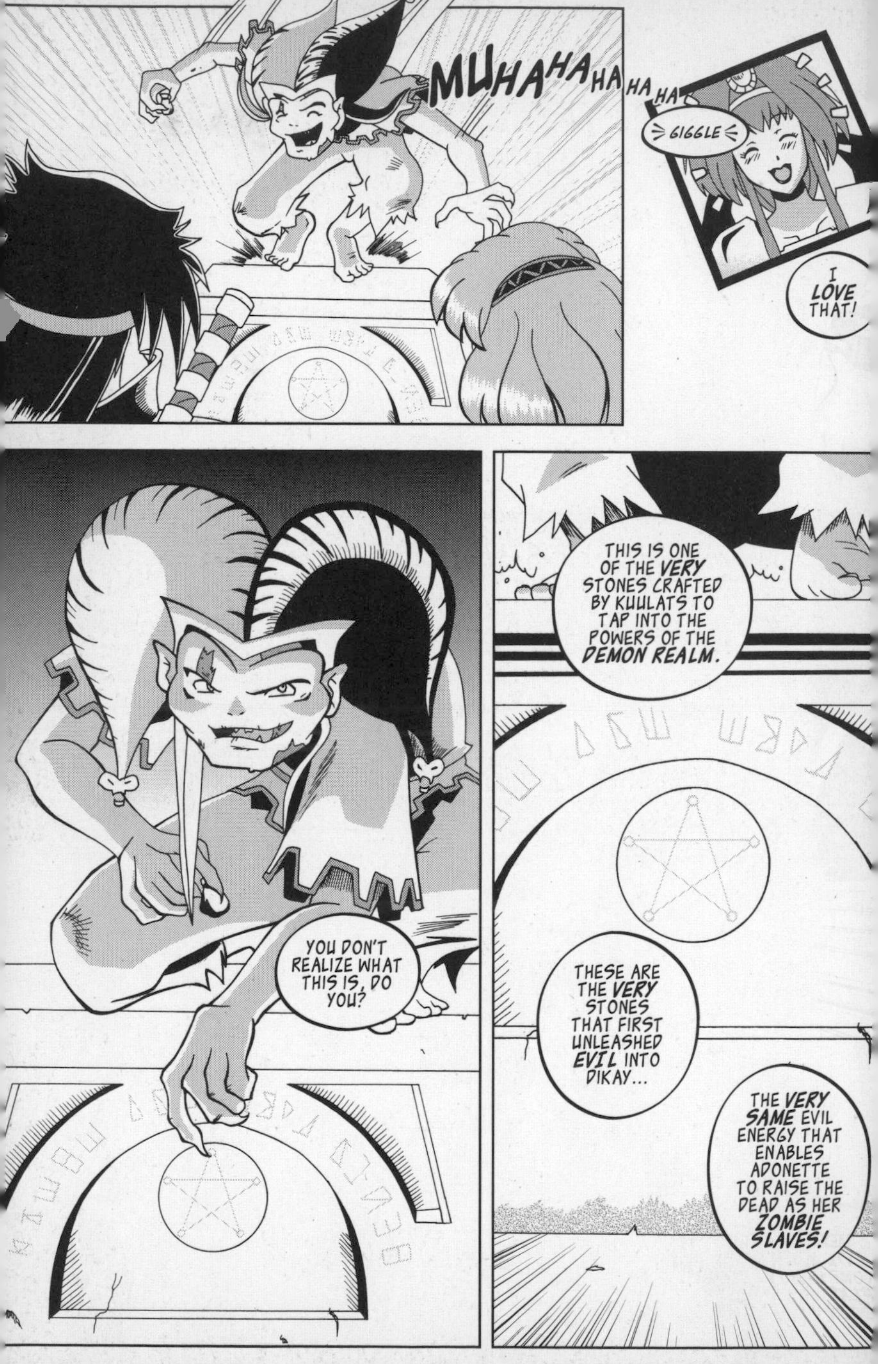
MUHAHAHAHAHA
GIGGLE
I LOVE THAT!
YOU DON'T REALIZE WHAT THIS IS, DO YOU?
THIS IS ONE OF THE VERY STONES CRAFTED BY KUULATS TO TAP INTO THE POWERS OF THE DEMON REALM.
THESE ARE THE VERY STONES THAT FIRST UNLEASHED EVIL INTO DIKAY...
THE VERY SAME EVIL ENERGY THAT ENABLES ADONETTE TO RAISE THE DEAD AS HER ZOMBIE SLAVES!

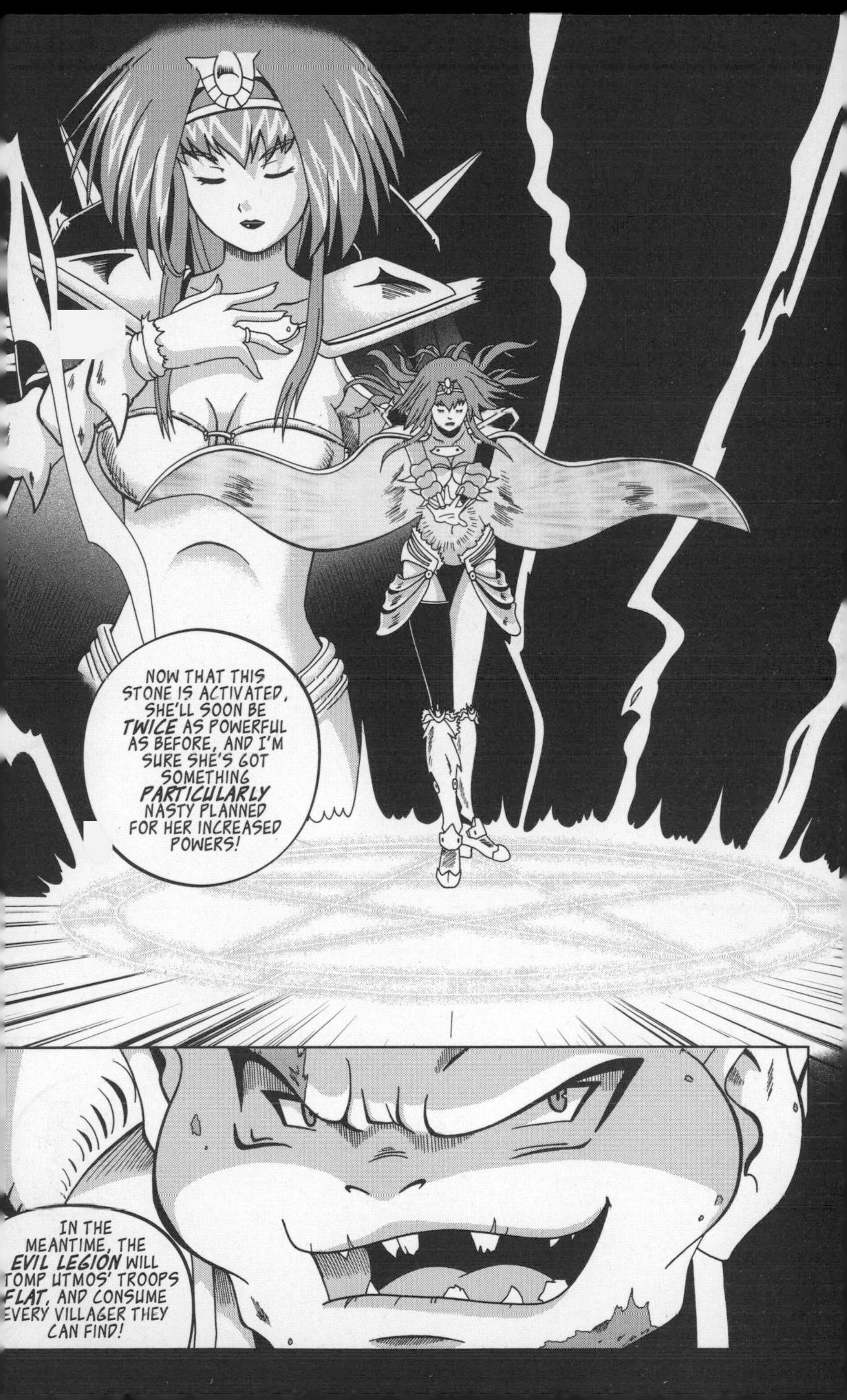
NOW THAT THIS STONE IS ACTIVATED, SHE'LL SOON BE TWICE AS POWERFUL AS BEFORE, AND I'M SURE SHE'S GOT SOMETHING PARTICULARLY NASTY PLANNED FOR HER INCREASED POWERS!
IN THE MEANTIME, THE EVIL LEGION WILL TOMP UTMOS' TROOPS FLAT, AND CONSUME EVERY VILLAGER THEY CAN FIND!

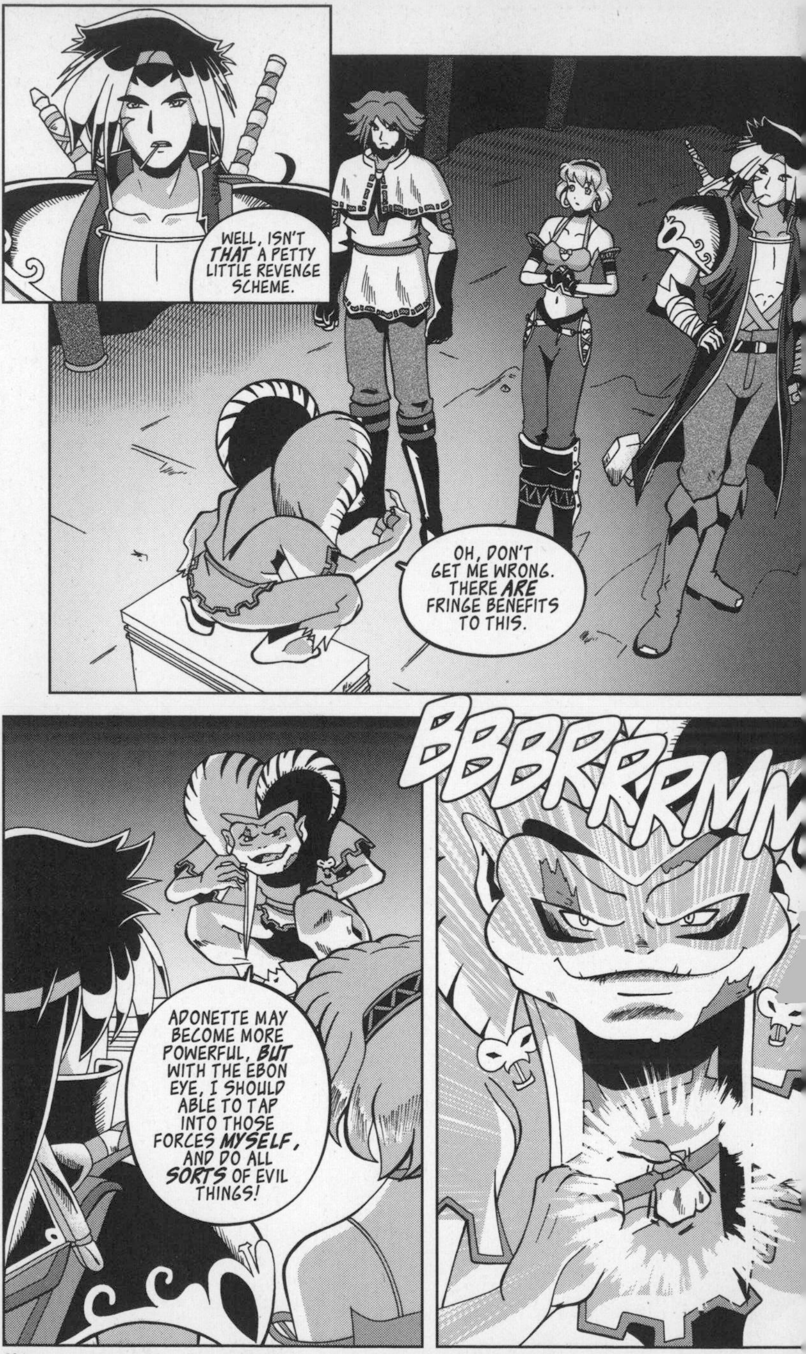
WELL, ISN'T THAT A PETTY LITTLE REVENGE SCHEME.
OH, DON'T GET ME WRONG. THERE ARE FRINGE BENEFITS TO THIS.
ADONETTE MAY BECOME MORE POWERFUL, BUT WITH THE EBON EYE, I SHOULD ABLE TO TAP INTO THOSE FORCES MYSELF, AND DO ALL SORTS OF EVIL THINGS!
BBBRRRRMN

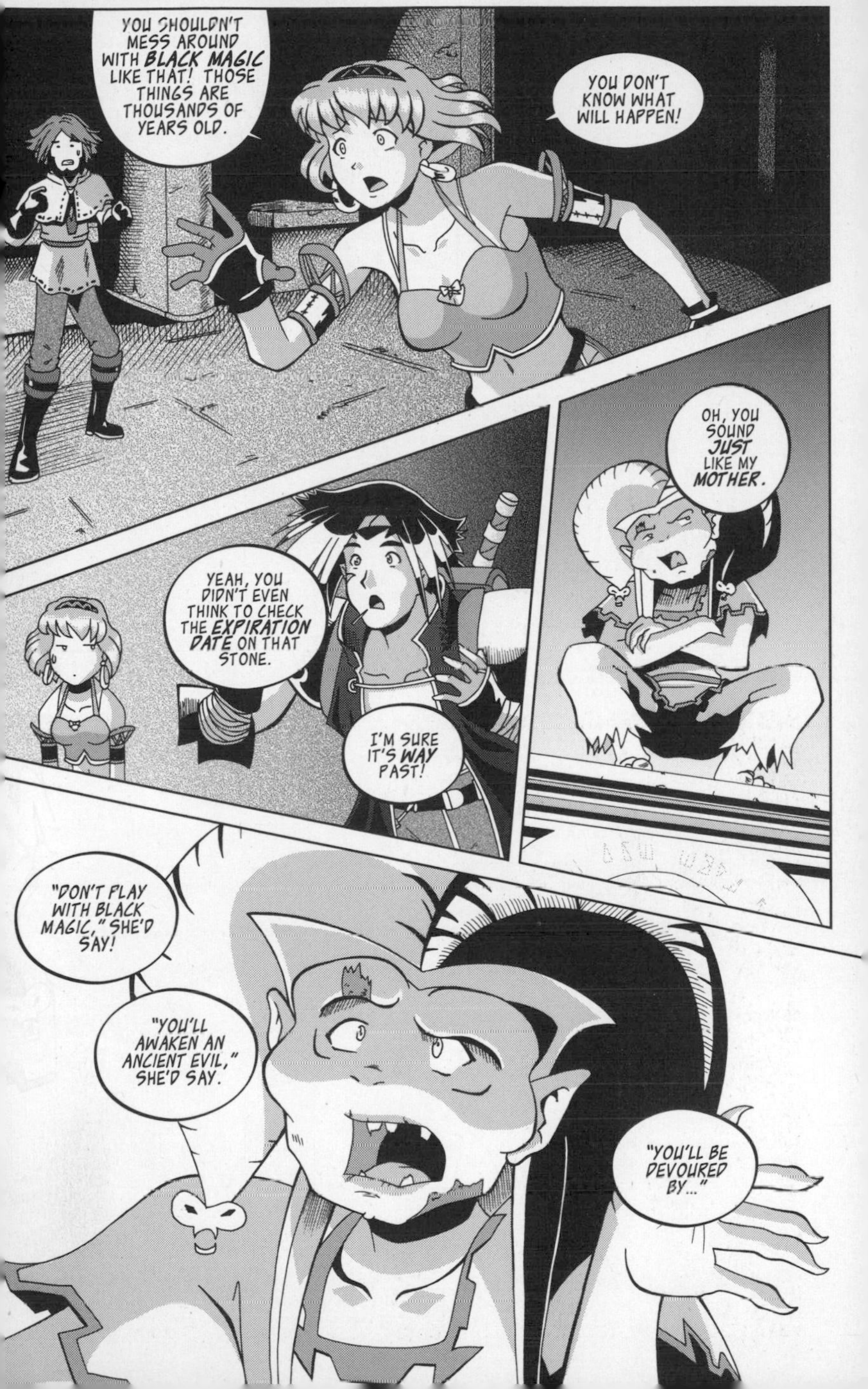
YOU SHOULDN'T MESS AROUND WITH BLACK MAGIC LIKE THAT! THOSE THINGS ARE THOUSANDS OF YEARS OLD.
YOU DON'T KNOW WHAT WILL HAPPEN!
YEAH, YOU DIDN'T EVEN THINK TO CHECK THE EXPIRATION DATE ON THAT STONE.
I'M SURE IT'S WAY PAST!
OH, YOU SOUND JUST LIKE MY MOTHER.
"DON'T PLAY WITH BLACK MAGIC," SHE'D SAY!
"YOU'LL AWAKEN AN ANCIENT EVIL," SHE'D SAY.
"YOU'LL BE DEVOURED BY..."

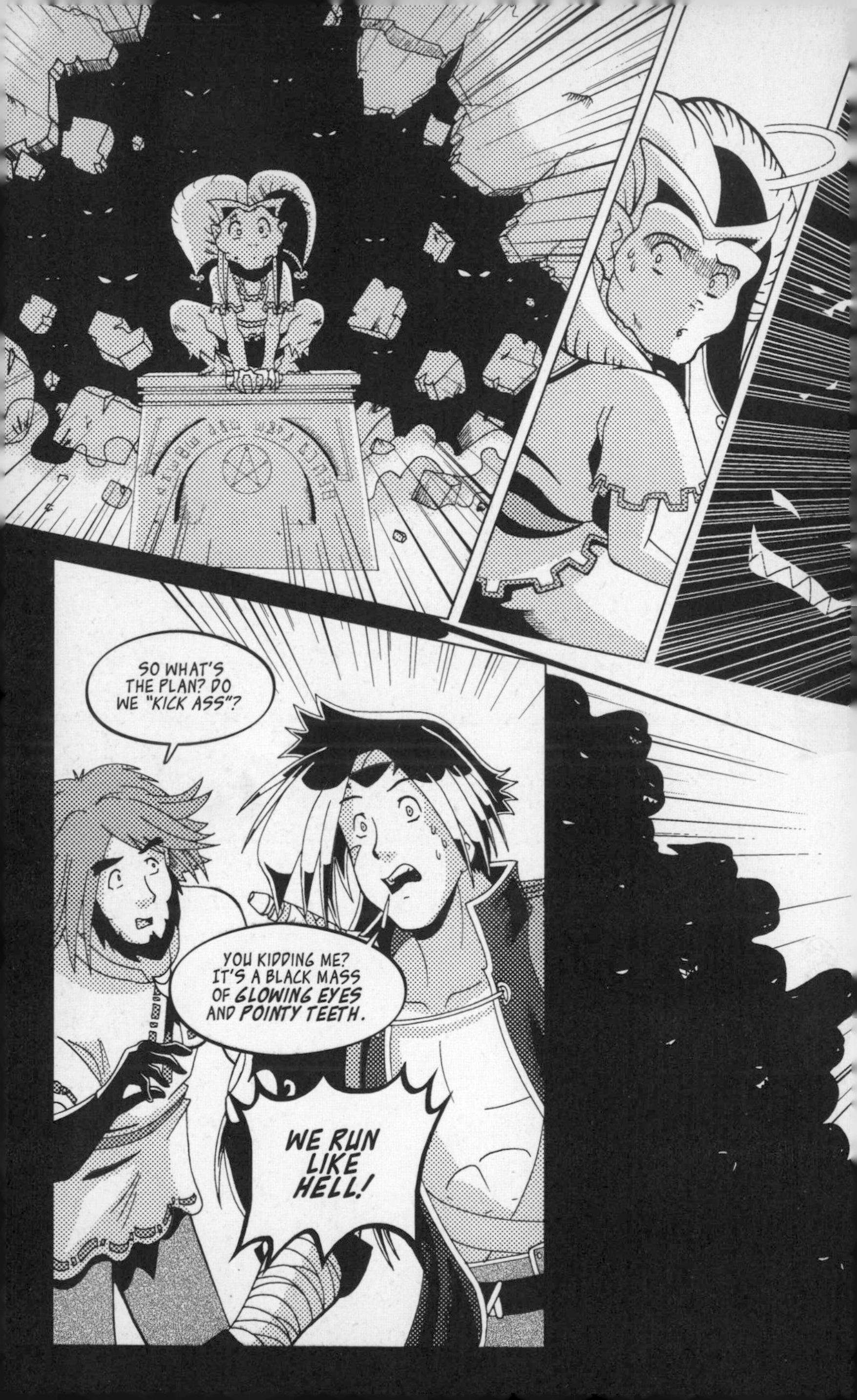

SO WHAT'S THE PLAN? DO WE "KICK ASS"?
YOU KIDDING ME? IT'S A BLACK MASS OF GLOWING EYES AND POINTY TEETH.
WE RUN LIKE HELL!

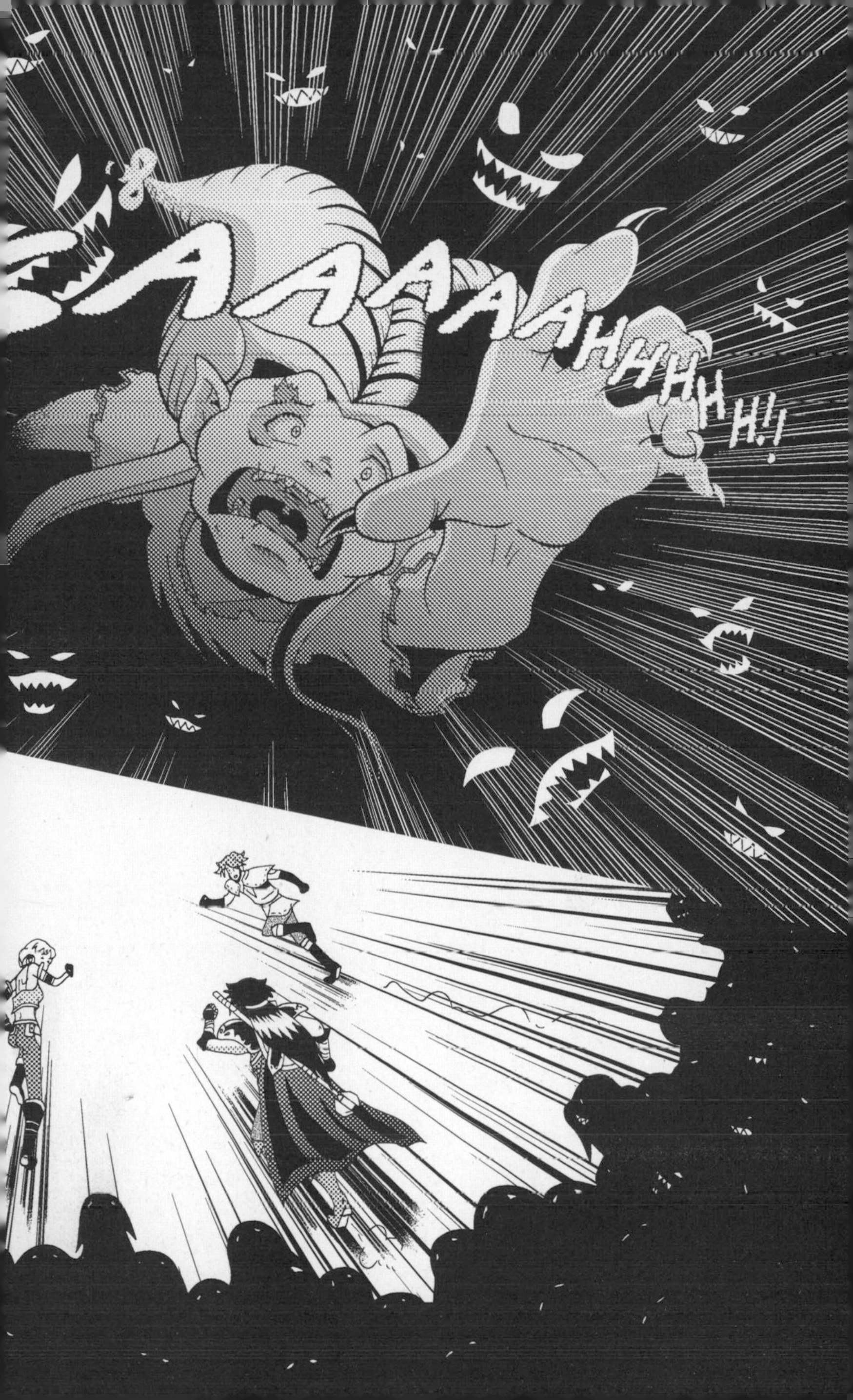
AAAAAAHHHHH!!

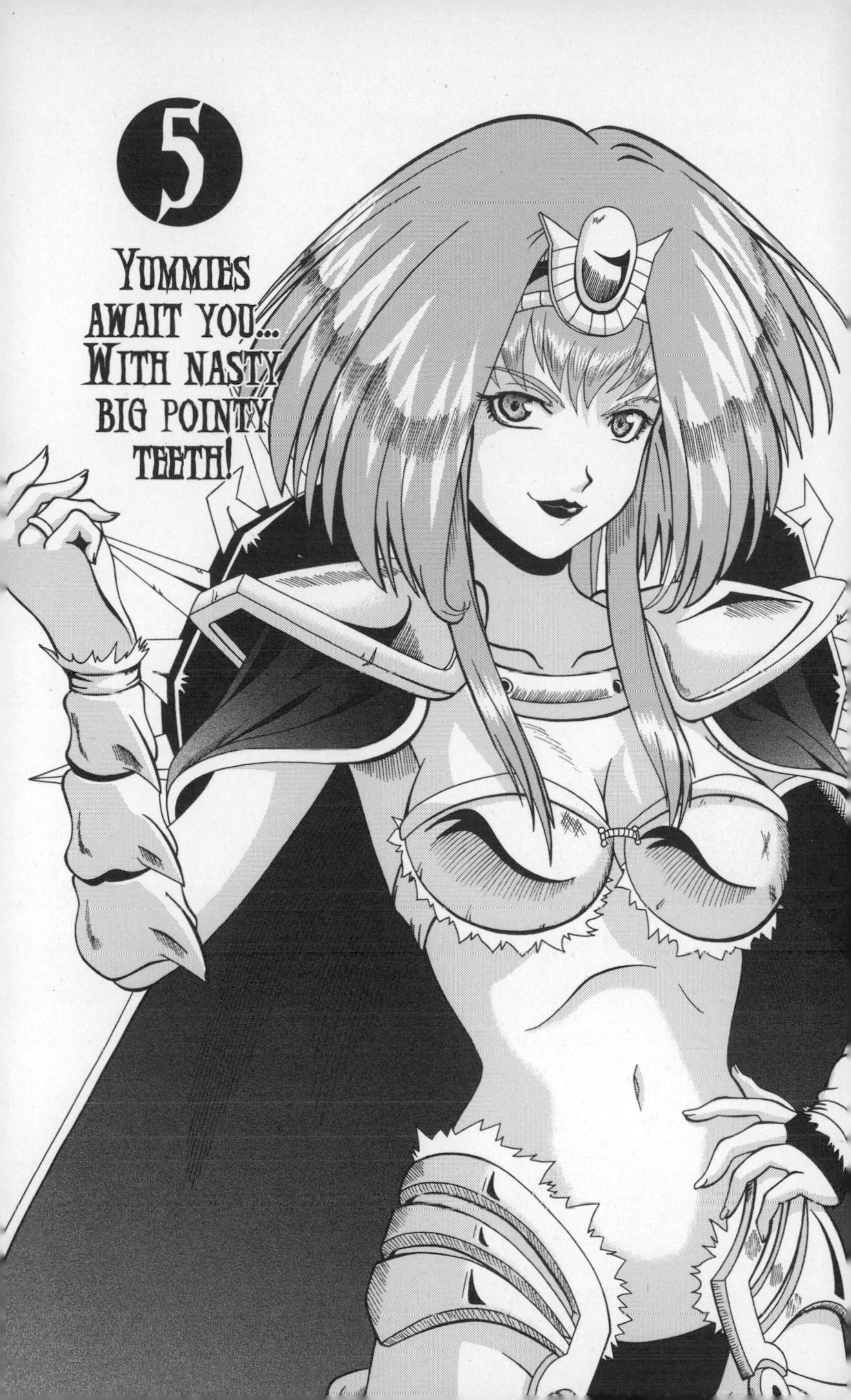
5
YUMMIES AWAIT YOU... WITH NASTY BIG POINTY TEETH!

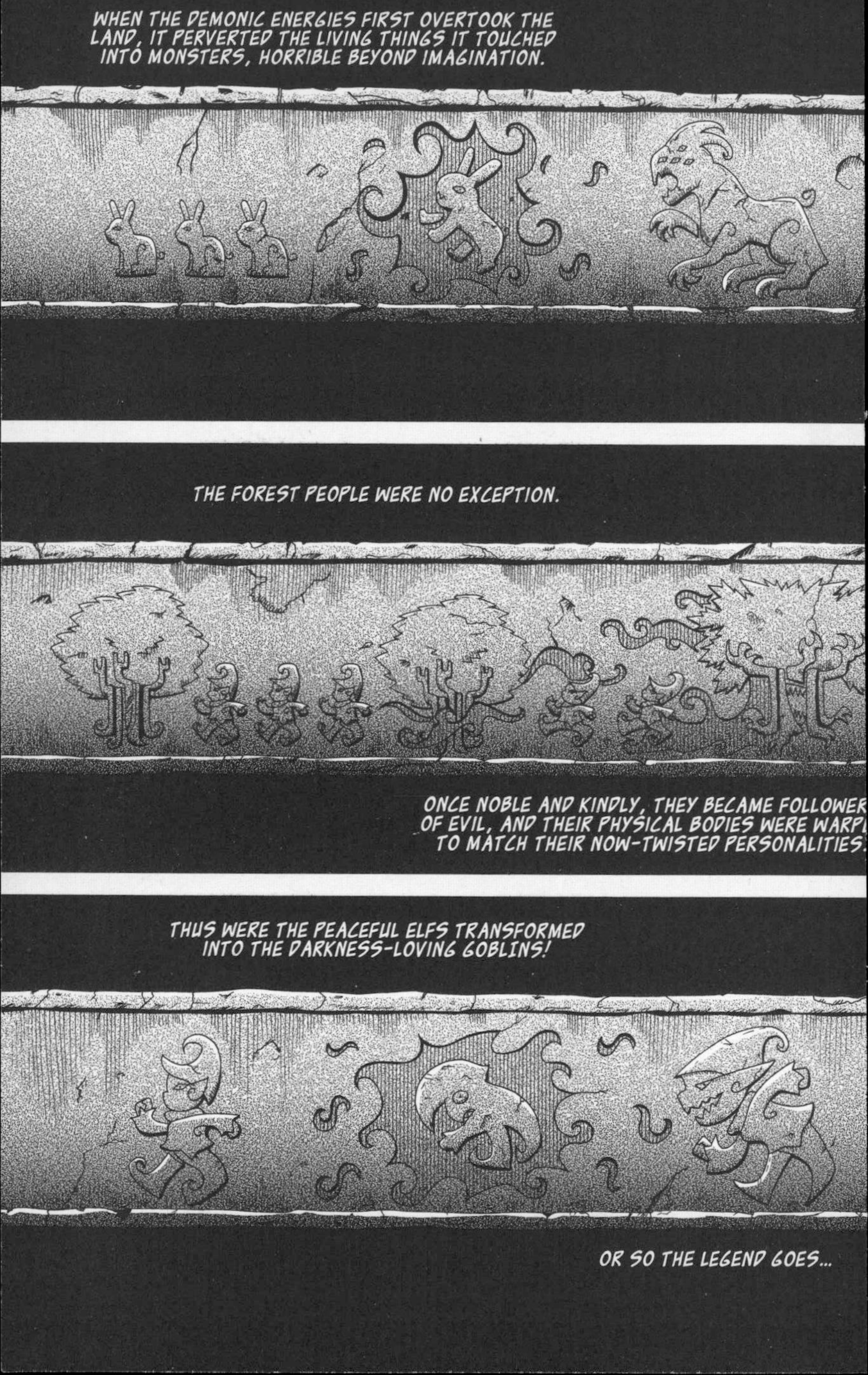
WHEN THE DEMONIC ENERGIES FIRST OVERTOOK THE LAND, IT PERVERTED THE LIVING THINGS IT TOUCHED INTO MONSTERS, HORRIBLE BEYOND IMAGINATION.
THE FOREST PEOPLE WERE NO EXCEPTION.
ONCE NOBLE AND KINDLY, THEY BECAME FOLLOWER OF EVIL, AND THEIR PHYSICAL BODIES WERE WARP TO MATCH THEIR NOW-TWISTED PERSONALITIES!
THUS WERE THE PEACEFUL ELFS TRANSFORMED INTO THE DARKNESS-LOVING GOBLINS!
OR SO THE LEGEND GOES...

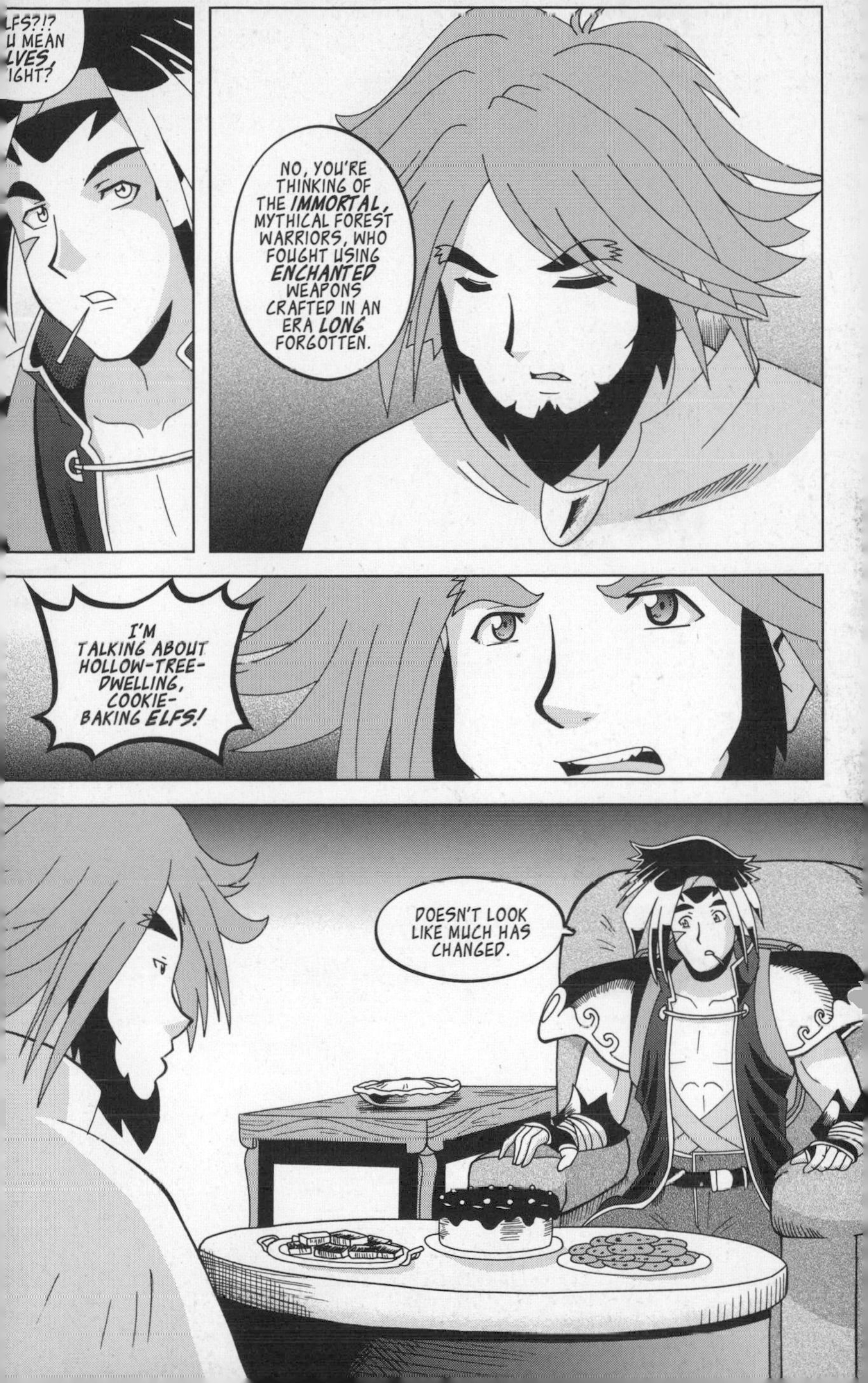

LFS?!? U MEAN LVES, IGHT?
NO, YOU'RE THINKING OF THE IMMORTAL, MYTHICAL FOREST WARRIORS, WHO FOUGHT USING ENCHANTED WEAPONS CRAFTED IN AN ERA LONG FORGOTTEN.
I'M TALKING ABOUT HOLLOW-TREE-DWELLING, COOKIE-BAKING ELFS!
DOESN'T LOOK LIKE MUCH HAS CHANGED.

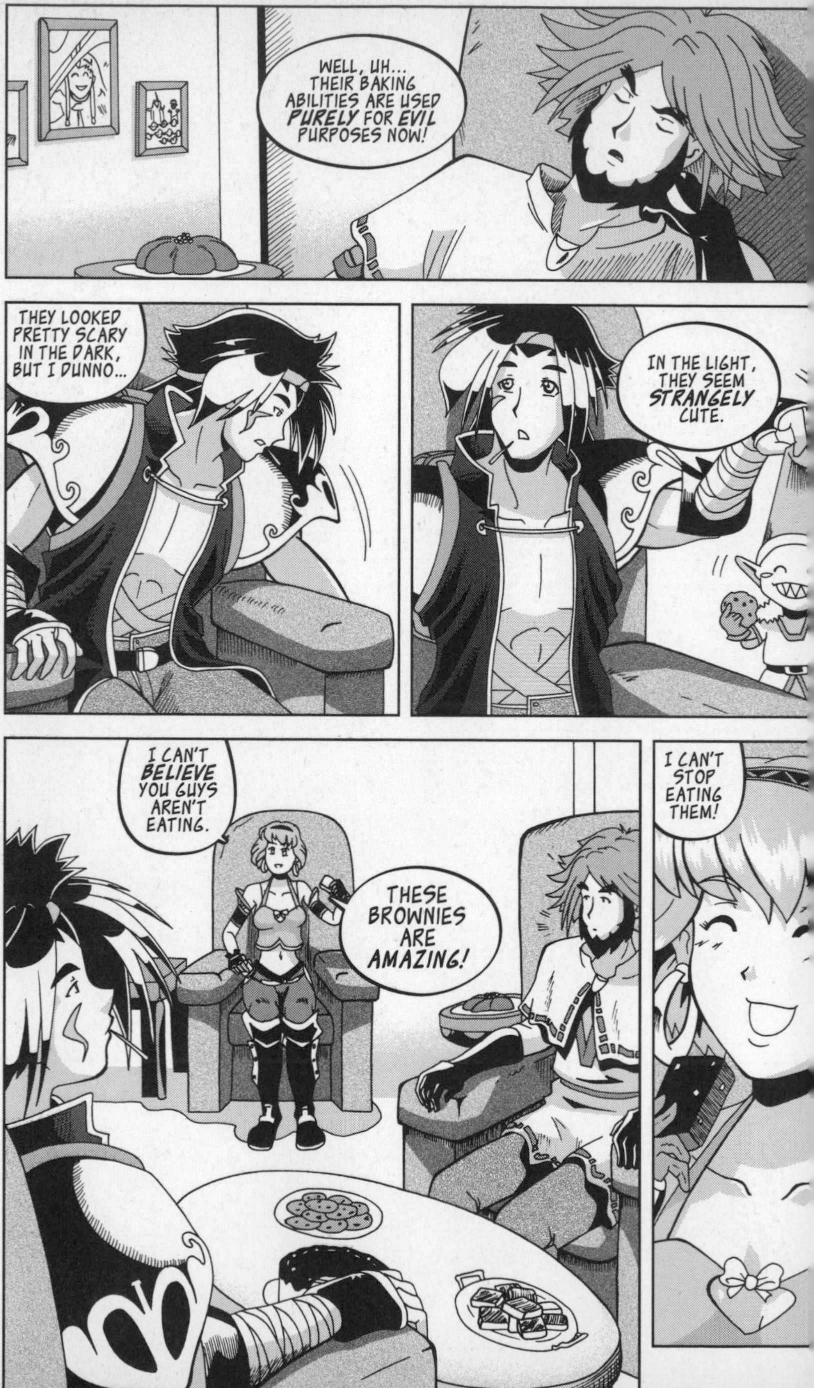
WELL, UH... THEIR BAKING ABILITIES ARE USED PURELY FOR EVIL PURPOSES NOW!
THEY LOOKED PRETTY SCARY IN THE DARK, BUT I DUNNO...
IN THE LIGHT, THEY SEEM STRANGELY CUTE.
I CAN'T BELIEVE YOU GUYS AREN'T EATING.
THESE BROWNIES ARE AMAZING!
I CAN'T STOP EATING THEM!

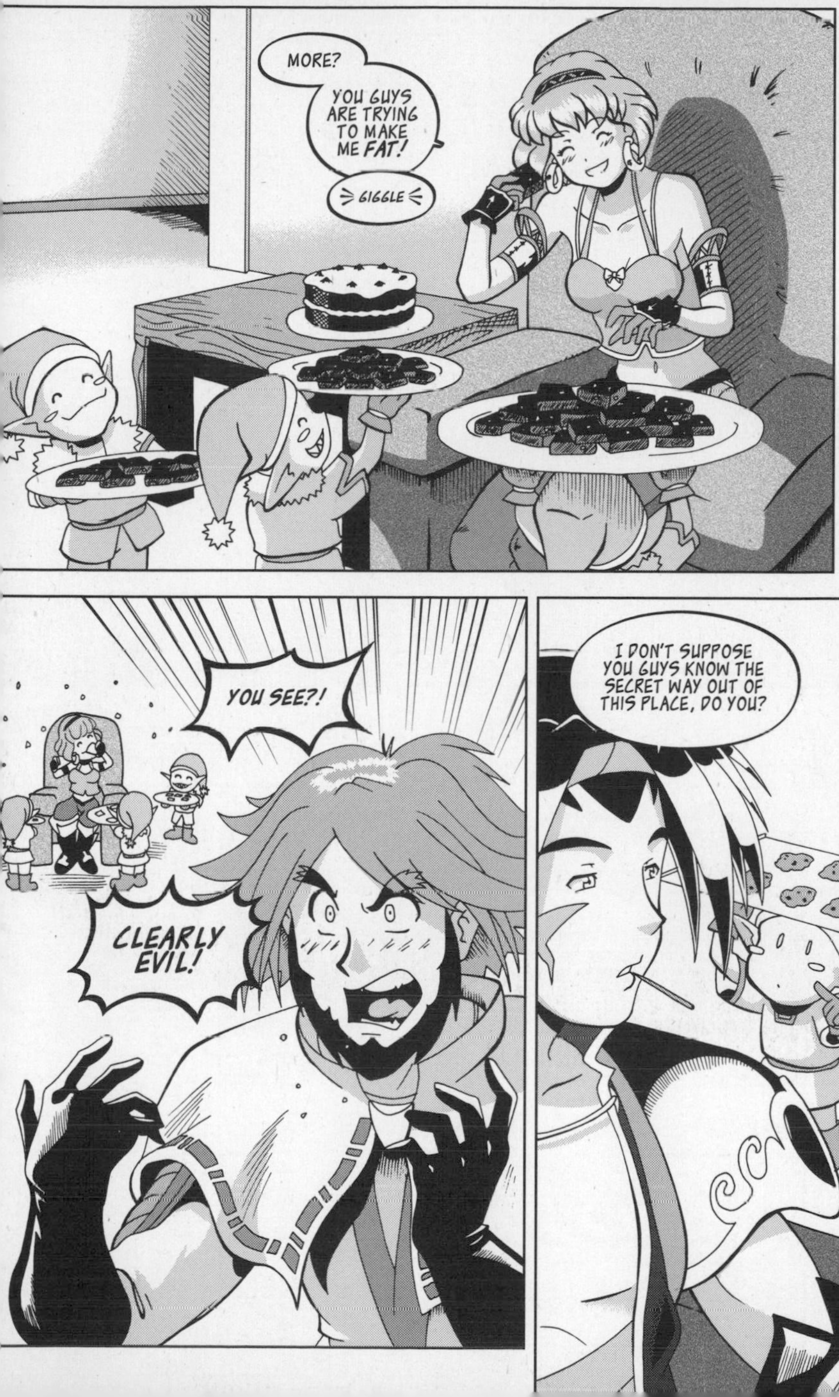
MORE?
YOU GUYS ARE TRYING TO MAKE ME FAT!
GIGGLE
YOU SEE?!
CLEARLY EVIL!
I DON'T SUPPOSE YOU GUYS KNOW THE SECRET WAY OUT OF THIS PLACE, DO YOU?

Dikay Museum of Natural History
Ancient Catacomb Exhibit
...WHICH BRINGS US TO THE CONCLUSION OF OUR TOUR.
Dikay Museum of Natural History
Ancient Catacomb Exhibit
DIKAY TOURS
I WOULD LIKE TO INVITE YOU ALL TO VISIT OUR GIFT SHOP, AND PICK UP A SOUVENIR TO COMMEMORATE YOUR VISIT.
HAVE A WONDERFUL AFTERNOON, AND I HOPE YOU ALL ENJOY YOUR STAY IN THE "PREVIOUSLY ACCURSED" LAND OF DIKAY!
CLNK
CLNK

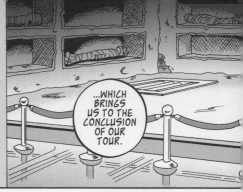

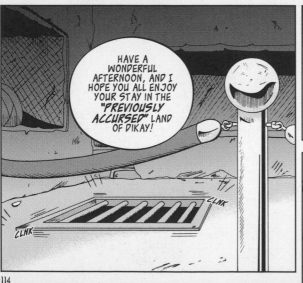

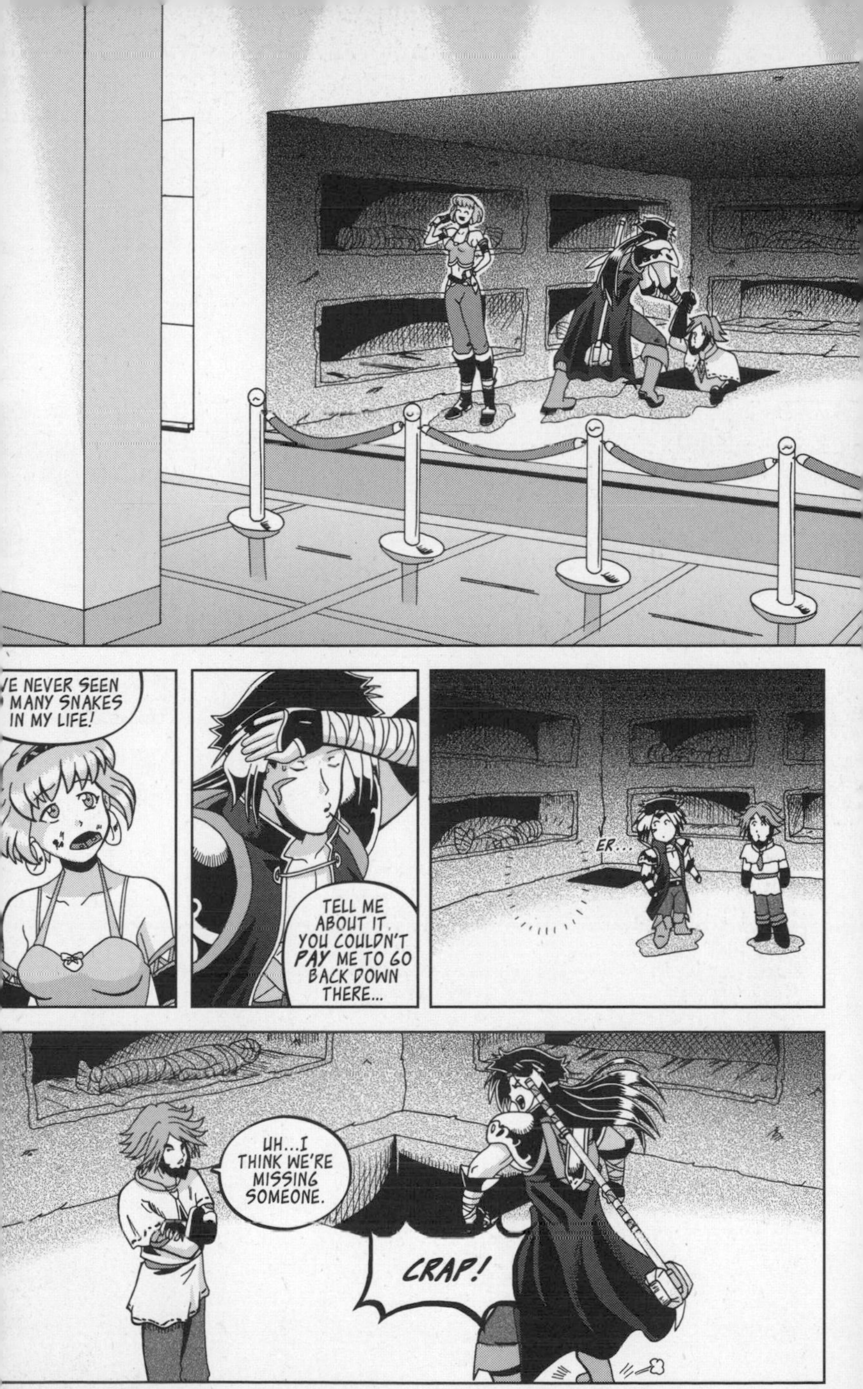
VE NEVER SEEN MANY SNAKES IN MY LIFE!
TELL ME ABOUT IT. YOU COULDN'T PAY ME TO GO BACK DOWN THERE...
ER...
UH...I THINK WE'RE MISSING SOMEONE.
CRAP!

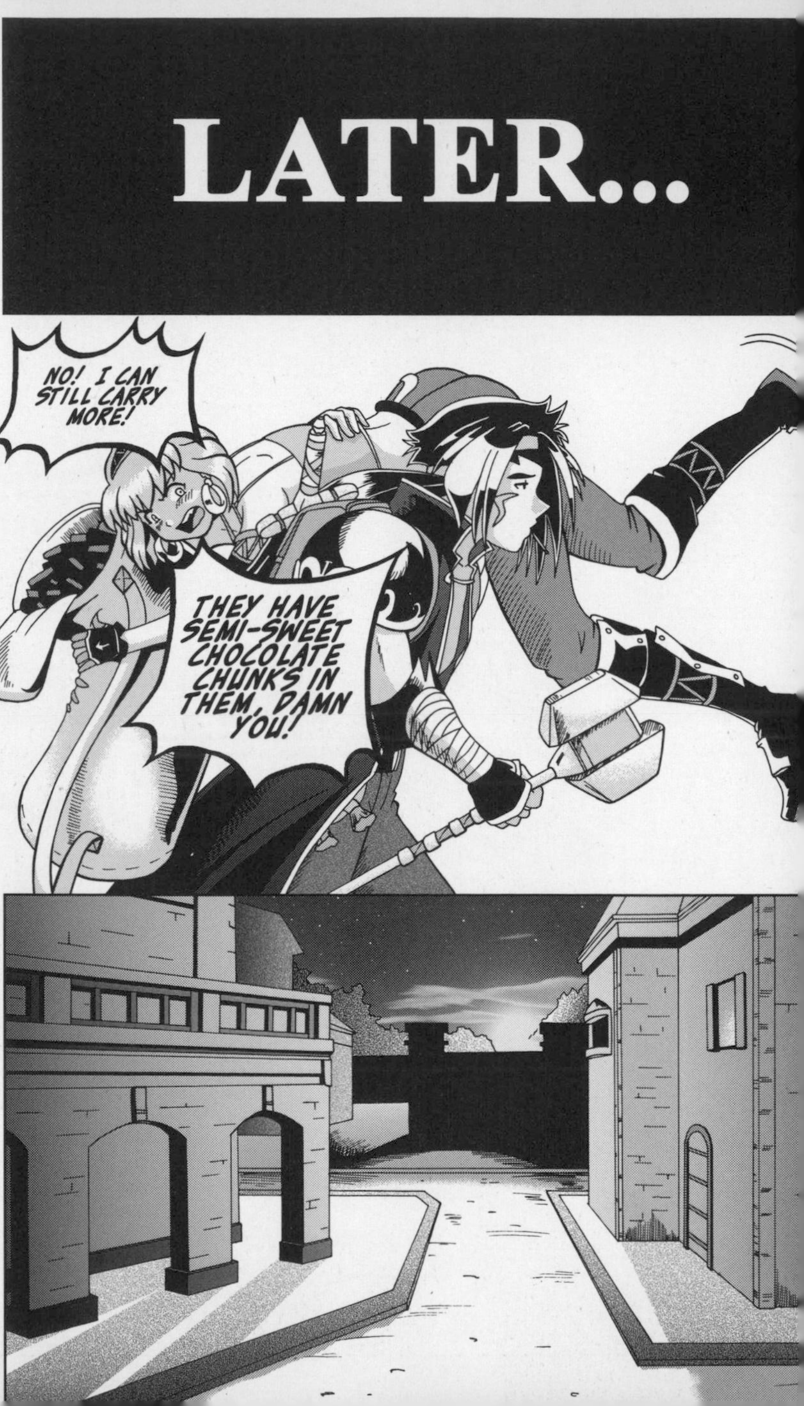
LATER...
NO! I CAN STILL CARRY MORE!
THEY HAVE SEMI-SWEET CHOCOLATE CHUNKS IN THEM, DAMN YOU!

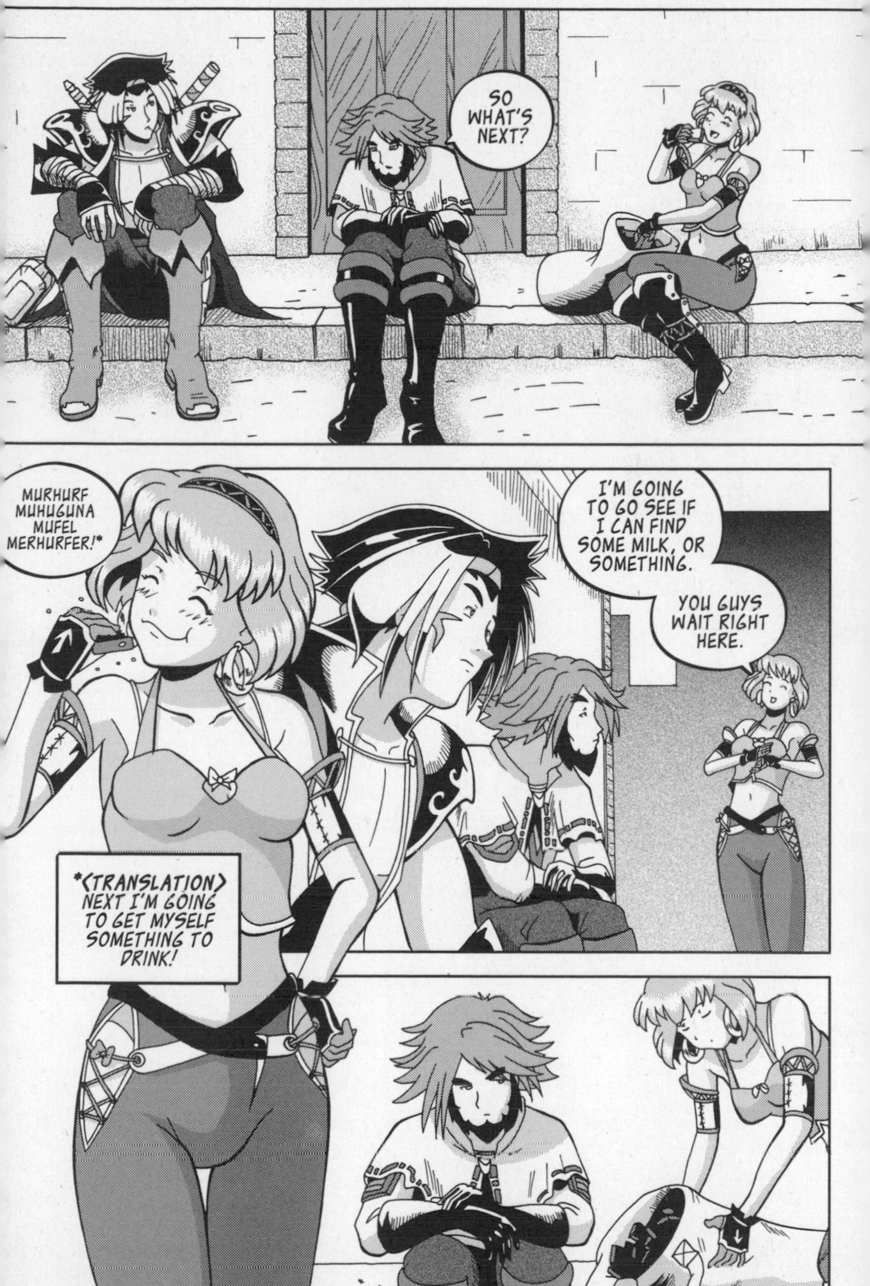
SO WHAT'S NEXT?
MURHURF MUHUGUNA MUFEL MERHURFER!*
I'M GOING TO GO SEE IF I CAN FIND SOME MILK, OR SOMETHING.
YOU GUYS WAIT RIGHT HERE.
*<TRANSLATION> NEXT I'M GOING TO GET MYSELF SOMETHING TO DRINK!

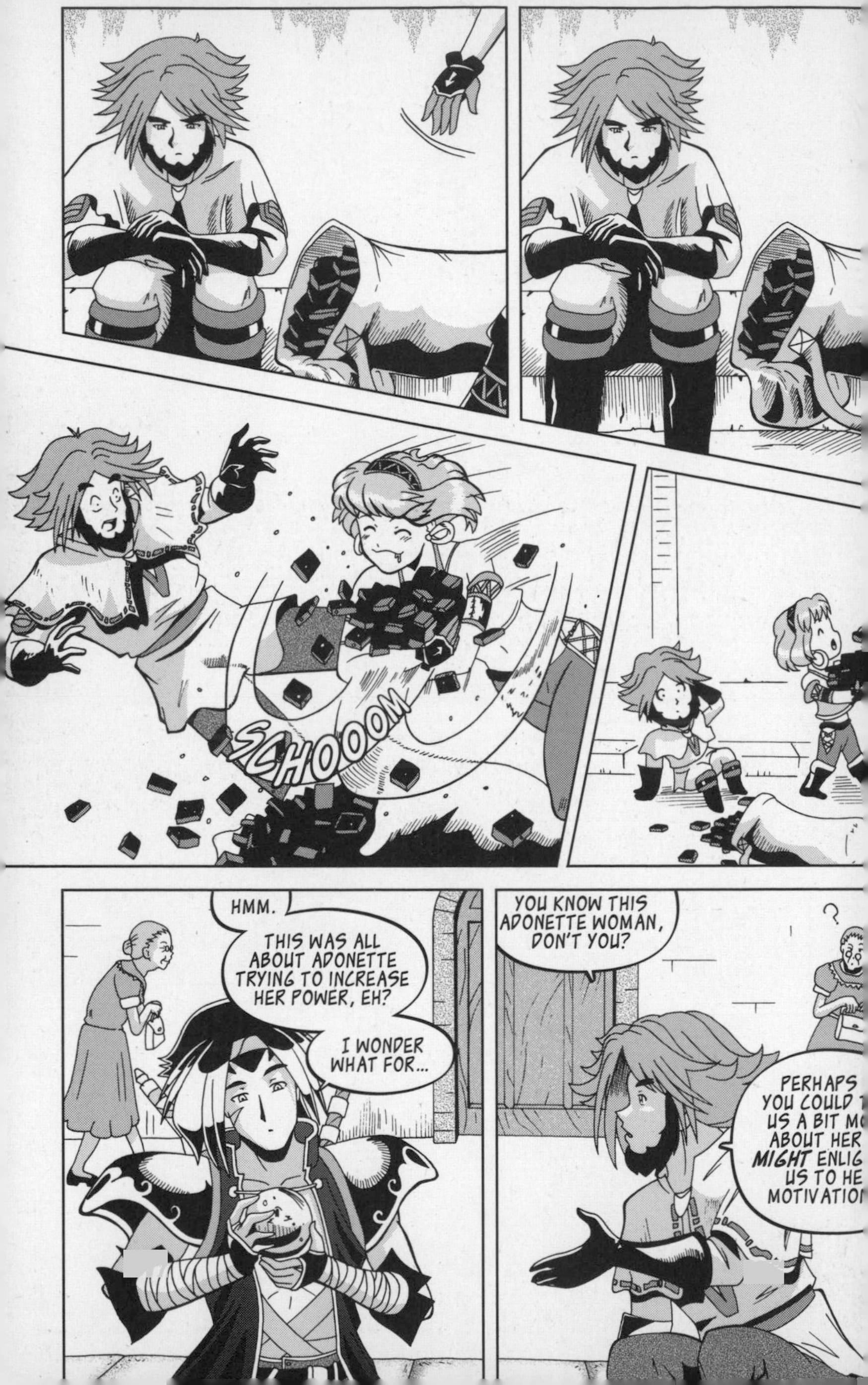
SCHOOOM
HMM.
THIS WAS ALL ABOUT ADONETTE TRYING TO INCREASE HER POWER, EH?
I WONDER WHAT FOR...
YOU KNOW THIS ADONETTE WOMAN, DON'T YOU?
PERHAPS YOU COULD T US A BIT MO ABOUT HER *MIGHT* ENLIG US TO HE MOTIVATION

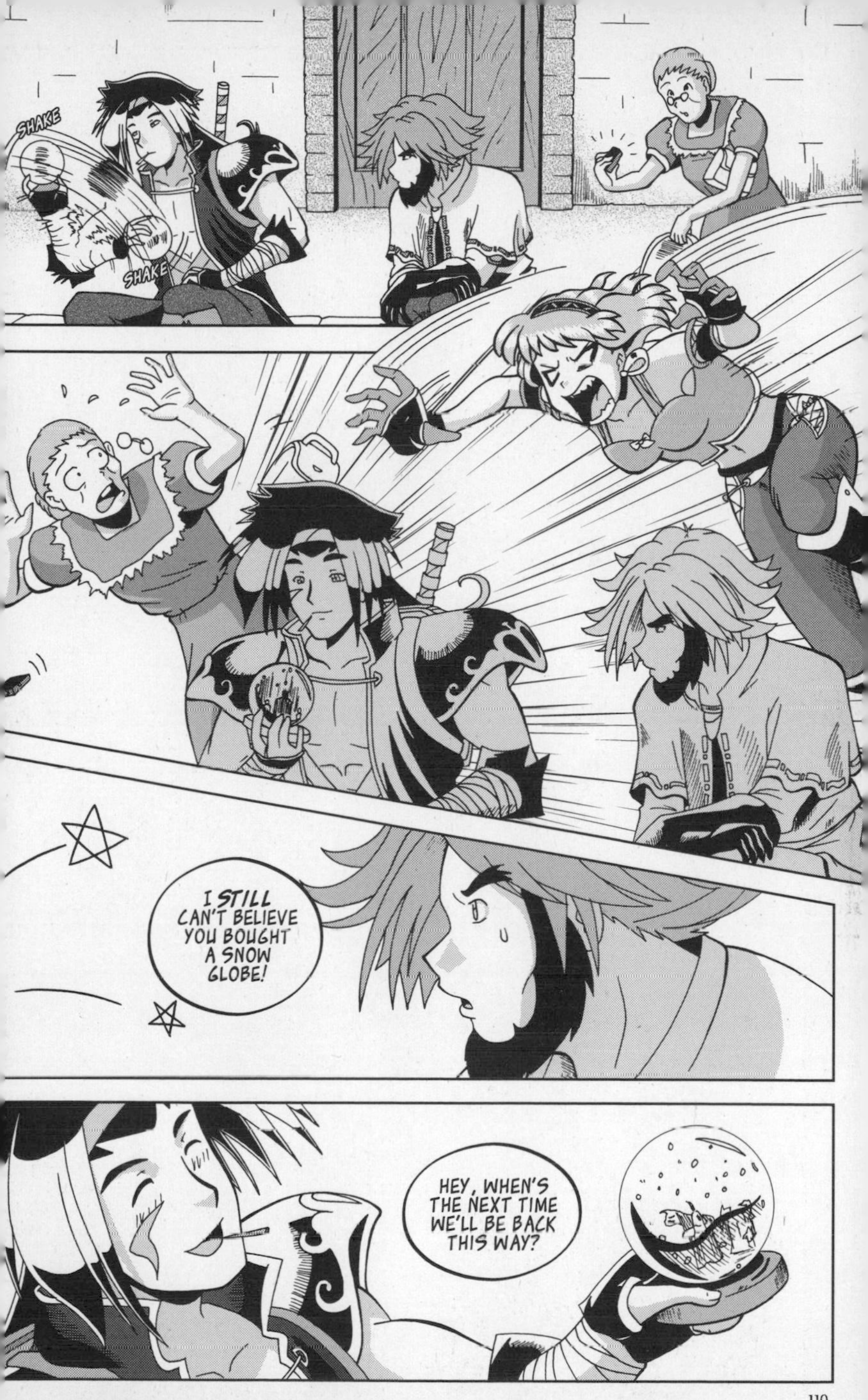
SHAKE
SHAKE
I STILL CAN'T BELIEVE YOU BOUGHT A SNOW GLOBE!
HEY, WHEN'S THE NEXT TIME WE'LL BE BACK THIS WAY?

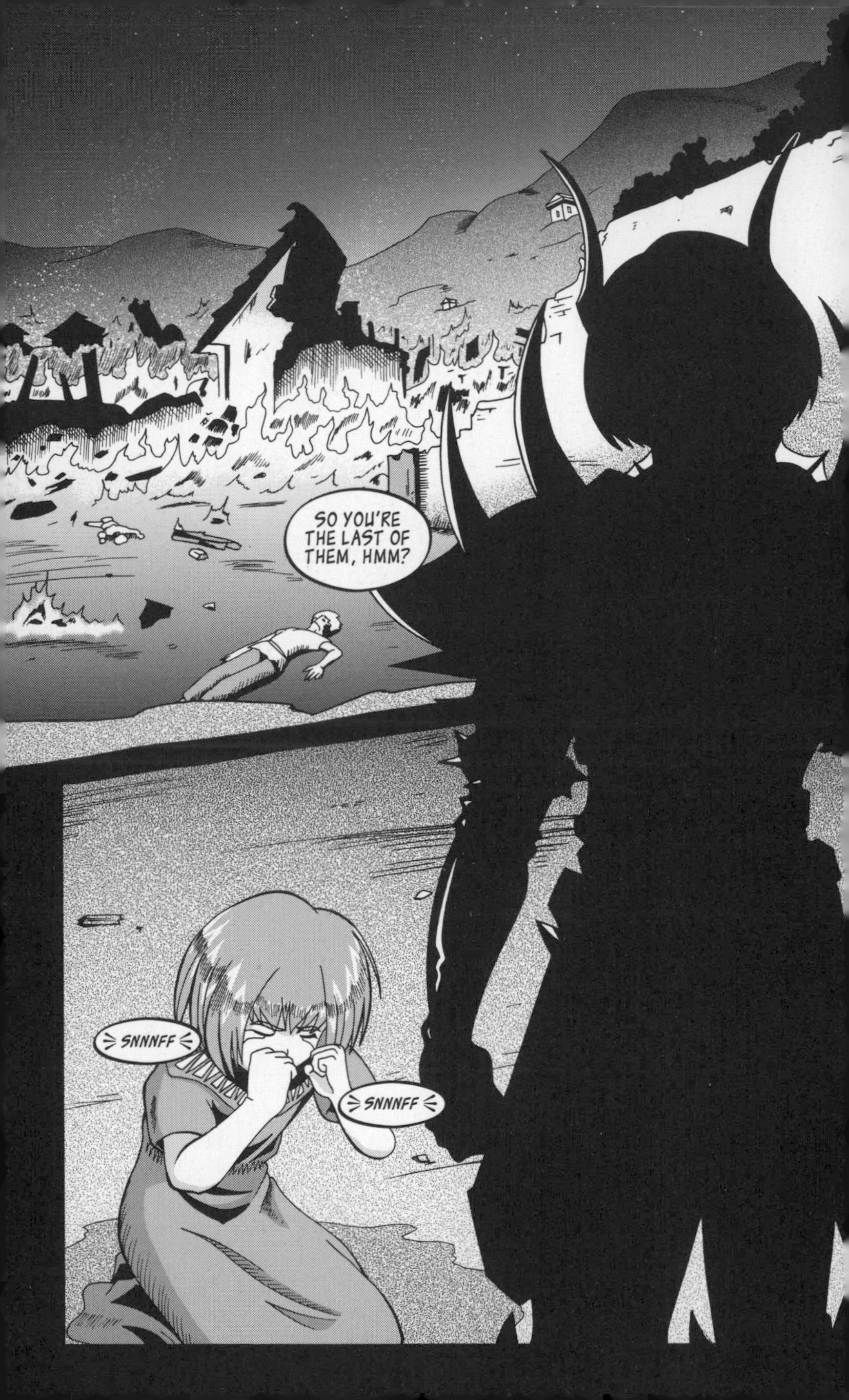
SO YOU'RE THE LAST OF THEM, HMM?
SNNNFF
SNNNFF

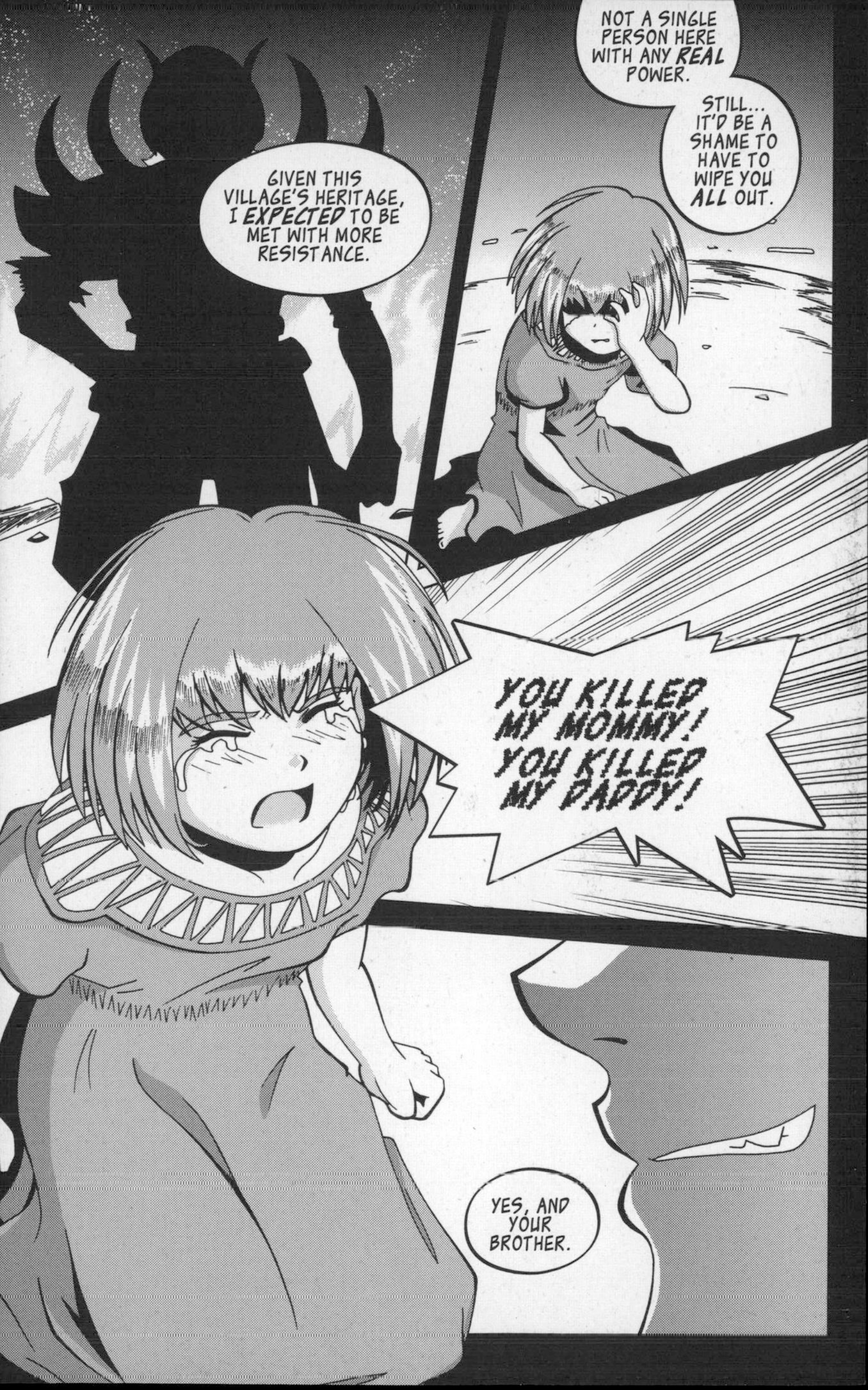
GIVEN THIS VILLAGE'S HERITAGE, I EXPECTED TO BE MET WITH MORE RESISTANCE.
NOT A SINGLE PERSON HERE WITH ANY REAL POWER.
STILL... IT'D BE A SHAME TO HAVE TO WIPE YOU ALL OUT.
YOU KILLED MY MOMMY! YOU KILLED MY DADDY!
YES, AND YOUR BROTHER.

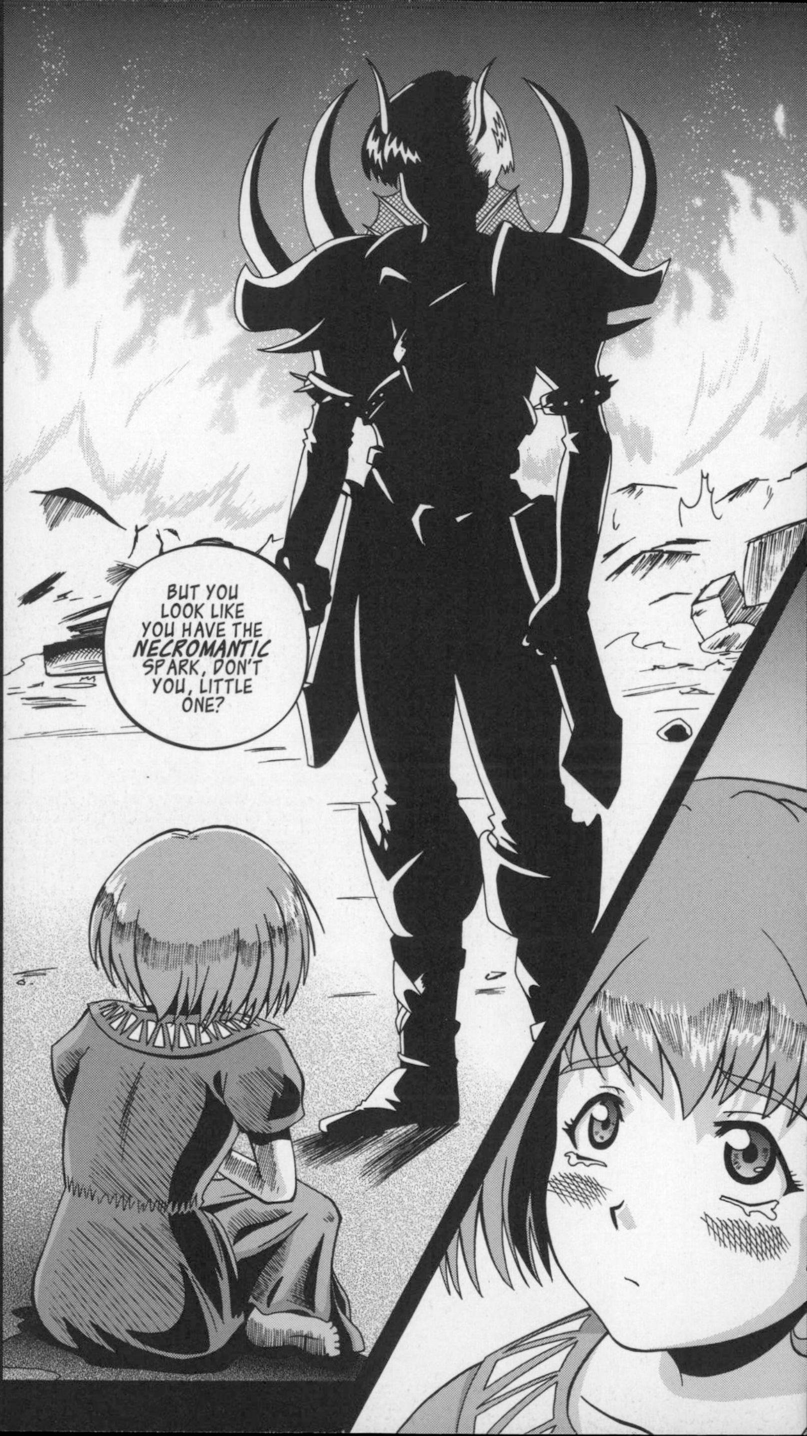
BUT YOU LOOK LIKE YOU HAVE THE NECROMANTIC SPARK, DON'T YOU, LITTLE ONE?

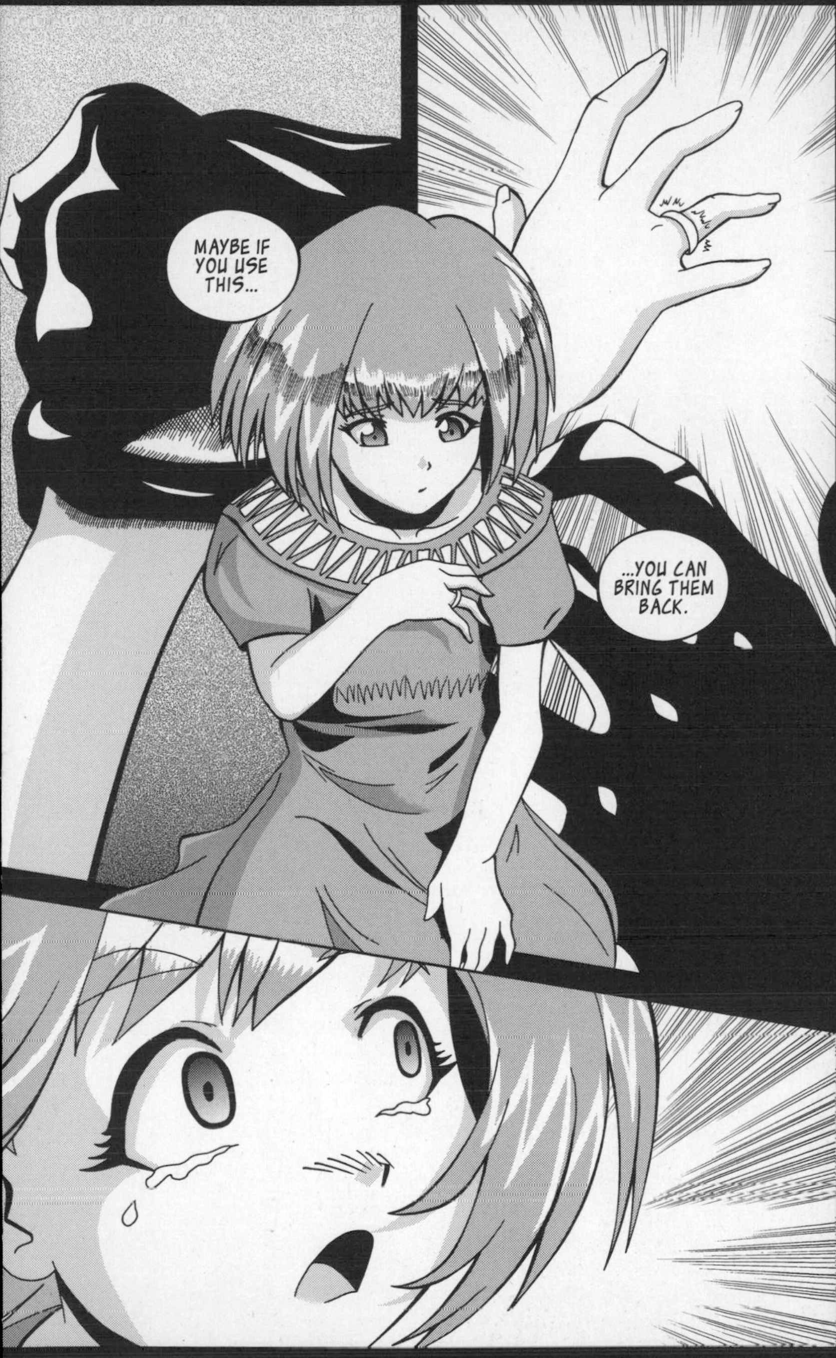
MAYBE IF YOU USE THIS...
...YOU CAN BRING THEM BACK.

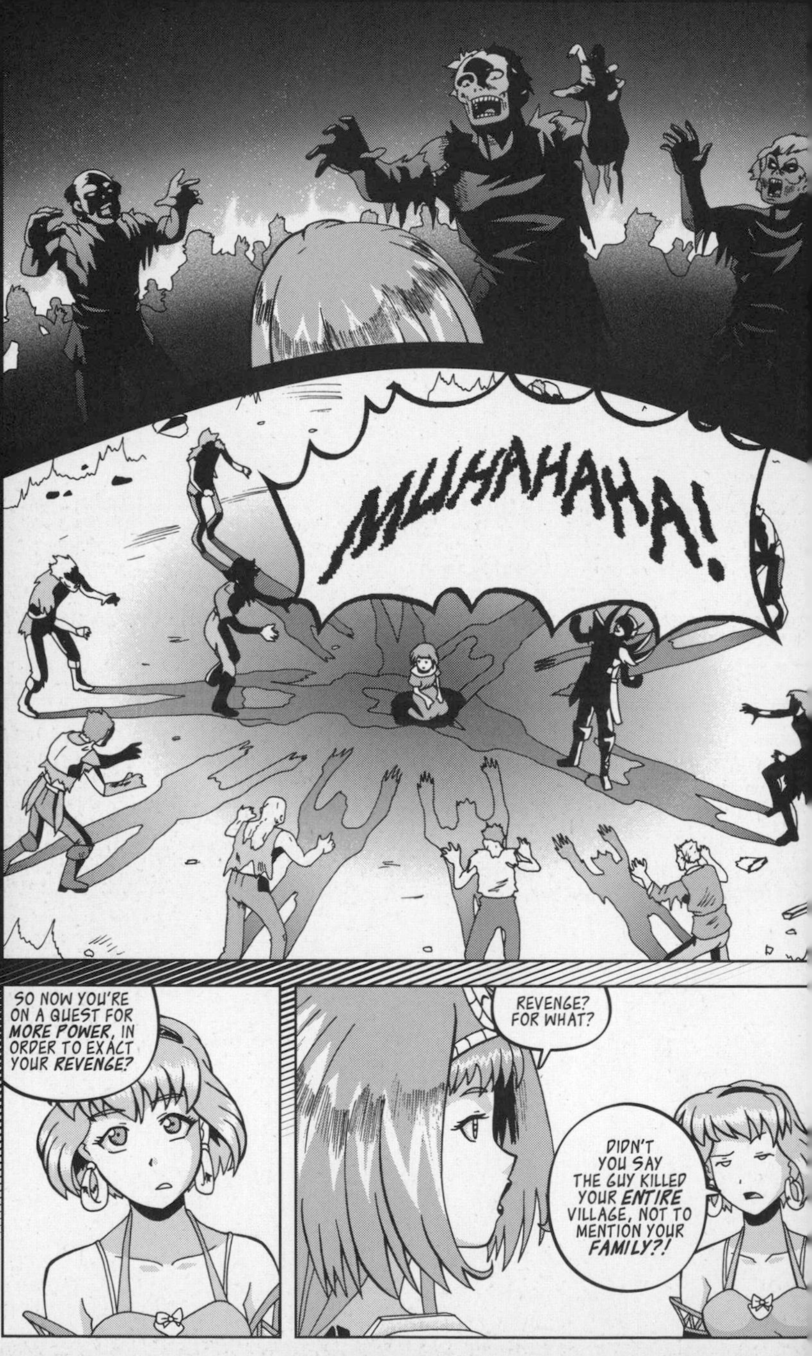
MUHAHAHA!
SO NOW YOU'RE ON A QUEST FOR MORE POWER, IN ORDER TO EXACT YOUR REVENGE?
REVENGE? FOR WHAT?
DIDN'T YOU SAY THE GUY KILLED YOUR ENTIRE VILLAGE, NOT TO MENTION YOUR FAMILY?!

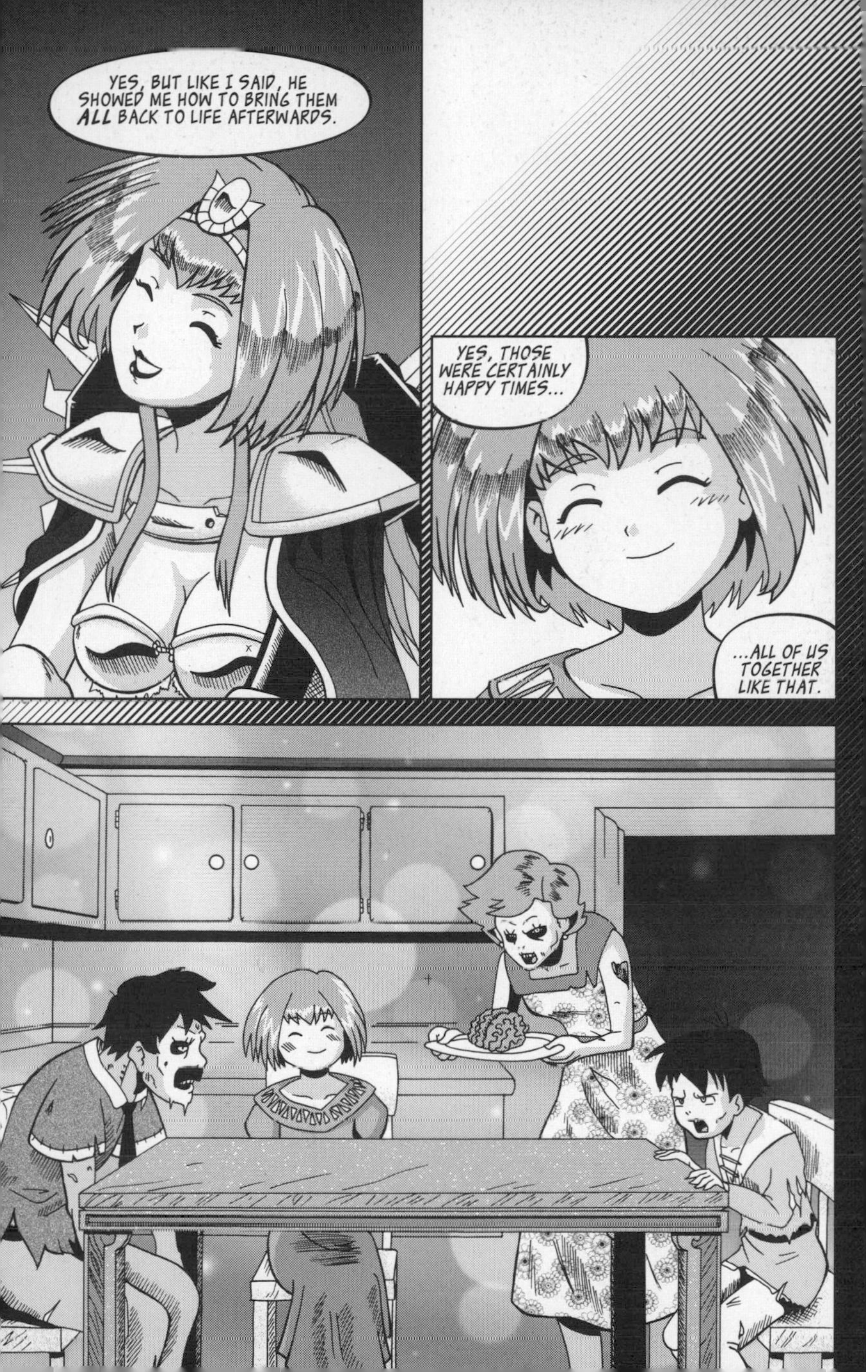
YES, BUT LIKE I SAID, HE SHOWED ME HOW TO BRING THEM ALL BACK TO LIFE AFTERWARDS.
YES, THOSE WERE CERTAINLY HAPPY TIMES...
...ALL OF US TOGETHER LIKE THAT.

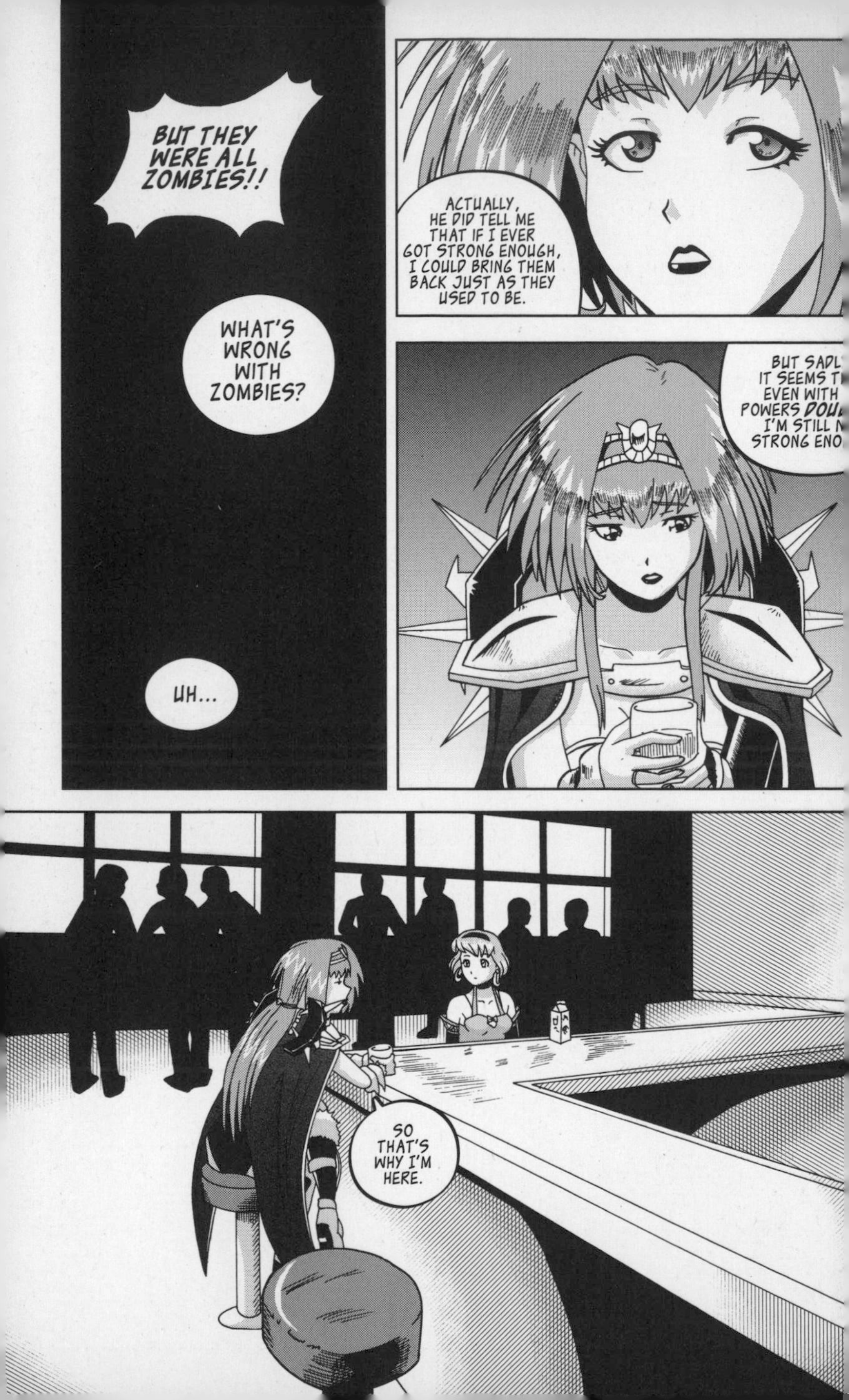
BUT THEY WERE ALL ZOMBIES!!
WHAT'S WRONG WITH ZOMBIES?
UH...
ACTUALLY, HE DID TELL ME THAT IF I EVER GOT STRONG ENOUGH, I COULD BRING THEM BACK JUST AS THEY USED TO BE.
BUT SADL IT SEEMS T EVEN WITH POWERS DOU I'M STILL N STRONG ENO
SO THAT'S WHY I'M HERE.

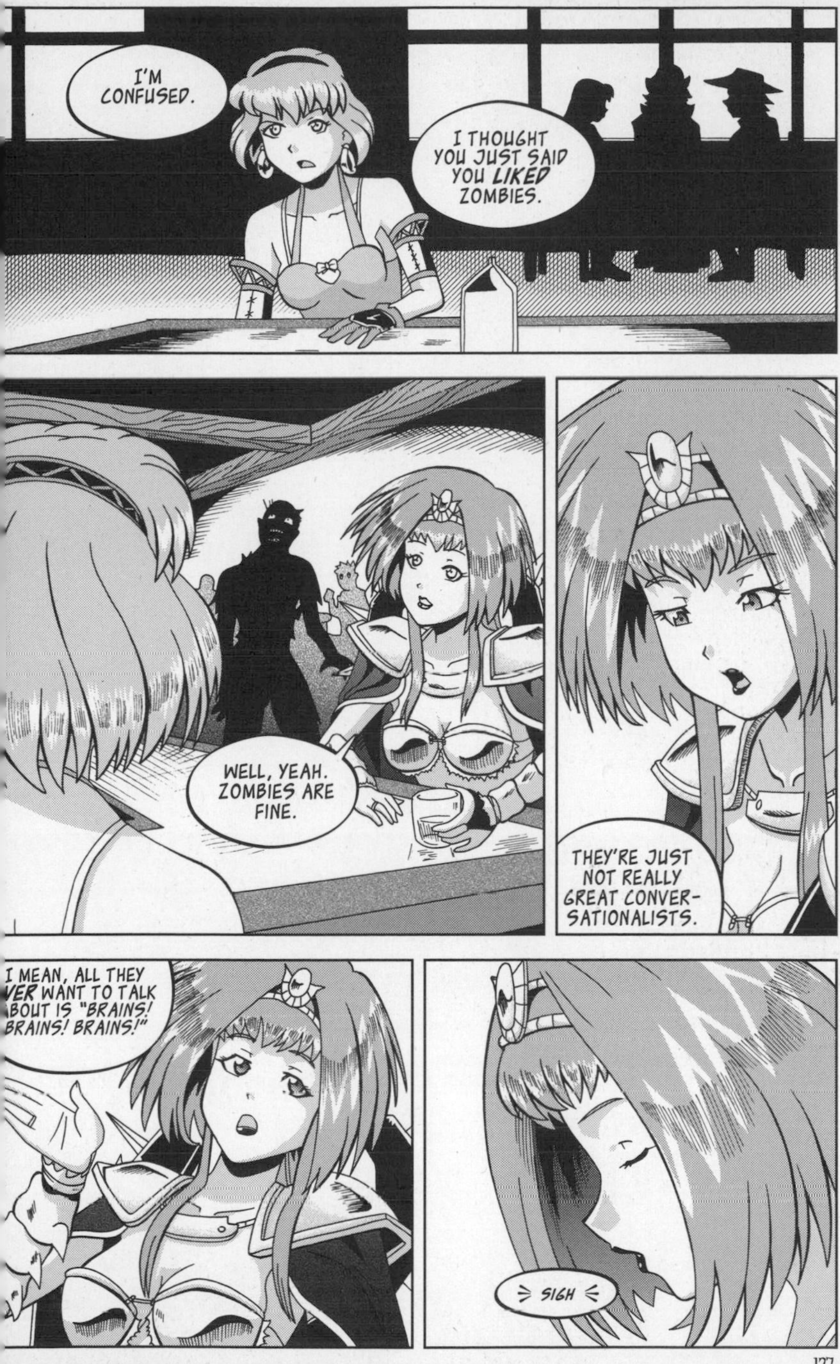
I'M CONFUSED.
I THOUGHT YOU JUST SAID YOU LIKED ZOMBIES.
WELL, YEAH. ZOMBIES ARE FINE.
THEY'RE JUST NOT REALLY GREAT CONVER-SATIONALISTS.
I MEAN, ALL THEY VER WANT TO TALK BOUT IS "BRAINS! BRAINS! BRAINS!"
SIGH

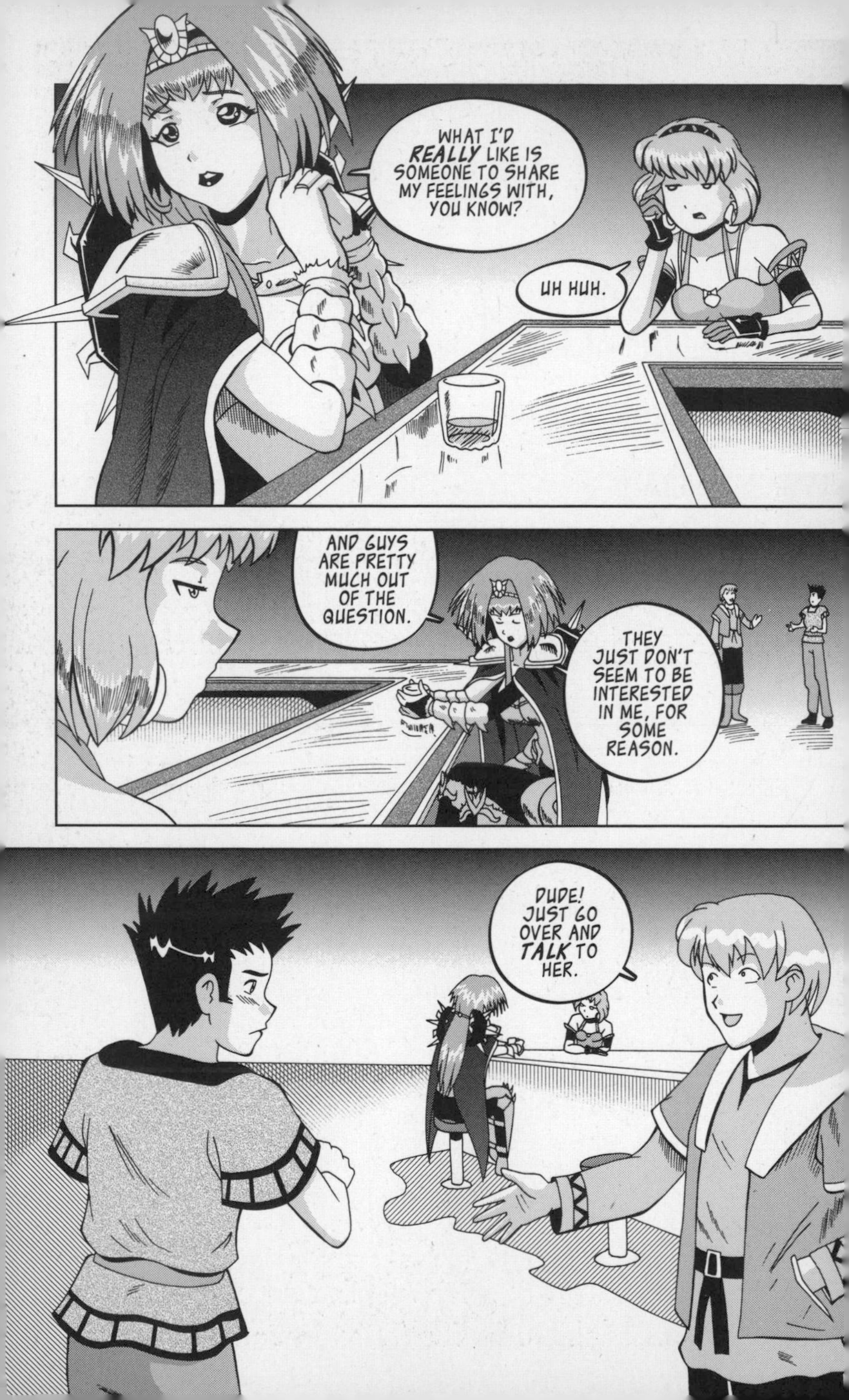
WHAT I'D REALLY LIKE IS SOMEONE TO SHARE MY FEELINGS WITH, YOU KNOW?
UH HUH.
AND GUYS ARE PRETTY MUCH OUT OF THE QUESTION.
THEY JUST DON'T SEEM TO BE INTERESTED IN ME, FOR SOME REASON.
DUDE! JUST GO OVER AND TALK TO HER.

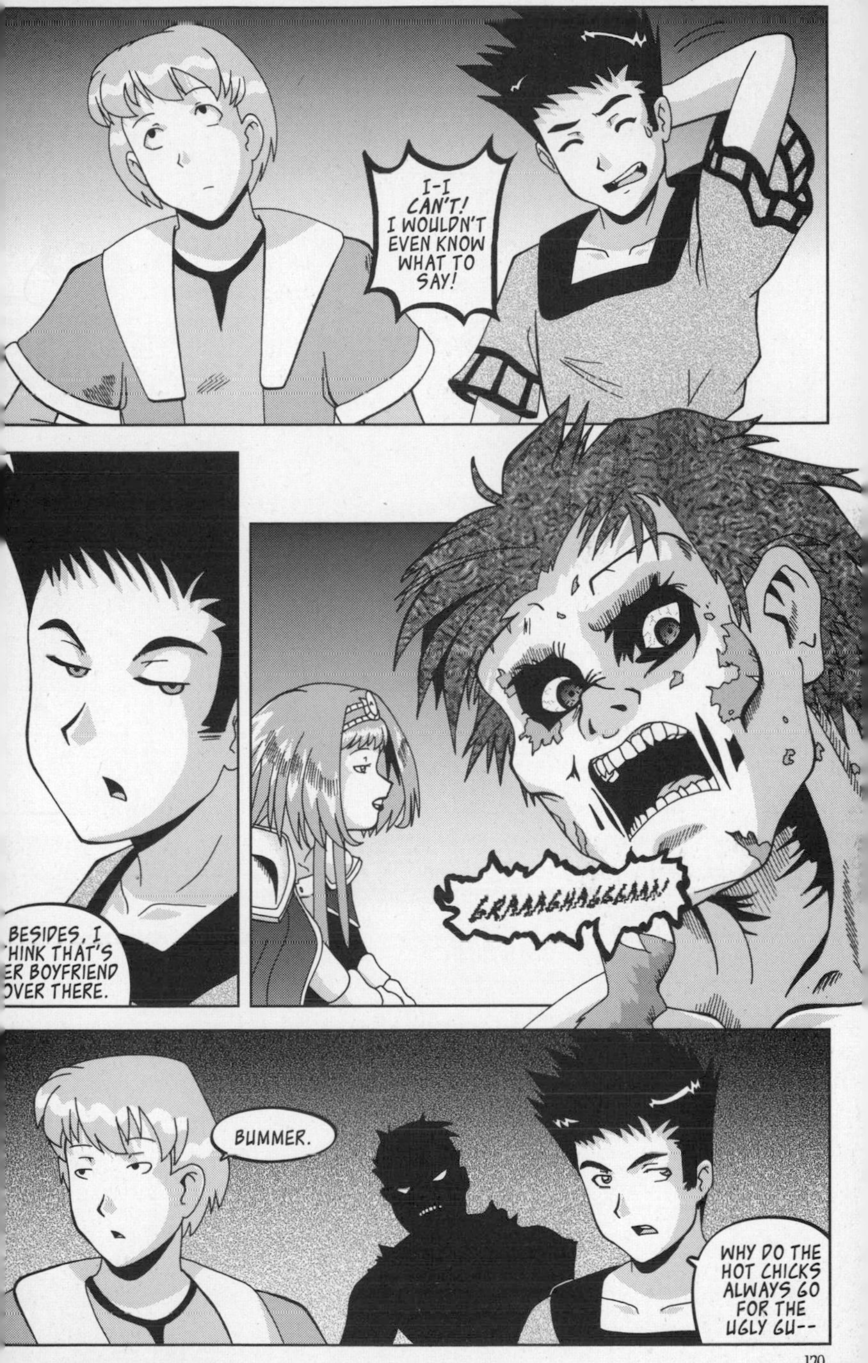
I-I CAN'T! I WOULDN'T EVEN KNOW WHAT TO SAY!
BESIDES, I HINK THAT'S ER BOYFRIEND OVER THERE.
GRAAAGHALGGAAN!
BUMMER.
WHY DO THE HOT CHICKS ALWAYS GO FOR THE UGLY GU--

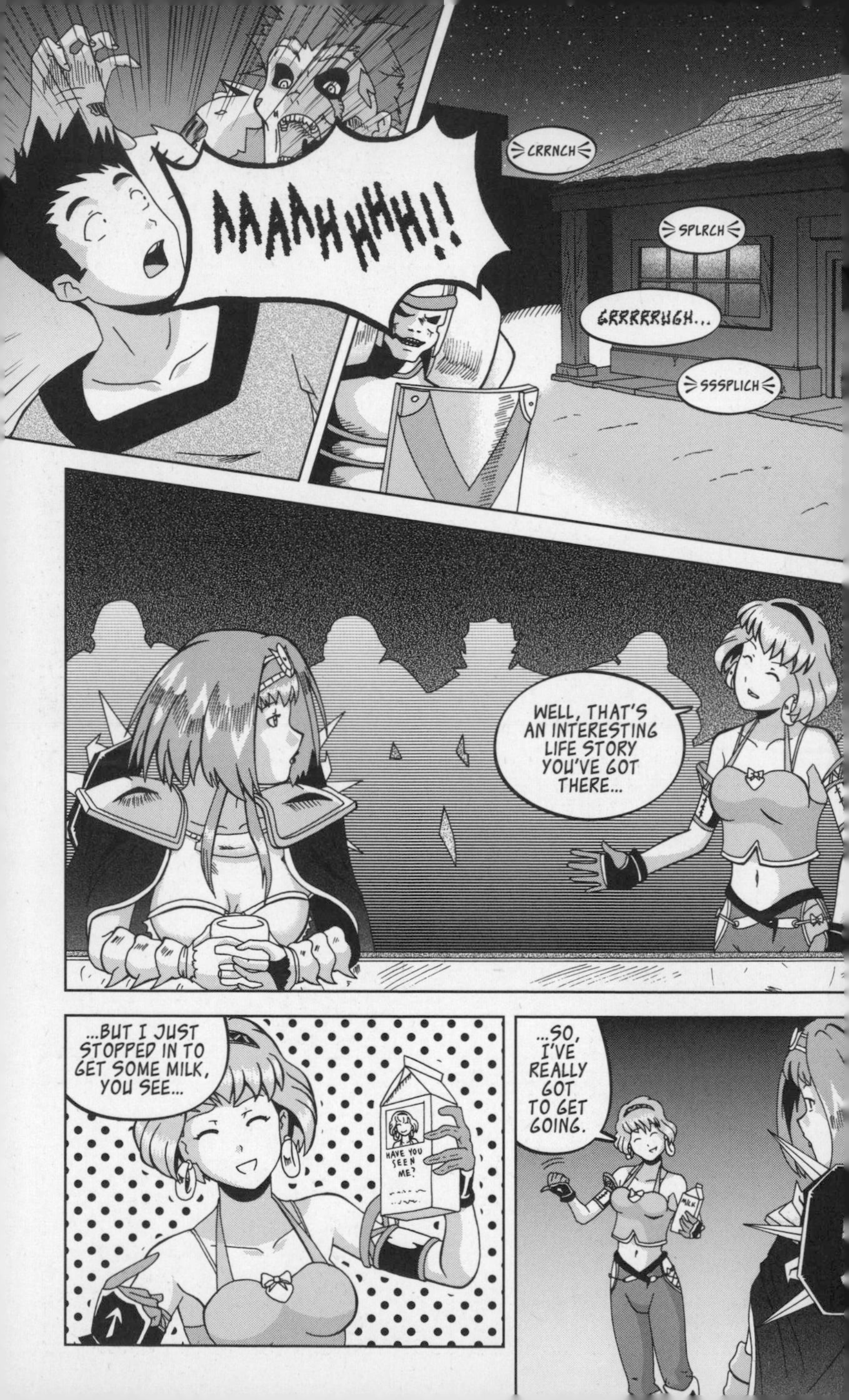
AAAAHHHH!!
CRRNCH
SPLRCH
GRRRRRUGH...
SSSPLICH
WELL, THAT'S AN INTERESTING LIFE STORY YOU'VE GOT THERE...
...BUT I JUST STOPPED IN TO GET SOME MILK, YOU SEE...
HAVE YOU SEEN ME?
...SO, I'VE REALLY GOT TO GET GOING.
MILK

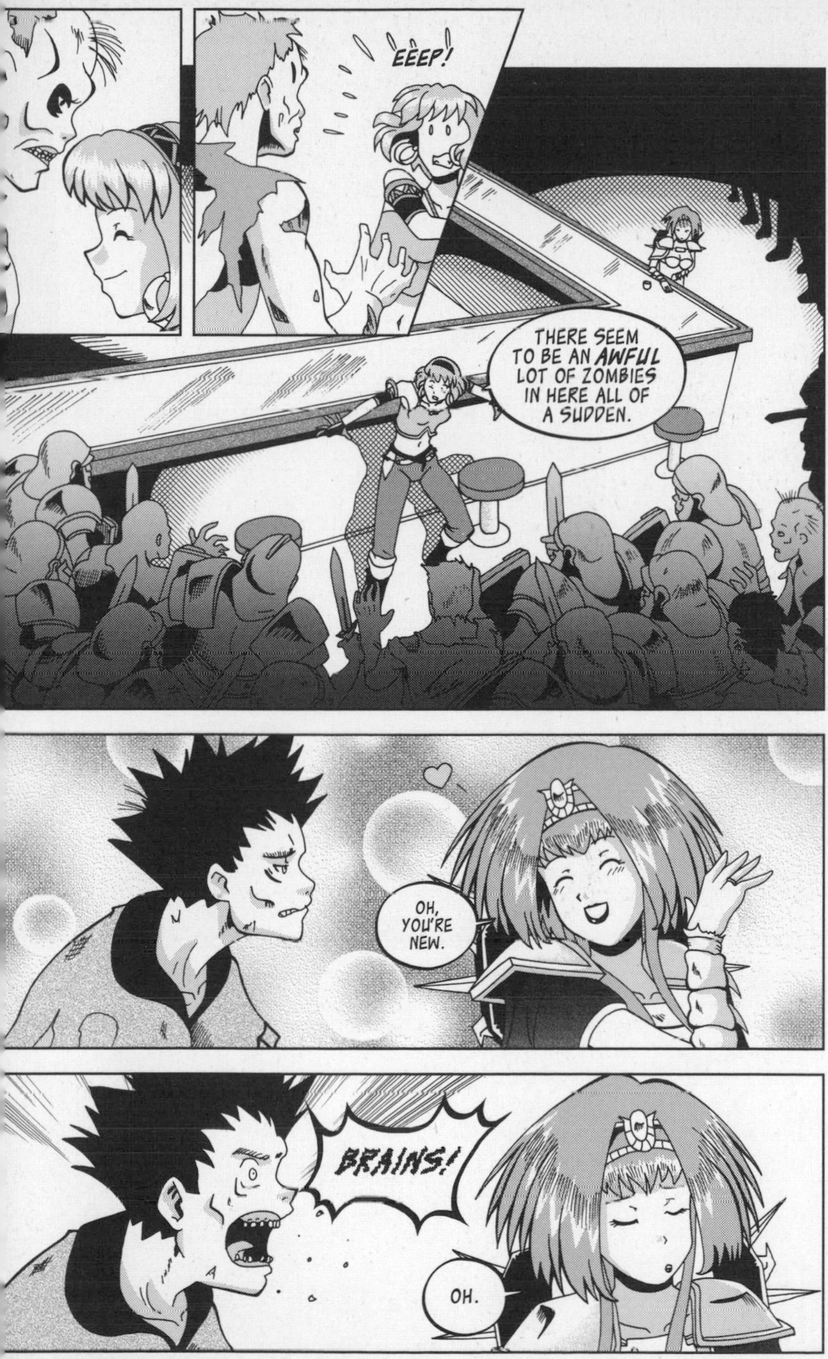
EEEP!
THERE SEEM TO BE AN AWFUL LOT OF ZOMBIES IN HERE ALL OF A SUDDEN.
OH, YOU'RE NEW.
BRAINS!
OH.

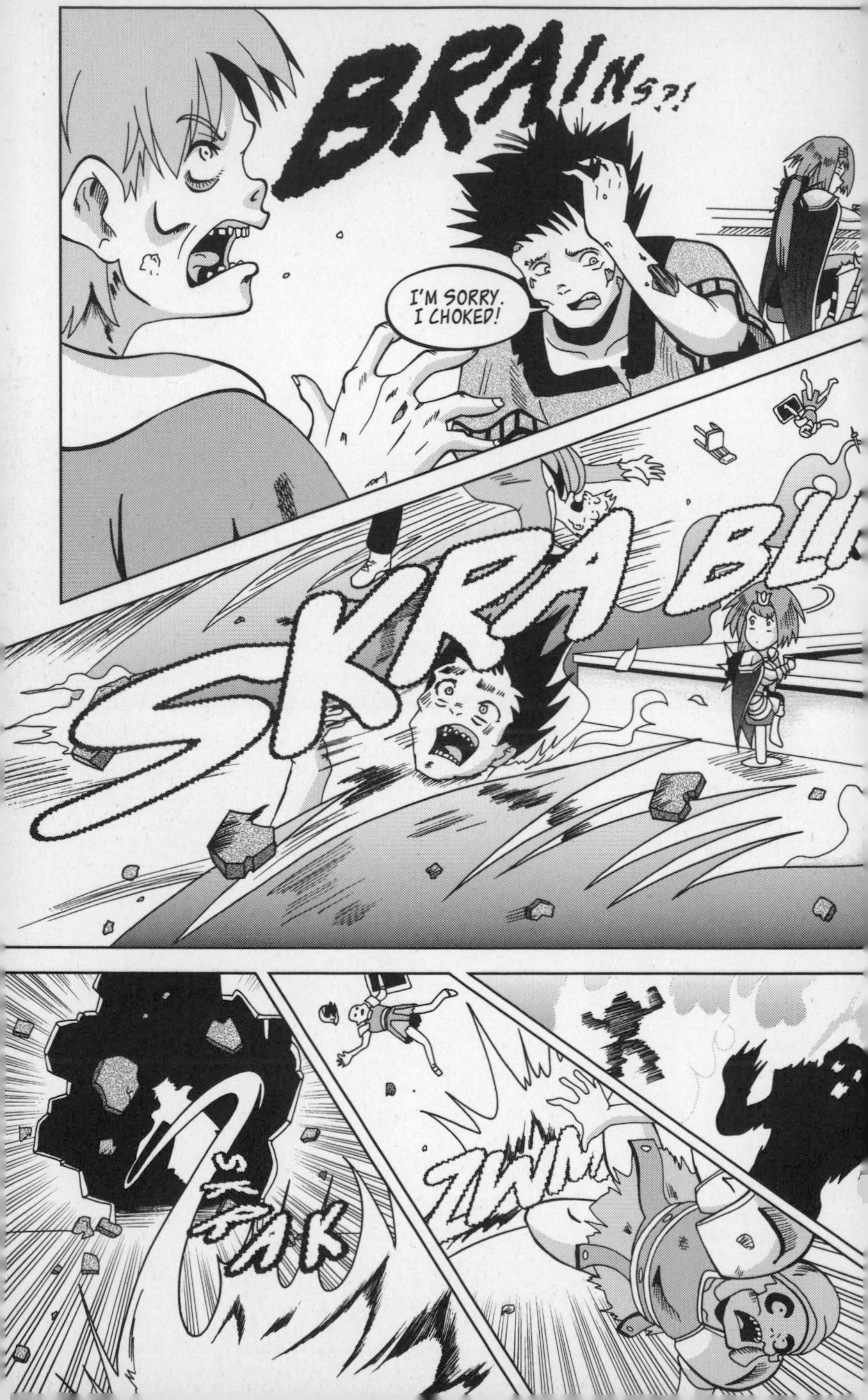
BRAINS?!
I'M SORRY. I CHOKED!
SKRABL
SKRAK
ZWM

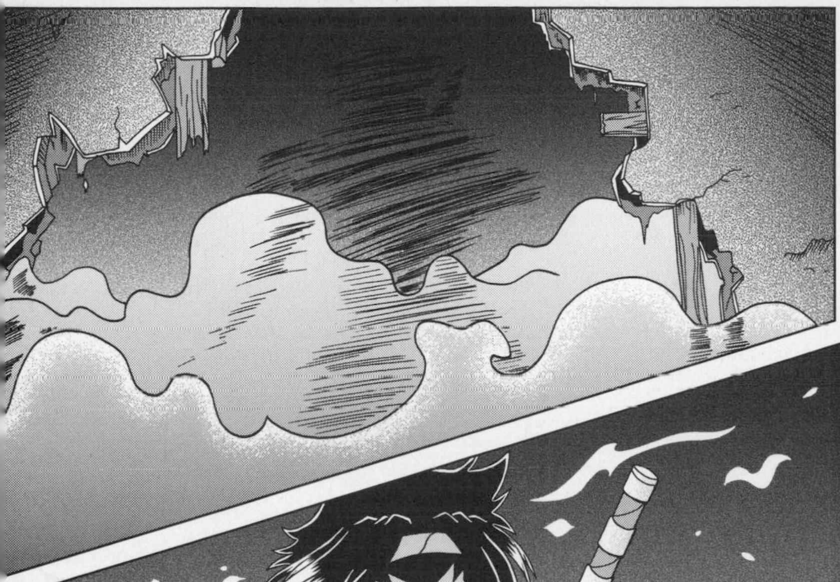
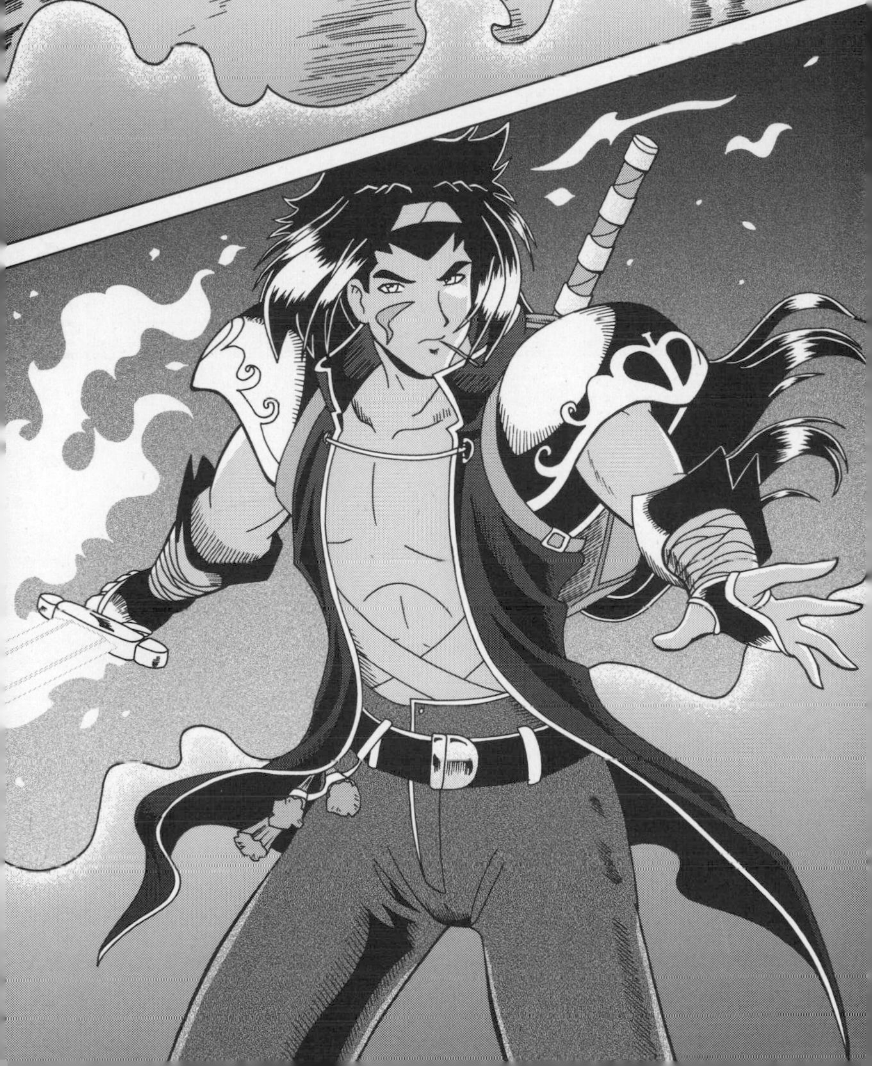

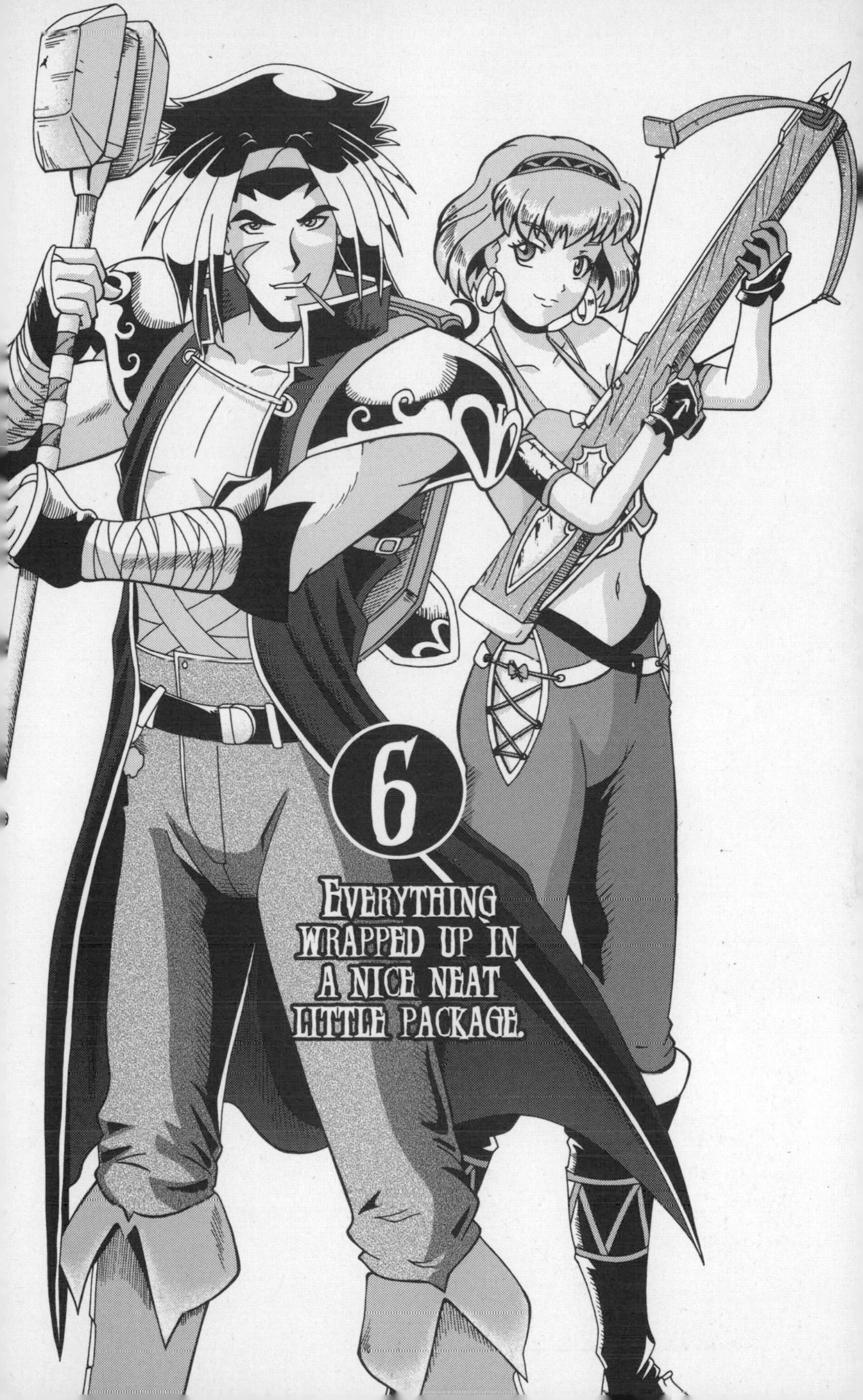
6
EVERYTHING WRAPPED UP IN A NICE NEAT LITTLE PACKAGE.

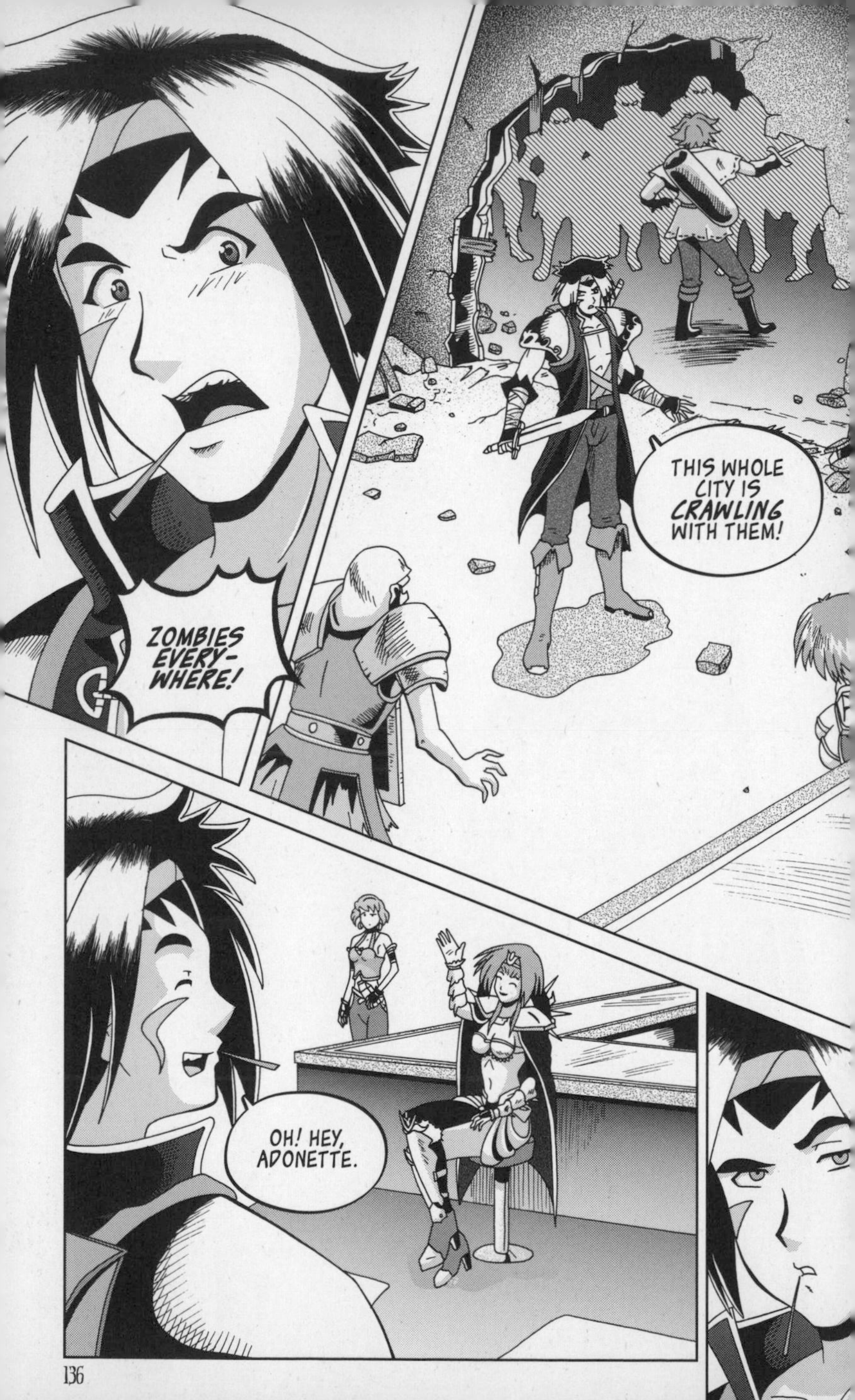
ZOMBIES EVERY-WHERE!
THIS WHOLE CITY IS CRAWLING WITH THEM!
OH! HEY, ADONETTE.

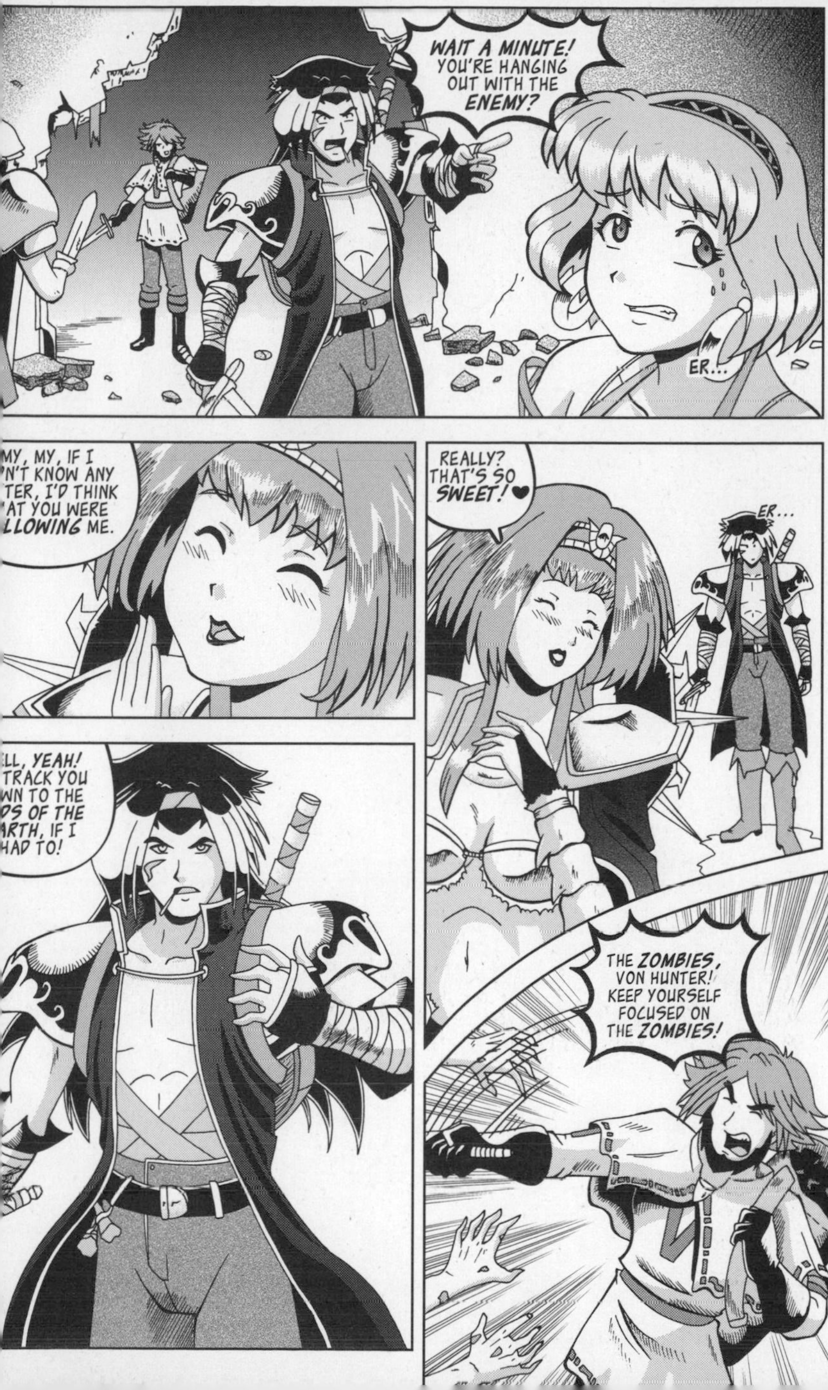
WAIT A MINUTE! YOU'RE HANGING OUT WITH THE ENEMY?
ER...
MY, MY, IF I
'N'T KNOW ANY
TER, I'D THINK
AT YOU WERE
LLOWING ME.
ELL, YEAH!
TRACK YOU
WN TO THE
DS OF THE
ARTH, IF I
HAD TO!
REALLY? THAT'S SO SWEET! ♥
ER...
THE ZOMBIES, VON HUNTER! KEEP YOURSELF FOCUSED ON THE ZOMBIES!

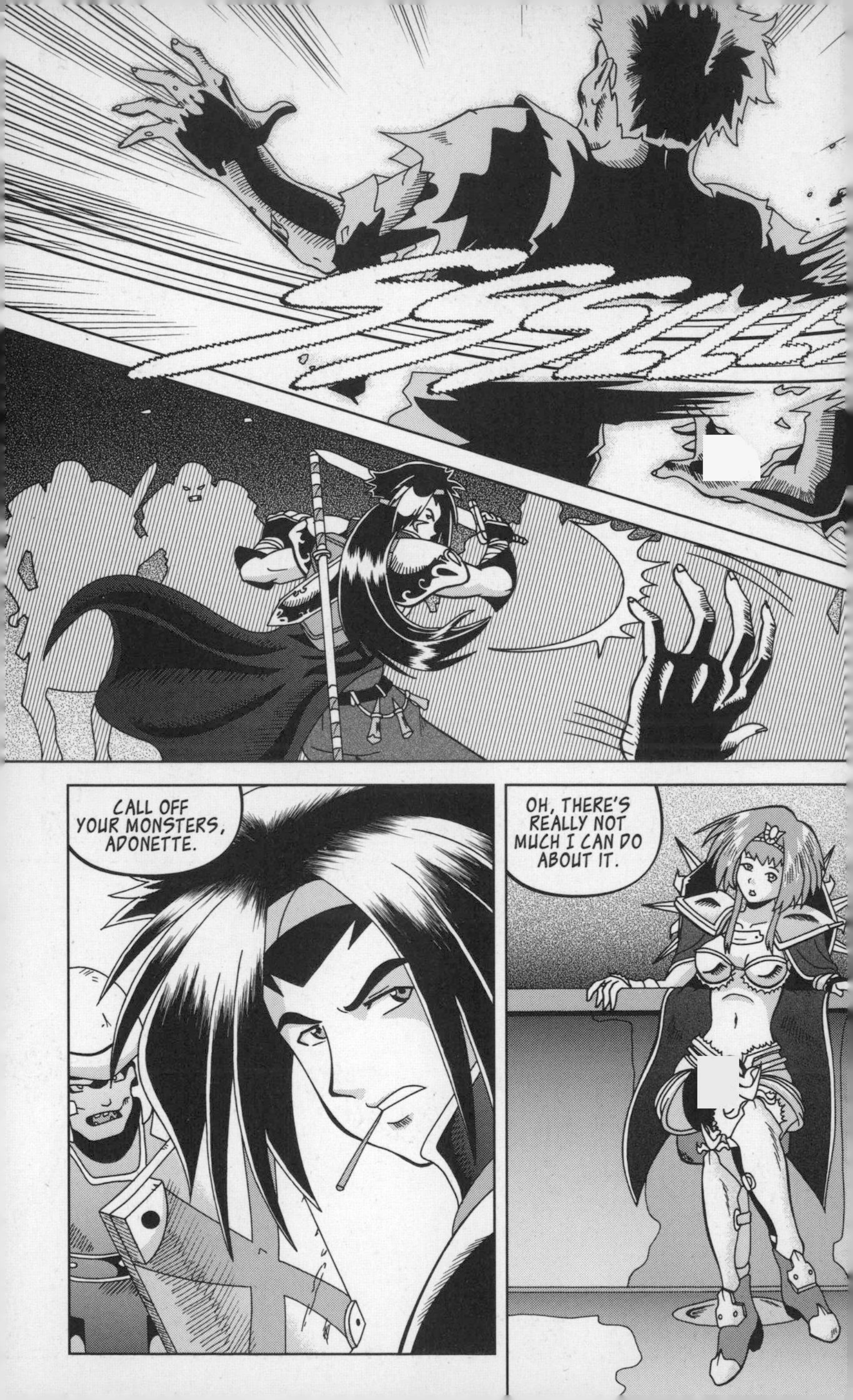
CALL OFF YOUR MONSTERS, ADONETTE.
OH, THERE'S REALLY NOT MUCH I CAN DO ABOUT IT.

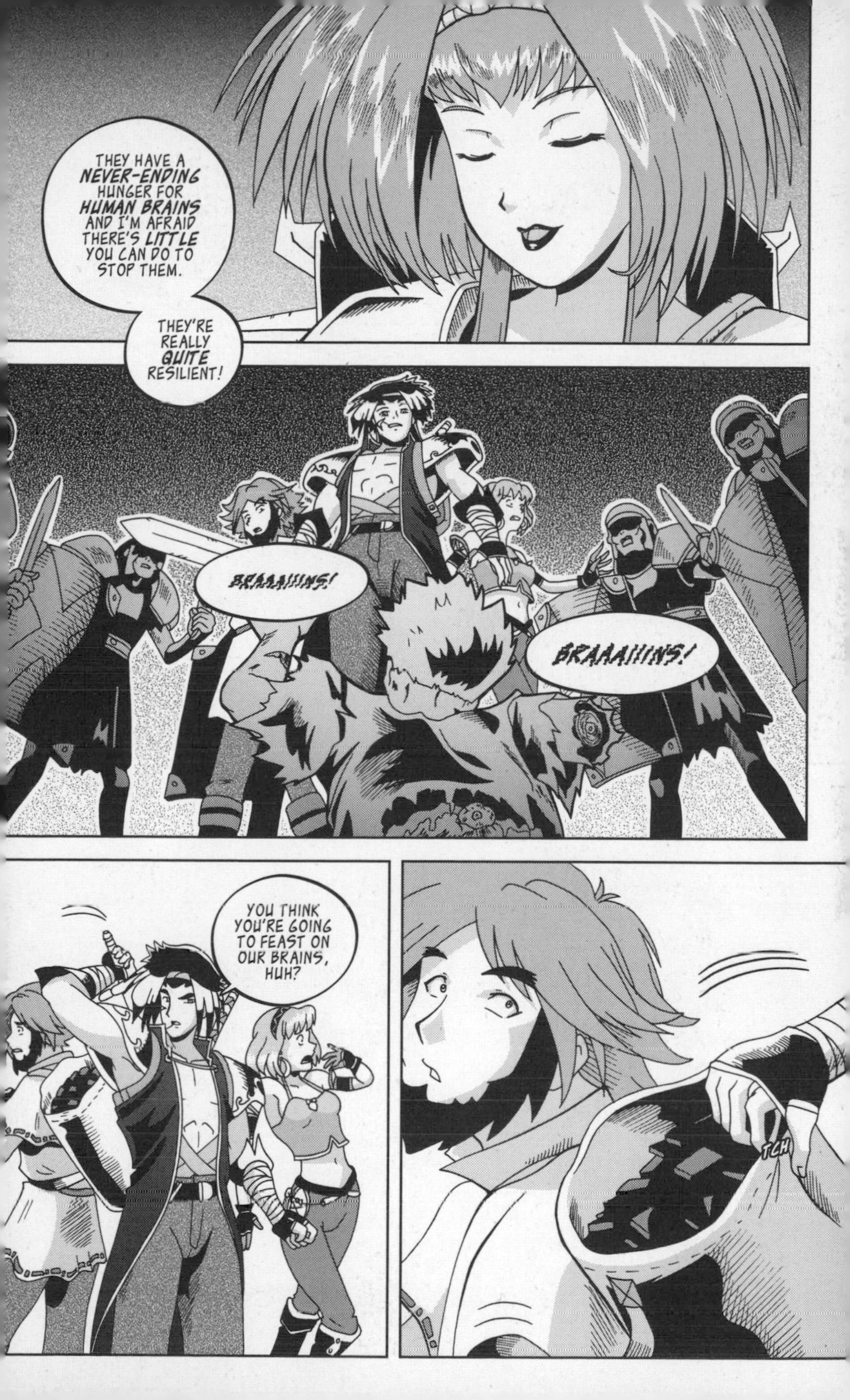
THEY HAVE A NEVER-ENDING HUNGER FOR HUMAN BRAINS AND I'M AFRAID THERE'S LITTLE YOU CAN DO TO STOP THEM.
THEY'RE REALLY QUITE RESILIENT!
BRAAAIIINS!
BRAAAIIINS!
YOU THINK YOU'RE GOING TO FEAST ON OUR BRAINS, HUH?
TCH

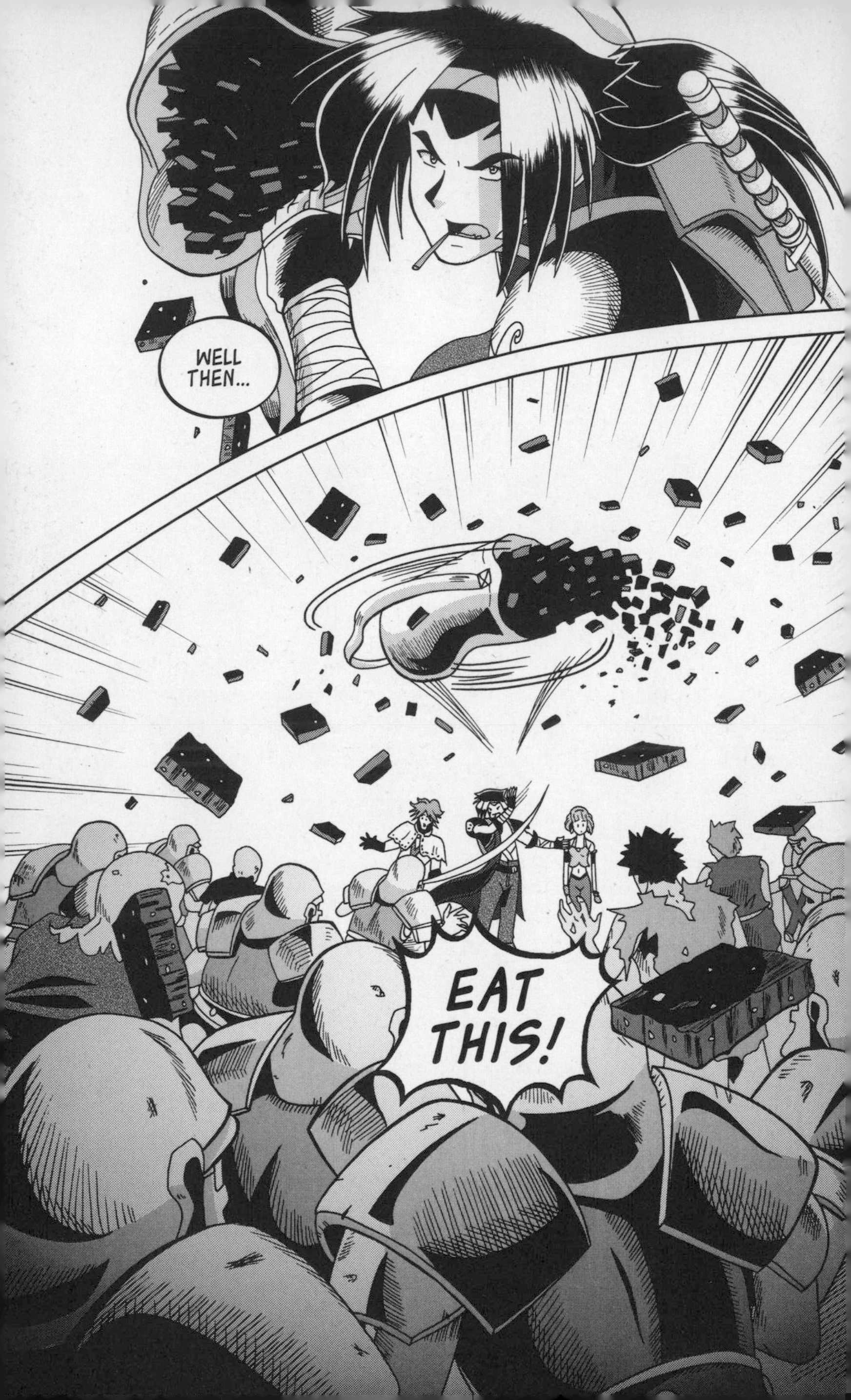
WELL THEN...
EAT THIS!

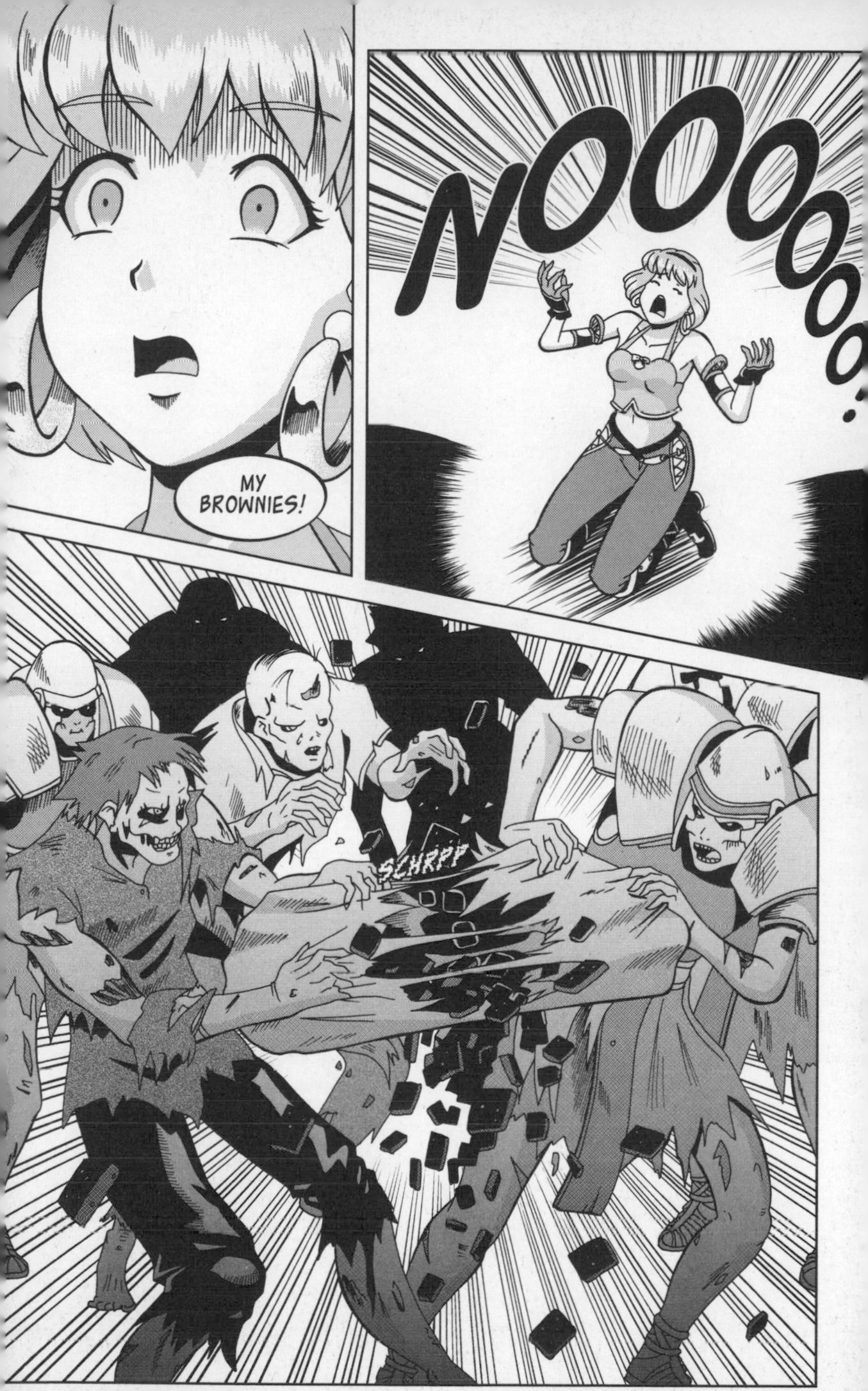
MY BROWNIES!
NOOOOOO...!
SCHRPP

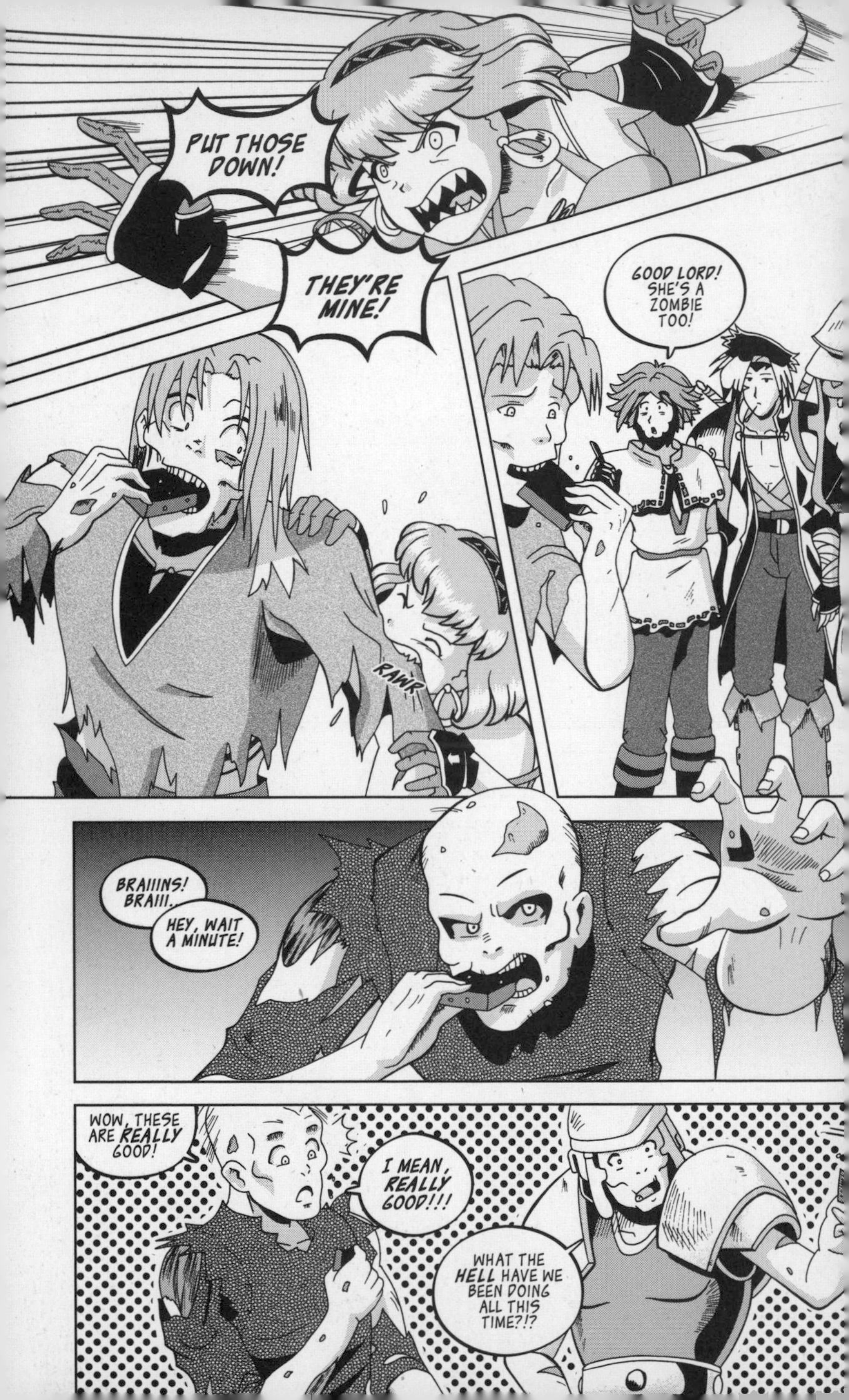
PUT THOSE DOWN!
THEY'RE MINE!
RAWR
GOOD LORD! SHE'S A ZOMBIE TOO!
BRAIIINS! BRAIII...
HEY, WAIT A MINUTE!
WOW, THESE ARE REALLY GOOD!
I MEAN, REALLY GOOD!!!
WHAT THE HELL HAVE WE BEEN DOING ALL THIS TIME?!?

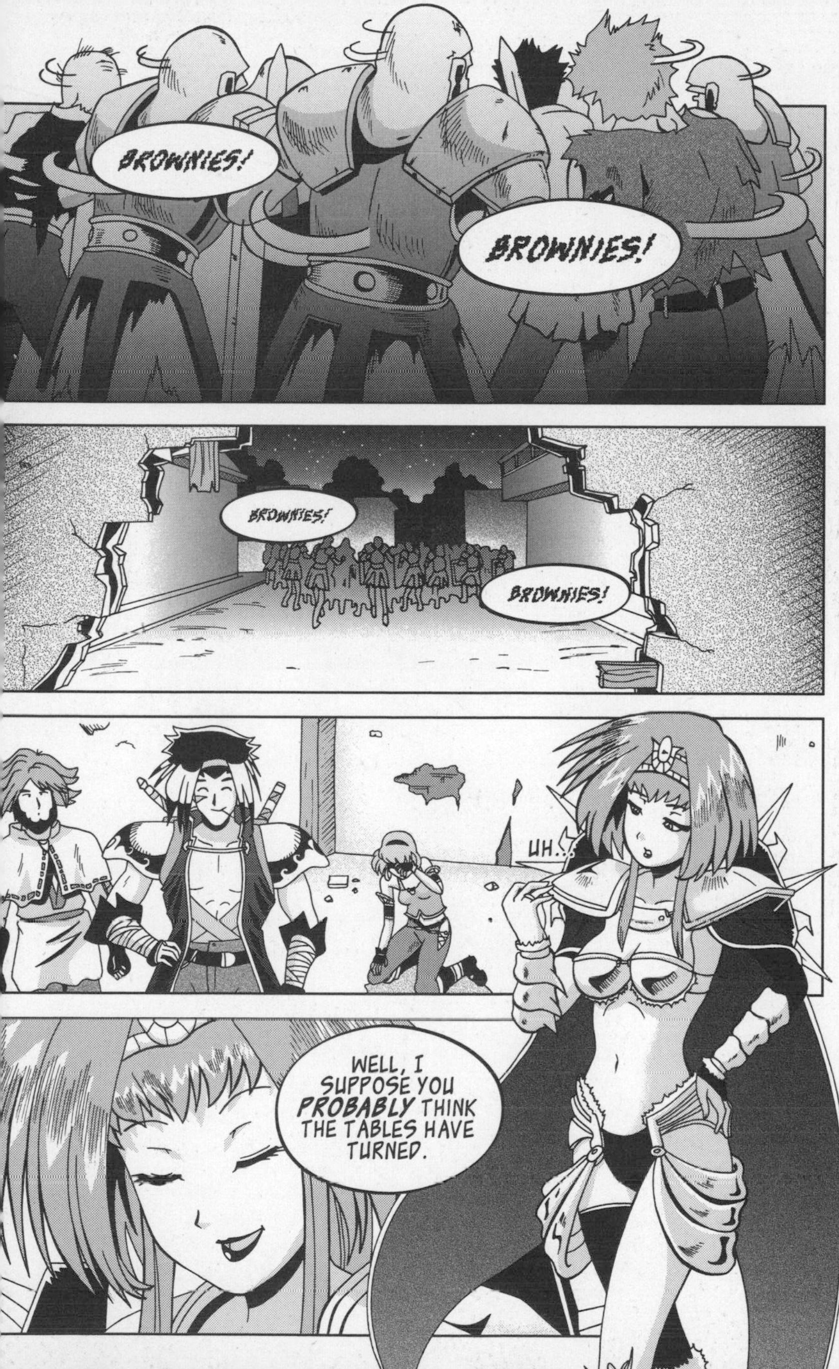
BROWNIES!
BROWNIES!
BROWNIES!
BROWNIES!
UH...
WELL, I SUPPOSE YOU *PROBABLY* THINK THE TABLES HAVE TURNED.

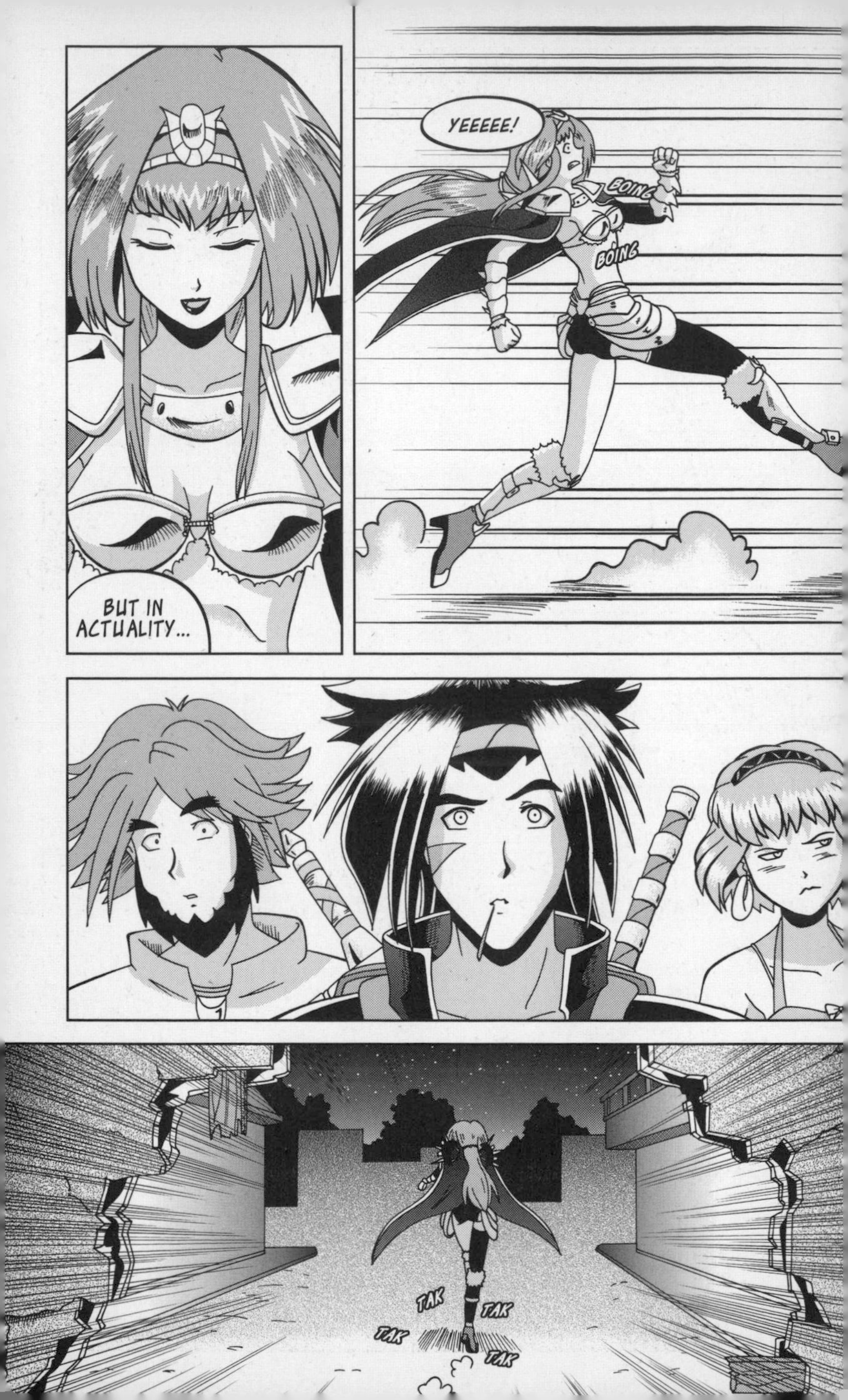

BUT IN ACTUALITY...
YEEEEE!
BOING
BOING
TAK
TAK
TAK
TAK

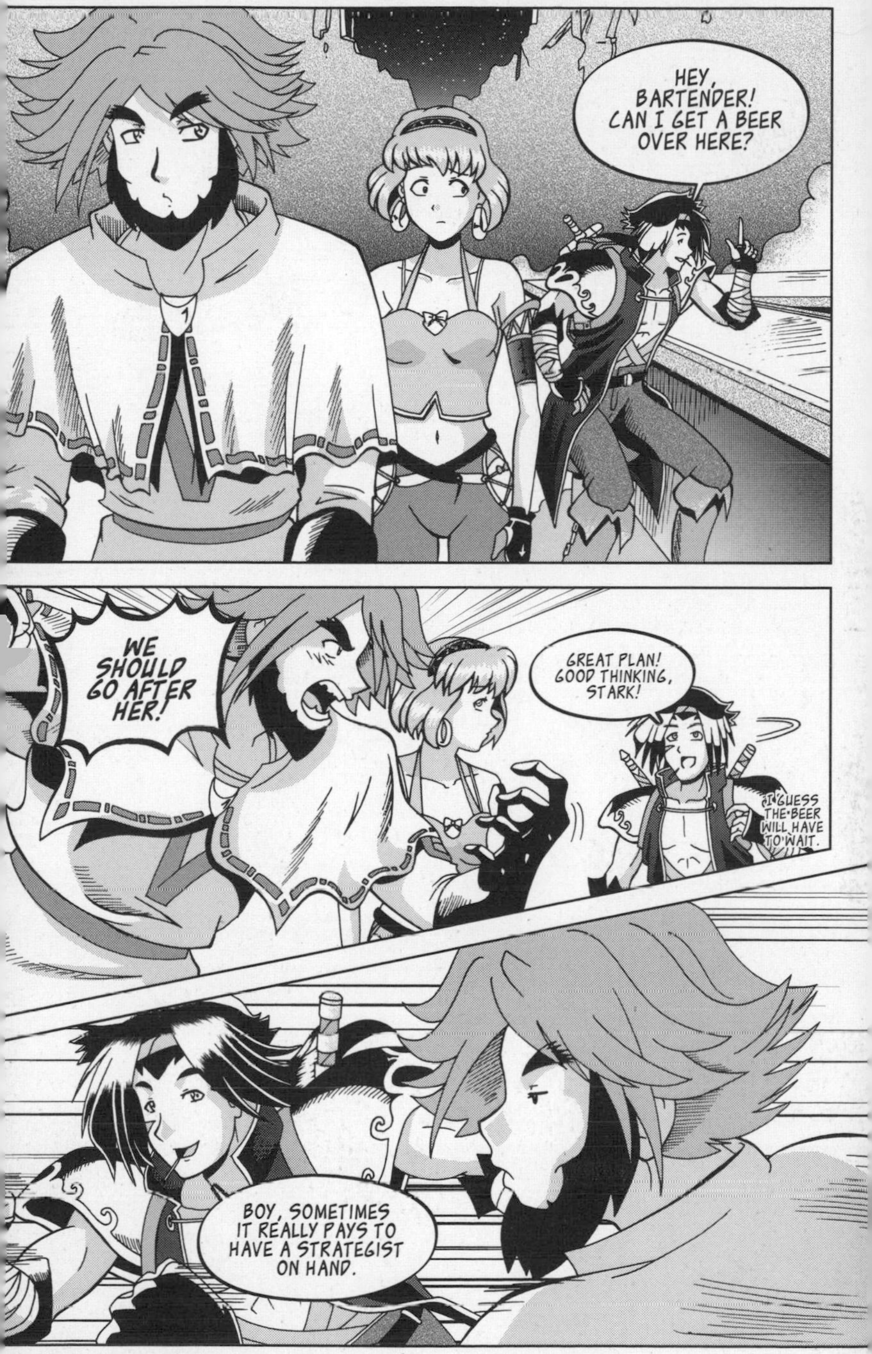
HEY, BARTENDER! CAN I GET A BEER OVER HERE?
WE SHOULD GO AFTER HER!
GREAT PLAN! GOOD THINKING, STARK!
I GUESS THE BEER WILL HAVE TO WAIT.
BOY, SOMETIMES IT REALLY PAYS TO HAVE A STRATEGIST ON HAND.

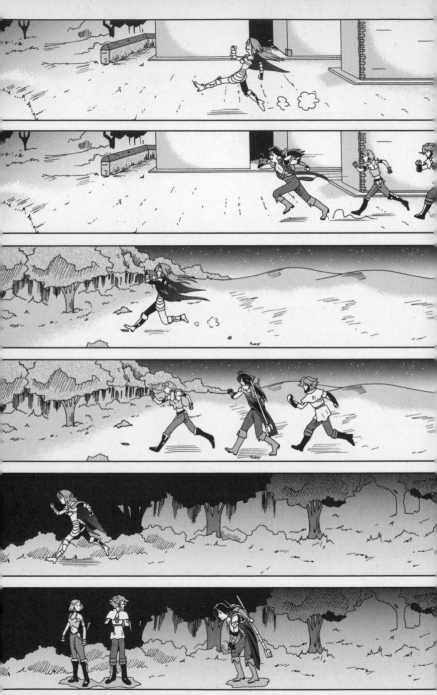

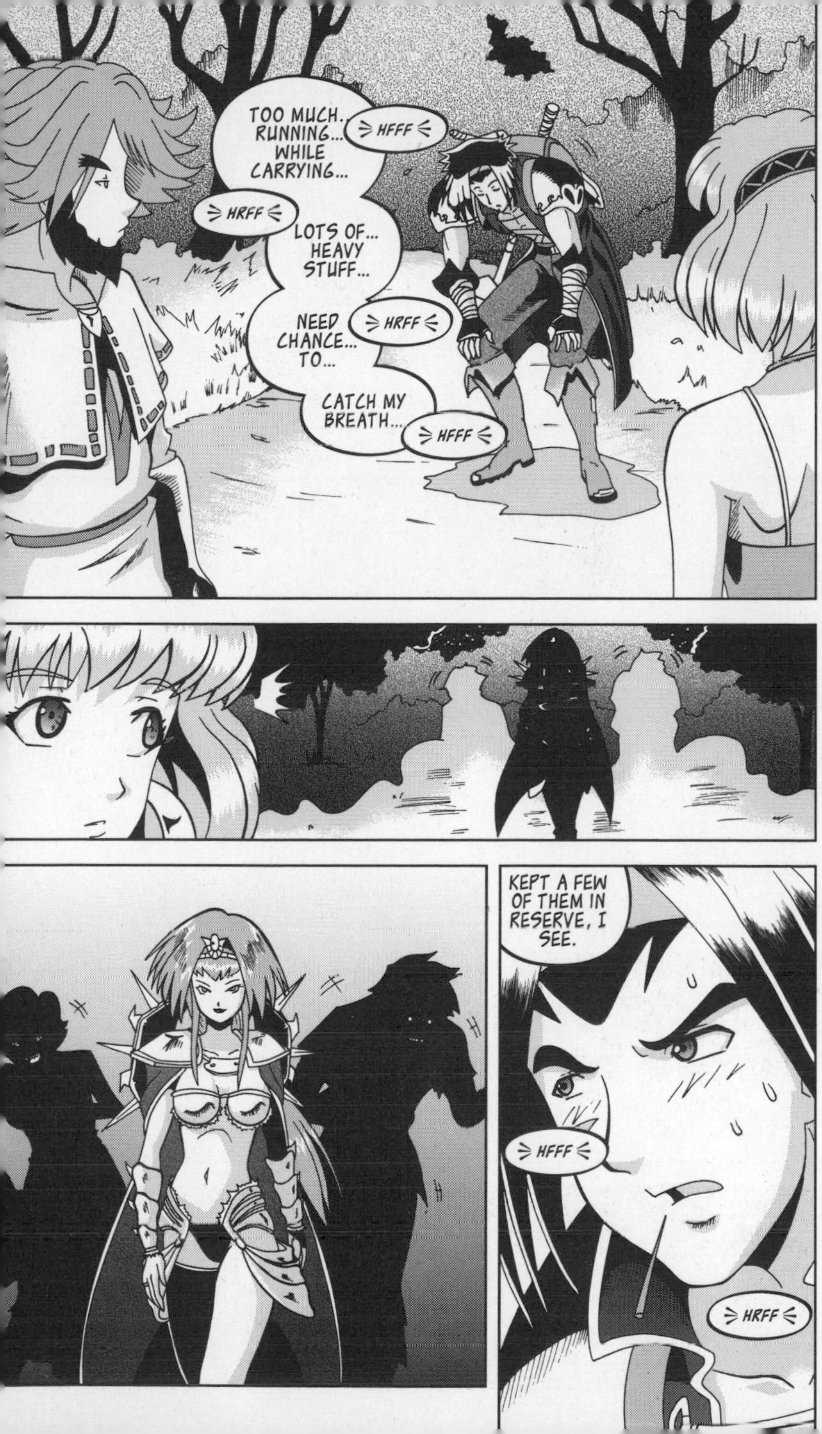
TOO MUCH.. RUNNING... WHILE CARRYING...
HFFF
HRFF
LOTS OF... HEAVY STUFF...
NEED CHANCE... TO...
HRFF
CATCH MY BREATH...
HFFF
KEPT A FEW OF THEM IN RESERVE, I SEE.
HFFF
HRFF

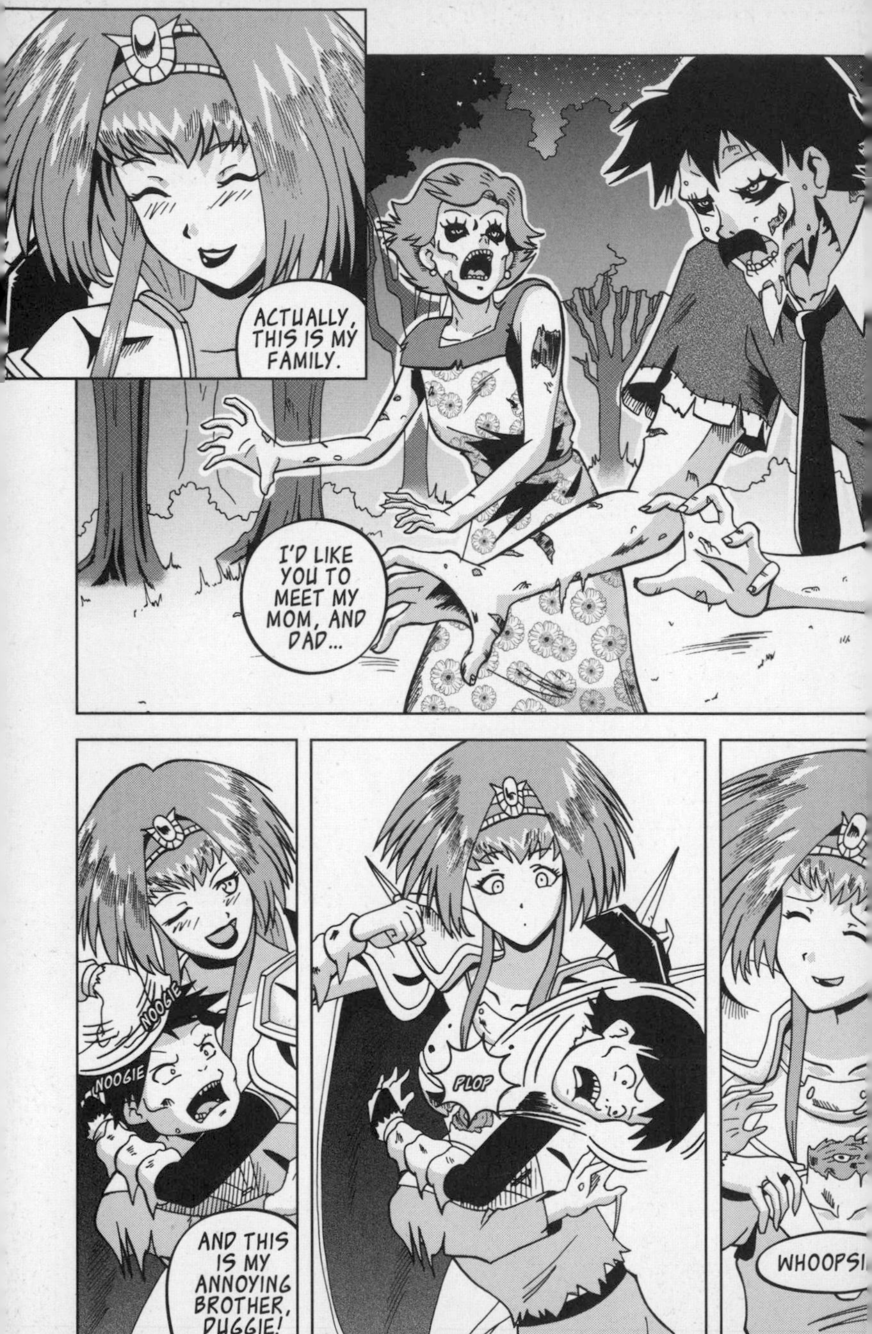
ACTUALLY, THIS IS MY FAMILY.
I'D LIKE YOU TO MEET MY MOM, AND DAD...
NOOGIE
NOOGIE
AND THIS IS MY ANNOYING BROTHER, DUGGIE!
PLOP
WHOOPSI

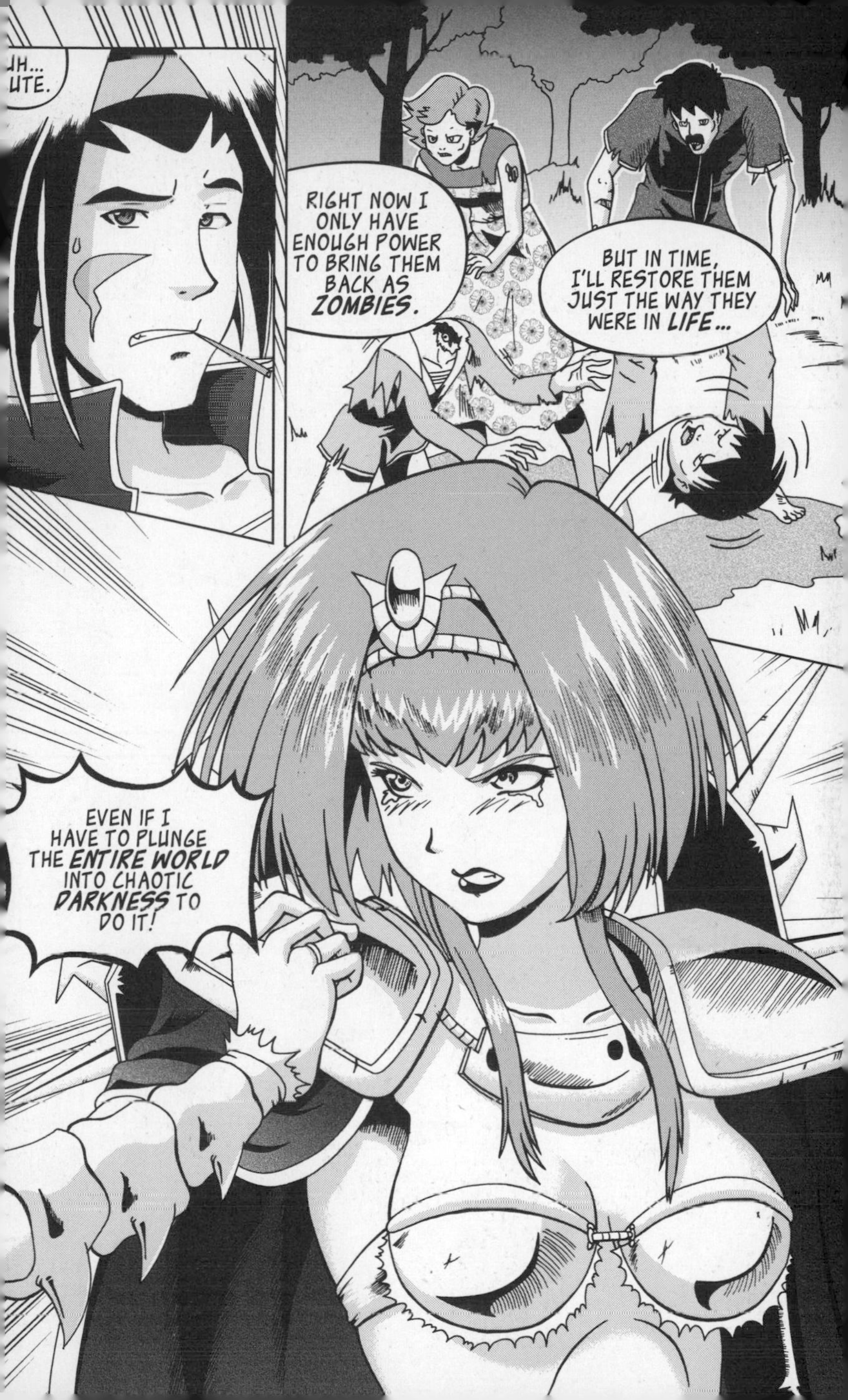
UH...
UTE.
RIGHT NOW I ONLY HAVE ENOUGH POWER TO BRING THEM BACK AS ZOMBIES.
BUT IN TIME, I'LL RESTORE THEM JUST THE WAY THEY WERE IN LIFE...
EVEN IF I HAVE TO PLUNGE THE ENTIRE WORLD INTO CHAOTIC DARKNESS TO DO IT!

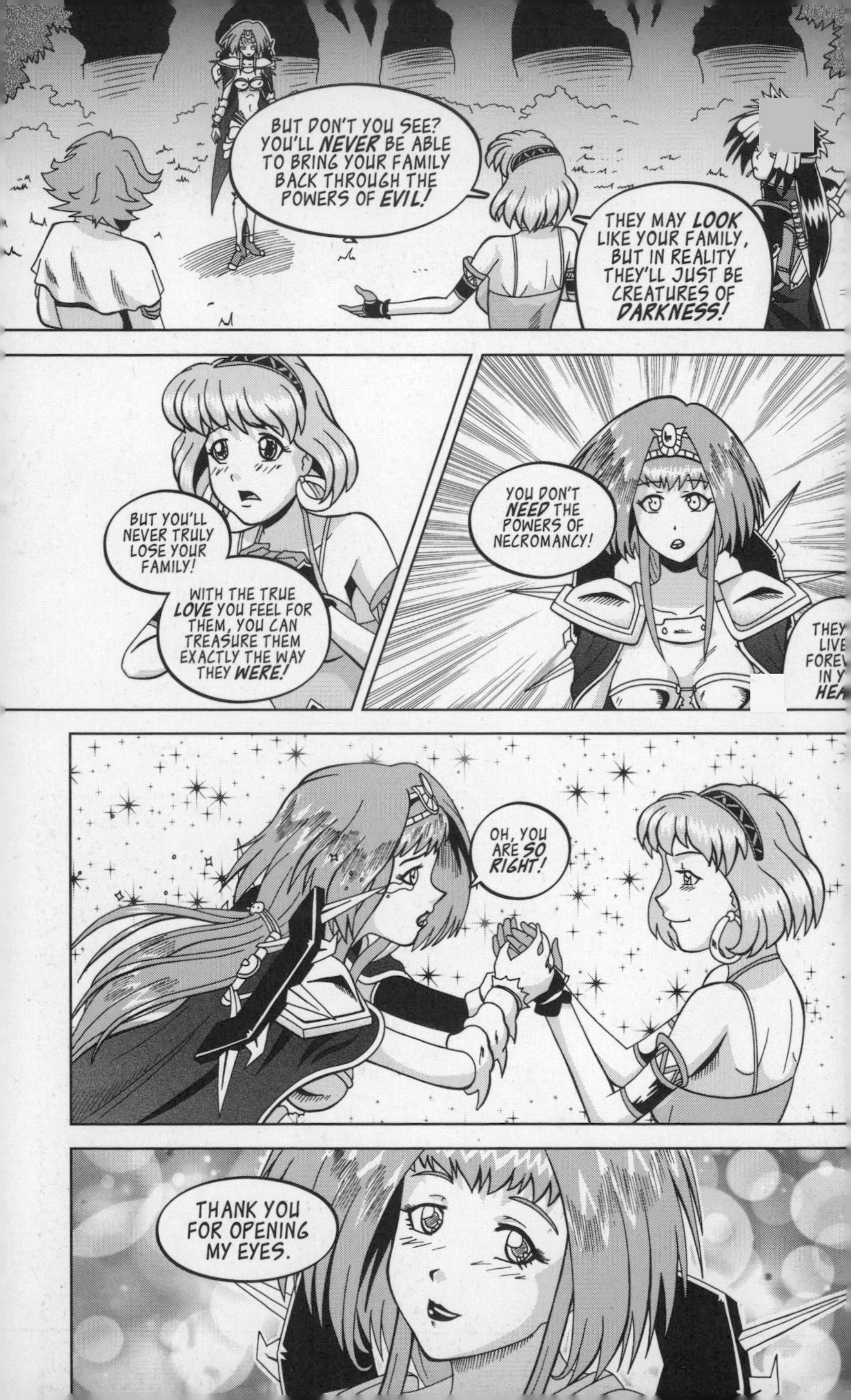
BUT DON'T YOU SEE? YOU'LL NEVER BE ABLE TO BRING YOUR FAMILY BACK THROUGH THE POWERS OF EVIL!
THEY MAY LOOK LIKE YOUR FAMILY, BUT IN REALITY THEY'LL JUST BE CREATURES OF DARKNESS!
BUT YOU'LL NEVER TRULY LOSE YOUR FAMILY!
WITH THE TRUE LOVE YOU FEEL FOR THEM, YOU CAN TREASURE THEM EXACTLY THE WAY THEY WERE!
YOU DON'T NEED THE POWERS OF NECROMANCY!
OH, YOU ARE SO RIGHT!
THANK YOU FOR OPENING MY EYES.

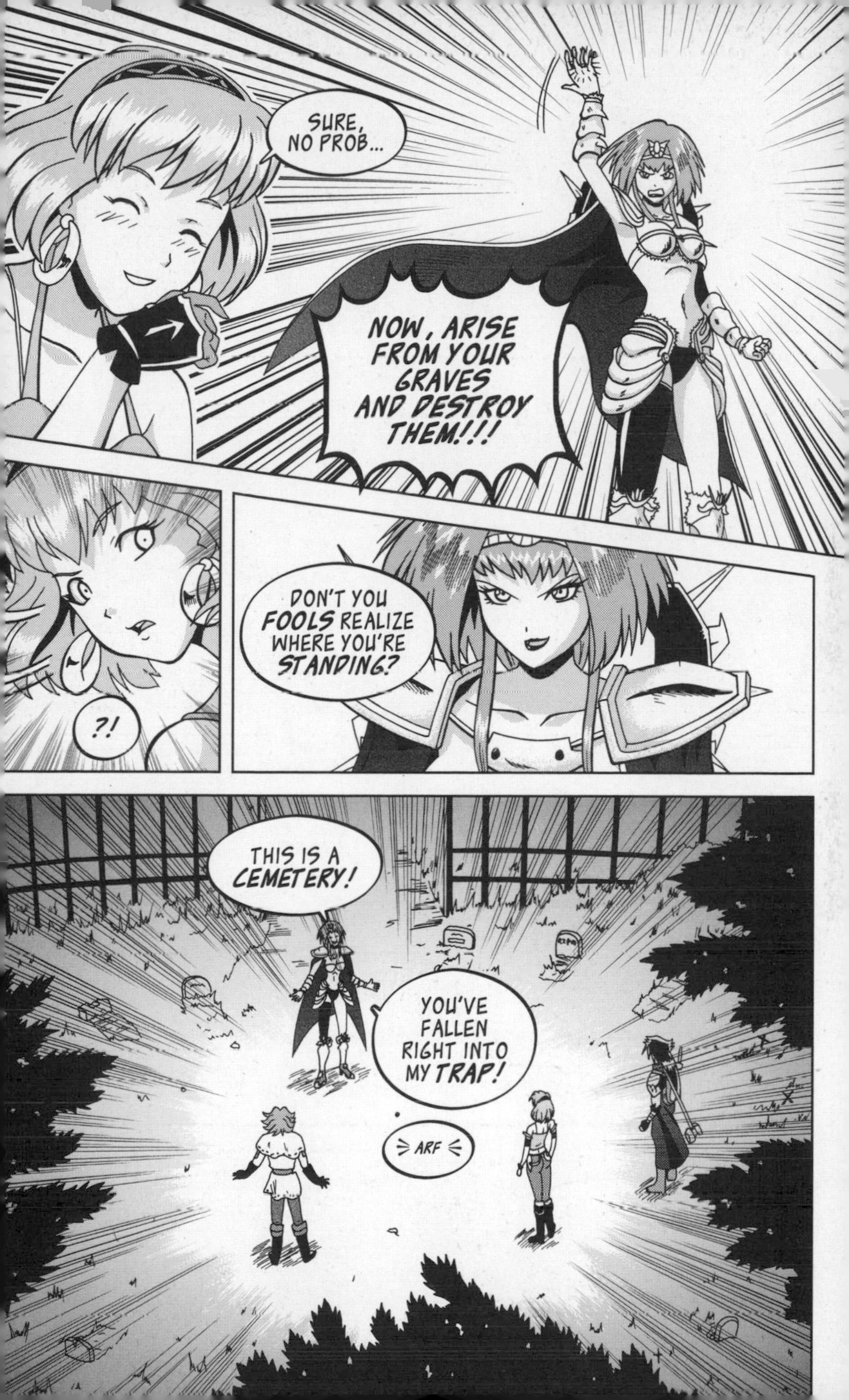
SURE, NO PROB...
NOW, ARISE FROM YOUR GRAVES AND DESTROY THEM!!!
?!
DON'T YOU FOOLS REALIZE WHERE YOU'RE STANDING?
THIS IS A CEMETERY!
YOU'VE FALLEN RIGHT INTO MY TRAP!
ARF

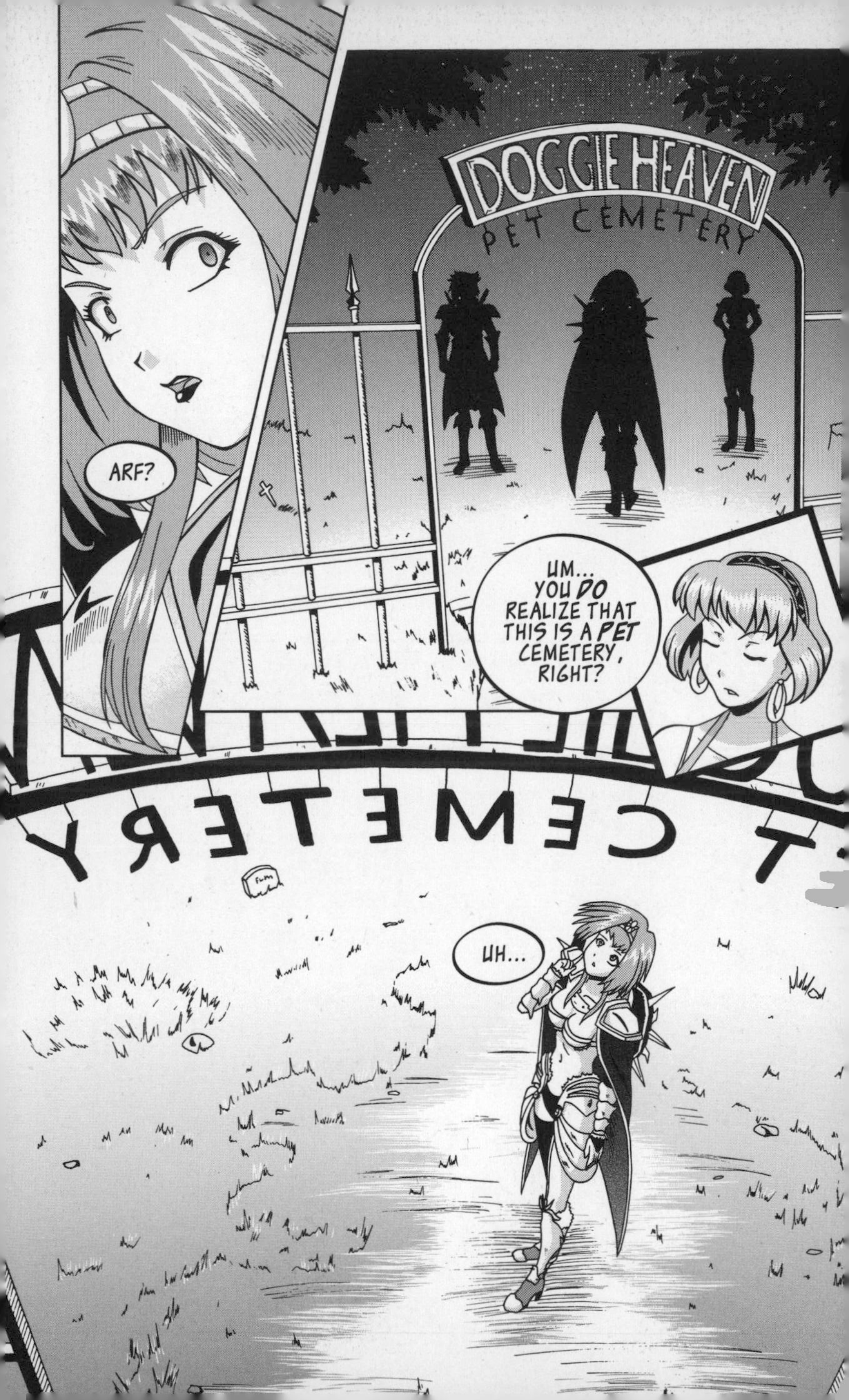
ARF?
DOGGIE HEAVEN
PET CEMETERY
UM... YOU DO REALIZE THAT THIS IS A PET CEMETERY, RIGHT?
UH...

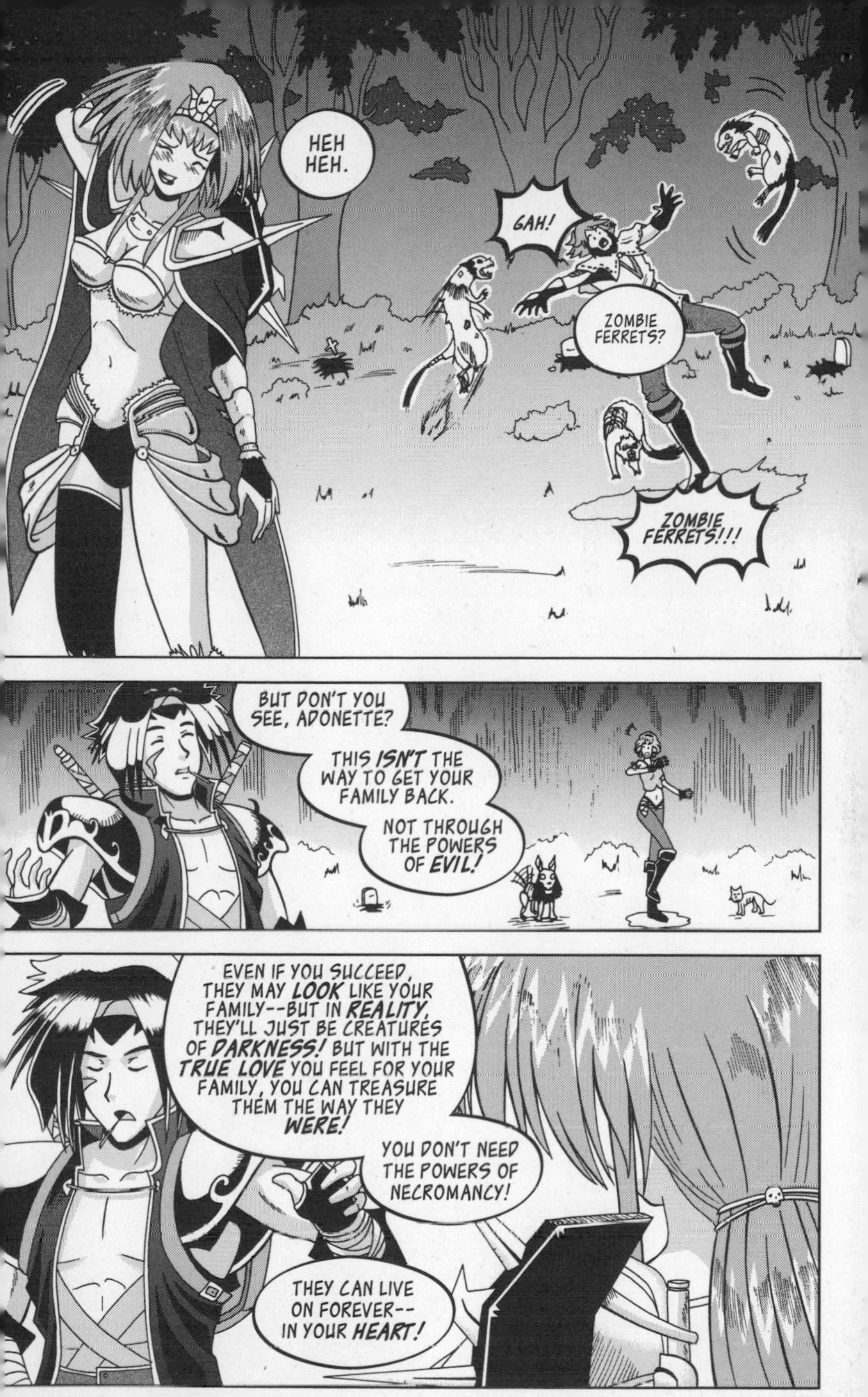
HEH HEH.
GAH!
ZOMBIE FERRETS?
ZOMBIE FERRETS!!!
BUT DON'T YOU SEE, ADONETTE?
THIS ISN'T THE WAY TO GET YOUR FAMILY BACK.
NOT THROUGH THE POWERS OF EVIL!
EVEN IF YOU SUCCEED, THEY MAY LOOK LIKE YOUR FAMILY--BUT IN REALITY, THEY'LL JUST BE CREATURES OF DARKNESS! BUT WITH THE TRUE LOVE YOU FEEL FOR YOUR FAMILY, YOU CAN TREASURE THEM THE WAY THEY WERE!
YOU DON'T NEED THE POWERS OF NECROMANCY!
THEY CAN LIVE ON FOREVER-- IN YOUR HEART!

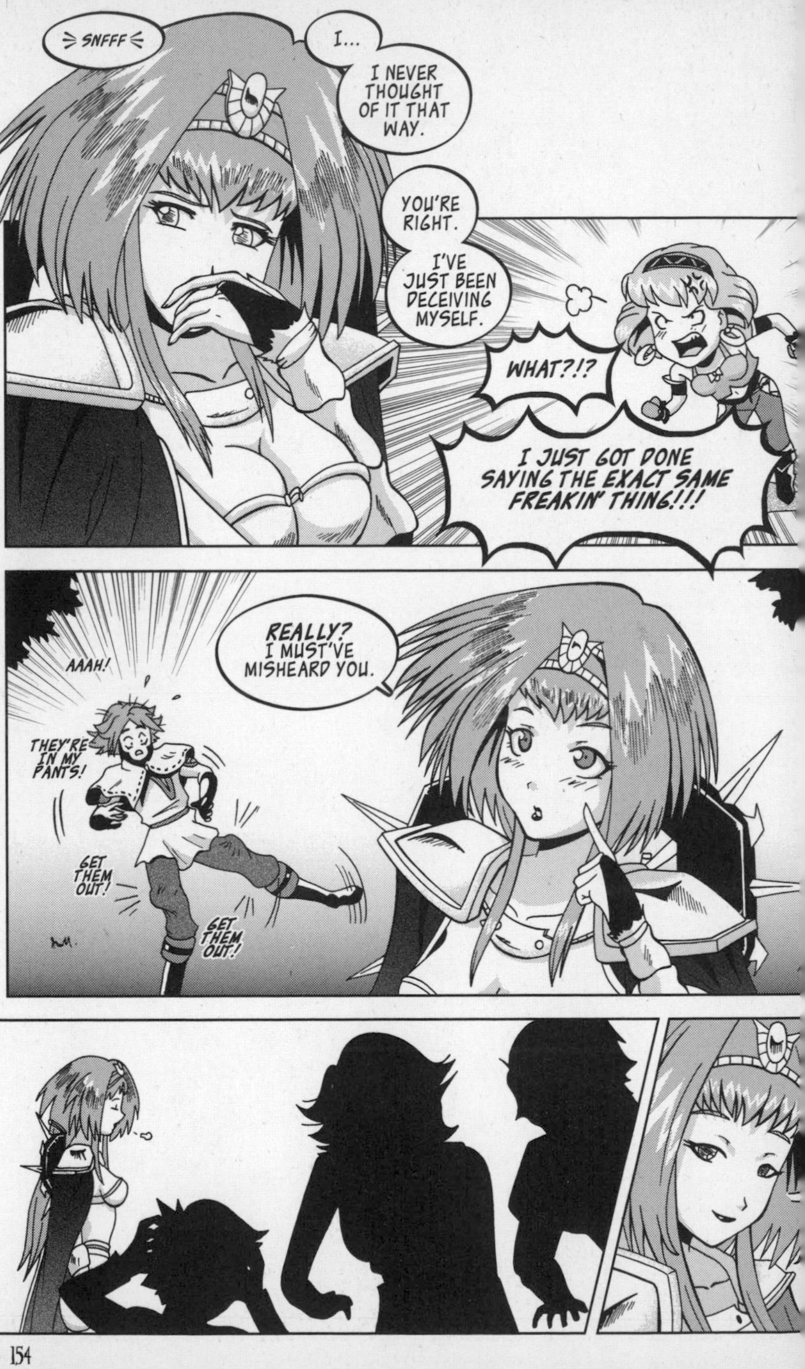

SNFFF
I...
I NEVER THOUGHT OF IT THAT WAY.
YOU'RE RIGHT.
I'VE JUST BEEN DECEIVING MYSELF.
WHAT?!?
I JUST GOT DONE SAYING THE EXACT SAME FREAKIN' THING!!!
AAAH!
THEY'RE IN MY PANTS!
GET THEM OUT!
GET THEM OUT!
REALLY? I MUST'VE MISHEARD YOU.

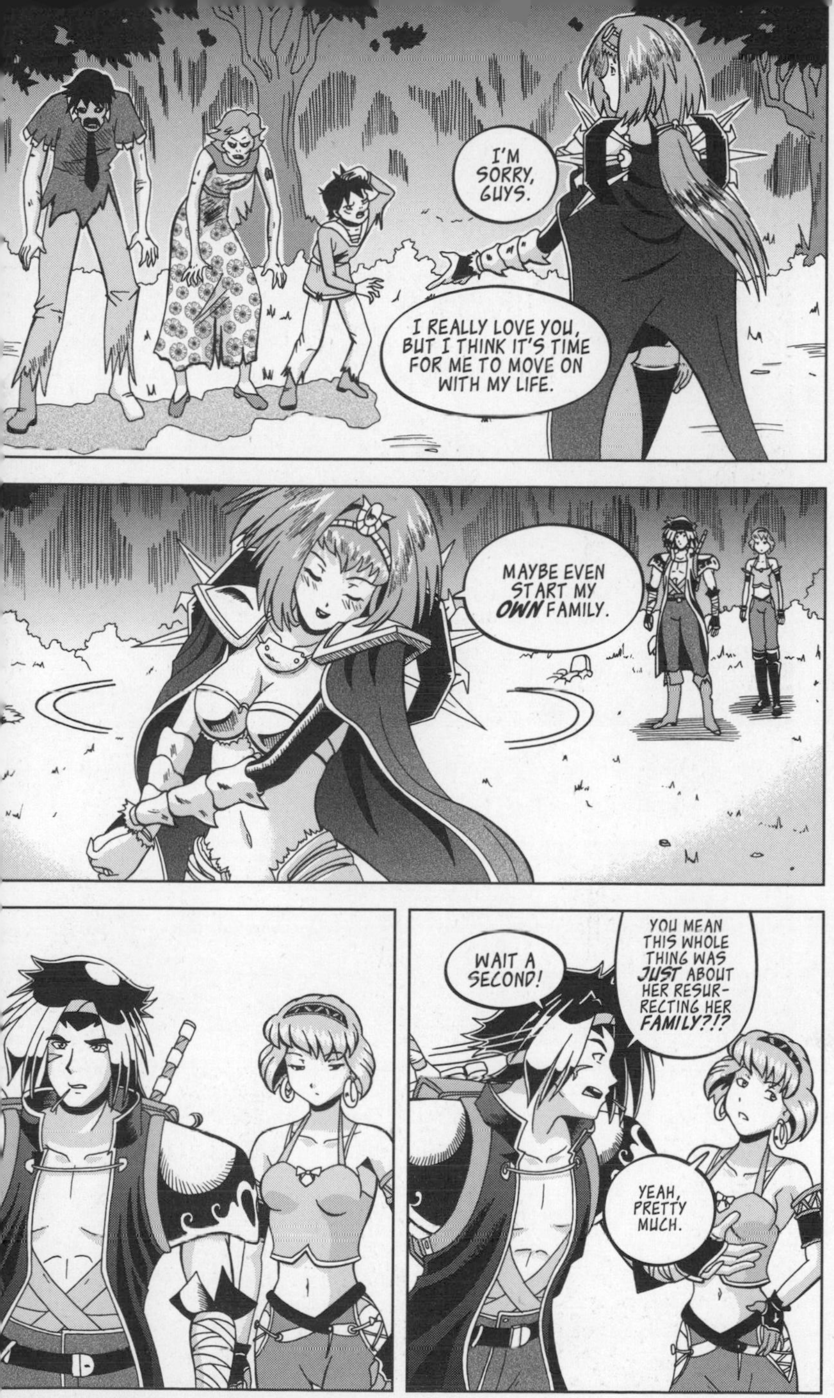
I'M SORRY, GUYS.
I REALLY LOVE YOU, BUT I THINK IT'S TIME FOR ME TO MOVE ON WITH MY LIFE.
MAYBE EVEN START MY OWN FAMILY.
WAIT A SECOND!
YOU MEAN THIS WHOLE THING WAS JUST ABOUT HER RESUR-RECTING HER FAMILY?!?
YEAH, PRETTY MUCH.

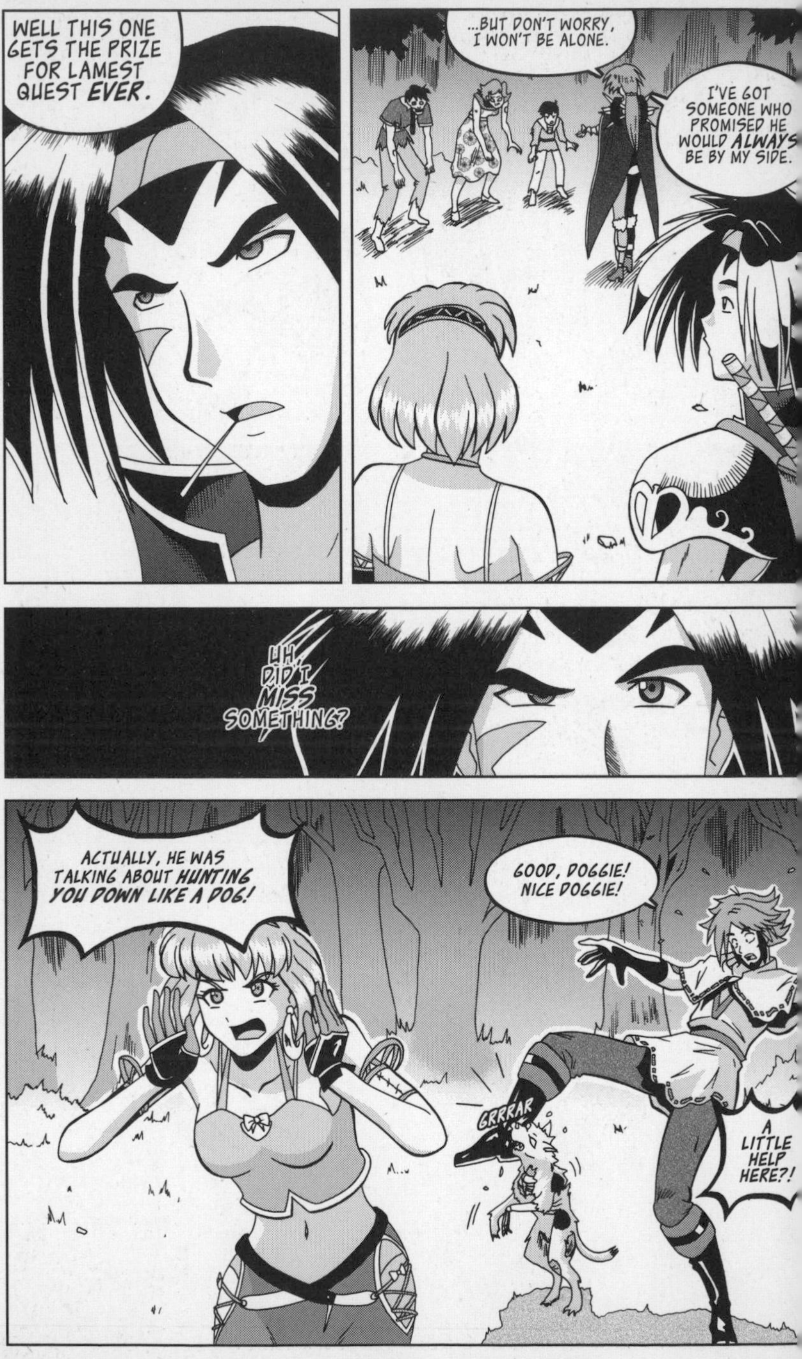
WELL THIS ONE GETS THE PRIZE FOR LAMEST QUEST EVER.
...BUT DON'T WORRY, I WON'T BE ALONE.
I'VE GOT SOMEONE WHO PROMISED HE WOULD ALWAYS BE BY MY SIDE.
UH, DID I MISS SOMETHING?
ACTUALLY, HE WAS TALKING ABOUT HUNTING YOU DOWN LIKE A DOG!
GOOD, DOGGIE! NICE DOGGIE!
GRRRAR
A LITTLE HELP HERE?!

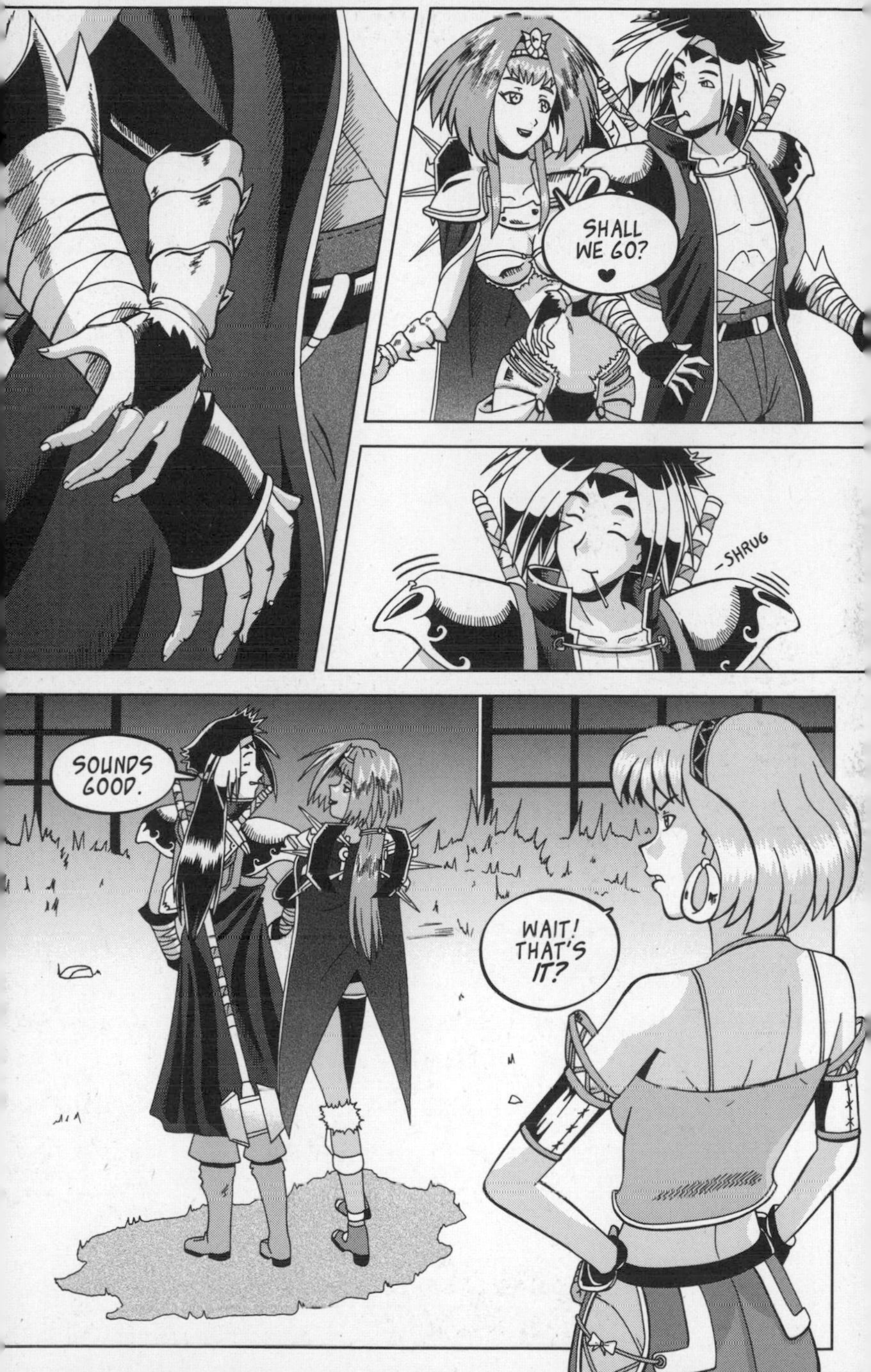
SHALL WE GO? ♥
-SHRUG
SOUNDS GOOD.
WAIT! THAT'S IT?

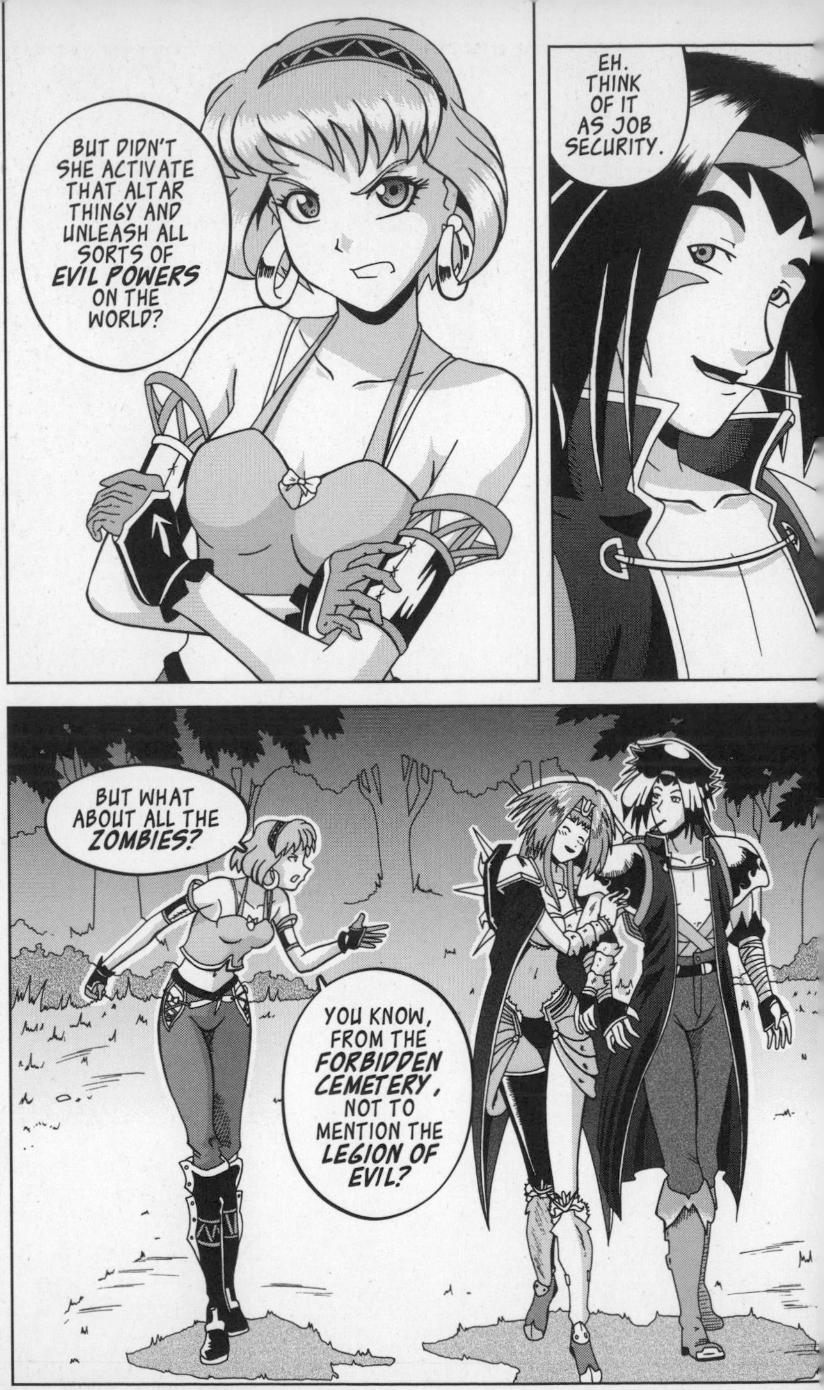
BUT DIDN'T SHE ACTIVATE THAT ALTAR THINGY AND UNLEASH ALL SORTS OF EVIL POWERS ON THE WORLD?
EH. THINK OF IT AS JOB SECURITY.
BUT WHAT ABOUT ALL THE ZOMBIES?
YOU KNOW, FROM THE FORBIDDEN CEMETERY, NOT TO MENTION THE LEGION OF EVIL?

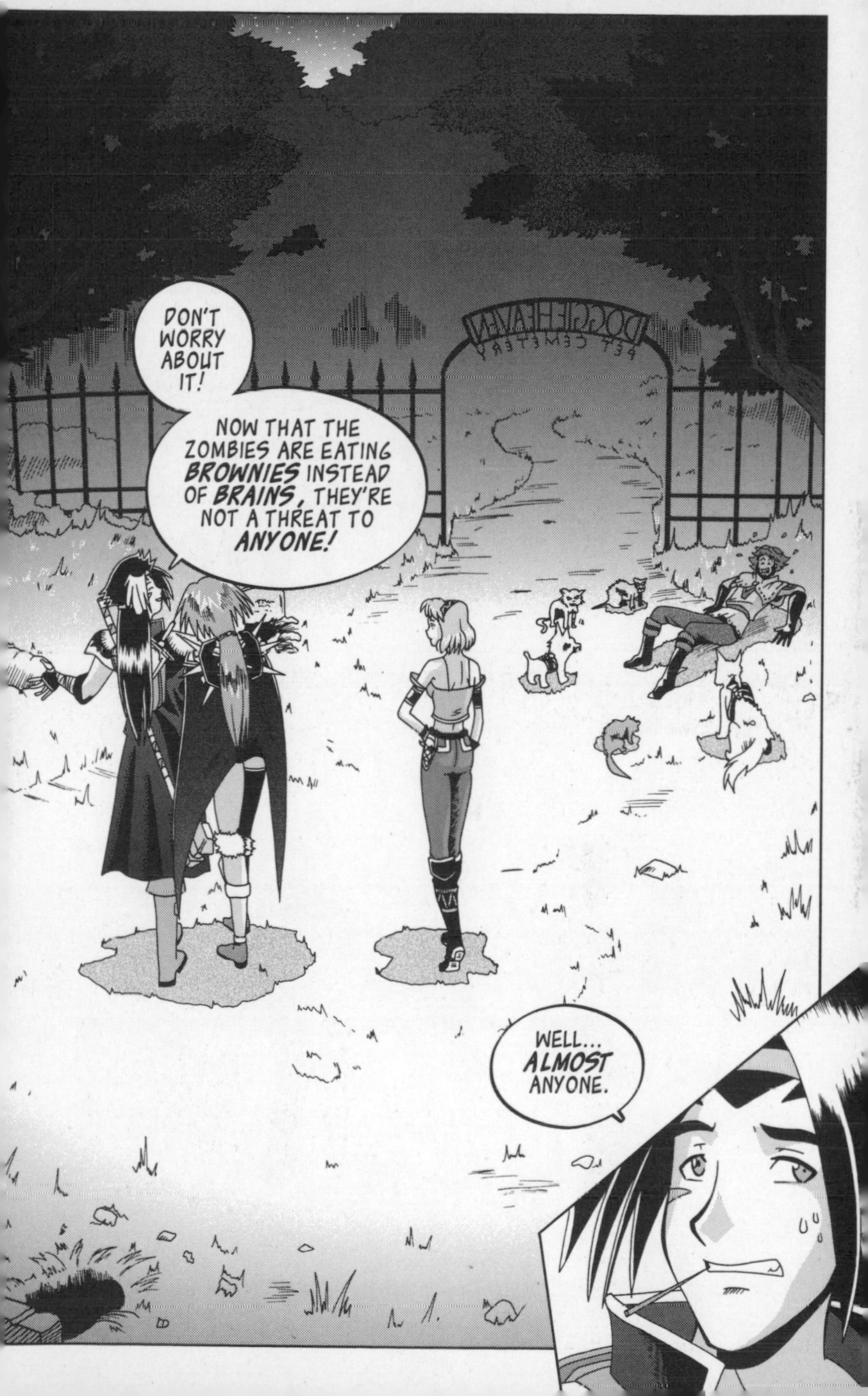
DON'T WORRY ABOUT IT!
NOW THAT THE ZOMBIES ARE EATING BROWNIES INSTEAD OF BRAINS, THEY'RE NOT A THREAT TO ANYONE!
WELL... ALMOST ANYONE.

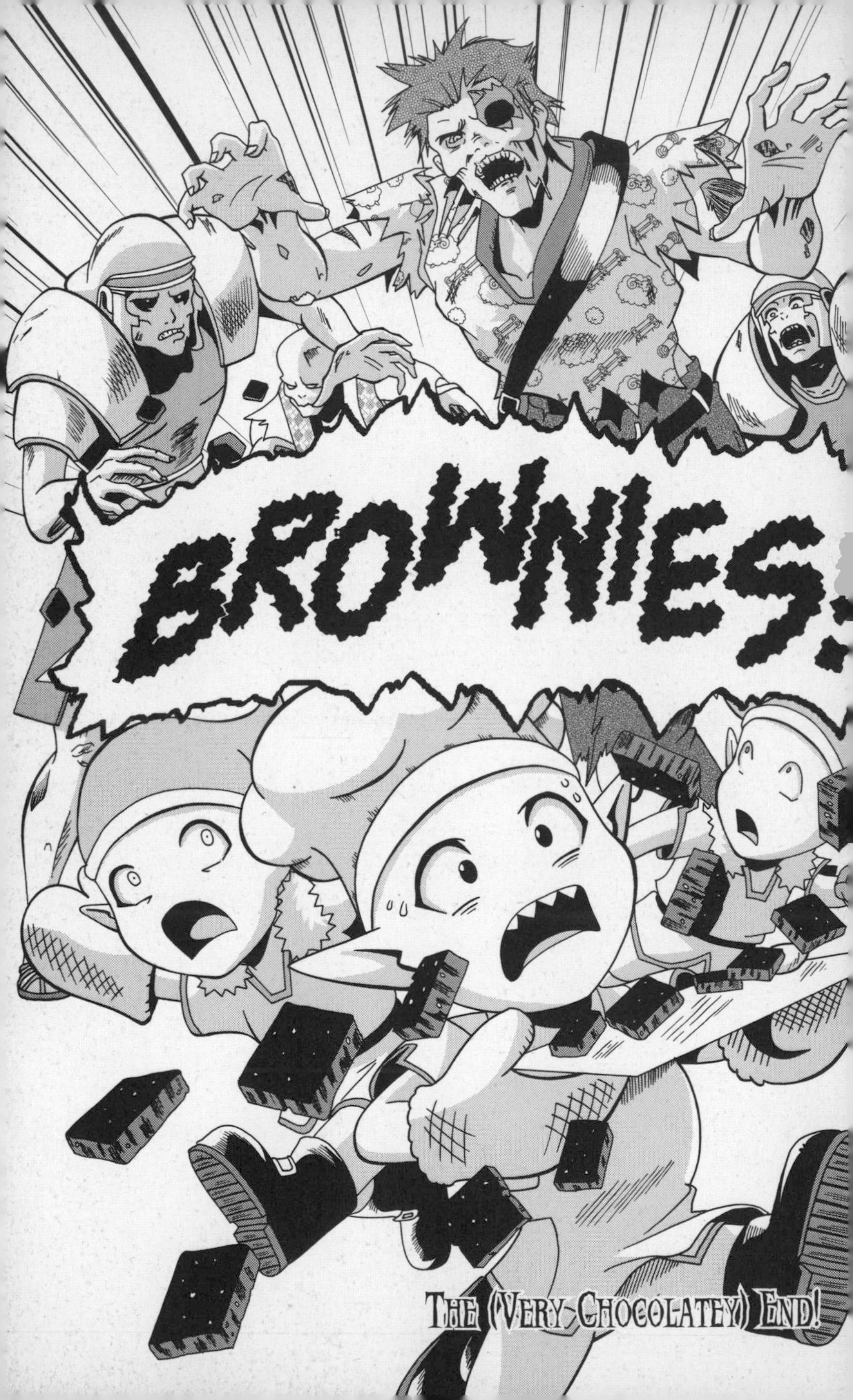
BROWNIES?!
THE (VERY CHOCOLATEY) END!

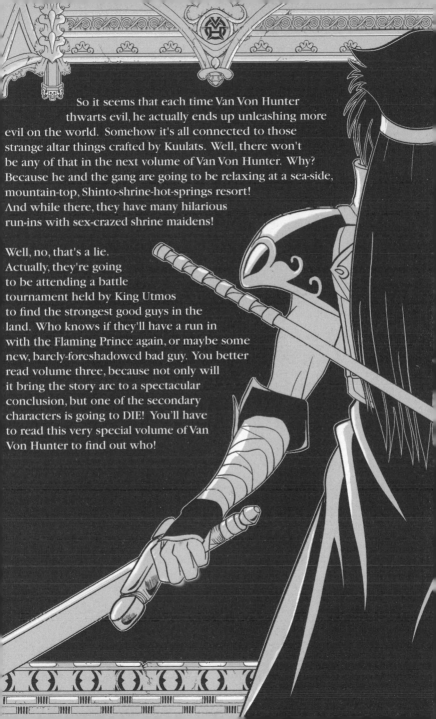

So it seems that each time Van Von Hunter thwarts evil, he actually ends up unleashing more evil on the world. Somehow it's all connected to those strange altar things crafted by Kuulats. Well, there won't be any of that in the next volume of Van Von Hunter. Why? Because he and the gang are going to be relaxing at a sea-side, mountain-top, Shinto-shrine-hot-springs resort! And while there, they have many hilarious run-ins with sex-crazed shrine maidens!

Well, no, that's a lie. Actually, they're going to be attending a battle tournament held by King Utmos to find the strongest good guys in the land. Who knows if they'll have a run in with the Flaming Prince again, or maybe some new, barely-foreshadowed bad guy. You better read volume three, because not only will it bring the story arc to a spectacular conclusion, but one of the secondary characters is going to DIE! You'll have to read this very special volume of Van Von Hunter to find out who!

ADONETTE

AH, HERE WE HAVE THE LOVELY, FETCHING YOUNG VIXEN KNOWN AS ADONETTE. YOU'LL NOTICE ON THIS OUTFIT HOW SHE HAS MANAGED TO KEEP THE WEIGHT OF HER ARMOR PLATING DOWN BY ONLY USING IT FOR KEY STRATEGIC SPOTS. AFTER ALL, SHE NEEDS TO KEEP THE WEIGHT OF HER OUTFITS TO A MINIMUM BECAUSE OF A COUPLE OTHER ITEMS THAT REALLY WEIGH HER DOWN. WHAT? I'M TALKING ABOUT THOSE THREE-BLADED EVISCERATORS SHE HAS MOUNTED BEHIND HER SHOULDER PADS.

HA! IT'S CHIBI-ADONETTE! I...HUH? OH, WE DON'T HAVE ONE OF THOSE? SO THIS WOULD BE...ADONETTE AS A CHILD. WOW. SHE SURE IS WEARING AN AWFULLY PLAIN-JANE, I-AM-SO-A-GENERIC-LITTLE-PEASANT-GIRL OUTFIT. HMM. THIS CERTAINLY IS A STRIKING DEPARTURE FROM HOW SHE DRESSES NOWADAYS. EH, BUT WHAT DO YOU WANT? BEING RAISED BY THOSE DAMN, DIRTY ZOMBIES WILL REALLY SCREW WITH YOUR MORAL VALUES.

DIKAY TOUR GUIDE & PRINCESS AUGEN

AH, THE RAVEN-HAIRED DIKAY TOUR GUIDE. LITTLE WOULD YOU SUSPECT THAT SHE'S ACTUALLY GOING TO BECOME THE ARCH VILLAIN IN THE NEXT VOLUME OF VAN VON HUNTER. LITTLE WOULD YOU SUSPECT IT BECAUSE, WELL...SHE'S NOT.

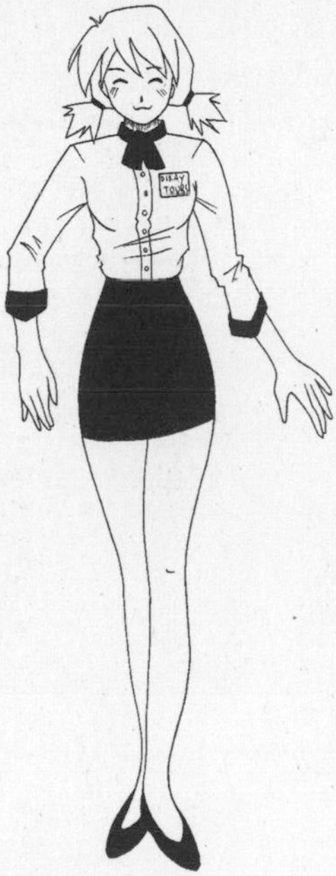
DIKAY TOUR

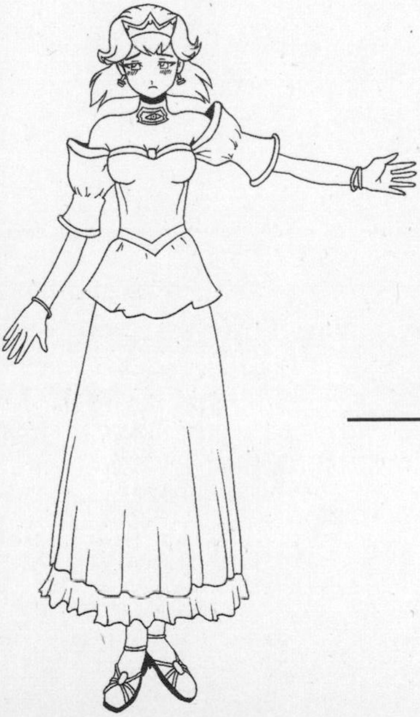

POOR, POOR PRINCES AUGEN. SHE WAS BORN WITH THE HORRIBLE CURSE OF SIGHT. SHE ALWAYS HAS TO SUFFER THE INDIGNITY OF LOOKING AT UGLY THINGS IN LIFE. BUT THEN AGAIN, THERE'S BEAUTIFUL THINGS IN LIFE TO LOOK AT TOO. SO IN THE END, I GUESS SIGHT REALLY ISN'T A CURSE. IT'S JUST A MATTER OF HOW YOU CHOOSE TO USE IT. KINDA LIKE LOVE, WHEN YOU THINK ABOUT IT.

Utmos & Chowse

This is the fabled King Utmos. He single-handedly took over the land of Dikay (with his massive armies) and swore that he would rejuvenate the land from a den of vile wickedness to a shining example of goodness and prosperity. But for all his good intentions, he seems to have a hard time finding a good jester.

The battle-hardened General Chowse, King Utmos' closest and most trusted general. Um... yup. That's who he is.

STARK & GOBLIN

STARK ITE IS THE CHIEF STRATEGIST FOR UTMOS' CAMPAIGNS IN DIKAY. HE ALSO MAKES FOR A GOOD JESTER IN A PINCH. STARK MAY SEEM LIKE A BIT OF A THROWAWAY CHARACTER, BUT IN ACTUALITY HIS INSIGHT INTO BATTLE STRATEGIES AND COMBAT TACTICS IS ABSOLUTELY INVALUABLE TO UTMOS AND VAN VON HUNTER. IF HE WERE TO EVER DIE UNEXPECTEDLY, IT WOULD BE A VERY, VERY BAD THING.

AWWWWW! IT'S A CUTE LITTLE GOBLIN! KNOWN HISTORICALLY AS THE MYTHICAL COOKIE—BAKING "ELFS," MODERN VERNACULAR REFERS TO THEM AS GOBLINS. WHATEVER THEIR NAME THEY'RE JUST SO DARN CUTE YOU WANT TO BUY A PLUSHIE DOLL VERSION OF THEM AND A BAG OF CHOCOLATE—CHIP, WALNUT MARSHMALLOW BROWNIES. YOU DO, DAGNABBIT! YOU DO!

GREETINGS FROM YOUR FRIENDLY NEIGHBORHOOD EDITOR:

I'M CO-OPTING THESE BONUS PAGES TO TALK A LITTLE BIT ABOUT HOW WE GO ABOU COMING UP WITH COVERS FOR OUR NEW BOOKS. YOU THINK THE LIFE OF AN EDITOR I AN EASY ONE OF GETTING PAID TO READ MANGA, EH? WELL, I'LL HAVE YOU KNOW THA THE ONEROUS TASK OF EVALUATING THE APPROPRIATE AMOUNT OF CLEAVAGE IN ANY GIVE IMAGE IS INTEGRAL TO MY DAILY ROUTINE! IT'S AWFUL, BELIEVE ME.

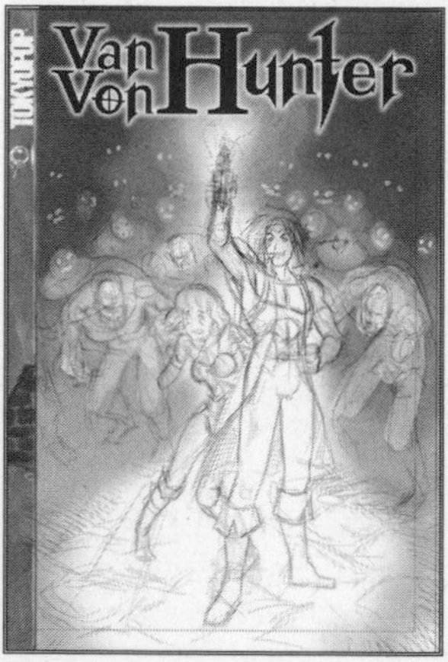
Van Von Hunter
TOKYOPOP

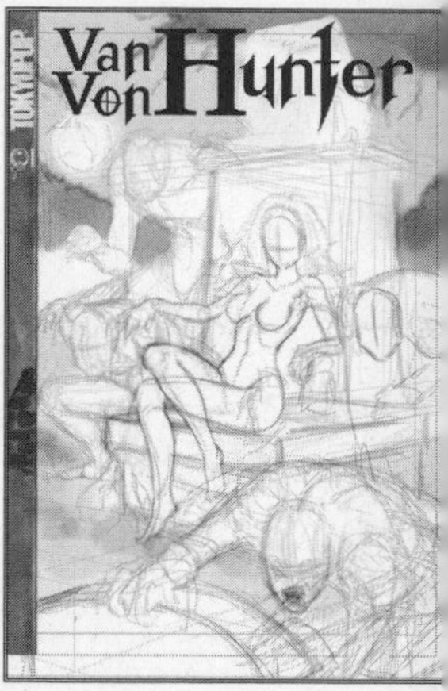
Van Von Hunter
TOKYOPOP

WHEN WE'RE THINKING COVERS, WE'RE THINKING SOMETHING THAT WILL JUMP OUT AT THE READER SAYING, "BUY ME! BUY ME!" THERE'S A LOT OF MANGA OUT THERE, AND HAVING AN ATTRACTIVE COVER (BY WHICH I MEAN ONE WITH THE MAGIC COMBINATION OF THE HIDEOUSLY ROTTING UNDEAD AND FAN SERVICE) HELPS GET CERTAIN FOLKS THEIR HARD-EARNED ROYALTIES. SO AS PART OF THE PROCESS, COVER DESIGN IDEAS ARE SUBMITTED TO ME, AND I SHOW THEM TO OUR TEAM OF DESIGNERS TO DETERMINE WHICH ONE IS THE MOST (AHEM) "APPEALING." I WAS REALLY FOND OF THE IMAGE ON THE LEFT, BECAUSE IT'S GOT A GOOD RATIO OF COOL:FUNNY (AND I'M FOND OF SIDEKICK), BUT ADONETTE IS A MAJOR FEATURE OF BOOK 2, AND SHE LOOKS PRETTY KICK-ASS SITTING THERE WITH HER MINIONS AT HER FEET, RIGHT?

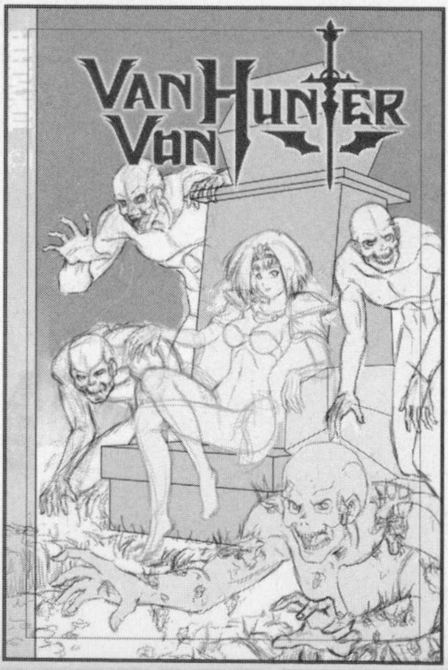

NEXT, WE GO TO THE REFINED PENCILS STAGE.

MIKE DOES A SECOND, MORE DETAILED SKETCH, SO WE CAN GET A BETTER IDEA OF WHAT THE FINAL IMAGE WILL LOOK LIKE (COMPLETE WITH UPDATED LOGO, RATHER THAN OLD ICKY ONE!), AND I CHECK TO MAKE SURE THE ANATOMY IS ACCURATE, THE ZOMBIES ARE SUFFICIENTLY MENACING, AND THAT EVERYTHING LOOKS SPIFFTACULAR BEFORE THE ARTIST GOES THROUGH THE EFFORT OF FINISHING IT. AND FEAR NOT, WE EDITORS ARE A THRIFTY BUNCH, AND SO EVEN THE REJECTED COVER SKETCH DOESN'T NECESSARILY GET WASTED. CHECK OUT OUR FIRST EDITION OF TAKUHAI MAGAZINE, FEATURING FULLY-RENDERED VAN ON THE BACK!

THE FINAL STAGE IS THE DIGITALLY PAINTED COVER.

THE FIRST VERSION CAME BACK A LITTLE TOO PASTEL (SEE? IT'S LIGHTER GREY THAN THE OTHER ONE!), SO WE WENT BACK AND DIRTIED IT UP A BIT! THERE WAS SOME CRAYON-ESQUE GREEN & PURPLE ZOMBIE HAIR GOING ON INITIALLY, AND EVERYTHING JUST LOOKED A LITTLE TOO CLEAN AND BRIGHT TO APPROPRIATELY CAPTURE THE HORROR THAT IS THE WALKING DEAD, BUT AN ADDED WROUGHT-IRON FENCE, EVEN CREEPIER TREES, SOME MIST, AND A WHOLE LOTTA MUD ON THE ZOMBIES HELPED TO BRING OUT THE EERIE TONE OF THE SCENE. EVERYONE'S FAVORITE BRAIN-EATERS LOOK LIKE THEY WERE FRESHLY DUG FROM THE GROUND! YUM! IRONICALLY, ADONETTE ACTUALLY GOT CLEANED UP A BIT SINCE HER ARMOR (SUCH AS IT IS) GOT A NICE LITTLE POLISH. OF COURSE, IT ONLY MAKES HER STAND OUT MORE BY COMPARISON, BUT WE WOULDN'T WANT IT ANY OTHER WAY!

BETCHA CAN'T WAIT TO SEE WHAT THE FINE FOLKS OF PSEUDOME STUDIOS HAVE IN THE WORKS FOR BOOK 3! I KNOW I'M CERTAINLY LOOKING FORWARD TO IT.

SIGNING OFF!
LDP

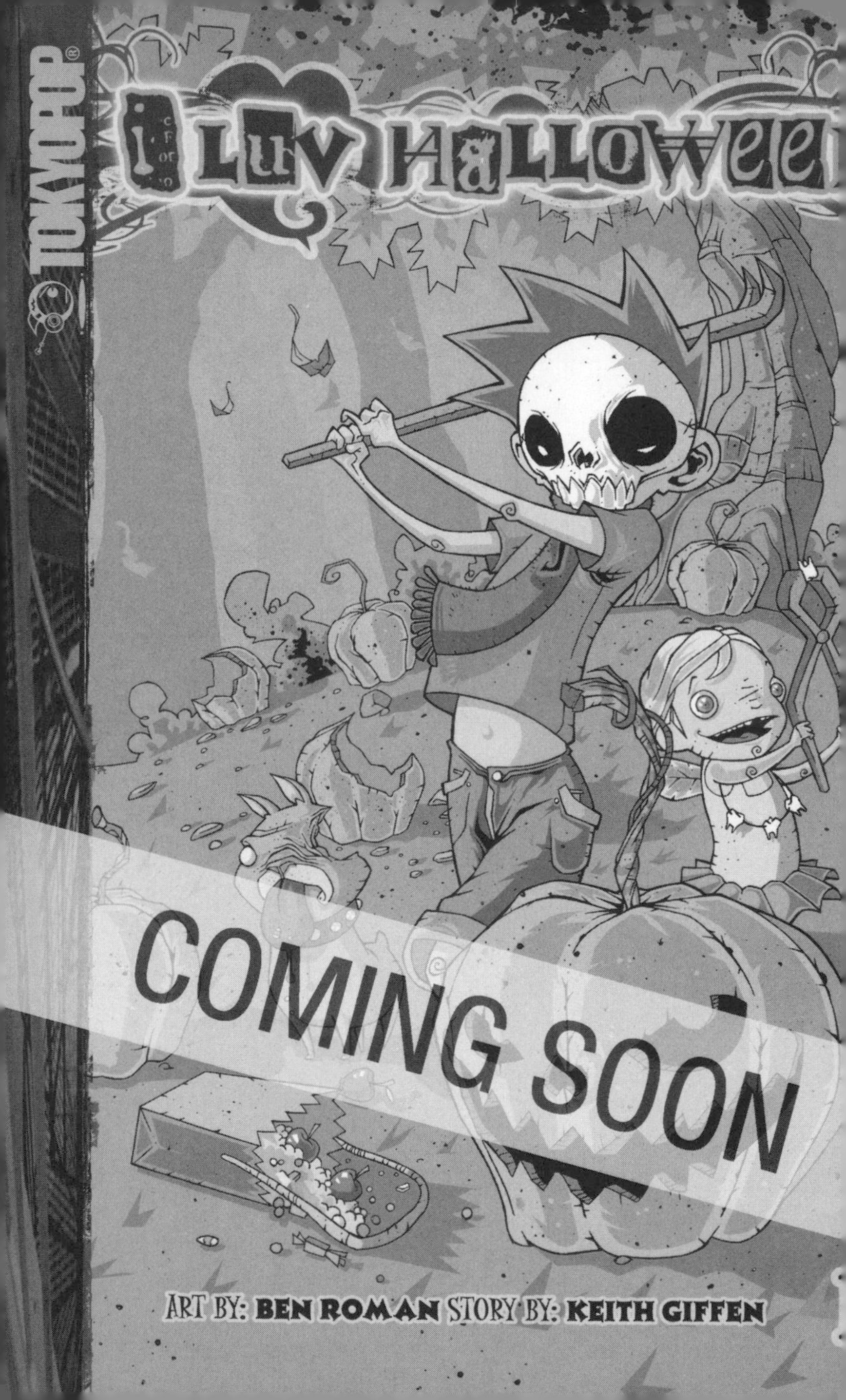
TOKYOPOP
I LUV HALLOWEE
COMING SOON
ART BY: BEN ROMAN STORY BY: KEITH GIFFEN

i LUV HALLOWEEN ™

HALLOWEEN HAS ALWAYS BEEN
AND WILL ALWAYS BE ABOUT
ONE THING...CANDY. HOWEVER,
THESE FIENDISH FRIENDS EXCEL
AT TRICKS IF THEY DON'T GET
THE RIGHT TREATS.

THIS HALLOWEEN,
JOIN THE MISADVENTURES OF
A GROUP OF PARTICULARLY
DISTURBING TRICK-OR-TREATERS
AS THEY GO ABOUT THEIR
MACABRE BUSINESS ON
HALLOWEEN NIGHT.

WRITTEN BY KEITH GIFFEN
(ENGLISH LANGUAGE
ADAPTATIONS OF
BATTLE ROYALE AND
BATTLE VIXENS) AND DRAWN
BY BENJAMIN ROMAN.

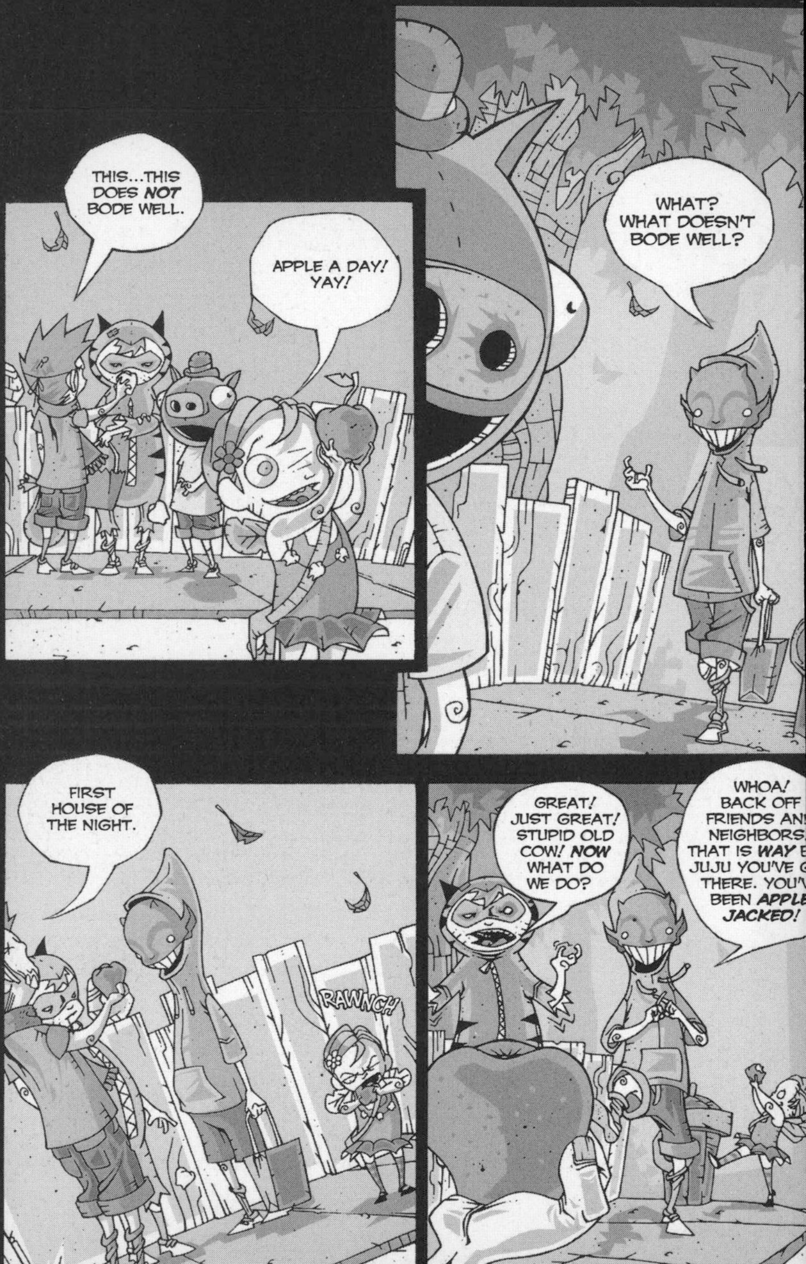

THIS...THIS DOES **NOT** BODE WELL.
APPLE A DAY! YAY!
WHAT? WHAT DOESN'T BODE WELL?
FIRST HOUSE OF THE NIGHT.
RAWNCH
GREAT! JUST GREAT! STUPID OLD COW! **NOW** WHAT DO WE DO?
WHOA! BACK OFF FRIENDS AN NEIGHBORS THAT IS **WAY** JUJU YOU'VE THERE. YOU' BEEN **APPLE JACKED!**

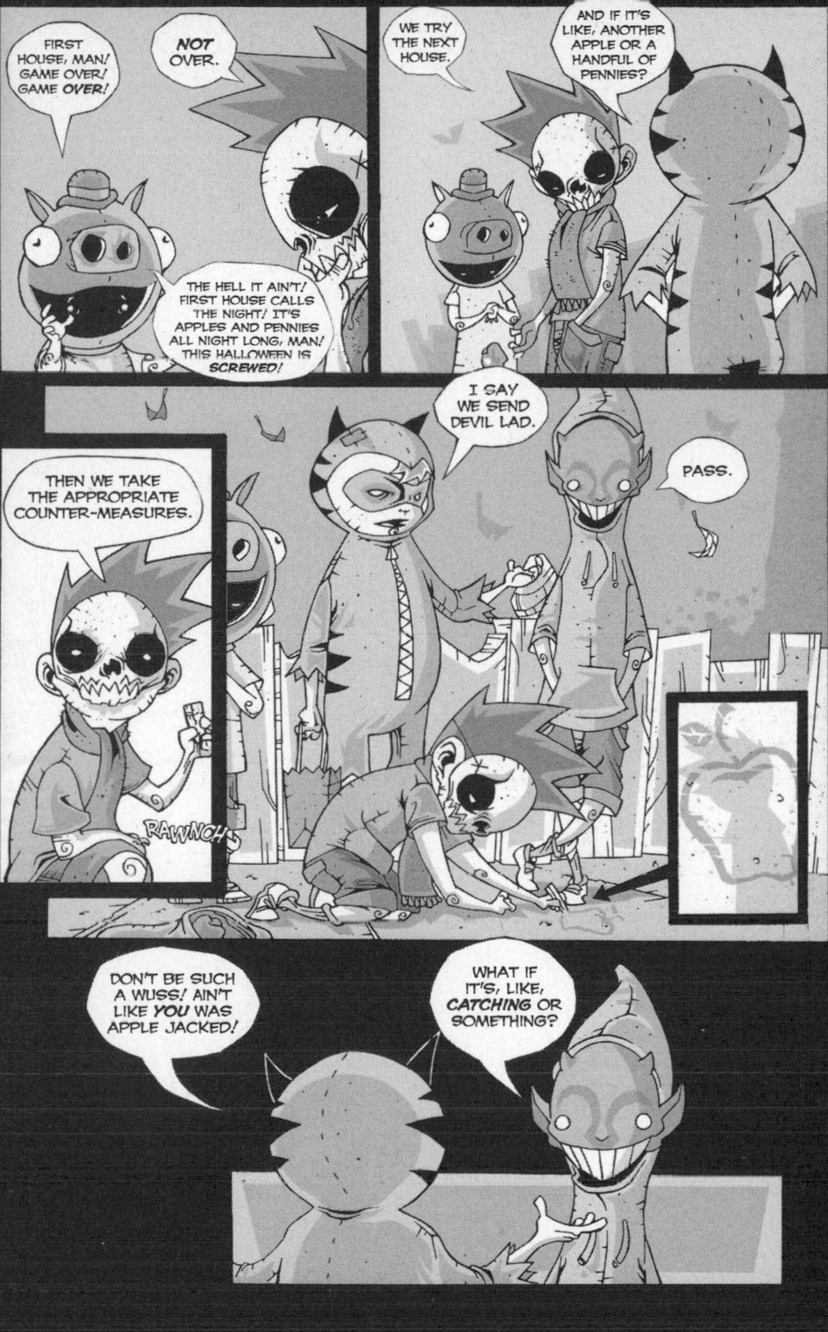

FIRST HOUSE, MAN! GAME OVER! GAME **OVER!**
NOT OVER.
THE HELL IT AIN'T! FIRST HOUSE CALLS THE NIGHT! IT'S APPLES AND PENNIES ALL NIGHT LONG, MAN! THIS HALLOWEEN IS **SCREWED!**
WE TRY THE NEXT HOUSE.
AND IF IT'S LIKE, ANOTHER APPLE OR A HANDFUL OF PENNIES?
THEN WE TAKE THE APPROPRIATE COUNTER-MEASURES.
RAWNCH
I SAY WE SEND DEVIL LAD.
PASS.
DON'T BE SUCH A WUSS! AIN'T LIKE **YOU** WAS APPLE JACKED!
WHAT IF IT'S, LIKE, **CATCHING** OR SOMETHING?

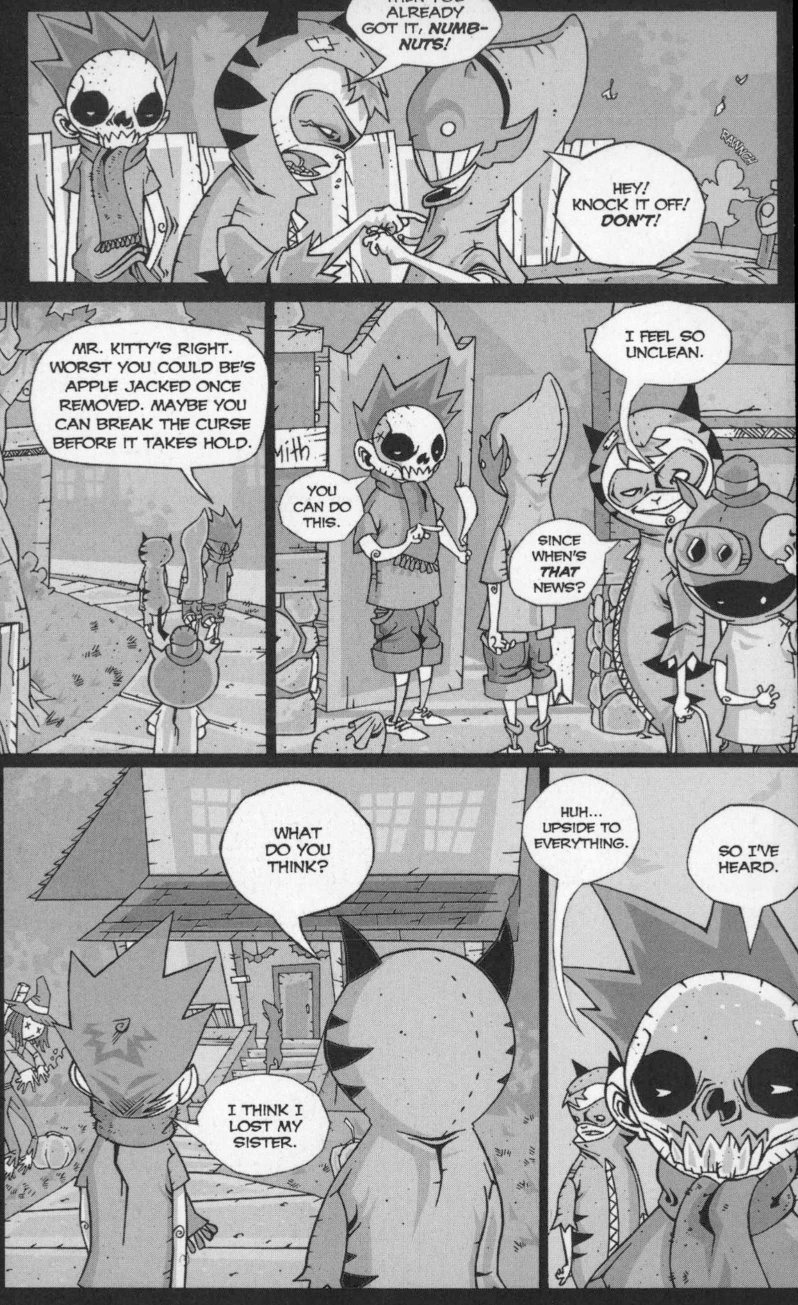
THEN YOU ALREADY GOT IT, *NUMB-NUTS!*
RAWNCH!
HEY! KNOCK IT OFF! *DON'T!*
MR. KITTY'S RIGHT. WORST YOU COULD BE'S APPLE JACKED ONCE REMOVED. MAYBE YOU CAN BREAK THE CURSE BEFORE IT TAKES HOLD.
I FEEL SO UNCLEAN.
YOU CAN DO THIS.
SINCE WHEN'S *THAT* NEWS?
WHAT DO YOU THINK?
I THINK I LOST MY SISTER.
HUH... UPSIDE TO EVERYTHING.
SO I'VE HEARD.

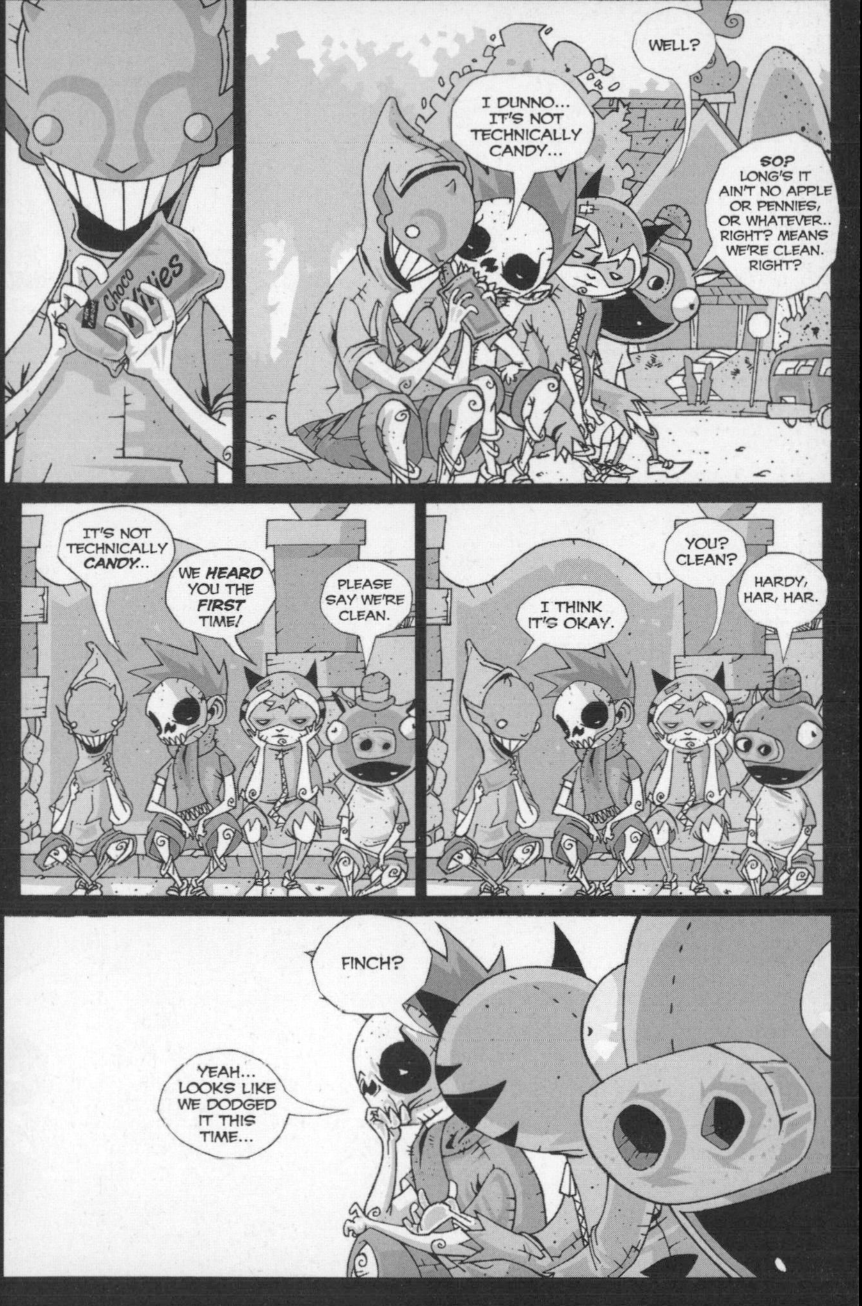
Choco
WELL?
I DUNNO... IT'S NOT TECHNICALLY CANDY...
SO? LONG'S IT AIN'T NO APPLE OR PENNIES, OR WHATEVER.. RIGHT? MEANS WE'RE CLEAN. RIGHT?
IT'S NOT TECHNICALLY *CANDY*...
WE *HEARD* YOU THE *FIRST* TIME!
PLEASE SAY WE'RE CLEAN.
I THINK IT'S OKAY.
YOU? CLEAN?
HARDY, HAR, HAR.
FINCH?
YEAH... LOOKS LIKE WE DODGED IT THIS TIME...

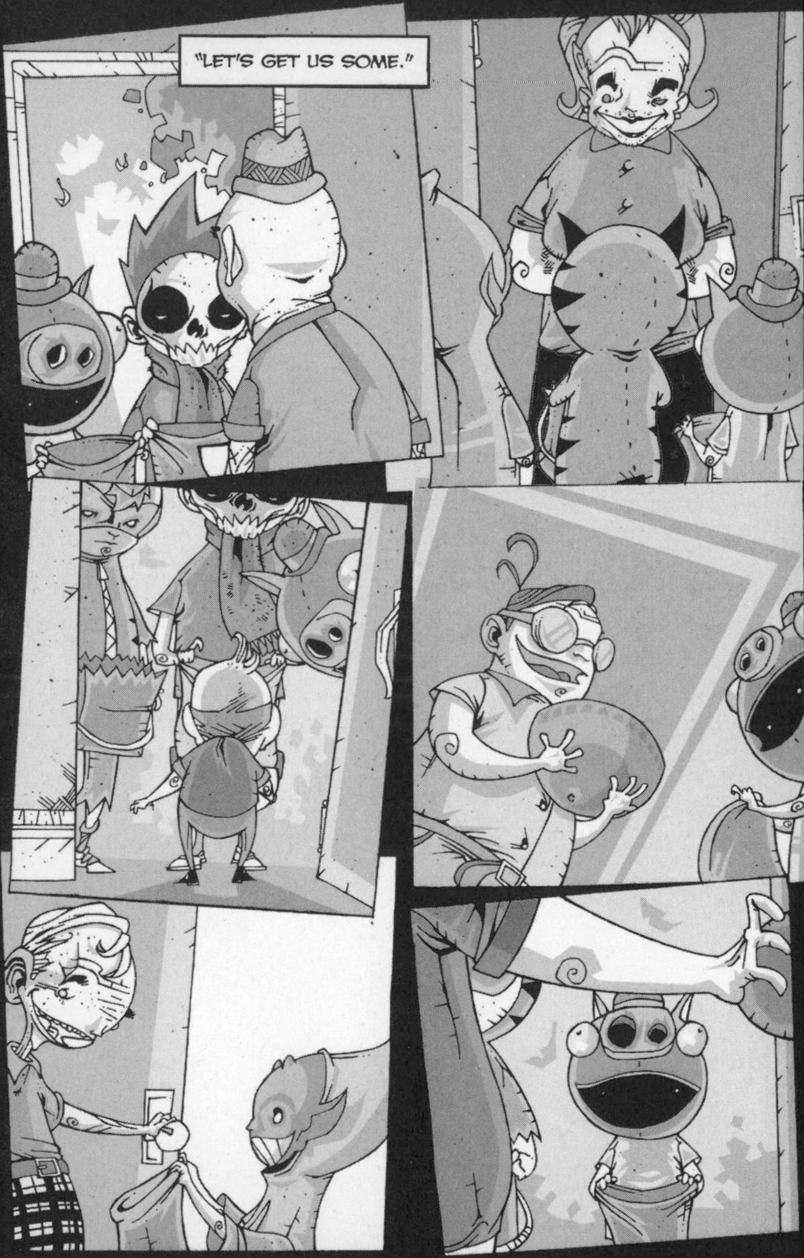
"LET'S GET US SOME."

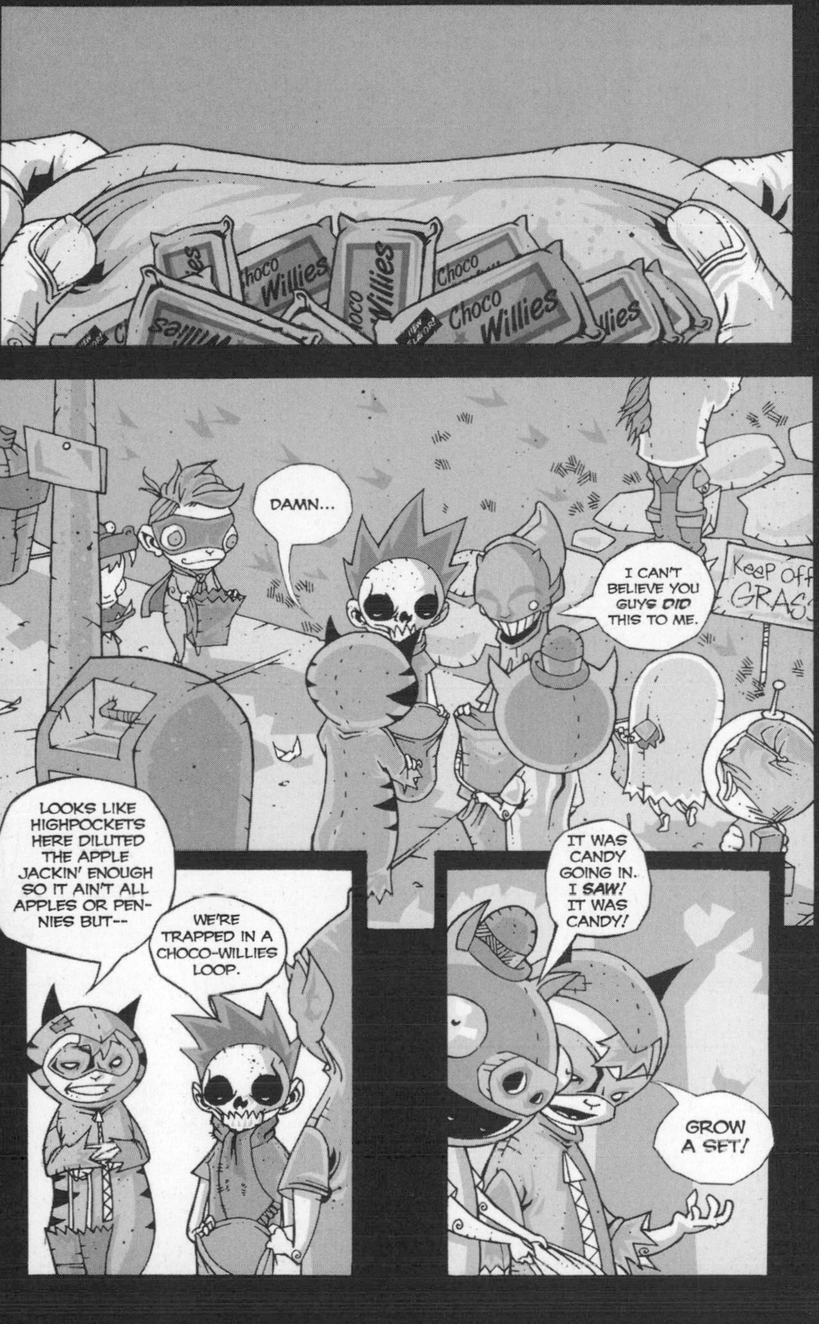

Choco Willies
NEW FLAVOR!
DAMN...
I CAN'T BELIEVE YOU GUYS *DID* THIS TO ME.
Keep off GRASS
LOOKS LIKE HIGHPOCKETS HERE DILUTED THE APPLE JACKIN' ENOUGH SO IT AIN'T ALL APPLES OR PENNIES BUT--
WE'RE TRAPPED IN A CHOCO-WILLIES LOOP.
IT WAS CANDY GOING IN. I *SAW!* IT WAS CANDY!
GROW A SET!

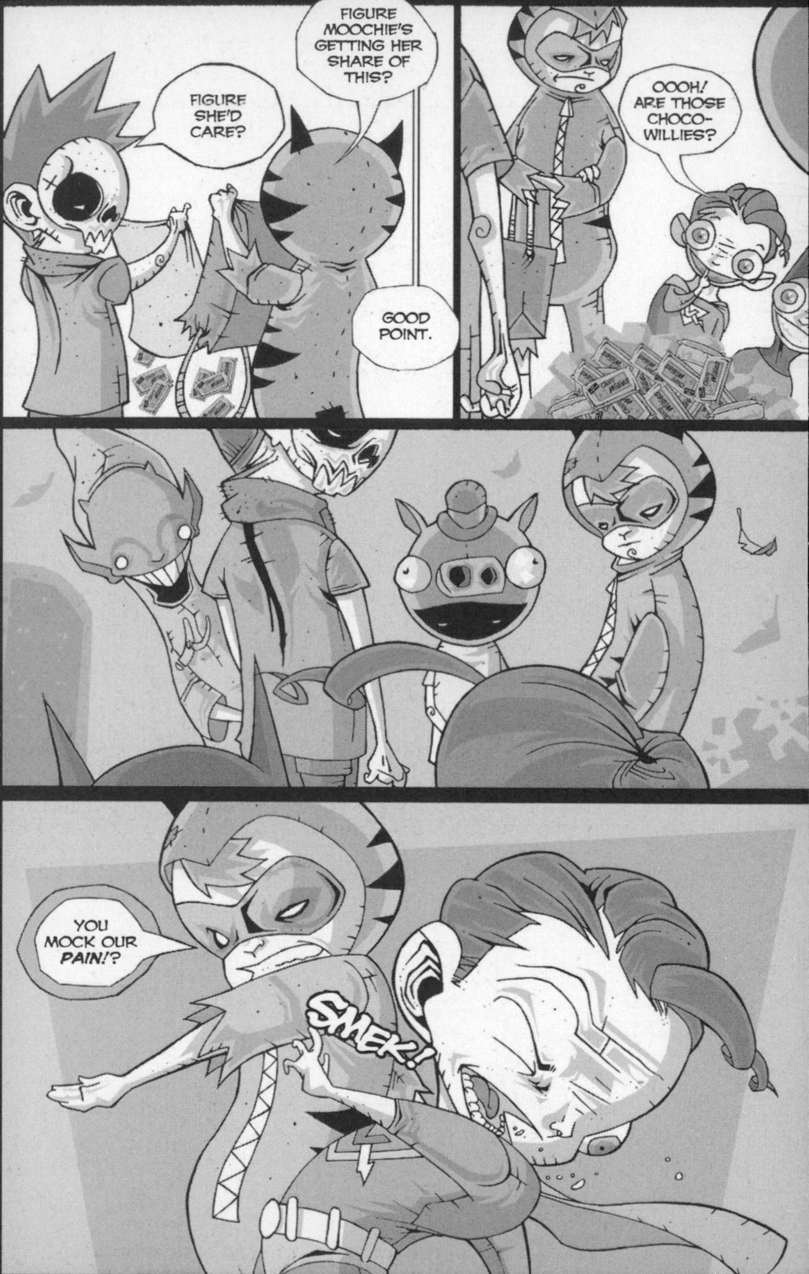
FIGURE SHE'D CARE?
FIGURE MOOCHIE'S GETTING HER SHARE OF THIS?
GOOD POINT.
OOOH! ARE THOSE CHOCO-WILLIES?
YOU MOCK OUR *PAIN!*?
SMEK!

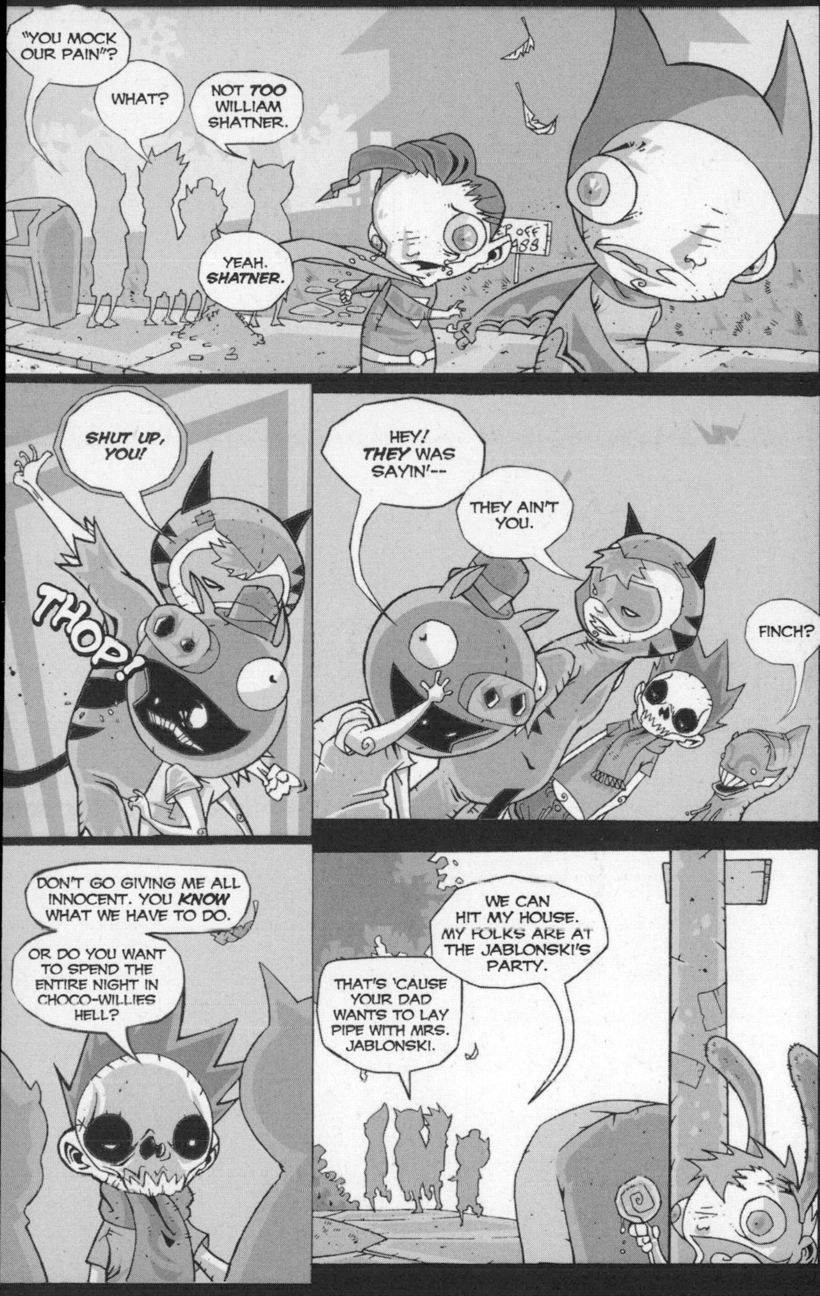
"YOU MOCK OUR PAIN"?
WHAT?
NOT TOO WILLIAM SHATNER.
YEAH. SHATNER.
EP OFF ASS
SHUT UP, YOU!
THOP!
HEY! THEY WAS SAYIN'--
THEY AIN'T YOU.
FINCH?
DON'T GO GIVING ME ALL INNOCENT. YOU KNOW WHAT WE HAVE TO DO.
OR DO YOU WANT TO SPEND THE ENTIRE NIGHT IN CHOCO-WILLIES HELL?
WE CAN HIT MY HOUSE. MY FOLKS ARE AT THE JABLONSKI'S PARTY.
THAT'S 'CAUSE YOUR DAD WANTS TO LAY PIPE WITH MRS. JABLONSKI.

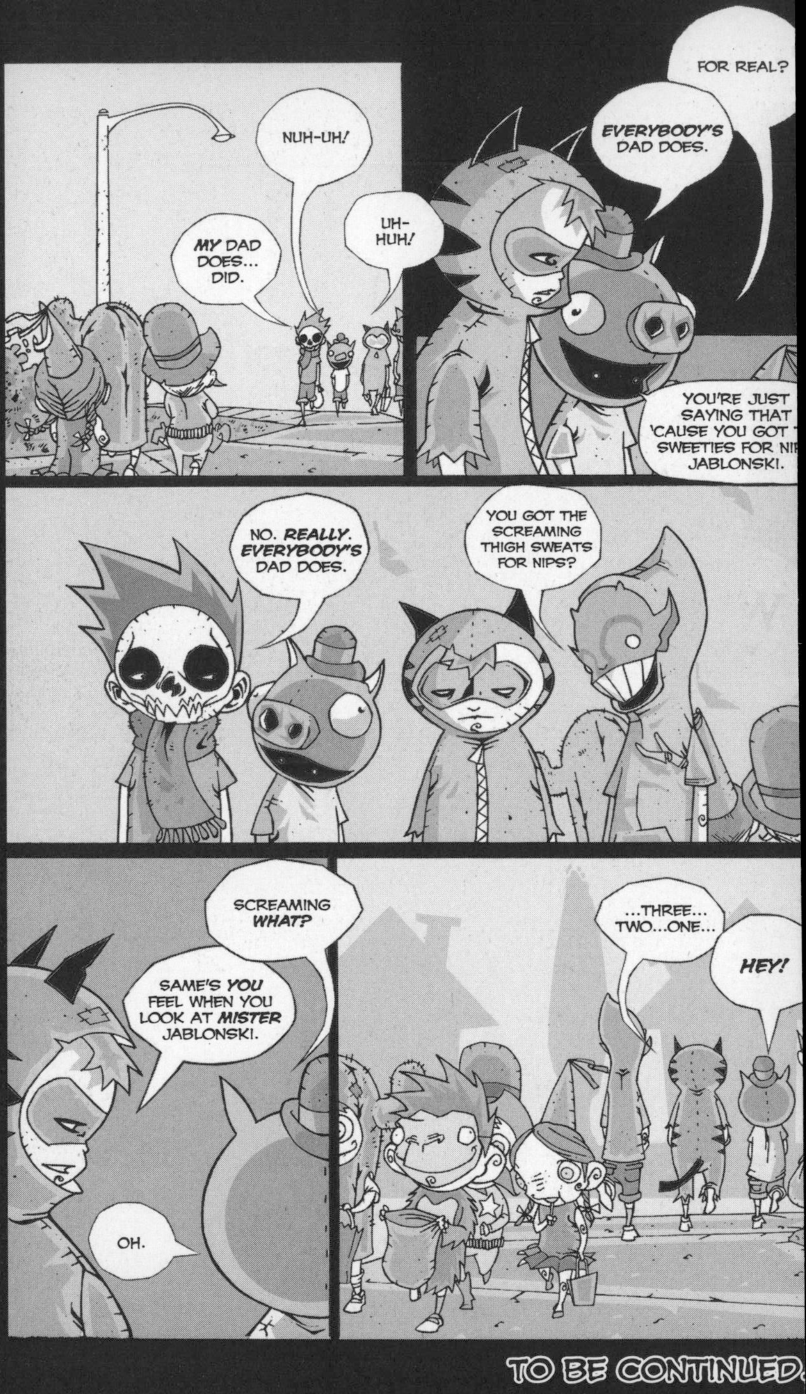
MY DAD DOES... DID.
NUH-UH!
UH-HUH!
EVERYBODY'S DAD DOES.
FOR REAL?
YOU'RE JUST SAYING THAT 'CAUSE YOU GOT
SWEETIES FOR NI
JABLONSKI.
NO. REALLY. EVERYBODY'S DAD DOES.
YOU GOT THE SCREAMING THIGH SWEATS FOR NIPS?
SCREAMING WHAT?
SAME'S YOU FEEL WHEN YOU LOOK AT MISTER JABLONSKI.
OH.
...THREE... TWO...ONE...
HEY!
TO BE CONTINUED

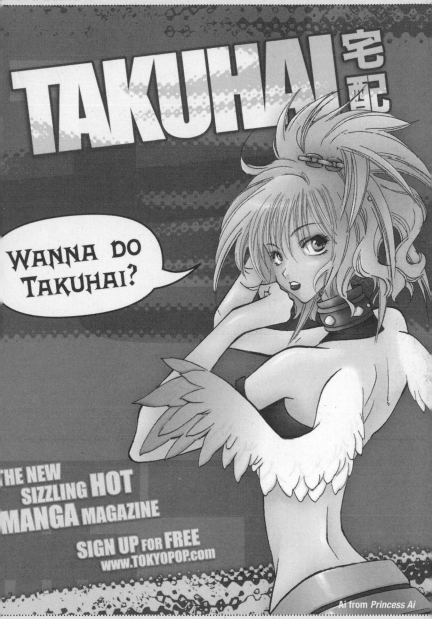

TOKYOPOP SHOP

WWW.TOKYOPOP.COM/SHOP

HOT NEWS!
Check out the
TOKYOPOP SHOP!
The world's best
collection of manga in
English is now available
online in one place!

GIRLS BRAVO

RIZELMINE

WAR ON FLESH

*War on Fl[...]
and other [...]
titles are
available [...]
the store [...]
never clos[...]*

- LOOK FOR SPECIAL OFFERS
- PRE-ORDER UPCOMING RELEASES
- COMPLETE YOUR COLLECTIONS

RAPPED PRINCESS

YABUKI, ICHIRO SAKAKI, AND YUKINOBU AZUMI

ER BIRTH FORETOLD THE DESTRUCTION OF THE WORLD!

Fifteen years ago, a set of twins—a girl and a boy—was born to the king of Linevan. Shortly after their birth, a prophecy foretold that when the girl turned 16, she would bring about the end of humanity. To avoid this terrible fate, the king ordered the girl disposed of—scrapped! She miraculously survived and was raised away from the kingdom that would kill her. But now she has turned 15, the king's guards have caught wind that she's still alive...and they set out to finish the job!

SCRAPPED
PRINCESS

CI-FI COMEDY THAT SPAWNED THE HIGHLY SUCCESSFUL ANIME! ALSO,
OUT FOR THE *SCRAPPED PRINCESS* NOVEL FROM TOKYOPOP IN NOVEMBER.

FOR MORE INFORMATION VISIT: WWW.TOKYOPOP.COM

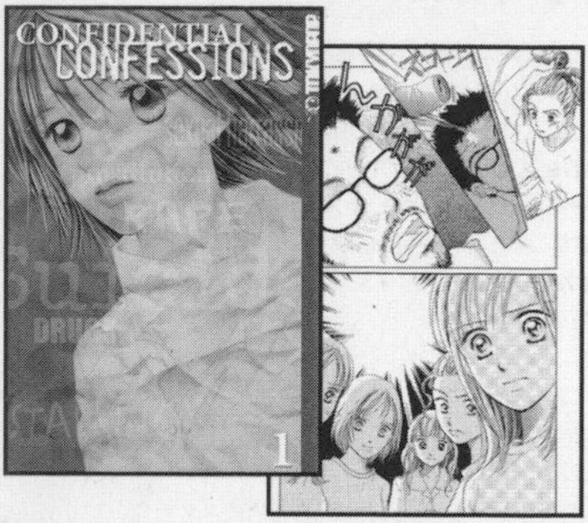
CONFIDENTIAL CONFESSIONS
1

BY REIKO MOMOCHI

CONFIDENTIAL CONFESSIONS

If you're looking for a happy, rosy, zit-fre look at high school life, skip this manga But if you're jonesing for a real-life view c what high school's truly like, *Confidenti Confessions* offers a gritty, unflinchin look at what really happens in thos hallowed halls. Rape, sexual harassmen anorexia, cutting, suicide...no subject is too hardcore for *Confidential Confessions*. While you're at it, don't expect a happy ending.

~Julie Taylor, Sr. Editor

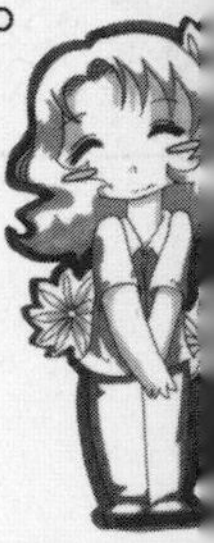

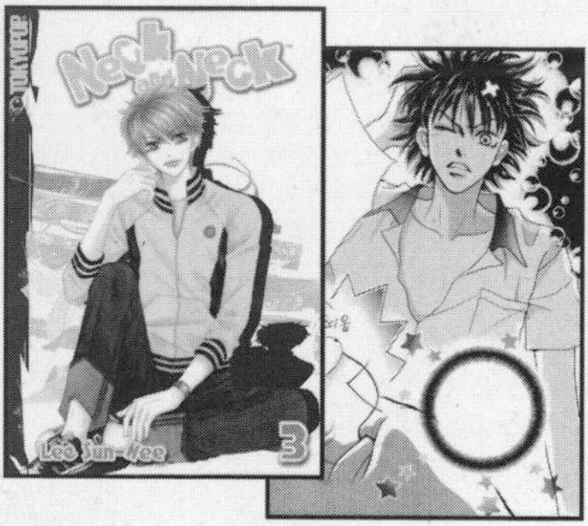
Neck and Neck
TOKYOPOP
Lee Sun-Hee
3

BY LEE SUN-HEE

NECK AND NECK

Competition can bring out the best c the worst in people...but in *Neck ar Neck*, it does both! Dabin Choi and Shih Myoung are both high school students both children of mob bosses, and eac is out to totally humiliate the other. Dabi and Shihu are very creative in their mutual tortures and there's more than a hint of romantic tension behind their attacks. This book's art may look somewhat shojo, but I found the story to be very accessible and very entertaining!

~Rob Tokar, Sr. Editor

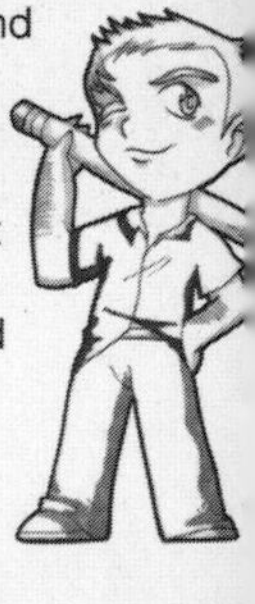

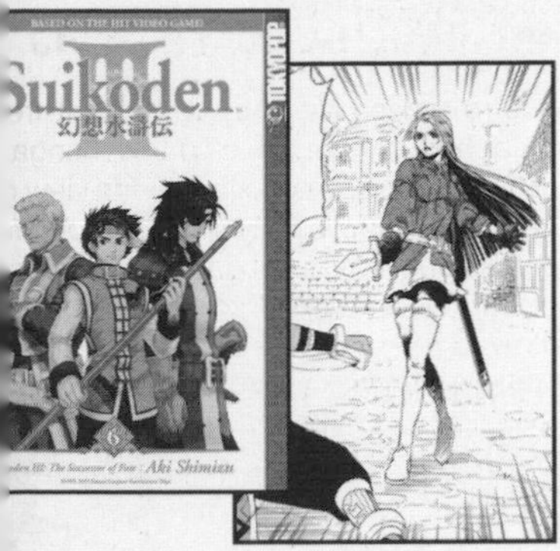
BASED ON THE HIT VIDEO GAME
Suikoden
幻想水滸伝
III
Aki Shimizu
TOKYOPOP

BY AKI SHIMIZU

SUIKODEN III

I'm one of those people who likes to watch others play video games (I tend to run into walls and get stuck), so here comes the perfect manga for me! All the neat plot of a great RPG game, without any effort on my part! Aki Shimizu, creator of the delightful series *Qwan*, has done a lovely, lovely job of bringing the world of Suikoden to life. There are great creatures (Fighting ducks! Giant lizard people!), great character designs, and an engaging story full of conflict, drama and intrigue. I picked up one volume while I was eating lunch at my desk one day, and was totally hooked. I can't wait for the next one to come out!

~Lillian Diaz-Przybyl, Editor

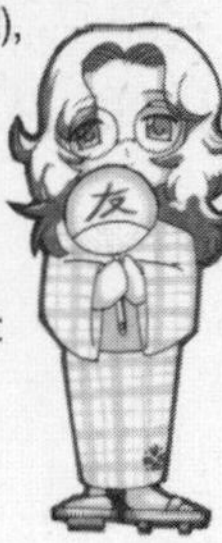

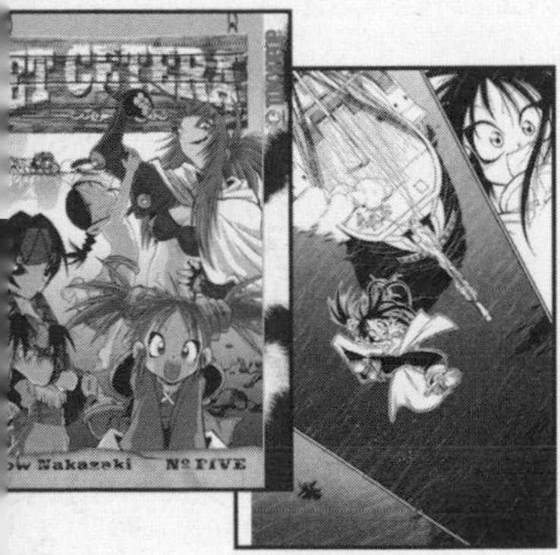
N° FIVE

BY TOW NAKAZAKI

ET CETERA

Meet Mingchao, an energetic girl from China who now travels the deserts of the old west. She dreams of becoming a star in Hollywood, eager for fame and fortune. She was given the Eto Gun—a magical weapon that fires bullets with properties of the 12 zodiac signs—as a keepsake from her grandfather before he died. On her journey to Hollywood, she meets a number of zany characters...some who want to help, and others who are after the power of the Eto Gun. Chock full of gun fights, train hijackings, collapsing mineshafts...this East-meets-wild-West tale has it all!

~Aaron Suhr, Sr. Editor

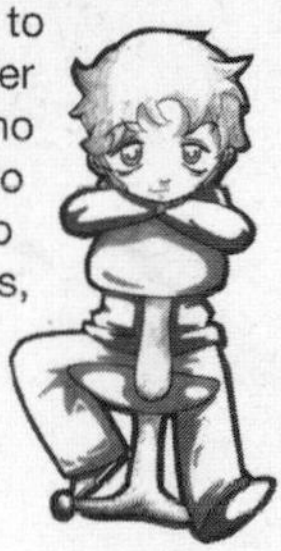

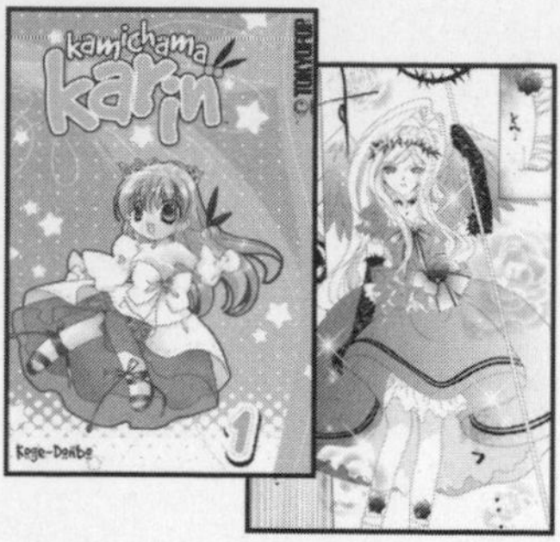
kamichama karin
Koge-Donbo
1

KAMICHAMA KARIN
BY KOGE-DONBO

Karin is an average girl...at best. She's not goo
at sports and gets terrible grades. On top
all that, her parents are dead and her belov
cat Shi-chan just died, too. She is miserabl
But everything is about to change—little do
Karin know that her mother's ring has the
power to make her a goddess!

From the creator of *Pita-Ten* and *Digi-Charat!*

Y YOUT AGE 10

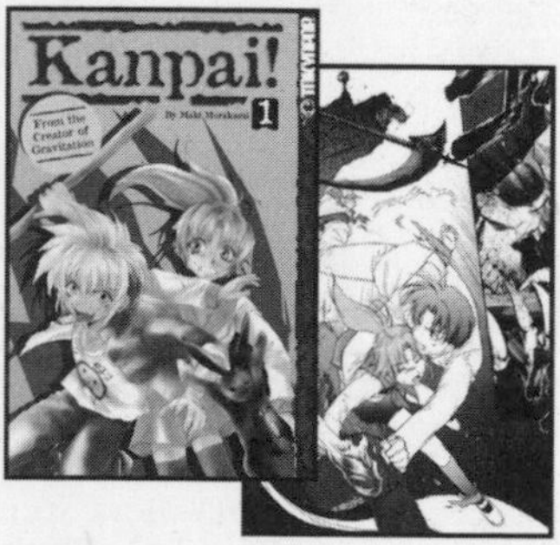
Kanpai!
From the Creator of Gravitation
1

KANPAI!
BY MAKI MURAKAMI

Yamada Shintaro is a monster guardian
training—his job is to protect the monsters fro
harm. But when he meets Nao, a girl from h
middle school, he suddenly falls in love...wi
her neckline! Shintaro will go to any lengths
prevent disruption to her peaceful life—ar
preserve his choice view of her neck!

A wild and wonderful adventure from the creator of *Gravitation!*

T TEEN AGE 13

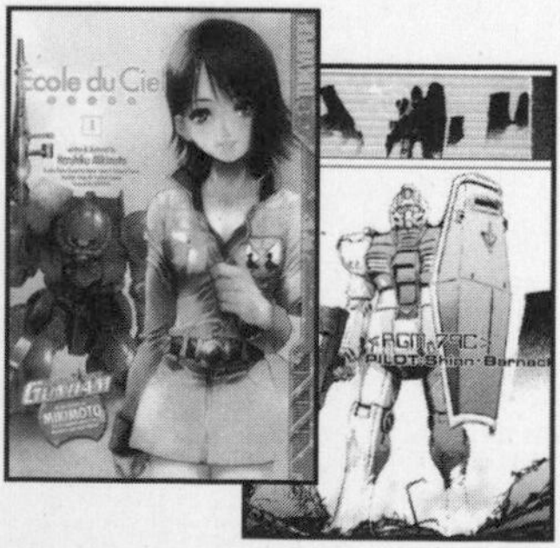
École du Ciel
MIKIMOTO

MOBILE SUIT GUNDAM ÉCOLE DU CIE
BY HARUHIKO MIKIMOTO

École du Ciel—where aspiring pilots train
become Top Gundam! Asuna, daughter of
brilliant professor, is a below-average student
École du Ciel. But the world is spiraling towa
war, and Asuna is headed for a crash course
danger, battle, and most of all, love.

From the artist of the phenomenally successful *Macross* and *Baby Birth!*

T TEEN AGE 13